THE HONEYWELL PROJECT
1519 E. FRANKLIN AVE.
MINNEAPOLIS, MN 55404
(612) 871 3753

FIRST STRIKE!
The Pentagon's Strategy For Nuclear War

minnehaha free space copy

FIRST STRIKE!
The Pentagon's Strategy For Nuclear War

BY
ROBERT C. ALDRIDGE

SOUTH END PRESS BOSTON, MA

Copyright © 1983 by Robert Aldridge

Copyrights are still required for book production in the United States. However, in our case it is a disliked necessity. Thus, any properly footnoted quotation of up to 500 sequential words may be used without permission, so long as the total number of words does not exceed 2000. For longer quotations or for a greater number of total words quoted, written permission from the publisher is required.

First printing
Library of Congress Number: 82-061148
ISBN paper: 0-89608-154-0
ISBN cloth: 0-89608-155-9

Cover design by Carl Conetta
Typeset by Nova Typesetting, Seattle
Produced by the South End Press collective

South End Press
302 Columbus Ave.
Boston, MA 02116

DEDICATION

For Tammi,
Joshua,
Poppy & John,
Tina,
Kristen,
Matthew,
Heather & Cortnie,
and Kyle;

that they and all the other children of the world may have a future.

CONTENTS

LIST OF FIGURES

ACKNOWLEDGMENTS

The history of this book reaches back many years. In 1975 the late Lord Philip Noel-Baker, Nobel Laureate of Britain, gave me the first spark of encouragement by saying he hoped I would write a book about my experiences. On January 29, 1977 Jim Douglass wrote a long letter from King County Jail in Seattle, where he was incarcerated for public witness against the Trident base, strongly suggesting that I put my research into book form. He outlined a prospectus for *First Strike* which is still the basic organization of this book. For this encouragement I am deeply grateful.

I am also indebted to many people who have corresponded with me to provide information and research which went into this book: Owen Wilkes, a New Zealand Researcher at Stockholm International Peace Research Institute, Sweden: Sam Warda, a concerned citizen and friend in San Francisco; Michael Klare, Director of the Militarism and Disarmament Program of the Institute for Policy Studies; Milton Leitenberg, Research Associate at Cornell University Center for International Studies; Kosta Tsipis, Associate Director of Massachusetts Institute of Technology program in Science and Technology for International Security; Fred Kaplan, Research Fellow at Massachusetts Institute of Technology Center for International Studies; Ingvar Botnen and Nils Petter Gleditsch of the Peace Research Institute of Oslo, Norway; Richard Falk, Milbank Professor of International Law at Princeton University; and George Kent, Professor of Political Science at University of Hawaii at Manoa.

I also wish to express my appreciation to those who have reviewed chapters of the *First Strike* manuscript to provide valuable criticism and suggestions: Jim and Shelley Douglass of Ground Zero Center for Nonviolent Action near Sub-Base Bangor, Marty and Marion Osberg of Shanti Community in British Columbia, Peter Chapman of Purcell Research in British Columbia, Ladon Sheats of Jonah House in Baltimore, Ched Myers of Bartimeus Community in Berkeley, Peter Conk of the San Jose Catholic Worker Community, Larry Purcell of the Redwood City (CA) Catholic Worker Community, William Epstein of the United Nations Institute for Training and Research (UNITAR), and Owen Wilkes of SIPRI and New Zealand.

Special recognition should go to Carl Conetta, my editor at South End Press, who helped me put an overwhelming mass of technical information into a readable form.

I also want to thank all the people too numerous to mention who have caused me to start thinking and have encouraged me along the way. I want to give a very special thanks to Janet for her help, encouragement, patience and love.

Robert C. Aldridge

Santa Clara, California
November 19, 1982

INTRODUCTION*
by Richard Falk

Ezra Pound, reflecting on the carnage and corruption exhibited in the course of World War I, wrote some famous lines about why those many died in battle:

For an old bitch gone in the teeth,
For a botched civilization...

We are still trying to unravel this riddle of a botched civilization. By now we realize that history does not stand still, that the flaws of Western civilization while not necessarily more severe, are now threatening a wider swathe of destruction, perhaps imperiling the entire future of the human species. Whether we are yet able to summon sufficient energy to transform this dismal prospect of an ending into a new beginning is, in a supreme sense, the encompassing political question of our time.

Most other civilizations, past and present, have been botched in a variety of ways. Perhaps the root flaw has been the pattern of

*I am grateful to Cindy Halpern and Carl Conetta for their editorial and substantive suggestions.

exploitation at the societal core that sustains privilege and inequality in a variety of vastly different class and technological circumstances across the reaches of time. The articulated justification of exploitation is the central lie told by the rulers of each civilization to explain and obscure their inhumanity. To the extent this lie is disbelieved by the people, it produces resistance and rulers must either divert the citizenry by mobilizing against foreign enemies or resort to some form of direct repression.

In addition to this shared circumstance there is the fateful working out in modern times of the Faustian bargain associated with the enterprises of science and technology. The acquisition of knowledge has been empowering in many respects for our civilization, but this empowerment reflects the distribution of values operative at a given moment. A dynamic technology linked to a political order that includes war within its repertoire of instruments is bound to result in an expanding capacity to inflict death and destruction (as is, incidentally, the parallel capacity to produce goods for human consumption by way of industrial processes). In Western civilization, progress in human society became viewed as providing an eventual cure-all for poverty and class antagonism; this progress was supposedly assured by growth, itself assured, save for cyclical adjustments, by continuous processes of technical innovation. Capitalism and war, even without any grand imperial design, then, incorporated the conviction that it was useful and necessary to expand as much as possible. From the ideas of Machiavelli, Hobbes, Darwin, and Clausewitz emerged a prevailing ideology able to reconcile power, progress and privilege.

The modern civilization drive did away with limits, whether imposed by the constraints of nature or religion. Faust's reliance on the prospect of continuous expansion of capabilities was so subversive, in part, because it denigrated humility as an essential human quality. Without cultivating the virtue of humility there is no understanding of the need for deference to elemental natural forces or sacred spiritual energies, and secular absolutism and idolatry are bound to result.

It was surprisingly easy to enter the nuclear age. The use of atomic bombs against Japan in 1945 appeared, at the time, breathtakingly "natural." Wasn't it natural to save American lives by inducing a rapid Japanese surrender? Wasn't it natural to let the Soviet Union know some facts of political life in planning a post-war world? After all, the United States government had a monopoly over this new extraordinary instrument of destruction, and monopolies over weapons can be used to achieve geopolitical results, as effectively as monopolies over markets can be used to realize economic goals. The United States believed it could achieve benevolent results through the spread of its influence. In some sense, this incredible new source of power seemed almost like a miraculous gift enabling the reshaping of the world in the moderate democratic direction.

It was equally natural for America's rival in the game of nations to devote its energies and resources to catching up as quickly as it could. The Soviet test explosion of a nuclear device in 1949 may have come sooner than Washington expected, but the process by which technology serves the pursuit of power made the Soviet adjustment virtually inevitable. As were the next rounds of feverish action by the United States to maintain its nuclear advantage. Indeed, the ongoing competition between "staying ahead" and "catching up" has produced what is generally described as "a nuclear arms race," with the perceptions of each side as to the capabilities and intentions of the other an intensifying factor at every stage.

The nuclear arms race is the most vivid expression of precisely what it means to live in a botched civilization at this time, but it is not itself the flaw. We would have reached this same terminal condition some decades or centuries later through the workings of the pre-nuclear system, by way of evolving non-nuclear weaponry that can inflict mass destruction, by laser weaponry, and by chemical and biological weaponry. Even aside from war, our material appetites would soon overwhelm the capacity of the biosphere to sustain a productive existence for human society at present population levels. Despite these other underlying threats, an emergency circumstance currently exists arising from the specific stage we are at in the evolution of nuclear arms technology. This emergency requires our most determined efforts at this time.

It is against this broad backdrop that Robert Aldridge has written such a stunning book. With a rare blend of technical mastery and engaged human feelings, Aldridge depicts the quest by American leaders for a first strike nuclear weapons capability. A first strike capability means the coordinated capacity to mount such a devastating initial attack on Soviet society that it would lack the will and capacity to respond effectively, especially as the United States would have taken steps to limit the effects of whatever damage could be inflicted by Soviet retaliation. As Aldridge explains, a first strike capacity allows leaders to "use" nuclear weapons as an instrument of foreign policy, rather than just as an ultimate hedge against either nuclear blackmail or attack by a rival. This first strike capability is intended mainly to intimidate adversaries rather than to serve necessarily as the basis for an actual attack plan, although Pentagon theorizing certainly doesn't exclude first strike scenarios from its so-called "menu of options," and at minimum, the task of intimidation depends, finally, on a manifest willingness to execute an attack if and when confronted by a Soviet refusal to back down.

For the United States to seek a first strike capability seems implausible when initially considered. It seems evident that the Soviet Union could and would take sufficient steps to ensure a secure retaliatory capability, or even if not wholly secure, one that any rational military planner in the United States would have to assume as secure. Given the catastrophic effects of a nuclear exchange, it would seem far more self-interested to stabilize or balance nuclear weapons capabilities at some level of parity than to gamble on making active use of nuclear weapons. This line of rational supposition is strengthened also by the dangerous side-effects of threatening a first strike. Even aside from the inflationary effect of the additional military expenditures on an already strained economy, the mere threat of first strike could lead unintentionally to disaster. To the extent that the other side believes that it is exposed to a credible threat of a first strike, it will take steps to discourage the temptation, especially in a crisis situation, by either attacking first so as to avoid losing its retaliatory capability or, at least, by adopting a "launch on warning" policy for its nuclear missile force. In either case, nuclear war is more likely than in the past to result from the interplay of nuclear strategies, anxieties, and vulnerability to disinformation in a crisis.

Our initial inclination, then, is to question Aldridge's thesis on first strike. After all, we live in a democracy. Our leaders seem reasonably honest. They are loyal and rational. Why would they embrace an approach to nuclear weapons that is both stupid and evil? And if they did make such a choice, wouldn't they at least explain their honest reasons for adopting a first strike doctrine? Even Richard Nixon argues that, despite our justifiable hatred of Communism and the Soviet system, during his presidency he understood that "our countries shared certain common interests ...Our central common interest was to ensure that our differences did not lead us into a shooting war. With tragic frequency, wars result from miscalculation. We were able to reduce that danger."[1] Nixon currently favors, to be sure, a military buildup that redresses "the nuclear military balance" so that the West "will not be subject to Soviet nuclear blackmail." Haig, Weinberger, and Reagan talk in a similar vein. The military buildup is declared as necessary to strengthen deterrence, to close "the window of vulnerability," and, generally, to make sure that the Soviet Union possesses no first strike temptations of its own. Alexander Haig, while he was Secretary of State, explained the Reagan Administration's opposition to the freeze proposal on these grounds: "A freeze at current levels would perpetuate an unstable and unequal military balance."[2]

There are three strong reasons, then, to doubt the contention that the United States is pursuing a first strike capability:

1.) It defies common sense, and seems unlikely given the generally intelligent quality of political leadership in this country;

2.) It involves genocidal planning of the most extreme sort, and seems inconsistent with the minimum sort of morality that has guided America's behaviour in the world;

3.) It contradicts official descriptions of United States national security policy, maintained by leaders of both political parties, and would require us to conclude that the entire leadership of the country was lying or somehow self-deceived.

And yet, we have Aldridge's calm, expert presentation of the various components of a comprehensive first strike strategy as operative in the United States, including super-accurate missiles, damage limitation policies, and anti-submarine warfare. The impact of his argument is, or should be, quite devastating. Not only does Aldridge make a case convincingly that we are creating a situation of grave danger, but his argument suggests that we are being governed in a grossly anti-democratic manner by leaders who are incompetent or depraved. To take Aldridge seriously is virtually to accept, it seems to me, Daniel Ellsberg's "call to mutiny" as a well-founded necessity if we value our status as citizens and our prospects for survival as sentient beings.

Finding Aldridge persuasive challenges us to give an account of why such a self-destructive path has been chosen. It seems stupid and evil from only certain points of view evidently quite removed from the concrete circumstances of those who possess the power of decision in this country. It is worth explaining why, despite the assault on common sense and the survival ethos, the United States seems, indeed, to be doing what Aldridge contends.

There is, to begin with, the essential techno-industrial momentum associated with "progress" in its military aspect. Bureaucratic forces possess great weight in shaping the choices presented to elected leaders. These forces are conditioned by career, habit, and collaborative relations with special interest groups to move ever forward in weaponry, to stay ahead and to achieve a maximum edge vis-a-vis potential international opponents. To achieve a first strike edge in the 1980s is "technologically sweet" (recalling Oppenheimer's words), requiring exquisite refinements in many spheres of weaponry. The adverse overall effects of these improvements on actual security are not really noticed because of the powerful built-in assumption that additions to *our* capabilities to inflict destruction are contributions to national security. To be stronger than one's rival is, in this strict Machiavellian sense, to be proportionately more secure. This militarist phenomenon does not seem exclusively tied to capitalism; it pertains, as well, in the Soviet variant of militarism, which if not properly called "socialist," is also not "capitalist." Profit margins, corporate special pleading, and a mutuality of outlook and access at the upper levels of government and business and finance, helps establish the *tone* of American militarism, but not its *essence*. Its essence is shaped by the logic of a world of competing sovereign states.

These general forces that shape official policy, and create a receptivity to first strike technology, are accentuated in the setting of nuclear weaponry. The United States as the first and only user of nuclear weaponry has a definite psycho-political stake in maintaining *the legitimacy* of this technology of mass destruction. It is not only the denial of guilt that is operative, it is also the sense of imperial predominance. Throughout the post-1945 period the United States rested its claims of predominance on its nuclear advantage. This advantage was, at first, absolute, and then since Soviet acquisition of nuclear weaponry, relative, but nevertheless real. It was in the 1970s under the aegis of detente and arms control, that the United States seemed to acknowledge temporarily its loss of a nuclear advantage by accepting parity as descriptive of U.S./Soviet strategic power. By the late 1970s, powerful domestic forces attacked nuclear equality as producing a circumstance of nuclear disadvantage or inferiority and consequent geopolitical decline for the United States. Paul Nitze, Eugene Rostow, and an array of retired generals, flamboyantly grouped in the Committee on the Present Danger, warned the country that it was becoming vulnerable to a Soviet first strike. The Reagan candidacy and presidency has accepted this mirage as the basis of its call for an arms buildup, and instituted a massive increase in defense spending at a time when unemployment was at post-depression peaks and the ranks of Americans living below the poverty level were rapidly swelling.

The nuclearist approach to militarism is especially confusing at this time because of deceptive patterns of public discourse. Despite the facade of detente and arms control, as Aldridge demonstrates, the American quest for a first strike option guided military laboratories and Pentagon planners even during the pre-Reagan period. It surfaced, to a certain extent, in Jimmy Carter's endorsement of a "flexible response" doctrine in Presidential Directive 59, which contained first strike implications, especially through its suggestion that Soviet command and control capabilities could be accurately targeted. That is, even in the pre-Reagan period there was a determined effort to assert a nuclear advantage (that is, a greater readiness to rely on nuclear weapons to achieve foreign policy ends), perceived by strategists and bureaucrats as a vital American "asset" ever since Hiroshima.

A further supporting argument for first strike arises from geopolitics. The United States' imperial position in the world deteriorated in the 1970s (the Vietnam defeat; the OPEC challenge; the erosion of dominance over capitalist rivals—and security partners—in Western Europe and Japan; the Indian nuclear explosion; and the anti-United States outcome of national revolutions in Angola, Iran and Nicaragua). In the teeth of that imperial deterioration, big government and big capital joined forces to support an accelerated defense effort as an urgent national priority. Even *Fortune* detected "a mental gap" in the call for added defense spending as advocates of a bigger budget were generally unable to connect the absence of American military power in any very concrete way to the process of American imperial decline. On a shallow level, the increased emphasis on military capabilities was claimed as necessary to show a new United States "resolve," a willingness, it would seem, to undertake in the future the same kind of costly and imprudent struggles against Third World nationalism that had culminated in the Vietnam debacle. And, in fact, the efforts to sustain the Duarte regime in power in El Salvador had been selected by the Reagan leadership as an easy way to manifest in concrete terms this new resolve. However, the Vietnam syndrome, as it is mockingly called by militarists, proved far more powerful at the grassroots level than was anticipated by official America. The intervention in El Salvador was unpopular from the start, and furthermore, it soom became evident that victory was not in the offing, and that America was about to sink its heavy boot into yet another quagmire.

But there is a more sinister, nuclear side to the argument for accelerated armament. It involves a kind of "desperado geopolitics" in which the nuclear option (in circumstances of international confrontation) becomes the basis for the defense of Western interests. Haig publicly reiterated this position in the course of denouncing the no-first-use proposal given prominence through its endorsement by four former national security heavies (Bundy, Kennan, McNamara, G. Smith): "Those in the West who advocate the adoption of a 'no first use' policy seldom go on to propose that the United States reintroduce the draft, triple the size of its armed forces and put its economy on wartime footing. Yet in the absence of such steps, a pledge of no first use effectively leaves the West nothing with which to counterbalance the Soviet conventional advantages and geopolitical position in Europe."[3] Leaving aside Haig's wild exaggerations of Western European vulnerability to conventional attack (many impartial experts regard Europe's non-nuclear capabilities as currently a match for the Soviets, and, in any event, discount the danger of such an attack), the statement is indicative of the persisting need for the United States to make use of its nuclear option to offset alleged Soviet military advantages flowing from their conventional superiority and geopolitical position. This same reasoning applies to other so-called theaters of conflict, particularly the Persian Gulf, where shorter Soviet interior lines of communication and supply are said to confer a tactical advantage to Moscow in the event an East-West encounter is confined to non-nuclear weaponry. In essence, the United States seeks to use its nuclear advantage to achieve what the strategists call "escalation dominance," that is, to make the Soviet Union back down or take upon itself the fateful decision to escalate the struggle by expanding the arena of conflict and combat. First strike is the culminating expression of this posture, a thoroughly frightening capability (or pseudo-capability) that threatens to attack the Soviet heartland (allegedly without fear of serious retaliation) if sufficiently provoked; "non-serious" retaliation is considered by first strike advocates to result in between 20 and 25 million dead. If the Soviets reject the implication or somehow call the bluff (possibily by producing their own first strike posture), then every regional crisis possesses the geopolitical tinder for general war.

This amounts to saying that American policy-makers and power-wielders evidently see no other way to sustain the imperial position of the United States than by an unprecedented reassertion of the nuclear option, ultimately in the form of a first strike posture. This "gamble" is a desperate one, not only because it risks nuclear catastrophe to promote overseas national interests (that is, interests unconnected with the defense of homeland), but also because the threat to these interests is predominantly political and indigenous in any event, and quite beyond the domain of deterrence. If Moscow doesn't control revolutionaries, and it doesn't, then threatening Moscow seems like a foolish response on our part that can only make us look silly or induce some irrational policy based on such a false presupposition. Having more ample military capabilities deployed for mobility and doctrines that rest on the nuclear option, only compounds the menace of this mode of thinking, and accounts for the label "desperado geopolitics."

One rebuke to this line of argument, and to Aldridge's indictment of national security as conceived by the Pentagon, is that it is so widely denied in official circles. The weaponry that Aldridge characterizes as "first strike" our leaders in Washington justify as contributions to "deterrence" or as giving American leaders choices in crises other than Armageddon or surrender. What are we to make of this divergence? There is a semantic abyss created by the word "deterrence." It can cover many distinct goals, including a commitment to deter Soviet leaders from taking actions they are *not*, in any event, taking. To hold Soviet (or even Cuban) leaders responsible for turmoil in Central America is to falsify the nature of the struggle—to find weaponry that will deter what is not being done in any event is to embark upon an *incoherent* course of policy. To back that up with first strike threats is to compound both the absurdity and danger, suggesting dire consequences if the Soviet Union doesn't stop doing what it's not doing! But an extension of deterrence beyond the strict limits of discouraging direct nuclear attack lends itself to such perverse applications.

Furthermore, let's concede that the weaponry, communications systems, and missile defense measures are motivated, in large part, by a philosophy of deterrence in the primary sense of inhibiting Moscow. Nevertheless, that undertaking, if pushed far enough, as it is indeed being pushed, is indistinguishable from planning a first strike posture. There is a lethal ambiguity that arises from this framework of doctrine and weaponry allowing for several parallel constructions. Naturally, our leaders stress the most benign possibility, whereas their leaders will stress (and presumably act upon) more ominous possibilities. Such is the nature of world politics.

Finally, our Pentagon/White house operatives have a rather low view of the citizenry, especially when it comes to accepting the burdens of the nuclear age. Every so often the national security establishment drops its guard and admits either that it is disappointed with the timidity of the public or that it is necessary for officials to dissemble to some extent to avoid alarmist reactions. Indeed, we have arrived at the scary circumstance where people serve at the pleasure and for the benefit of the rulers; to speak of government as consisting of delegated or representative powers is now only true in the most formal of senses. The fact, for instance, that our leaders don't clearly acknowledge first strike ambitions is no assurance that they are not being pursued. And when we check the reassuring words out against the realities of the overall pattern of the arms buildup, it is difficult to deny the force of Aldridge's conclusion that we are embarked on a coordinated effort to achieve a first strike capability.

There is a final possibility. The government itself may be in a state of willful or capricious confusion. It may actually be the case that most elected leaders sincerely believe that our nuclear motivations are retaliatory in character. The real power of decision on national security policy seems defintely to lie hidden in the recesses of the bureaucracy. Not long ago, it was reported that the official search for the MX basing methods was being aided by recommendations to be made by a civilian group headed by a conservative scientist, Charles Townes, and including among its rank three of the most unbalanced nuclear extremists that are currently loose in our midst—namely, Edward Teller, Herman Kahn, and Colin Grey.[4] Since consultants are often selected to give the kind of advice that is sought, we gain some insight into the outlook of these rulers operating from the deep cover of Washington's bureaucracy. Our conception of government may itself be too antiquated to capture the processes by which weapons programs and strategies are shaped and determined. These hidden militaristic bureaucrats—positioned to uphold imperial status and position—seem scornful of the formal governmental machinery consisting of politicians with short tenure and some public and electoral accountability; individuals who show only scant comprehension of the fine points of strategy and geopolitics. Many of us have grown disillusioned with the two-party system and the ritual of elections when it comes to questioning the fundamental postulates of national security policy. The roots of first strike planning exist so deep as to suggest that even the posts of President and Secretary of Defense and Senator have become largely ornamental in relation to national security policy. Throwing "the rascals" out, accordingly, becomes a much more formidable task, even, than organizing a new political party that seeks to build popular support in defiance of the prevailing bipartisan power structure. The evidence increasingly suggests that the American people are being held captive by a bureaucratic coup whose exact character, goals, and methods we have yet to comprehend, or even to identify accurately.

In this disturbing book, Robert Aldridge does much more than frighten or anger. He suggests that a refusal to go along with nuclearism, given the way the world is divided between "haves" and "have nots," is an intensely demanding challenge. He questions, correctly I feel, whether we can ever hope to free ourselves of this death-dealing militarism until we are genuinely ready to live and share with all others on this planet as brothers and sisters. He is convinced that there is a deep connection between our prosperity and our nuclearism and that we are not free in our personal lives of complicity in the curse of nuclearism (and specifically, first strike) until we adopt a simple life style for ourselves and decide to withhold resources (taxes and labor) from this killing ground of official defense activities. A radical message for a radical time!

1. *NYT*, August 18, 1982, p. A21.
2. Text of Haig's speech to International Club of Georgetown University's Center for Strategic Studies, *NYT*, April 7, 1982, p. A8.
3. Ibid., p. A8.
4. *NYT*, August 10 1982, pp. A2, A15; note, also the absence of any skeptical comment in the news report.

PROLOGUE

The means may be likened to a seed, the end to a tree; and there is just the same inviolable connection between the means and the end as there is between the seed and the tree.

—Mohandas K. Gandhi

I hestitated at the gate and let my gaze wander down the chain-link fence. Dew clung to the barbed tips of the wires topping off the fence. A knot turned in my stomach. It had been plaguing my arrival at work for months. But today was different. I took a deep breath and stepped inside the perimeter.

I flashed my ID card at the guard and entered the engineering building. Climbing the stairs my feet were slow and heavy. I negotiated down the hall and absently punched the four-digit combination to the secret room where missile reentry bodies were designed. I trudged to my desk, my hands quivering.

The clock on the wall showed fifteen minutes until shift time. I turned the page of my new desk calendar. The date glared at me in red characters—January 2nd, the first working day of the year. This was the day when . . . the knot tightened. I settled deeper in my chair and began to review, once again, the sequence of events that had brought me to this day.

For years I had watched discontent smolder in the aerospace industry as employees were called upon to build hideous weapons while suppressing moral doubts. The corporate salary, coupled with lavish fringe benefits, seduces the defense workers as they are swept up in the game of nuclear brinkmanship. I was once proud to be an engineer. After my discharge following the second world war I attended California State Polytechnic University in San Luis Obispo and received a technical degree in aeronautics. Janet and I married during that time. The 1948 recession was gripping the country as I left Cal Poly and I was forced to take other employment. It was nine years later, in 1957, that I returned to aeronautics and obtained an engineering job at Lockheed Missiles and Space Company, a subsidiary of the Lockheed Corporation located at the southern tip of San Francisco Bay. I took courses at San Jose State Univesity to receive my Bachelor of Science degree in 1962; graduating magna cum laude with honors in aeronautics.

Design studies on the first Polaris missile were just getting underway when I hired-on at Lockheed. As we advanced through three generations of Polaris and into the Poseidon submarine-launched weapons, I became a veteran engineer on sea-based missiles and leader of an advanced design group. At the time I valued my work, but how it was evaluated troubled me: the Poseidon weapons system was given an "effectiveness rating" of 80-million fatalities. Still, I looked upon America as the hope of the world, and I put my work in service to that ideal.

When the Strategic Arms Limitation Talks (SALT) were convened in Vienna on April 16, 1970, the Poseidon missile with its multiple Mark-3 warheads was nearing production status. Lockheed and the Navy became concerned that SALT developments might outlaw the multiple individually-targeted reentry vehicles (MIRVs). Such a ban could ultimately stop deployment of the Poseidon missile which, besides depriving the Navy of its newest weapon, would be financially disastrous for Lockheed. The decision was made to keep a jump ahead and find alternatives that would satisfy any treaty restriction. A working group was set up for that purpose and I was selected as the design engineering representative.

Shortly after being assigned to SALT studies, as it was openly called at first, I grew uneasy. During a meeting in my supervisor's office, the Assistant Chief Engineer stopped by. He and the Navy had just hammered out a set of options for the working group to investigate. One area to receive attention was the possibility of putting MIRVs on a missile without the Soviets finding out. I was appalled. How could we be serious about disarmament if we were willing to cheat on a treaty? This was my first glimpse at the lack of candor in

US policy. Nevertheless, I pursued the study as outlined because my moral qualms were still not strong enough to override my attachment to the weekly paycheck.

It wasn't long before public opposition to stepped-up weapons production brought the security lid down. The task force was given an innocuous code name: CAFE, to deflect public scrutiny. As this happened I was removed from the CAFE operation and given the design responsibility for the Mark-500 maneuvering reentry vehicle (MARV) to be used on the Trident missile. Unknowingly, I had entered the final phase of my aerospace career.

MARVs were ostensibly being designed to evade enemy interceptors during reentry when the earth's atmosphere allows aerodynamic maneuvering. At that late time in flight, however, there are only a few seconds left to find and fire at the incoming warhead. That fact, coupled with the complex arrays of penetration aids and decoys which accompany US reentry bodies, would render interception of even existing warheads more theoretical than practical. Seen in that light, the cost of MARVs could not be justified. The evasion story was further weakened after the 1972 ABM Treaty severely limited the number of anti-ballistic missiles allowed each country.

To update my knowledge on maneuvering technology I reviewed numerous secret documents. I soon discovered that Pentagon strategists have a keen interest in more accurate weapons and it didn't take much deduction to see that a homing MARV was their ultimate goal. The precision they desired could only be useful for destroying hardened targets such as missile emplacements or command posts. This was a departure from our stated deterrent policy of only firing when fired upon. This was before the time of public confusion over winning limited nuclear wars, reloading missle silos, and the alleged vulnerability of US silos. I was unhampered in my perception that going after the Soviets' land-based missiles meant shooting first because it made no sense to retaliate against empty silos. I was also outraged that this move toward first strike was kept secret from the public.

Other influences had heightened the tension between my beliefs and my career. My children challenged my part in designing weapons. "Someone must have the courage to start," said my oldest daughter about abandoning that kind of work. Those words troubled me. A good friend once said that when someone made him uncomfortable he found it advantageous to listen. I was more than uncomfortable. I felt trapped. All of my career preparation had been in the engineering field, and all of my experience in engineering had been in the production of weapons.

My doubts chipped away at the technology-oriented mentality that my profession had engendered in me, and nurtured the growth of more people-centered concerns. I became more critically aware of what was happening at work. The pride which once welled-up in me when a successful missile flight was announced began giving way to questions. Why were we constantly working overtime to correct failures if everything was going so well? Or, while diplomats were relating how scrupulously the United States abides by the Atmospheric Test Ban Treaty, I would find myself witnessing another underground *event* that vented into the atmosphere. I discussed these contradictions with my colleagues but seldom in any depth. Some cheating and deception was an accepted norm in our society and, as regards international treaties and global justice, the defense worker's field of interest rarely reached beyond the immediate job assignment. I began to see that not only was the public being deceived but that we defense workers were also uninformed.

Most of my colleagues did not seem to really think of their efforts in terms of preventing war. Patriotic feelings were subordinated to a concern for winning more contracts and working more overtime. Investigating new business opportunities received high priority and many of our present weapons originated as unsolicited proposals to the Pentagon from a military contractor.

I could see very little joy within the guarded gates of Lockheed. Only intellectual activity was visible and that was strictly shunted along the lines of the project at hand. This one-dimensional concern, along with tough-line competition for more responsibility, was the general rule. The drive to gather more and more work under one's wing always amazed me until I finally diagnosed this *empire building* as a groping for security—a need to become indispensible. But I knew of very few who actually achieved any degree of permanence. A budget cut or administrative reshuffle could result in one being laid off or squeezed out of line in the pecking order. Fear constantly charged the atmosphere while the healthy fulfillment of seeing one's efforts benefit humanity was denied.

As my awareness moved to curiosity and finally to disdain, I sensed that my engineering career was drawing to a close. I yearned for the end even while I dreaded the loss of security that would accompany it. I hadn't begun to appreciate the security I had achieved, or its hold on me, until I assessed what I would lose if I quit: months of accumulated sick leave, medical and dental insurance, and life insurance; all covered by the company in addition to a large weekly salary. If it had been only Janet and me the decision would have been more manageable. But what about the kids?

Nevertheless, I recognized fear as the main obstacle to the obvious solution. Janet and I started planning our escape. We itemized objectives, areas to investigate, library research to perform, and people with whom we should discuss our plans. My engineering skills began to find a new objective. While both of us realized we would have to share wage-earning we were determined not to allow economic considerations to dominate our choice of occupations.

We wanted our children to be part of this decision so we discussed my work, my crisis of conscience and our social responsibility, at family meetings. They contributed suggestions, asked questions, and brainstormed ways they could help. A minor crisis arose when our teenagers confronted the prospect of a more austere lifestyle, but as the issues became clearer they became supportive.

Janet and I set the date for January of 1973. Immediately after Christmas vacation I would give notice of my resignation. We would start the new year with a new life.

We set aside the four days following Christmas as a time to unify our intentions. We rented a cabin in the Santa Cruz Mountains and retired into the wilderness to read and talk and contemplate—to center our moral feelings and religious beliefs on our family and what we were about to do. We strengthened our bonds to face the future.

January 2, 1973: Those crimson characters still glared at me. I was getting impatient. Clark, my supervisor, should have arrived ten minutes ago. I wanted to finish it—to get past that point where there would be no turning back.

Clark rushed in at twenty after. From his face I could tell he had been sidetracked by the department manager. Now I had to catch him before he left again. I walked hesitatingly to his door.

"I'd like to talk with you, Clark."

He invited me to have a seat. Clark was a good supervisor. He was approachable and listened to what a person had to say. His sensitivity to subordinates was hampered only by his affinity to company philosophy. My words faltered.

"I've decided to leave Lockheed." Now, the bridge was crossed. I continued: "Guess you could tell something's been bugging me."

Clark showed only mild surprise. His head nodded slowly as he admitted he realized I'd been unhappy but didn't know why. I'd been a lead engineer under him for five years and worked for him longer than that. We'd had our differences but he had always been fair.

"Nothing personal, Clark. Guess I'm developing a conscience—getting concerned about people." His eyes popped open. I continued: "I like engineering and all that but we've got weapons up to our gazoo. We're just finding excuses to keep the business going . . ."

I cut loose then and told him my feelings about the arms race and how we had already saturated the deterrent capability; how I felt about the military being glutted with money while critical human needs were not being met. ". . . Now we're in the Trident program. That'll gobble up more billions. Meanwhile, global relations are strained by our skyrocketing defense budget."

Clark listened. When I finished he leaned back in his chair and stared at the ceiling thoughtfully. Then he said: "You may be right, Bob. I've thought about those things too. But I keep telling myself we won't really use these weapons—this is just a game we're playing."

His words were not new to me. I had had these same thoughts many times myself. Now they stood clearly as a weak defense against moral crisis. Pentagon objectives are very real and clear. The military exists for only one purpose—as any general or admiral can tell you. Most defense workers realize, at least subconsciously, that when we align our priorities with those of the Pentagon we are going to be pressed into service to that purpose. But to people engaged in that service it takes a moral/spiritual crisis to deflect their activity because it means sacrificing their careers, forfeiting seniority benefits and status, and facing financial insecurity.

During my remaining time at Lockheed I discussed my reasons for leaving with co-workers. I told them I had decided to stop kidding myself and act on the truth as I saw it. Most of them respected my decision and some even congratulated me. They said they'd like to do likewise but were the first to admit they couldn't give up the paycheck.

Clark and my other friends took me out to lunch on my last day. After the final goodbyes I made my way to the badge office—the last step in the checkout procedure. The cold, bare office was empty except for one clerk who nonchalantly accepted my ID badge while jerking a thumb toward the one-way door leading outside the fenced perimeter.

"Through there," he grunted. As I turned a loud clang echoed through the bare office. My badge had hit the bottom of an empty metal waste container. "Thus ends the Lockheed chapter of my life," I thought. A couple more steps, a twist of the knob, and I was out in the dim winter sunshine. The springloaded door banged with finality behind me.

Anticipation of this moment had been the worst. I now emerged from that deathly atmosphere with a new feeling of freedom. I would no longer have to censor my speech or my way of thinking to conform to company policy. I was my own man, so to speak, and I resolved that my engineering experience would not be wasted. I started doing full time research and used the information to write articles and give talks. I started gathering highly technical and isolated facts and putting them together using common language so people could understand what is happening. As I delved deeper into Pentagon activity I discovered a pattern more sinister than I had imagined. Evidence indicated that the Pentagon is looking far beyond what is needed for defense. It is developing the instruments which will allow the United States to fight and win a nuclear war; if survival after any type of nuclear conflict can be called a victory.

That is what this book is about. Throughout these pages I will share with you how I have discovered that evolving technologies are putting this country in a position to launch a disabling and unanswerable first strike.

What I depict in this book is not science fiction. It is real and is moving toward its ultimate climax. Stopping it will be up to all of us and I hope this book will help supply the knowledge and motivation. It is not just the people at Lockheed and other such places who are making the first strike machinery. It is all of us—we who pay the taxes that buy the weapons; and we who sit quietly by and leave the running of this country to the "experts." What is happening affects every one of us and our concerns are the area in which we are the most qualified experts.

The decision to stop first strike and all that it implies will come only from the grass roots level. It will not be based on technology or politics or economics. As it was in my case, it will be in everyone's case—the decision will be a spiritual/moral choice. It will happen when we face the truth and correct our lives accordingly. I feel that it is happening already. Each of us can make it happen sooner.

THE FIRST STRIKE SYNDROME

Should you read upon an encounter with an elephant, a sign saying Buffalo, believe not your eyes.

—Alexei Konstantinovich Tolstoy

"I have become death, the destroyer of worlds," quoted Dr. Robert Oppenheimer from the Bhagavad Gita as he witnessed the first atomic explosion. Oppenheimer headed the project which culminated in that blaze of light across the New Mexico desert on July 16, 1945. At that instant the United States entered the nuclear age. Three weeks later history's second atomic blast ripped through the Japanese city of Hiroshima. Only three days after that the nuclear specter struck again as Nagasaki disappeared in a fiery massacre. Those first three tests of the United States' newly found power took place in less than a month and left behind misery and mutilation that has lasted for decades.

For at least the first decade of the nuclear age the U.S. monopolized the ability to start and win a nuclear war. It exercised that ability when it escalated World War 2 to atomic weapons, purportedly to bring that war to a quick end. A deeper reason for this escalation, however, appears to have been a warning to Russia not to overrun Europe and Asia during the final days of the war. Had the USSR not stopped its advances more cities might have been incinerated. These events serve as a grim reminder that when the United States had the ability to launch an unanswerable nuclear strike there was no reluctance to do so if it served its purpose.

Gradually, as the Soviet Union followed in the development of nuclear weapons, the United States lost its strategic edge. The announced nuclear policy of each country shifted to *deterrence*—the threat of mutual annihilation that was supposed to keep either nation from striking first. The truth, however, is that the Pentagon has pursued a more aggressive *counterforce* policy since the mid-1950s at least. Such a policy has not been generally advertised, however. What information is available in the public domain is usually couched in military/scientific jargon and is buried deep in technical journals, congressional hearing transcripts, military posture statements, and government reports. Furthermore, the Pentagon has been successful in keeping the various weapons programs isolated from one another so that even the more professional critics have a difficult time seeing how they interrelate to provide an aggressive capability.

Nevertheless, it is a prerequisite of democratic processes that the populace be informed. It may even fall as a duty on each taxpayer and voter to have at least a working knowledge of the military activities which consume over half the federal tax dollar. Correct evaluation of how elected representatives and government officials are performing is essential for democracy to be participatory.

The average person, however, still believes the two superpowers are operating under the nuclear strategy of *deterrence*. The Pentagon, at least, has publicly offered deterrence as its strategic doctrine since shortly after the beginning of the nuclear age. Deterrence is the nuclear stalemate whereby both superpowers refrain from shooting nuclear weapons first because they fear the massive retaliation which would follow. Since retaliatory weapons must survive a nuclear first attack in order to fulfill their mission, they are stored in underground silos, are on alert in heavy bombers, and are carried aboard submarines hiding at sea.

In order to deter an attack on the U.S., the Pentagon would aim strategic weapons at targets whose destruction would be most unacceptable—Soviet cities and manufacturing areas. Because these are vulnerable targets, American missiles wouldn't have to carry a very big bomb or be too precise in their aim. The 40-kiloton* bombs or submarine-launched Poseidon missiles, for example would serve the purpose.

The deterrent policy has been dubbed MAD; an appropriate acronym which stands for "mutual assured destruction." It was this

---

*A kiloton is the nuclear explosive force equal to one-thousand tons of conventional explosives. A megaton is equal to one-million tons.

principle upon which the first Strategic Arms Limitation Talks (SALT) agreements were based. By limiting defenses against ballistic missiles and restricting the number of offensive weapons, each country was supposedly guaranteed the ability to inflict unacceptable retaliation even after absorbing a nuclear attack.

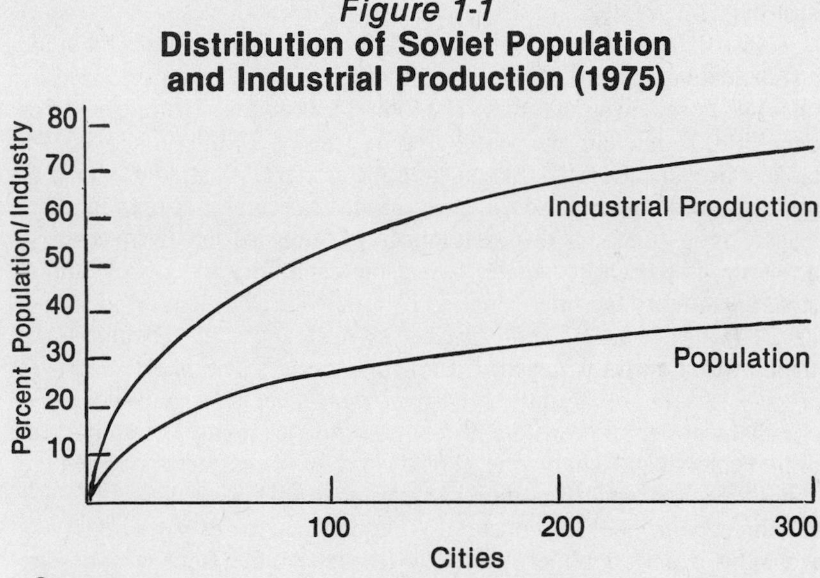

Figure 1-1
Distribution of Soviet Population and Industrial Production (1975)

Source:
Department of Defense Annual Report Fiscal Year 1981, by Harold Brown, Secretary of Defense (January 29, 1980) p. 79.

What is the "unacceptable retaliation" that would deter the Soviets from launching a nuclear attack? In 1957, then Defense Secretary Robert McNamara testified: "It seems reasonable to assume that in the case of the Soviet Union, the destruction of, say, one-fifth to one-fourth of its population and one-half to two-thirds of its industrial capacity would mean its elimination as a major power for many years.[1] McNamara's definition of a credible deterrent is not arbitrary. According to a paper published by Cornell University, about 25 percent of the Soviet population and half its industry are concentrated in the top 100 cities.[2] Figure 1-1 illustrates that the concentration of population and industry falls off sharply for additional cities. Whereas destroying the largest 100 eliminates about a quarter of the Soviet population and half its industry, obliterating the next hundred largest cities would only eliminate an additional 7 percent of the population and 13 percent of the industry. Destroying the third set of 100 cities according to size would only liquidate an additional 4 percent of the population and 7 percent of the industry. It can be seen from this that McNamara's definition of deterrence is based on the fact that only the largest 100 cities could be destroyed efficiently.

It would seem that 400 deliverable hydrogen bombs would provide an adequate deterrent. More than this number, however, are carried on only two Poseidon submarines. The total US weapons stockpile contains over 30,000 nuclear warheads: approximately 22,000 deployed for tactical use and about 10,000 on strategic carriers.* A strategic force of this size does not make sense if the US doctrine is, indeed, to retaliate against cities under a deterrence policy. Such a force is necessary, however, if the United States wants the capability to destroy Soviet strategic military facilities.

This brings us to *counterforce*. As a nuclear strategy, counterforce means aiming attack missiles at military targets. The word means to *counter* the enemy's military *forces* which includes missile silos, command posts, nuclear storage depots, strategic air bases, communications centers, and submarine pens. Many of these targets are called "hard" because they are buried deep in bunkers or silos and are reinforced with steel and concrete. Weapons used to destroy hard targets would have to be extremely precise. Although counterforce weapons are not necessarily first strike weapons (which will be discussed below), counterforce does have offensive connotations because many counterforce targets would have to be destroyed *before* they are used or their destruction would be of no significance. Furthermore, these are the installations which would be targeted if either the US or the USSR were contemplating an unanswerable nuclear first strike.

First strike is an ambiguous term which has been assigned several meanings. In one sense it is used to describe whatever country initiates

*Tactical and strategic weapons are distinquished by the range over which they can be delivered. Tactical weapons are used over relatively short distances in theatres of operation such as Europe or against opponents at sea. They are sometimes called theatre weapons. Strategic weapons refer to those which would be used during a major confrontation between the superpowers and are capable of reaching the opponent's homeland.

nuclear war. It is also associated with a (hoped for) limited use of nuclear weapons to stop a massive attack with conventional armament. This is more often called "first use."

Use of the term "first strike" in this book will be in the more technical military sense of a strategic first strike: a capability to inflict a *disarming* or *unanswerable* first strike against a rival nation.*

Counterforce is not necessarily equated with first strike because there are degrees of counterforce. The ability to destroy bomber bases, for instance, would require counterforce weapons or counterforce targeting. But destroying a bomber base does not constitute a disarming first strike because silo-based and submarine-based missiles would be certain to retaliate.

A disarming first strike capability can be described as the ultimate in counterforce. That is, it would comprise an arsenal of counterforce weapons capable of destroying the entire strategic force of the other superpower. Although counterforce does not necessarily mean first strike, first strike is counterforce in its maximum sense.

It has been general public belief that United States strategic policy is one of deterrence. There is evidence, however, that strategic counterforce targeting has been practiced for decades. Recent Senate testimony by General David C. Jones, at the time chairman of the Joint Chiefs of Staff, confirms this fact:

Senator Tower: General Jones, what is your opinion of the theory of mutual assured destruction?

General Jones: I think it is a very dangerous strategy. It is not the strategy that we are implementing today within the military, but it is a dangerous strategy.

Senator Tower: Your professional military judgment is that it is a dangerous strategy and that it is not one that we should follow?

General Jones: I do not subscribe to the idea that we ever had it as our basic strategy. I have been involved with strategic forces since the early 1950s. We have

*The question often comes up of whether the Soviet Union is also pursuing a first strike posture to which the US must respond. It is true that the Soviets try to emulate the United States' progression of weapons but they lacked many technologies, which the US is rapidly acquiring, that are significant for a first strike capability. I will show in subsequent chapters that the exaggerated Soviet threat is not a valid excuse for the extensive weapons development programs being pursued by the United States.

always targeted military targets. There has been a lot of discussion—it is interesting that, when I was out in the field, in Washington you would hear a lot of rhetoric about different strategies. We followed orders, but basically, the strategy stayed the same in implementation and targeting.

Senator Tower: Unfortunatey, I am not sure that your opinion was always shared by your civilian superiors.

General Jones: I agree there were some, including some in government, who have felt that all we required is a mutual assured destruction capability. I am separating that from our targeting instructions to the field, approved by civilian authorities, which always included targeting military targets.[3]

An early 1956 issue of *Foreign Affairs* magazine pointed out that in any discussion of American strategic policy one must distinguish between the two related but different meanings of the word "policy." The magazine quoted then Deputy Defense Secretary Paul Nitze, now the Reagan Administration's chief arms control negotiator, as saying, "In one sense, the action sense, it refers to the general guidelines which we believe should and will in fact govern our actions in various contingencies. In the other sense, the declaratory sense, it refers to policy statements which have as their aim political and psychological effect."[4]

Cities were undoubtedly the main targets when nuclear bombs were carried only on bombers during the late 1940s and the beginning of the 1950s because the number of nuclear weapons was limited and they were atom (fission) bombs with a lower explosive yield. In addition, the cities were vulnerable and could not be hidden. But as the US nuclear stockpile grew there were enough weapons to assign to other targets. The "softer" military targets became the next logical choice. For these, the added explosive power of hydrogen (fusion) bombs made up for what the weapons then lacked in accuracy.

By the mid-1950s the Strategic Air Command (SAC) was again preparing for a first strike against the Soviet Union with the result that "virtually all of Russia would be nothing but a smoking, radiating ruin at the end of two hours."[5] This planning was revealed in two recently declassified top secret reports.

The first report, a 1954 Navy memorandum of an Air Force briefing on SAC's plans and capabilities for war, said that then SAC commander,

General Curtis LeMay, "has complete confidence in SAC's ability to crush Russia quickly by massive atomic bombing attacks. No aspect of the morals or long-range effects of such attacks were discussed, and no questions on it were asked."[6]

The second document, a briefing of the Weapons System Evaluation Group's (WSEG) Report No. 12, of February 1955, called for twice the allocation of nuclear bombs against USSR air bases in order to preclude retaliation against the US and its allies. It warned that even "this additional allocation cannot prevent the Soviets launching a strike unless we hit first."[7]

These documents demonstrate that a strategic counterforce policy actually predominated during the mid-1950s while the *announced* policy of deterrence elicited the desired political and psychological effects from the American people.* That was in the age of aircraft and the United States was on the verge of deploying the world's first jet bombers, the B-52s. The Soviets were far outclassed. But counterforce met a setback a few years later when the intercontinental ballistic missile (ICBM) entered the picture. A missile race ensued that introduced not only a faster delivery vehicle which could be launched very quickly, but also a new set of targets—the very small, numerous, and hard missile silos. The imminence of a first strike capability receded as missile accuracy became a more stringent requirement. The Pentagon's pursuit of a greater counterforce capability continued, however, and was evident in its nuclear targeting plans.

By December 1960 the first Single Integrated Operational Plan (SIOP) was drawn up. The SIOP is probably the Pentagon's most secret document. It assigns every nuclear weapon to a specific target under any given set of circumstances. In the summer of 1961 a revision of the SIOP was completed by Daniel Ellsberg and two other Rand Corporation strategists. It was approved by the Pentagon late that year and officially adopted in January 1962. Among the options it contained were the following counterforce targeting provisions:[8]

> Soviet strategic retaliatory forces such as missile silos, bomber bases and submarine tenders.

---

*I do not mean to imply that the Pentagon is independent in the development of more counterforce weapons. What is actually leading the United States toward an aggressive and destabilizing first strike capability is the influence of the military-industrial complex. I'll deal with this in more detail in Chapter 11.

Soviet air defenses away from cities which would cover US bomber routes.

Soviet air defenses to protect cities.

Soviet command and control centers and systems.

In January 1962, the month the revised SIOP was adopted, Defense Secretary McNamara made the first official reference to a counterforce capability: "A major mission of the strategic retaliatory forces is to deter war by their capability to destroy the enemy's warmaking capabilities."[9] The following month, on February 17th, McNamara indicated that in order to deter Soviet aggression the United States needed a larger stockpile of weapons than the USSR. "We may have to retaliate with a single massive attack," he claimed, "or we may be able to use our retaliatory forces to limit damage* done to ourselves, and our allies, by knocking out the enemy's bases before he has time to launch his second salvos . . ."[10]

This argument of preventing counter-retaliation is still being used today. But what must be remembered is that the capability to hit missile silos before the second salvo is fired is exactly the same as that required to destroy them before any of the missiles are fired. As one former aide to McNamara pointed out: ". . . there could be no such thing as a primary retaliation against military targets after an enemy attack. If you're going to shoot at missiles you're talking about first strike."[11] President Kennedy didn't clear up the ominous implications of US strategic doctrine when he told reporters in March 1962 that "Krushchev must not be certain that, where our vital interests are threatened, the United States will not strike first."[12]

McNamara again alluded to this "damage limiting," or counterforce, strategy during his now famous commencement address at Ann Arbor, Michigan on June 16, 1962. He said the United States' "principal military objectives in the event of a nuclear war stemming from a major attack on the Alliance, should be the destruction of the enemy's military forces, not his civilian population. The very strength and nature of the

---

Damage Limitation is a tranquilizing term introduced by the Pentagon to mean counterforce. While "damage limitation" sounds like a restrained approach to nuclear strategy it actually means limiting damage to *American* cities. That, of course, requires the destruction of the opponent's assault forces *before they can be used*. For referring to a counterforce capability on the part of the Soviets the Pentagon has coined the more aggressive-sounding term, *war fighting*. Both damage limitation and war fighting, however, mean the same: counterforce.

Alliance forces makes it possible for us to retain . . . sufficient reserve striking power to destroy an enemy's society if driven to it."[13] Even when examining that statement in the context of the entire paragraph from which it was extracted, it is not possible to determine if the "major attack on the Alliance" needs to be a nuclear attack. Also, he openly admitted that the US strategic forces contain more weapons than are necessary for deterrence.

In 1967, when the US had already deployed 1,054 land-based intercontinental ballistic missiles (ICBMs) and forty-one Polaris missile-launching submarines, McNamara changed the emphasis on weapons procurement from quantity to quality. He said the US had enough nuclear weapons delivery systems—missiles, submarines, bombers—and that the effort from that time forth would be to make them perform better. This shift in policy had several advantages for the Defense Department. First, it allowed more open development of counterforce weapons. Second, given the obvious numerical overkill for Soviet cities, it would be easier to sell the idea of making existing weapons more effective. Third and perhaps most important from the Pentagon's viewpoint, it opened a new avenue of reponse to Soviet weapons development. The Soviets had a huge production program underway to build up their ICBM force and were just beginning to increase the number of submarine-launched ballistic missiles (SLBMs). In addition, they were installing anti-ballistic missile interceptors around Moscow. All this activity gave the Soviets a more credible second strike capability while causing the United States' counterforce ability to deteriorate.

The Soviet weapons buildup presented a growing number of military targets that would have to be destroyed before they could launch weapons if nuclear hostilities appeared imminent. To counter that increase the U.S. began development of the multiple individually targeted reentry vehicles (MIRVs).* Although MIRVs were rationalized as a means of overwhelming ABM defenses around Moscow (a prime target under a deterrence strategy) with multiple warheads, as we shall see they have capabilities more suited to a counterforce role.

---

*MIRVs changed the concept of one missile destroying one target to one missile being able to destroy many targets. Many MIRVs can be put on one missile so that more targets can be destroyed without increasing the number of missiles. Although missile numbers do not increase, the actual number of warheads, or bombs, continue to multiply.

McNamara's change of emphasis opened the door for deployment of MIRVs and other potent strategic weapons which enhance a counterforce capability. Quality improvements have now expanded to include maneuvering reentry vehicles, target sensing warheads, computerized guidance systems, penetration aids, and many more innovations which will be discussed in later chapters.

McNamara's announcement reflected a shift in weapons development which had already been initiated. In 1966 he had ordered the Strategic Exercise Study (Strat-X) to look at follow-on generations of strategic weapons. Deputy Defense Secretary David Packard put the Underwater Long-range Missile System (ULMS) into advanced (early) development in 1968. ULMS later became known as Trident. The B-1 bomber soon followed and mobile Missile-X (MX) development started in 1972. Sea-launched cruise missiles were also started in 1972 with the air-launched version following in 1973. The development and deployment of these counterforce weapons are moving the US toward the capability to launch an unanswerable first strike against the Soviet Union.

Counterforce made significant advances under the Nixon Administration. Only three months after taking office in early 1969, Richard Nixon's newly appointed Defense Secretary, Melvin Laird, requested funds to "significantly improve the accuracies of Poseidon missiles" which were then being flight tested. Later, however, apparently recognizing that the aggressive implications of that move were not being well received, he withdrew his request. He again submitted it the following year only to have it defeated in the House Armed Services Committee.[14] At the same time Richard Nixon introduced what was later to be known as the doctrine of selectivity and flexibility during his annual foreign policy report to Congress:

> Should the President in the event of nuclear attack be left with the single option of ordering the mass destruction of enemy civilians in the face of the certainty that it would be followed by the mass slaughter of Americans? Should the concept of assured destruction be narrowly defined and should it be the only measure of our ability to deter the variety of threats we might face?[15]

Possibly thinking that the third try would be charmed, in early 1971 Representative James Buckley introduced an amendment to the fiscal 1972 defense authorization bill which would have started research and development programs to increase the guidance accuracy of Poseidon and Minuteman 3 missiles. But again the Defense Department backed off after correctly assessing that the groundwork was still not properly laid for such a blatant counterforce program. Nevertheless, President Nixon pursued the campaign toward greater counterforce by again alluding to a need for more "flexible" strategic options during a report to Congress. He said: "I must not be, and my successor must not be, limited to the indiscriminate mass destruction of enemy civilians as the sole possible response to challenges. . . ."[16] Under the guise of seeking more humanitarian nuclear alternatives he pushed for a more lethal policy.

Although the Nixon Administration was not successful in getting Congressional backup for its more aggressive weapons programs during 1971, the drive continued into the following year. For the third time during his annual foreign policy report to Congress Nixon stressed a wider range of nuclear choices. This time he was more emphatic:

> . . . A simple assured destruction doctrine does not meet our present requirements for a flexible range of strategic options. No President should be left with only one strategic course of action, particularly that of ordering the mass destruction of enemy civilians and facilities. Given the range of possible political-military situations which could conceivably confront us, our strategic policy should not be based solely on a capability of inflicting urban and industrial damage presumed to be beyond the level an adversary would accept. We must be able to respond at levels appropriate to the situation.[17]

In May of 1972 the first Strategic Arms Limitation Talks (SALT-1) documents were signed. Immediately therafter, Melvin Laird appeared before Congress with a list of "SALT-related adjustments to strategic programs." He was seeking to accelerate nine programs because, in the words of then Director of Defense Research and Engineering Dr. John Foster, the only way in which the SALT accords would work was if the US was strong and had a "timely and credible hedge" against those agreements expiring or being abrogated.[18] When the Senate defeated these proposals the administration presented supplemental proposals to increase warhead accuracy. These, too, were defeated in a House-Senate conference. This time, however, the Pentagon's attempt at a major reversal in defense doctrine was leaked to the press. Media reports highlighted a desire to increase the accuracy and explosive force of US nuclear warheads. Defense Department spokesman Jerry Friedheim tried to mollify the implications of these reports by asserting that this was only a research program to develop the ability, within the next five years, to knock out hard military targets. Friedheim called it a "hedge" against possible failure to reach a permanent agreement with the Soviet Union on offensive nuclear arms since the SALT-1 Interim Agreement was only effective for five years. He downplayed any Pentagon desire to obtain a first strike force but did concede that "if you develop the capability to attack hard targets then the option would be there for some future president to determine whether to deploy that capability." He said, however, that because of the time needed to complete the research such a decision would be up to someone other than Richard Nixon even if he were reelected to a second term.[19]

In spite of that pre-election disclaimer, shortly after his inauguration for a second term, Nixon proclaimed that the deterrent philosophy based on the ability to kill tens of millions of people was "inconsistent with American values." In his May 1973 foreign policy speech to Congress he declared that a president needed greater flexibility in his choice of options.[20] Shortly thereafter James Schlesinger, the new defense secretary, started programs to improve the accuracy of strategic missiles—a full year before Congressional approval was obtained.

In January of 1974, the intrepid Schlesinger, employing his battering-ram diplomacy, moved the development of counterforce weapons into greater visibility. On the tenth of that month he told the Overseas Writers Association luncheon in Washington, D.C. that "in the pursuit of symmetry we cannot allow the Soviets unilaterally to obtain a counterforce option which we ourselves lack." In presenting the menu of options he thought was required, he said "military targets, whether silos or other military targets, are, of course, one of the possible target sets." He then implied that at present the United States only had massive retaliation against Soviet cities as a response option.[21] That was stretching the truth a bit. Since its inception the blueprint for thermonuclear war—the SIOP—contained counterforce options but they were still within the context of mass retaliation. What Schlesinger and Nixon envisioned was limited nuclear war whereby only one or two missiles could be launched against selected targets. Schlesinger's philosophy was that the strategic forces are an integral part of an interdependent triplet of forces: conventional, theater (tactical) nuclear, and strategic nuclear. Although the SIOP, which targets both strategic and tactical weapons, had always aimed some strategic weapons at theater targets, he visualized their more selective use to supplement the other two forces. But that would require missiles with greater precision.

The tune changed somewhat in February, however, when a Senate committee asked if this newly announced counterforce policy would have a destabilizing effect on the current round of SALT talks. Schlesinger's reply was: "We have no *announced* counterforce strategy, if by counterforce one infers that one is going to attempt to destroy silos. We have a new targeting doctrine that emphasizes selectivity and flexibility."[22] (emphasis added) Schlesinger advocated that the MAD response to a limited nuclear attack is not feasible. He said we needed a response-in-kind. He then constructed the premise that if the Soviets destroyed the US submarine base at Groton, Connecticut we should be able to retaliate against a similar target such as their counterpart at Murmansk. But regardless of Schlesinger's carefully chosen words, the history of US strategic doctrine shows that the failure to announce a strategy is no assurance that it does not exist.

The real utility of limited nuclear war and enhanced counterforce options became apparent on May 30, 1975 when Schlesinger finally acknowledged publicly that the US would consider "first use" of nuclear weapons to stop a large scale communist advance with *conventional* armaments in Europe.[23] This raised cries of indignation from people who had believed the US was adhering strictly to the deterrent philosophy. Schlesinger's proclamation was later extended to Korea and was quickly supported by then President Ford. Although Schlesinger admitted at that time that first use of nuclear weapons by either NATO or the Warsaw Pact would pose grave risks of escalating into major nuclear war, that threat to fire first still stands today.

Let us look closer at the Nixon-Schlesinger targeting doctrine of selectivity and flexibility. Besides opening the door wider for more overt development of counterforce weapons, it is designed to make limited nuclear war seem to be a more acceptable option. Aiming at military targets sounds like the way a war should be run. It seems more humane than obliterating population areas. And if it is limited that is better yet. But the chances of it remaining limited are practically zero. NATO Commander General Bernard Rogers said that "the use of theater nuclear weapons would in fact escalate to the strategic level, and very quickly."[24]

The whole concept is based on the supposition that the Soviets might launch a handful of missiles at the United States. There was no explanation given as to why they would launch such an attack in the first place, nor did anyone ask for one. The hypothesis was blindly accepted by an unquestioning people. But firing one or two missiles at the United States is a preposterous notion for two reasons. First, if the Soviets did initiate limited nuclear war they would have no assurance that US response would be equally limited. It could well be massive retaliation. Even if US commanders wanted to keep it limited they might not be able to maintain control of the nuclear forces to prevent massive retaliation.

Secondly, a limited Soviet attack on the US is unrealistic because even if US retaliation were also limited it could still be more severe. In that case hostilities would not be likely to end there. If the response inflicted greater damage the Soviets would undoubtedly feel it necessary to even things up. This escalation could develop into total war which would devastate both sides. It is highly improbable that a potential belligerent would discount such a risk and gamble on a limited exchange. The hypothetical set of circumstances used to justify the targeting doctrine of selectivity and flexibility cannot stand close scrutiny.

A more plausible explanation for the Pentagon's interest in selective targeting, and for the administration's blatant first use threats, is to pave the way toward using or threatening to use nuclear weapons in some future Third World insurrection. Reestablishing the first use policy in Europe, which has its precedent in the years immediately following World War II, was a step toward making Americans feel that limited nuclear war is a reasonable alternative. The threat was quickly expanded to include Korea when that country became a hotbed of discontent during 1975-76 and the US nuclear stockpile was increased in the south. According to Choson Soren (the General Association of North Korean Residents in Japan) there were at that time 150 nuclear mines planted along the 38th Parallel.[25] Aircraft and ships bearing nuclear weapons were also dispatched to cover the Korean peninsula. The Brookings Institute estimated that there were 720 nuclear weapons in Korea in 1975 with a combined explosive yield of 13,000 kilotons—1,000 times as powerful as a Hiroshima-type bomb.[26] This is an unmistakable violation of the Korean Armistice Agreement.[27]

It has been reported that in the early 1950s General Douglas MacArthur wanted to use the atom bomb to end the Korean war in the same manner that World War II was ended. Also, according to Daniel Ellsberg, Richard Nixon planned to end the Vietnam war in 1969 by devastating Hanoi with nuclear weapons.[28] Both MacArthur's and Nixon's ambitions were thwarted because of public opposition.

The need to properly prepare the sentiments of the populace may have been the most important lesson the Pentagon learned from the Indochina war. A principle aim of the doctrine of selectivity and flexibility has been to neutralize the small amount of restraining power associated with the MAD policy by removing the fear of unacceptable retaliation. That is not to say, of course, that such fear is not still justified.

Viewed in this context, Presidential Directive No. 59 (PD-59), signed by President Carter in mid-1980, was not a new policy. Harold Brown, Secretary of Defense at the time, explained that "PD-59 is *not* a new strategic doctrine; it is *not* a radical departure from US strategic policy over the past decade or so. It *is*, in fact, a refinement, a codification of previous statements of our strategic policy."[29] (emphasis his) He further emphasized: "Previous Administrations, going back well into the 1960s, recognized the inadequacy of a strategic doctrine that would give us too narrow a range of options."[30]

There are frightening circumstances surrounding the issue of PD-59, however. It was preceded by an 18-month study ordered by the White House that sought to:

> Determine the nuclear strategy that would eliminate the USSR as a functioning national entity.
>
> Investigate promoting separatism by destroying areas in the USSR which support the present Soviet government.
>
> Identify the targets which would "paralyze, disrupt and dismember" the Soviet government by annihilating the ruling group.[31]

Those don't sound like objectives for a defensive strategy; or even for a limited nuclear war. They sound more like international assassination plots gone nuclear.* When viewed in the light of counterforce trends and the aspirations of the Pentagon to achieve a disarming first strike those objectives have startling implications. Their connection with PD-59 tends to substantiate that that directive is more far reaching than

---

*The Pentagon's new strategic master plan for fighting a prolonged nuclear war, prepared in accordance with a late 1981 presidential directive and sent to the Reagan White House in August 1982 (CF. *Los Angeles Times*, 15 April 1982, p.1), is attributed as being the first detailed plan of how a nuclear war might be won by destroying enemy political centers. Actually, however, a nuclear strike to decapitate Soviet leadership and its political infrastructure dates back to at least the Ford Administration (CF. *Fiscal Year 1977 Authorization for Military Procurement, Research and Development, and Active Duty, Selected Reserves and Civilian Personnel Strengths*, hearings before the Senate Armed Forces Committee, 11 March 1976, Part 11, pp. 5931-5932). What is actually happening seems to be a systematic public revelation of long standing military ambitions.

Secretary Brown asserts. It lends credibility to the belief that the use or threat to use nuclear weapons in localized areas is not the Pentagon's final goal.

The counterforce capability to destroy hard targets during limited nuclear exchanges is indistinguishable from that needed to launch a knockout nuclear attack against Russia. More than precision is required, however. A highly complex system of weapons so thoroughly automated and integrated as to be almost beyond belief would be necessary. Outside of the defense establishment few seem to view such a network as more than science fiction fantasy. Nevertheless, there is potent evidence that the Pentagon is not only thinking about it but is actually working to achieve it. Shortly before his resignation in early 1977, former Defense Secretary Donald Rumsfeld had this to say about the concept of damage limitation:

> The most ambitious (damage limiting) strategy dictates a first strike capability against an enemy's strategic offensive forces which seeks to destroy as much of his megatonnage as possible before it can be brought into play. An enemy's residual retaliation, assumed to be directed against urban-industrial targets, would be blunted still further by a combination of active and passive defenses, including ASW, ABMs, anti-bomber defenses, civil defense, stockpiles of food and other essentials and even the dispersal and hardening of essential industry.[32]

With only two sentences Rumsfeld has outlined the scenario for a disabling first strike: very precise strategic weapons to destroy Soviet land-based missiles in silos and other critical targets, anti-submarine warfare (ASW) to sink Russia's missile-launching submarines before they can fire their weapons, and anti-ballistic missile (ABM) and bomber defenses to stop any weapons that survived the first assault and were launched in retaliation. Although Rumsfeld did not admit that these were the Pentagon's goals, there is a plethora of evidence that the necessary technology and hardware are being developed. Subsequent chapters will describe the evolution of accurate missiles and other elements of the strategic nuclear triad, as well as undersea warfare and defenses against enemy missiles and bombers. Space warfare will likewise be discussed because elimination of Soviet early warning, communications and navigation satellites also fits into the first-strike scenario. Finally, we'll look at the command, control, and communication networks needed to tie all these systems together and synchronize their use. The evidence will stand on its own that the United States will begin to achieve the capability to launch a disarming, disabling and unanswerable first-strike against the Soviet Union by the later 1980s.

As pointed out above, our existing weapons have some counterforce capability against softer military targets. Soviet missiles also have this capability—a fact that is constantly emphasized by the Pentagon. Neither side, however, can presently destroy the opponent's hard military targets, such as missile silos, with any degree of certainty. Nevertheless, the Pentagon's argument for enhancing US counterforce capabilities rests on a hypothetical case of a Soviet first-strike against the US land-based Minuteman force. This hypothetical scenario unfolds something like this: If the Soviets initiated an all out attack against US silo based missiles but held back a sizeable portion of their land-based ICBM force to deter retaliation, then, according to military planners, when the US retaliates it would have to destroy those missiles held in reserve in hardened silos to prevent counter-retaliation against US cities. This idea of destroying Soviet missile silos during a second strike is known as second strike counterforce.

But the likelihood of the Soviets initiating such an attack is open to serious question. One must take into consideration the strategic warheads on bombers and submarines. About three-quarters of US strategic warheads are so based—only one-quarter of the US compliment of strategic bombs would be lost if all silo-based Minuteman missiles were destroyed. The remainder would be adequate for retaliation and counter-counter retaliation and therefore would deter any Soviet attack. Former Defense Secretary Harold Brown pointed out the futility of a Soviet attack on U.S. silos in his fiscal year 1980 report:

> Even without Minuteman, our surviving second strike capability would remain large—in the thousands of warheads. Not only could we still destroy a wide range of targets; we could also cause catastrophic damage to the Soviet urban-industrial base. It is difficult, in the circumstances, to see how the Soviets could expect to gain any meaningful advantages from starting such a mortal exchange.[33]

Of course, analysis of a second strike counterforce strategy should start by questioning why the Soviets would want to destroy only US silo-based missiles in the first place. Even accepting Defense Department predictions that 90 percent of US Minuteman ICBMs will be vulnerable to a Soviet first strike by the mid-1980s, there still is no logical reason for a Soviet attack considering the certainty of massive US retaliation. The only reasonable explanation for such an attack would be a perception on the part of the Soviets of a threat to their ICBM force. But Minuteman-3 warheads—even with yield and accuracy improvements—have only a 44 percent probability of destroying a silo-based missile and cannot therefore be considered a first strike weapon.

While the alleged need for greater US counterforce capability collapses under scrutiny, the dangers posed by the development of such a capability are very real. As pointed out in a paper published by the Congressional Budget Office, the development of weapons and systems capable of destroying silos and submarines are destabilizing in two ways:

> . . . Perhaps the most serious problem with US forces designed for second strike counterforce stems from the possibility that they would be seen as first strike weapons, and thus be destabilizing. Two types of nuclear stability might be threatened by the development of US counterforce capability: crisis stability and arms control stability[34]

The destabilizing impact of counterforce weapons on arms control can be seen by the inability to negotiate an effective SALT-2 Treaty; even if it had been ratified it would not have stopped the first strike weapons. A nation cannot be sincere about controlling arms while at the same time opening a new front in the arms race and pursuing the development of more aggressive weapons.

The second type of instability pertains to times of international crisis when the very presence of first strike weapons makes nuclear war more imminent. As noted in the Congressional Budget Office paper, deploying first strike capable missiles under the guise of second strike counterforce could very well prompt the USSR to fire first in crisis circumstances:

> There may be an inescapable dilemma involved in the procurement of second strike counterforce capability: a US arsenal large enough to attack Soviet ICBMs after having absorbed a Soviet first strike would be large enough to threaten the Soviet ICBM force in a US first strike. Moreover, the Soviet Union, looking at capabilities rather than intentions, might see a US second strike capability in this light. *Faced with a threat to their ICBM force, Soviet leaders facing an*

> *international crisis might have an incentive to use their missiles in a preemptive strike before they could be destroyed by the United States*. (emphasis added)[35]

The upshot of this analysis is that the development of "second strike counterforce capability" which has been justified as a necessary precaution against a hypothetical Soviet first strike may create the only conditions under which such an attack would be launched. The second strike counterforce scenario is in a very real sense a self-fulfilling prophecy.

More importantly, despite all the talk about a second strike counterforce capability, *there is no practical difference between such a capability and a first strike counterforce capability*. If the US can destroy a sizeable portion of the Soviet ICBM force after absorbing a Soviet first strike, under the stress of a going war and when atmospheric conditions created by nuclear explosions are far from favorable, then it would have a far greater chance of destroying all Soviet silo-based missiles with a preemptive first strike when the element of surprise and choice of time are in its favor and Soviet missiles are not in a high state of readiness. This is a first strike capability even if the intention is not there to use it. Furthermore, attempts by the Soviet Union to match US development of a greater strategic counterforce capability might provide the pretext for the Pentagon to launch a preemptive first strike.

In order to defuse Congressional opposition to the development of counterforce capabilities, Pentagon officials have worked hard to discredit the possibility of mounting a successful unanswerable first strike. During hearings on the fiscal year 1979 military budget, Under Secretary of Defense for Research and Engineering, Dr. William J. Perry, told Congress:

> In the last four Defense Reports, the Secretaries have stated that so long as we and the Soviets maintain diversified, survivable, second strike forces, neither is likely to obtain a disarming first strike capability. To do so would require:
>
> a. Absolute secrecy—the ability to generate the required forces without providing strategic warning to the other side;
>
> b. The ability to pretarget and destroy the (missile launching submarines) in a coordinated attack;
>
> c. The ability to interdict the bomber forces, either on the ground or in the air; and
>
> d. The ability to destroy the ICBMs. Neither side seems likely to acquire all these capabilities in the near future.[36]

Again the scenario for a disarming first strike has been postulated. Dr. Perry's "near future," however, certainly doesn't project into the latter 1980s because that is when today's emerging technologies will start becoming operational. So with this brief introduction to strategic nuclear policies—both public and announced—I will now proceed to a chapter by chapter, weapon by weapon description of how a US disarming first strike capability is being constructed.

Notes

1. *The Fiscal Year 1968-72 Defense Program and 1968 Defense Budget,* by Defense Secretary Robert McNamara before a joint session of the Senate Armed Services Committee and the Senate Subcommittee on Department of Defense Appropriations, (January 23, 1967), p. 39.
2. Jarvenpaa, Pauli; *Flexible Nuclear Options: New Myths and Old Realities,* Cornell University Peace Studies Program Occasional Paper No. 7, (September 1976).
3. *Military Implications of the Treaty on the Limitation of Strategic Offensive Arms and Protocol Thereto (Salt II Treaty),* Hearings before the Senate Armed Services Committee (July 24, 1979) Part 1, pp. 169-170.
4. Cited in *Foreign Affairs,* (January 1956), pp. 187-189.
5. US Navy *Memorandum Op-36/jm,* signed by Navy Captain W. B. Moore, 18 March 1954. Originally classified TOP SECRET. Declassified in January 1979. Appended to Rosenberg, David Alan; "A Smoking Radiating Ruin at the End Of Two Hours," *International Security,* Center for Science and International Affairs, Harvard University, Winter 1981-82, pp. 3-38.
6. Ibid.
7. *Briefing of WSEG (Weapons Systems Evaluation Group) Report No. 12,* 1955. Originally classified TOP SECRET. Declassified 20 October 1980. Appended to Rosenberg, Op. Cit.
8. For a thorough discussion of the early SIOP see Ball, Desmond; *Deja Vu: The Return to Counterforce in the Nixon Administration,* (California Seminar on Arms Control and Foreign Policy, December 1974), pp. 10-13 (Herafter referred to as *Deja Vu.*)
9. *Department of Defense Appropriations for 1963,* hearings before the House Appropriations Committee, (January 1962), Part 2, pp. 249-250.
10. Cited in *Deja Vu,* op, cit., p. 14.

11. Cited in *Deja Vu,* op. cit., p. 15.
12. Cited in *Newsweek,* (April 9, 1962), p. 32.
13. Commencement address by Defense Secretary Robert McNamara at the University of Michigan, Ann Arbor, Michigan on June 16, 1962. Reprinted in the *Department of State Bulletin,* (July 9, 1962), XLVII, pp. 64-69.
14. For a fuller discussion of the history of proposed legislation to improve missile accuracies see Ball, Desmond; "The Counterforce Potential of American SLBM Systems," *Journal of Peace Research,* (International Peace Research Institute, Oslo, Norway; Vol. XIV, No. 1, 1977), pp. 31-32.
15. *US Foreign Policy for the 1970s: A New Strategy for Peace,* a report to Congress by President Richard M. Nixon, (February 18, 1970), p. 122.
16. *US Foreign Policy for the 1970s,* a report to Congress by President Richard M. Nixon, (February 25, 1971), pp. 54-55.
17. *US Foreign Policy for the 1970s,* a report to Congress by President Richard M. Nixon, (February 9, 1972), p. 22.
18. Leitenberg, Milton; "The Race to Oblivion," *Bulletin of the Atomic Scientists,* (September 1974), p. 9.
19. See UPI dispatch "Nuclear Policy Switch: New Accuracy, Power Sought for Warheads," *San Jose Mercury,* (August 10, 1972) p. 1. Also see Beecher, W.; "Major War Plans are being Revised by White House," *New York Times,* (August 5, 1972).
20. Foreign policy address to Congress by President Richard M. Nixon (May 1973).
21. Address by Defense Secretary James R. Schlesinger at the Overseas Writers Association luncheon in Washington, D.C. on January 10, 1974. Excerpts reprinted in "Flexible Strategic Options and Deterrence," *Survival,* (Vol. XVI, No. 2, March/April 1974), pp. 86-90.
22. *Fiscal Year 1975 Authorization for Military Procurement, Research and Development, and Active Duty, Selected Reserve and Civilian Personnel Strengths,* hearings before the Senate Armed Services Committee (February 5, 1974) Part 1, p. 265.
23. UPI dispatch, "US Favors First Use of N-Weapons," *San Jose Mercury,* (May 31, 1975)
24. "Rogers Says 'Limited' Nuclear War Would Escalate." *Defense Daily,* (November 12, 1981), p. 60.
25. The author attended an all-day briefing with Chosen Soren in Tokyo during August 1975 at which these issues were discussed.
26. Statement on withdrawal of nuclear weapons from the Korean Peninsula by the 25th Pugwash Conference held in Kyoto, Japan toward the end of August 1975.
27. Article 2, Paragraph 13, Item D of the Korean Armistice Agreement

prohibiting introduction of material into Korea from abroad.

28. Sweeney, Frank; "Nixon's Secret Plan: Nukes," *San Jose Mercury*, (November 11, 1975), p. 21.
29. Remarks by Secretary of Defense Harold Brown at the Naval War College, Newport, Rhode Island, on August 20, 1980. Published in *Selected Statements,* prepared by the Air force for Department of Defence personnel, (September 1, 1980), p. 46.
30. Ibid, p. 47.
31. *Chicago Sun-Times,* 12 February 1979. (A *Washington Post* Special by Walter Pincus.)
32. *Annual Defense Department Report Fiscal Year 1978,* by Secretary of Defense Donald H. Rumsfeld, (January 17, 1977), pp. 76-77.
33. *Department of Defense Annual Report Fiscal Year 1980,* by Harold Brown, Secretary of Defense, (January 25, 1979), p. 15.
34. *Counterforce Issues for the US Strategic Nuclear Forces,* a background paper published by the Congressional Budget Office, (January 1978), p. 32.
35. Ibid.
36. *Department of Defense Authorization for Appropriations for Fiscal Year 1979,* hearing before the Senate Armed Services Committee, (February 21, 1978), Part 2, p. 1089.

THE STRATEGIC NUCLEAR TRIAD

The unleashed power of the atom has changed everything save our modes of thinking, and we thus drift toward unparalleled catastrophe.
—Albert Einstein

Understanding the strategic triad, as it is called, is a first step in comprehending the aggressiveness of the new weapons which are being developed. For both the United States and the Soviet Union the triad is a three-pronged assault force for nuclear war and is composed of carrier vehicles to deliver nuclear bombs from land, sea and air. The three components of the US strategic triad contain approximately 10,000 nuclear warheads. These are the primary weapons that would be used to destroy land-based military targets in the Soviet Union if nuclear hostilities should errupt. Figure 2-1 lists the inventory of US strategic missiles and bombers projected for mid-1983. Figure 2-2 does the same for the Soviet strategic carrier vehicles.

The land leg of the US strategic triad is presently made-up of 1,054 intercontinental ballistic missiles (ICBMs). They are stationed in concerete and steel silos which are buried deep underground. The latest version Minuteman ICBMS—the Minuteman-3s—occupy 550 of these silos; each missile holding three warheads which can be sent to diffferent targets. The remaining silos contain 450 Minuteman-2 missiles equipped with a single one-megaton bomb each, and 54 Titan-2s* which are each loaded with a gigantic nine-megaton device.

The air wing consists of 316 heavy B-52 bombers (not counting over 200 B-52s and four B-1s in storage or used for other purposes), all with intercontinental range, operated by the Strategic Air Command. Originally each B-52 carried four large hydrogen bombs in the 25-megaton class which were dropped on their targets by gravity. Currently, B-52s have been modified to carry at least 12 nuclear-tipped short-range attack missiles (SRAMs), which can travel a hundred miles to their target, under their wings. Later model B-52s have been converted to substitute eight additional SRAMs for gravity bombs in one bomb bay. That increases the total SRAM capacity to twenty. Some of the later B-52s are being converted to interchange air-launched cruise missiles (ALCMs) for SRAMs. At least 496 B-52s were built but some were lost during the Indochina war while others have been transferred to other missions such as ocean surveillance and mine laying. Still others have been mothballed.

By mid-1983 there will be thirty-three ballistic missile launching submarines to comprise the sea leg of the US strategic triad. Nineteen will carry a Poseidon missile in each of their sixteen launch tubes which are, in effect, seagoing silos. Each Poseidon missile is loaded with 14 warheads that can be dispatched against separate targets.† Every one of these so-called multiple individually-targeted reentry vehicles (MIRVs) contain a 40-kiloton hydrogen bomb. A single Poseidon submarine can cause catastrophic devastation to 224 cities or moderately hard military

*Two of the Titan-2 missiles and their silos have been destroyed by accidental explosions. However, in this text I will use the figure of 54 even though two of them are not in service. There is talk that the Reagan Administration intends to phase out the Titan-2s by 1987 and replace 50 Minuteman-2s with triple-MIRV Minuteman-3s, for a net increase of 46 warheads.

†Poseidon missiles were originally deployed with two warhead "mixes": the full load of 14 on some missiles to reach targets within 2,500 nautical miles, and a reduced load of 10 warheads on others to achieve greater range for destroying targets farther away. Since the longer range Trident-1 missiles have been back-fitted into twelve Poseidon submarines and can cover the farther targets, it seems logical that the remaining nineteen Poseidon submarines would carry a full load. This would acount for media reports that the number of warheads on Poseidon missiles have been increased. (Cf. *New York Times*, 30 October 1980, p. 23.) Therefore, the net number of warheads deployed in submarines would probably remain about the same, although Trident-1 missiles carry fewer. The capabilities of the latter, however, are much greater.

Figure 2-1

US Strategic Missiles and Bombers Projected (Mid-1983)

Name	Category	Range (Naut. Mi.)	Number Deployed	Warhead Yield	Warheads/ Missile	Remarks
Titan-2	ICBM	6,300 +	54	9 MT	1	Liquid fuel
Minuteman-2	ICBM	7,000 +	450	1-2 MT	1	Solid fuel Penetration Aids
Minuteman-3	ICBM	7,000 +	250 300	170 KT 335 KT	3 MIRVs	Solid fuel Radiation hardened Penetration Aids Improved Accuracy
Poseidon	SLBM	2,500	304**	40 KT	14 MIRVs	Solid fuel Radiation hardened Penetration Aids
Trident-1	SLBM	4,000	240***	100 KT	8 MIRVs	Solid fuel Radiation hardened Penetration Aids
B-52	Bomber	Inter-continental	316*		Bombs/SRAMs/ ALCMs	8 turbofan/turbojet engines Subsonic

TOTAL: 1914*

KT = Kilotons MT = Megatons SRAM = Short Range Attack Missile ALCM = Air Launched Cruise Missile

*Number does not include B-52 or B-1 bombers in storage or used for other purposes.
**Carried 16 each in 19 Poseidon submarines.
***Carried 16 each in 12 converted Poseidon submarines and 24 each in two new Trident submarines.

Sources:

"Specifications," *Aviation Week & Space Technology,* (March 8, 1982), pp. 142-143.

The Military Balance 1981/82, (International Institute for Strategic Studies, London, England).

Department of Defense Annual Report Fiscal Year 1982, by Harold Brown, Secretary of Defense, (January 19, 1981), pp. 48-54.

Department of Defense Annual Report Fiscal Year 1981, by Harold Brown, Secretary of Defense, (January 29, 1980), pp. 19, 71-77, 131.

SALT II Agreement, US Department of State Selected Documents No. 12 A (June 18, 1979), p. 16.

Figure 2-2

USSR Strategic Missiles and Bombers Projected (Mid-1983)

Name	Category	Range (Naut. Mi.)	Number Deployed*	Warhead Yield	Warheads/ Missile	Remarks
SS-11	ICBM	5,700 Mod 2 5,400 Mod 3	518 total	Mod 2 1-2 MT Mod 3 300 KT	1 3 MRVs	Liquid fuel Hot launch
SS-13	ICBM	5,400	60	1 MT	1	Solid fuel Hot launch
SS-17	ICBM	5,400 Mod 1 5,900 Mod 2	150 total	Mod 1 900 KT Mod 2 5 MT	4 MIRVs 1	Liquid fuel Cold launch
SS-18	ICBM	6,500 Mod 1 5,900 Mod 2 8,600 Mod 3 5,900 Mod 4	308 total	Mod 1 18-25 MT Mod 2 2 MT Mod 3 18-25 MT Mod 4 500 MT	1 8-10 MIRVs 1 10 MIRVs	Liquid fuel Cold launch
SS-19	ICBM	5,200 Mod 1 5,400 Mod 2	362 total	Mod 1 550 KT Mod 2 5 MT	6 MIRVs 1	Liquid fuel Hot launch
SS-N-5***	SLBM	700	48	1 MT	1	Liquid fuel On 13 Golf (diesel) and 3 Hotel submarines
SS-N-6	SLBM	1,300 Mods 1 & 2 1,600 Mod 3	453 total	Mods 1 & 2 1-2 MT Mod 3 350 KT	1 3 MRVs	Liquid fuel On 28 Yankee-1 & 1 Golf-4 (diesel) submarines

Name	Category	Range (Naut. Mi.)	Number Deployed*	Warhead Yield	Warheads/ Missile	Remarks
SS-N-8	SLBM	4,300	267	1 MT	1	Liquid fuel On 1 Hotel-3, 16 Delta-1, 4 Delta-2, and 1 Golf-3 submarines
SS-NX-17	SLBM	1,700	12	1 MT	1	Solid fuel On 1 Yankee-2 submarine
SS-N-18	SLBM	4,500	208 total	Mod 1 200 KT Mod 2 450 KT	3 MIRVs 1	Liquid fuel On 13 Delta-3 submarines
Tu-95 (Bear)	Bomber	Inter-continental	105**	—	—	Subsonic 4 turboprop engines
Mya-4 (Bison)	Bomber	Inter-continental	45**	—	—	Subsonic 4 turbojet engines
			2536**			

KT = Kilotons MT = Megatons ICBM = Intercontinental Ballistic Missile SLBM = Submarine-Launched Ballistic Missile
MRV = Multiple Reentry Vehicles (not separately targeted) MIRV = Multiple Independently-targeted Reentry Vehicle

*Assuming SALT limits are not exceeded. **Does not include aircraft configured as tankers or reconnaissance. ***Not SALT accountable in Golf submarines.

Sources:

Department of Defense Annual Report Fiscal Year 1982, by Harold Brown, Secretary of Defense, 19 January 1981, pp. 45-46.

Hearings on Military Posture and HR 10929, before the House Armed Services Committee, 27 January 1978, Part 7, p. 82.

Counterforce Issues of the U.S. Strategic Nuclear Forces, a Congressional Budget Office background paper, January 1978, pp. 16-19.

Retaliatory Issues of the U.S. Strategic Nuclear Forces, a Congressional Budget Office background paper, June 1978, pp. 6-9.

Library of Congress tables published in *Aviation Week & Space Technology*, 18 April 1977, pp. 18-19. *The Military Balance:* 1976/77; 1977/78; 1978/79; 1979/80; 1980/81; 1981/82. Published by the International Institute for Strategic Studies, London, England.

Aviation Week & Space Technology: 3 April 1978, p. 17; 16 June 1980, pp. 75-76; 22 September 1980, pp. 14-15; 17 November 1980, p. 13; 1 December 1980, p. 15; 16 February 1981, pp. 98-100; 12 October 1981, pp. 82-83; 4 January 1982, pp. 20-21; 11 January 1982, p. 26; 8 March 1982, pp. 129 & 147.

"Gallery of Soviet Aerospace Weapons," *Air Force Magazine*, March 1982; by John W.R. Taylor, editor of *Jane's All The World's Aircraft*.

Air Force Magazine, March 1980, pp. 47-50.

Desmond Ball, "Research Note: Soviet ICBM Deployment," *Survival*, July/August 1980, pp. 167-170.

Walter Pincus, "US Downgrades Soviet ICBM Yield," *Washington Post*, 31 May 1979.

Walter Pincus, "Soviets Believed to Have Problems With New Typhoon Missile," *Washington Post*, 18 January 1982, p. 13.

William Parham, "A Soviet Threat From The Arctic?" *Norwich Bulletin* (CT), 29 November 1981, p. 11.

targets using bombs with two to three times the explosive power of those dropped on Hiroshima and Nagasaki.

Another twelve Poseidon submarines will have been converted to carry sixteen new Trident-1 missiles each by mid-1983. The Trident-1s are loaded with eight 100-kiloton warheads apiece. In addition, another 48 Trident-1 missiles will be stowed on two new Trident submarines. Ten older submarines which carried Polaris missiles have been retired and some are being converted to attack subs. Those ten older submarines taken together had the capability of attacking 160 targets (10 submarines × 16 missiles × one warhead per missile). A single Trident submarine, however, can attack 336 targets (24 missiles per sub X 14 warheads per missile). One Trident submarine can threaten over twice as many targets with a greater probability of destruction than the whole fleet of ten Polaris subs.

The Soviet Union also has strategic missiles stationed in silos, submarines and intercontinental bombers. (See figure 2-2) For many years the land leg of the USSR's triad consisted of SS-7, SS-8, SS-9, SS-11 and SS-13 missiles. SS-7s and SS-8s are very old heavy missiles which have been dismantled as more submarine based weapons were built. This is in accordance with the SALT-1 Agreements. The SS-9 has often been called the "silo buster" but the new generation SS-18s have now replaced SS-9s. The SS-18 carries 8 to 10 MIRVs or one very large warhead in the 25-megaton range. Some Soviets have told me that up to thirty MIRVs can be carried on the SS-18. They would, of course, have to be much smaller with an accompanying increase in accuracy; and would require extensive testing which has not been done and which could be readily monitored. SALT 2, however, limits the number of MIRVs on an ICBM to ten, and the number of very heavy ICBMs to 308 (including test launchers). Although the United States has not ratified SALT 2, both countries have been abiding by its limits.

Many of the smaller SS-11 ICBMs have been replaced by SS-17s and SS-19s, the latter being about the same size as MX. The SS-11 has been tested and probably deployed with three multiple reentry vehicles (MRVs) which detonate in a triangular pattern to distribute their destructiveness more "efficiently." MRVs all go to the same target—they cannot be sent to separate targets as MIRVs can. The SS-17s and SS-19s, however, are both MIRVed.

There is some speculation that the sixty solid fueled SS-13s have been replaced with SS-16s, also using solid propellant. These are the only two Soviet silo-based missiles which use solid propellent. It should be noted that all US missiles except the 54 old Titan 2s have the more versatile solid propellant which improves readiness and reliability of the weapons. Nevertheless, because the SS-16 is solid fueled it has been alleged by the Pentagon that this missile is destined to be land mobile. By the same token the US Minuteman missiles could also be deloyed in the mobile mode and that, in fact, has been considered.

The SS-20 intermediate range ballistic missile (IRBM), of which the Soviets have reportedly deployed 300 in Europe, consists of the first two stages of the SS-16. Ostensibly by adding the third stage these theater nuclear weapons could be transformed to a strategic ICBM. During early April of 1982 there were U.S. intelligence "leaks" to the media that 200 of the SS-20s had been so converted. Some columnists nibbled at this bait and splashed the news across the nation's newspapers. By the end of that month, however, official sources and a congressional inquiry established that the SS-16 missile had never been deployed in a mobile mode. There are apparently as many as a couple of dozen still at the test site in various stages of readiness but they are far from being operational.

The SS-16 is a solid propellant missile which was supposed to be a successor to the SS-13, of which only 60 were deployed. Soviet engineers, however, have never mastered solid propellant technology. The SS-16 is the least accurate and least reliable of the latest generation Soviet ICBMs. It has a single warhead and was tested between 1972 and 1976—only once since 1975. The latest tests indicated serious problems and it has not been tested since. As one columnist remarked: "The new SS-16 'threat' is a particularly egregious example of the impudence with which these 'intelligence' sources try to manipulate public debate. Vigilance against such manipulation is vital if the arguments for a freeze are to be conducted rationally."[1]

Turning now to the submarine-launched ballistic missiles, the oldest SLBMs in the Soviet Navy are the SS-N-5s. They are such short range that they can hardly be classified as strategic and, indeed, they were not counted in the SALT quotas. Moreover, many of them are carried in diesel-powered submarines which are vitually obsolete in modern warfare because of their vulnerability. The prime components of the Soviet SLBM force are the SS-N-6, SS-N-8, and SS-N-18 missiles. The former are carried, sixteeen each, on Yankee submarines and have been tested with three MRVs. Twelve SS-N-8 SLBMs are carried on each Delta-1 submarine and sixteen on each of the stretched Delta-2 boats. SS-N-18 missiles are carried on Delta-3 subs—sixteen per boat.

The Soviets have encountered many problems in developing the sea leg of their strategic triad. Less than one-quarter of their strategic warheads (as opposed to about one-half for the US) are in submarines although they have more submarines and more launch tubes than the United States. Also, only a very small percentage of their subs are at sea at any given time. The first of a new class of Typhoon submarine, which began construction in 1975, was not launched until September 1980. It is still being fitted out and is not expected to be operation until at least 1985.

Typhoon submarines are larger and heavier than the United States' new Trident. Some analysts believe that Typhoon is designed to operate beneath the Arctic ice and then break through as it surfaces when ready to launch its missiles. Each submarine will carry 20 missiles which is fewer than the 24 on Trident.

These 4,900 nautical-mile-range missiles, designated the SS-NX-20 by NATO—are also having development problems. Like the SS-16 these missiles use solid propellant and share the problems that have plagued Soviet solid-fuel technology. Two recent launches of the SS-NX-20 were complete failures—one had to be blown up in flight and the other didn't even get off the pad.

I have already explained the difficulties encountered by the USSR in introducing solid propellant into their ICBM forces. Their experience with SLBMs is just as sad. Their first try was the SS-NX-17 which was originally designed to replace the SS-N-6s. In 1977 or early 1978 one Yankee-class submarine was outfitted with these missiles for development launches but that was as far as the program went. There are still only twelve SS-NX-17s deployed in submarines. The SS-NX-20 designed for the Typhoon was the Soviets' second try at a solid fuel SLBM but it seems to be encountering similar difficulties.

Finally, in the bomber catagory, the Soviets only have 150 heavy bombers with intercontinental range. The new supersonic Backfire bomber we have heard so much about (not shown in figure 2-2) is a medium bomber with limited range which was not counted under previous SALT negotiations. Some proponents for a harder line against the Soviets contend that the Backfire has strategic significance with refueling capabilities. But given the limited Soviet inventory of only 45 tankers,[2] that threat seems more hypothetical than real.

When we compare the totals of figures 2-1 and 2-2 we can see that the Soviets outnumber the US as far as delivery vehicles (missiles and bombers) are concerned. That is misleading, however. Figure 2-3 illustrates that the United States surpasses the USSR as far as deliverable warheads are concerned, which means that the American strategic force is able to attack more targets.

The uploading of warheads on Poseidon missiles, the operational capability of air-launched cruise missiles on B-52s, and the commissioning of the first Trident submarine has now boosted US strategic warheads close to the 10,000 mark. Soviet warheads have now reached about 7,000. Both countries are closer to "equivalence," however that may be defined, than they have been in decades. It is at these times of perceived balance, or near-balance, that moratoriums, freezes, and even arms reduction agreements are most likely to be negotiated.

Figure 2-3
US & USSR Strategic Nuclear Warheads

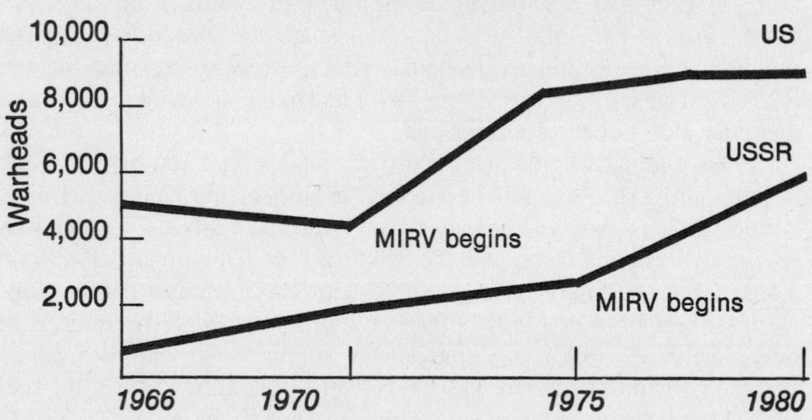

Source:
Department of Defense Annual Report Fiscal Year 1982, by Harold Brown, Secretary of Defense, 19 January 1981, p. 54.

The balance is not static, however, and the Soviet gain cannot be expected to continue. In the absence of restraining agreements the action-reaction cycle of the arms race will cause another escalation. The Soviet warhead inventory can be expected to start leveling off soon with deployment of their new ICBMs reaching the final stages and the delay-causing problems encountered with their new MIRVed SLBMs. On the other hand, US warhead inventories are expected to surge with

MX deployment looming in the mid-1980s and the plans to put long-range nuclear cruise missiles on ships and attack submarines. The curve will rise even steeper if the Trident-2 missile starts entering the fleet during the late 1980s. An analysis of the Reagan Administration's budget request indicates a plan to build 17,000 more nuclear bombs during the next ten years.[3] According to the Center for Defense Information, there are presently about 12,000 tactical and strategic nuclear warheads that can be delivered to the Soviet homeland and that number will approach 20,000 after the scheduled buildup.[4] There are no Soviet tactical warheads that can reach the United States—they tried to install some in Cuba but were forced to withdraw them under the U.S. threat of military confontation. The planned US buildup will set off a new phase in the nuclear arms race which can only lead to greater instability and insecurity.

Some writers who try to justify US weapons programs allude to possible Soviet cheating on the number of ICBMs reported. They imply that the older missiles which have been replaced might still be available for launch.[5] Former Defense Secretary Harold Brown discredited such allegations in his fiscal year 1981 report:

> The Soviets are believed to have a substantial number of excess missiles. Most of these missiles are older ICBMs that have been replaced by newer models and cannot be launched operationally because they are not compatible with existing launchers. There is no evidence that production of missiles for which there are existing launchers (SS-17, SS-18 and SS-19) is significantly greater than the number of those launchers. Although the SS-17 and SS-18 are designed for cold launch and could therefore in principle take reloads in a relatively short time, there is no evidence that the Soviets have any plan or capability to use excess missiles as reserve, or refires. We are quite confident they have not tested or trained in those ways.[6]

That statement also puts to rest another argument used to justify second strike counterforce—the argument that when the US retaliates it must have the accuracy to destroy cold launch* silos so they cannot be

*Cold launch means the missile is popped out of the tube or silo by a gas generator—a small rocket motor not part of the missile—and the missile's first stage motor is ignited after clearing the silo muzzle. This technique has been used on US submarines since the early 1960s. The real advantage of cold launch for fixed land-based missiles is that the pop-up energy gets the missile moving. That is why it is often called a "zero stage." The saving of on-board fuel can then be used to increase range or payload.

reloaded. Nevertheless, reports of an alleged Soviet reload capability persist. During alleged exercises the Soviets were reported to have removed some SS-18 missiles from their silos and replaced them with others—something that is done routinely with ballistic missiles if they develop a malfunction. This report played up these missile switches as a reload exercise.[7] It said, however, that the reload procedure took 2 to 5 days. If that is so I don't have much confidence in the competency of Soviet technicians. I have been responsible for testing SLBMs from launch tubes and quite often we had to remove and replace a missile overnight. It can be done that quickly in a tube that has not been fired. It would take somewhat longer to clean up and repair the silo after igniting the gas generator but 2-5 days seems like a leisurely pace. Even if the reload capability was credible, it couldn't justify prompt response, super-precise ballistic missiles. The slower traveling cruise missiles would be adequate for destroying empty silos. Cruise missiles would not be so destabilizing in crisis situations, but they do generate other arms control problems.

Tactical nuclear weapons are also assigned their targets by the SIOP and are part of the total nuclear balance. They comprise a wide spectrum of arms ranging from rockets that can be fired by one person to depth bombs, artillery shells, demolition charges, mines, torpedoes, rockets, and the neutron bomb. Many are in the hands of battlefield commanders, ships' captains, and airplane pilots. Some are more powerful than strategic bombs although they don't have a comparable range. But even that distinction is becoming blurred. 400 Poseidon strategic warheads are aimed at theater targets in Europe because of their accuracy. As pointed out above, some theater weapons can reach Russian territory. This will be aggravated if the 464 ground-launched cruise missiles and 108 Pershing-2 IRBMs with precision maneuvering warheads are ever deployed in Europe because they will be able to reach all of the USSR west of the Ural Mountains.

On the Soviet side, two new theater weapons have entered their inventory. One is the SS-20 which has been discussed above. The other is the shorter range SS-21 which uses the two upper stages of the SS-16. Neither, however, can reach the United States. Although this book focuses mainly on strategic nuclear weapons, it is not possible to completely ignore tactical devices. As shall be shown later, many of the less dramatic arms play a vital role in a disarming first strike capability.

The characteristics of a counterforce weapon can now be addressed. For either country to successfully execute a disarming first strike it would need at its command a missile force that could precisely "kill" every missile silo and other military target with no, or very little, warning. To assess strategic counterforce capability we need to look at both the size and quality of a nation's strategic arsenal. We read many Pentagon dispatches which emphasize the Soviet lead in *megatonnage, throw weight,* and *number of missiles.* Not nearly so well emphasized are other important characteristics such as *numbers of warheads, reliability, readiness* and *accuracy.* It is in these areas where the United States excells—and where, in the final analysis, lie the main contributing factors to the counterforce capability of weapons.[8]

Let us look first at *number of missiles* vs. *numbers of warheads.* Because the US had three times as many warheads, the Soviet Union was allowed more ballistic missile submarines and more silo-based ICBMs in the 1972 SALT-1 Agreement. One reason for the US lead in warheads was the vastly superior bomber force and another, which has already been discussed, was the deployment of MIRVs on Minuteman-3 and Poseidon missiles. The USSR will, by mid-1983, have 2,536 strategic missiles and bombers. At the same time the United States will have 1,914 delivery vehicles. The apparent Soviet edge in carriers is misleading because the US, with a commanding lead in numbers of warheads, can attack almost half again as many targets. John Newhouse, one time counselor for the Arms Control and Disarmament Agency, highlighted: "It is difficult to overstate the importance of this kind of advantage; missile warheads, the actual weapons, not missile launchers, the means of delivery, represent the more critical measure of overall strategic power."[9]

Throw weight means the same as payload. When used with reference to a missile it is the weight remaining after the last rocket stage has burned out and separated. While the Soviet Union leads in pounds of throw weight, they do not use it efficiently. The United States, on the other hand, through miniaturization and advanced technology, has increased the overall effectiveness of the throw weight at its disposal. *Sea Power,* the official publication of the Navy League of the United States, emphasizes the US advantage:

> Properly prepared, a TNT explosion is reliably efficient . . . Such efficiency depends on the degree of combustion of the explosive mass. If only that part of the charge nearest the detonator explodes, throwing off and scattering the unexploded balance, efficiency suffers.

> In nuclear blasts, so incomplete an explosion would be a "dirty" bomb, which scatters "fallout" radioactive components. A "clean" bomb, on the other hand, would mean complete or nearly complete combustion, with little or no unexploded fallout. In other words, an efficient bomb with a much greater effect on the target and much less radioactive contamination. American tests have been gratifyingly "clean." Russian bombs have been notoriously "dirty."
>
> Bomb efficiency modifies "throw weight." An efficient bomb of, say, 200 kilotons could be even more destructive to an enemy silo and its contents than a "dirty" bomb of one or even two megatons . . . A near miss by a hostile bomb might not crush the concrete silo or even throw the poised misile off its pad, but the microwave radiation of an efficient bomb exploding at a distance of a few hundred meters could either destroy or so seriously disturb the guidance of a MIRVed missile, or "bus," that it would become useless.[10]

Reliability is the predicted percentage of missiles that will reach their target after the launch button has been pushed. It is the final score of a probability game which weighs the chances of all the myriad missile components—from the two-bit computer chip to the multi-million dollar guidance package—working properly. The reliability of US missiles varies between 75 and 80 percent. Soviet missiles are not as good—only 65 to 75 percent reliable. It can be summed up that Russia's best works only as well as America's worst.

Readiness is somewhat related to reliability. There are always some missiles or submarines that are out of service for one reason or another—maintenance, breakdown, overhaul. Readiness indicates the number of missiles that are "on target" and ready to fire at any given time. The overall readiness of US strategic forces is reported to be 95 percent while for the Soviet Union it is only 75 percent.[11] Figures 2-1 and 2-2 indicate there are 1,598 strategic missiles in the US forces and 2,386 for the USSR. When we apply the readiness percentages the gap narrows—1,518 American missiles ready to use compared to 1,789 for Russia. That certainly pares down the Soviet superiority in numbers of delivery vehicles. Furthermore, the 75 percent readiness estimate for the USSR's strategic forces may be too high. One strategic weapons expert who served as a SALT negotiator says the alert rate for USSR ICBMs has often been estimated at 30 percent, but indicates it is climbing, and indicates the alert rate of Minuteman missiles is 90 percent.[12] The late General George S. Brown, as chairman of the Joint Chiefs of Staff, reported that "only about 15 percent of the Soviet first line nuclear fleet, as compared to over 50 percent for the United States, operates away from port at any given time."[13] More recently Harold Brown, as Defense Secretary, said the Soviets "have roughly 15 percent of their ships at sea in a ready condition at any one time."[14] These figures tip the balance in favor of the United States for numbers of missiles ready to launch when the command is given.

To summarize thus far, we can see that although the Soviet Union has 1.5 times the number of missiles, the United States has about 1.5 times the number of warheads (estimated from numbers in Figures 2-1 and 2-2). When readiness and reliability are considered the United States has slightly more missiles ready to launch on command with an average of more bombs per missile, each of which has a better chance of reaching the target than its Soviet counterpart.

We can now move on to the last two measures of strategic power: *megatonnage* and *accuracy*. Because these are the most important aspects when it comes to destroying hard targets, they have the greatest influence on the first strike characteristics of a weapon.

As mentioned earlier, the Soviets have bigger bombs on the average; partly because they lack the expertise to miniaturize them and make them more accurate. That has been the technique the US has pursued. Until their latest generation of missiles, Soviet warheads could go as wide of the targets as 0.7 nautical miles with some as far off their mark as one to two nautical miles.* The new generation of ICBMs have a smaller miss error. Figure 2-4 lists the accuracies of US and USSR missiles now deployed. It does not reflect the new generation of US weapons—Trident-2 and MX—which will be discussed in detail in later chapters.

Lethality is the term used to describe the ability of a missile to destroy hard military targets. This can be quantified by a computation based on the megatonnage of the warhead and the accuracy of the missile. Accuracy is expressed as circular error probability (CEP) and is the radius of a circle, centered on the target, in which the warhead has a 50-50 chance of hitting.†

When the hardness of the particular target and the missile's

---

*A nautical mile equals 1.15 statute miles or 1.85 kilometers.

†Lethality is directly proportional to the two-thirds power of the warhead explosive yield (megaton equivalent) and inversely proportional to the accuracy (CEP) squared. The resulting equation for lethality (K) is:[15]

$$K = Y^{2/3} / (CEP)^2$$

where: Y = warhead yield in megatons
CEP = accuracy in nautical miles

reliability are taken into consideration, lethality can be translated into probability of kill: the likelihood of a single warhead taking-out a particular silo.* In actual practice it is common to aim two warheads—one from each of two missiles—at harder targets to increase the kill probability. This is called 2-on-1 cross-targeting and, like single-shot targeting, it can be translated into a kill probability.† Figure 2-4 tabulates the counterforce capabilities for US and Soviet missiles and includes columns detailing single-shot and cross-targeting probabilities of kill.

We can examine Figure 2-4 in several ways. First let us pick out what appears to be the most counterforce weapon. At first glance it would appear to be Mods 1 & 3 of the SS-18 and Mod 2 of the SS-19 because they have the highest probability of kill per warhead. We must remember, however, that these are single warhead missiles. It would take two missiles to have an 87 percent chance of destroying one silo. If all SS-18s and SS-19s were of these Mods, which they aren't, the entire force could destroy fewer than 300 silos. That is not an efficient countersilo system.

Next let us look at Mods 2 & 4 of the SS-18 and Mod 1 of the SS-19. They all have approximately 50 percent cross-targeting probability of kill. The SS-18s carry ten warheads each which means two missiles have a 50 percent chance of destroying 10 silos—or 5 silos; an average of 2½ per missile. At that rate the force of 308 SS-18s could ostensibly destroy 770 silos.

In like manner, two SS-19, Mod 1 missiles with six warheads each would have a 50 percent chance of destroying 6 silos, or 1½ per missile average. That implies 543 silos could be destroyed by the 362 SS-19s. The cumulative destruction is 1,313 silos which is 259 more than the US

*The equation for single-shot probability of kill (SSP_k) is:[16]

$$SSP_k = 1 - e^{-z}$$

where: $z = K \times r/2H^{2/3}(0.19H^{-1} - 0.23H^{-1/2} + 0.068)^{2/3}$

r = reliability expressed as a decimal

H = hardness of the target expressed in pounds per square inch (PSI) overpressure capability

†The equation for cross-targeting probability of kill (CTP_k) is:[17]

$$CTP_k = 1 - (1 - P_{k_1}r)^2$$

where: $P_{k_1} = SSP_k$ assuming the reliability is equal to 100%

r = reliability of the two missiles expressed as a decimal. (Assuming they are the same.)

Figure 2-4

Counterforce Capability of Ballistic Missiles (Mid-1983)

		Missile	Explosive yield of warhead (megatons) Y	Accuracy of reentry vehicle (Naut. Mi.) CEP	Lethality per reentry vehicle K	Reliability of missile (%) r	Probability of silo kill per reentry vehicle (%) SSP_k**	Probability of silo kill for 2-on-1 cross targeting (%) CTP_k**
US	ICBMs	Titan-2	9.0	0.5	17.30	75	18	31
		Minuteman-2	1.0	0.3	11.11	80	13	23
		Minuteman-3	0.17	0.1	30.69	80	31	51
		Minuteman-3	0.335	0.1	48.24	80	44	67
	SLBMs	Poseidon	0.04	0.3	1.30	80	2	3
		Trident-1	0.1	0.25	3.45	80	4	8
USSR	ICBMs	SS-11, Mod 2	2.0	0.7	3.24	70	3	7
		SS-11, Mod 3	3 × 0.3	0.5	3.73	70	4	8
		SS-13	1.0	1.0	1.00	70	1	2
		SS-17, Mod 1	0.9	0.27	12.79	75	13	25
		SS-17, Mod 2	5.0	0.27	40.11	75	36	56
		SS-18, Mod 1	25.0	0.23	125.00*	75	76	87
		SS-18, Mod 2	2.0	0.23	30.01	75	29	47
		SS-18, Mod 3	25.0	0.19	125.00*	75	76	87

Figure 2-4 (continued)

Counterforce Capability of Ballistic Missiles (Mid-1983)

		Missile	Explosive yield of warhead (megatons) Y	Accuracy of reentry vehicle (Naut. Mi.) CEP	Lethality per reentry vehicle K	Reliability of missile (%) r	Probability of silo kill per reentry vehicle (%) SSP_k**	Probability of silo kill for 2-on-1 cross targeting (%) CTP_k**
USSR		SS-18, Mod 4	0.5	0.14	32.14	75	30	49
		SS-19, Mod 1	0.55	0.14	34.25	75	32	51
		SS-19, Mod 2	5.0	0.14	125.00*	75	76	87
	SLBMs	SS-N-5	assume 1.0	2.0	0.25	assume 65	0.25	0.5
		SS-N-6, Mods 1 & 2	2.0	1.0	1.59	70	2	3
		SS-N-6, Mod 3	3 × .35	1.0	1.03	70	1	2
		SS-N-8	1.0	0.84	1.42	70	2	3
		SS-NX-17	1.0	0.5	4.00	70	4	8
		SS-N-18, Mod 1	0.2	0.76	0.59	70	0.6	1
		SS-N-18, Mod 2	0.45	0.76	1.02	70	1	2

*Use cutoff value for lethality, $K_{max} = 125$. For a thorough discussion of K_{max} due to the cratering effect of nuclear weapons see *Nuclear Explosion Effects on Missile Silos* listed in sources below.
**Silo hardness assumed to be 3,000 pounds per square inch (PSI) overpressure capability.

Sources for Figures 2-1 and 2-2:

Offensive Missiles: Stockholm Paper 5, (Stockholm International Peace Research Institute, Stockholm, Sweden; 1974), pp. 16 & 18.

Kosta Tsipis, *Nuclear Explosion Effects on Missile Silos,* (Center for International Studies, Massachusetts Institute of Technology; February 1978), pp. 83-87.

has. It looks like the Soviets have the resources to eliminate our ICBM force. But there are serious fallacies in this number juggling.

The foregoing scenario assumes that all the SS-18s and SS-19s are MIRVed which is not the case. Even more unrealistic is that the scenario requires a perfect distribution of about a thousand sets of four warheads—each set having one warhead that would work properly and hit close enough while the other three would be duds or fall too far away. That would be impossible to predict before the fact. This actually amounts to cross-targeting four MIRVs on each silo which only raises the kill probability to 74 percent. After all the SS-18s and SS-19s have been fired there would still be over 250 US ICBMs unscathed and ready to launch.

Another fallacy is that cross-targeting four warheads to one silo is not wise because of a phenomenon called *fratricide*—where one nuclear explosion destroys other incoming warheads. Say, for instance, that the first warhead explodes too far away to cause damage. But it kicks up debris and ionizes the atmosphere so that the next warhead is destroyed by flying objects or has its fuzing circuit burned out by a tremendously high electromagnetic pulse generated in the circuitry. It has not yet been determined how fratricide can be plugged into the lethality equation other than to limit the number of warheads sent to each target. That is why it is only considered feasible to send two warheads to each silo—the first timed for an air burst to maximize overpressure and radiation while minimizing debris; the second a ground burst to produce shock and cratering effects.

Now let us look at the overall, comparative counterforce threat posed by each of the two strategic superpowers. Let us grant, as Pentagon officials allege, that the Soviets will be able to destroy 90 percent of our land-based missiles by the mid-1980s. The U.S. has about one-quarter of its approximately 10,000 strategic warheads on those missiles so that would mean loss of roughly 2,250 warheads (.9 × .25 × 10,000)—actually 2,154.

Looking the other way, US Minuteman-3 missiles alone could destroy about an equal number (2,257) of Soviet strategic warheads.*

---

*The US has 900 335-kiloton warheads and 750 170-kiloton warheads on Minuteman-3 missiles. The Soviets have 1,398 silos. If 900 silos were attacked by the 335-kiloton warheads (at a SSP_k of 44%) there would be 396 destroyed. Another 250 silos attacked by 250 170-kiloton warheads (SSP_k = 31%) would result in 77 destroyed. The 500 remaining 170-kiloton warheads cross-targeted against the last 248 silos (with a CTP_k = 51%) would destroy 126 of them. In all 599, or 43% of all

The purpose of this discussion is to demonstrate that neither superpower's most counterforce missiles can be perceived as a credible first strike threat against the other's silos. The standoff is pretty equal right now with no assurance that a countersilo attack would be worth the risk. That is with existing weapons, however. The US is developing new weapons and other military technologies which will upset the equilibrium. Those will be discussed in later chapters.

Increasing the warhead explosive yield and decreasing the miss distance both improve the lethality of a warhead. However, increasing the accuracy (decreasing the miss distance) is the more effective. Making a weapon twice as accurate has the same effect on lethality as making the warhead eight times as powerful. Phrased another way, making the missile twice as precise would only require one-eighth the explosive power to maintain the same lethality. Hence miniaturization of warheads and precision of delivery has been the course of US nuclear weapons development. An example may help.

The Minuteman-2 missile has a one-megaton warhead and a CEP of 0.3 nautical miles. Its lethality rating is 11. When converted to a Minuteman-3 with three 170-kiloton MIRVs and a CEP of 0.2 nautical miles, the total lethality of the missile—counting all three warheads—rose to 23. By narrowing the CEP one-third and MIRVing, the hard target kill probability for the full payload has almost doubled—from 13% to 24%—with only half the megatonnage. Subsequently, the NS-20 guidance system has been installed on all Minuteman-3s and the more powerful 335-kiloton warheads (which, through miniaturization, only occupy as much space as the other 170-kiloton bombs) have been fitted to 300 of them. These improvements have significantly improved the hard target kill probability.

Minuteman-3s are the most accurate ballistic missiles deployed. That is why fewer of them, with smaller warheads, can destroy more of the opponent's strategic bombs than all the SS-18s and SS-19s put together. The Soviets still rely heavily on megatonnage to achieve their counterforce capability. Pentagon spokesmen often allude to Soviet missiles having "demonstrated" tighter CEPs than previously determined. Such reports usually imply that the Soviets have surpassed us in accuracy or at least are catching up fast.[18] The key word here is

---

Soviet silos, would be destroyed. Since the Soviets deploy about three-quarters of their approximate 7,000 strategic nuclear warheads in silos, the Minuteman-3s would have destroyed 2,257 (.43 × .75 × 7,000) of those strategic bombs.

demonstrated. Only *test* CEPs are "demonstrated"—and there must be enough tests to plot a distribution curve. Operational CEPs can never be "demonstrated" unless there is a nuclear war. They have to be extrapolated based on test CEPs. That process considers all the differences between operational and test parameters—the direction of firing (test ICBMs are never flown over the North Pole as operational missiles would be), the variance in gravity effects (flying over a land mass as opposed to an ocean mass), weather conditions, and the distance flown. Furthermore, test missiles are usually laboratory specimens—as opposed to mass production models—and are flown under ideal conditions. The difference between test and operational CEPs is often called "bias."[19]

Even the operational CEP varies with different mission charcteristics. The range to the target has an effect on accuracy, as does the sequence in which the MIRVs are released from the missile. So it can be seen why a nominal CEP must be used for comparison purposes as in Figure 2-4. It can also be seen why we mustn't be too gullible about Pentagon tales of Russian missiles "demonstrating" a smaller CEP than previously determined.

To better understand how missile development has migrated toward better accuracy it might be helpful to trace the evolution of ballistic missiles. There are three basic segments to their flight trajectory: *powered flight* (also called the *boost phase*), *coast through space*, and *reentry* into the earth's atmosphere. After launch, rocket motors "boost" the missile to the required speed and in the proper direction—up and out of the atmosphere and on the way to its target. This is the first phase. When the booster motors burn out and fall off, all that was left of early missiles was the hydrogen bomb packaged in a special capsule so it wouldn't burn up from air friction as it reentered the earth's atmosphere. This reentry vehicle, as it was called, then went through the long coast phase, zipping through space in an arc and reaching altitudes of hundreds of miles. Eventually it would fall back into the earth's atmosphere for the final reentry phase. Figure 2-5 illustrates the flight path of a ballistic missile.

The early ballistic missiles were launched along a predetermined trajectory toward a desired impact point. All of the necessary "aiming" was done during powered flight when swivel nozzels or other similar steering control put the missile on the right heading at the proper velocity. But after the motors burned out it was no longer possible to

Figure 2-5
Flight Path of a Ballistic Missile

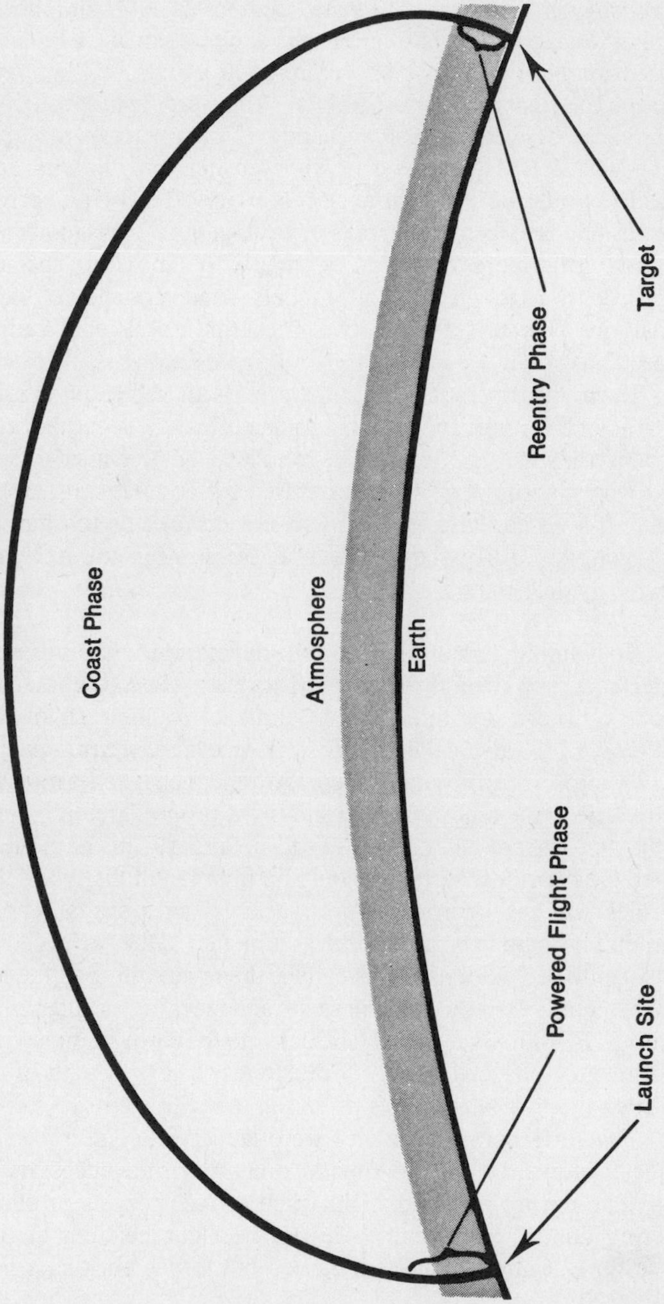

correct any errors in their course. From that point on the reentry body, carrying its hydrogen bomb, sped on to the target like a bullet. That is why these missiles are called *ballistic*. Also, like a bullet, it could be easily deflected from its intended path.

During the last half of the 1960s the multiple individually-targeted reentry vehicle (MIRV) was developed by the United States. Several of these MIRVs can be mounted on a portion of the missile called the "bus." They are then covered and protected by the missile's nose cone. (See Figure 2-6) By the time the last booster motor drops off, the nose cone has also been removed. All that is left to enter the long coast phase is the bus with its load of MIRVs. It maneuvers around the sky to drop these deadly passengers off for their separate destinations.

At first the Pentagon claimed that the reason MIRVs were needed was to get past the enemy's defensive anti-ballistic missile (ABM) interceptors. By spacing the reentry bodies one behind the other at sufficient distance, they explained, it would not be possible for one interceptor to destroy more than one warhead. Then when the supply of interceptors was exhausted, the remaining MIRVs would destroy the target. Spacing would be accomplished by backing the bus up along the flight path every time a body is released. After MIRVs were operational, however, the bus proved easy to reprogram to move sideways rather than back up. That put each bomb in a different flight path leading to a different target. Each missile could then destroy as many targets as it carried MIRVs. The following mid-1968 question and answer testimony confirms the fact that the Pentagon had the destruction of more targets in mind when it started the development program for MIRVs.

> *Senator Mike Mansfield:* Is it true that the US response to the discovery that the Soviets had made an initial deployment of an ABM system around Moscow and possibly elsewhere was to develop the MIRV system for Minuteman and (Poseidon)?
>
> *Dr. John S. Foster (Director of Defense Research and Engineering):* Not entirely. The MIRV concept was originally generated to increase our targeting capability rather than to penetrate ABM defenses. In 1961-62 planning for targeting the Minuteman force, it was found that the total number of aim points exceeded the number of Minuteman missiles.
>
> By splitting up the payload of a single missile (censored) each (censored) could be programmed (censored) allowing us to cover those targets with (censored) fewer missiles. (Censored) MIRV was originally born to implement the payload split-up (censored). It

> was found that the previously generated MIRV concept could equally well be used against ABM (censored).[20]

Despite the censor's intervention, enough remains of the testimony to show that MIRVs were conjured up to increase the counterforce potential of the US. They were clearly conceived to fill in the blanks when the SIOP went through its 1961 revision.

A preprogrammed flight path is adequate for a deterrent missile designed to retaliate against a limited number of cities. But counterforce weapons need better accuracy. The stellar inertial guidance (SIG) system helps to provide that accuracy. It was developed in 1969 although funds for the project were obtained without congressional approval. SIG is now on Trident-1 missiles. As the missile rises above the earth's atmosphere and all booster motors have been detached, SIG gets a reading from a star to correct the missile's on-board navigation computers. Course corrections are then made by the bus as it maneuvers to drop each MIRV off for its target.

Test flights of Trident-1 were also used to develop a new satellite navigation system called Navstar. Navstar will be used on newer missiles such as Trident-2 and MX and will be discussed in a later chapter. It may also, however, be back-fitted into Trident-1 and even Poseidon to give those weapons greater accuracy; to say nothing of the Minuteman missile force.

The external fixes provided by SIG offer more precise navigation than self-contained inertial guidance packages. Submarines are also handicapped by not knowing their own exact location at the time they launch a missile. With fixes from a star, however, each warhead can be better aligned on its target after launch but before it is released from the bus.

None of the accuracy improvements mentioned so far can foresee deviations from the desired flight path while the warhead is reentering the earth's atmosphere. These excursions can be profound. Under certain conditions one side of the reentry body may melt or erode away faster than the other and cause it to veer from its target. Rain, sleet and dust can also cause abnormal erosion of the nose tip which is very sensitive in keeping the reentry vehicle on course. Wind can blow the vehicle sideways and air turbulence also has an effect on accuracy. I won't go into detail on these phenomena but one should be aware that they do occur at unpredictable times and with varying intensity in many combinations. To make corrections for very finite accuracy during this phase of flight requires a maneuvering reentry vehicle (MARV). For precisely that reason the Navy and Air Force are developing a MARV. In addition, the Army's Pershing-2 missile, if deployed in Europe, will use the first operational MARV to increase its accuracy. We'll discuss MARVs more in the next chapter.

Since the early days of the Nixon Administration there has been effort and activity to improve the accuracy of Poseidon missiles in much the same manner that Minuteman-3 ICBMs have been updated. (This is not meant to imply that all potential accuracy improvements for Minuteman-3 have been exhausted.) Although recent accuracy improvement programs are enshrouded with secrecy it makes sense that the most available technology for Poseidon is SIG. Former Director of Defense Research and Engineering, Dr. Malcolm Currie, said in 1976: "The Improved Accuracy Program . . . has as its objective examination of the potential accuracy which can be achieved by SLBMs, as well as development of components and subsystems needed to achieve that accuracy. By far the largest share of our request is earmarked to asesss the accuracy of the Trident-1 and Poseidon missiles on test flight trajectories."[21] Although there is no evidence that SIG has been installed on Poseidon as an operational system, it does seem possible that some Poseidons have been tested with SIG navigation.

More recent testimony at the beginning of the Reagan Administration shows a focus on improving Trident-1 missiles—also known as the C-4—although there could be the possibility of extending these improvements to the Poseidon. Admiral Glenwood Clark, a technical director at the Strategic Systems Project Office, stated in testimony before the House Armed Services Committee in March 1981 that: "The modernization plan as it now sits and as approved by the Secretary of Defense is to at least—in the modernization—to at least improve the accuracy of C-4. . ."[22] Since the Trident-1 already has a SIG sensor that follows a preselected star towards its target, it is reasonable to deduce that the "modernization" will involve the more advanced and more accurate *two-vector SIG* and/or Navstar. Nevertheless, the evidence seems clear that there are strong moves toward giving existing SLBMs a hard target capability. Let us now take another look at the present US ICBMs.

Activities to increase the hard target kill potential of Minuteman-3 ICBMs are more visible. I have already discussed the introduction of NS-20 guidance systems and Mark-12A 335-kiloton warheads. A

Command Data Buffer computer controller, which stores flight trajectories for numerous targets, has been developed to allow retargeting of a Minuteman-3 missile in 25 minutes. Using this system, this full Minuteman-3 complement can be retargeted in under ten hours—a task that used to take weeks. The Strategic Air Command Digital Network (SACDIN) provides a greater number of computerized "target sets" to further speed-up retargeting. The development of a computer link with an airborne launch control center (called the "Looking Glass" aircraft)* will permit target switching from the air.

Minuteman-3 improvements may even include putting maneuvering warheads on existing missiles. In early 1974, Defense Secretary Schlesinger said: ". . . we plan to initiate advanced development of a terminally homing guided MARV *for possible retrofit into both ICBMS and SLBMs*. This MARV could give Minuteman-3 a very high accuracy, if such a capability should be needed in the future."[23] The late General George S. Brown indicated in his fiscal year 1978 posture statement that MARVing the Minuteman-3 missiles is still a live issue. He said: "Improvements in Minuteman-3 accuracy continue to be pursued to assure greater effectiveness per missile. Additional efforts are focusing on a terminally guided maneuvering reentry vehicle."[24]

In the fiscal year 1975 Pentagon budget presentation the development of the Mark-20 warhead was mentioned as part of the five-year plan for the Minuteman program.[25] When initial funding would take place was secret but over a quarter-billion dollars was proferred as the "broad planning figure." Air Force officials said that the Mark-20 has no direct relation to existing Minuteman MIRVs but that the technology being developed in its program would be used. The Mark-20 could well be the target-sensing precision MARV to which James Schlesinger and General Brown were alluding.

The aforementioned activities do not exhaust the improvements to Minuteman missiles that have been envisioned. During the mid-1970s, for instance, a program called PAVE PEPPER tested seven smaller MIRVs on Minuteman-3 missiles. *Air Force* Magazine proposed using the new high energy propellant developed for Trident-1 in Minuteman missiles to allow their throw weight to be doubled.[26] Other proposals suggested extending airborne launch control of Minuteman-3 to all 550 missiles instead of just 200; and putting Mark-12A reentry bodies on all

---

*Military humor perceives that this aircraft, like Alice who went through the looking glass, can take us into a different world.

550 instead of just 300. As regards Minuteman-2, it has been proposed to replace 100 of them with Minuteman-3 and to upgrade another 300 of the -2s for airborne launch control.[27] The Reagan Administration plans to replace 50 Minuteman-2s with the -3s as the Titan-2s are deactivated. Boeing was awarded a contract during mid-1982 to make this change. That will increase US counterforce-capable warheads by 150 and the total strategic inventory by 46.

One of the more exotic possibilities involves redesigning the Minuteman system so that missiles can be launched when a warning of attack is received but held in a parking orbit in space, or flying by remote control as a "cruise ballistic missile" in the atmosphere, until an attack is verified.[28] This would supposedly make the silo-based ICBMs less vulnerable but would require extensive testing and would be extremely expensive, to say nothing of being very dangerous. Nevertheless, it appears that Boeing Company has been given an Air Force contract to conduct preliminary wind tunnel testing.[29]

Are all these improvements necessary? Are they really needed to counter the "Russian threat"? Or do they support other interests? And do they increase the risk of war and other dangers? These are questions that people are beginning to ask. On February 27, 1978 then Under Secretary of Defense for Research and Engineering, Dr. William J. Perry, provided what could be a lead to the answer. He put the Soviet threat into proper context:

> We don't anticipate any problems with accuracy. . . We already have sufficient accuracy. If the Soviet Union had today the accuracy we have on Minuteman-3 they would already pose a threat to us in our silos.[30]

Clearly, the United States has at least an adequate deterrent defensive force. But as formidable as the present strategic forces are, and as far reaching as are all the programs to improve those forces, the Pentagon's thirst for the ultimate counterforce capability will not be sated. It has programs to modernize every leg of the triad to be more aggressive. The next three chapters will look at these modernization programs.

Figure 2-6
MIRVs Attached to Bus

Source: U.S. Department of Defense

NOTES

1. Andrew Cockburn, "Treat SS-16 Warnings Warily," *New York Times,* 27 April 1982, p.23.
2. *The Military Balance 1981/82,* prepared by the International Institute for Strategic Studies (IISS), London, England. Published in *Air Force Magazine,* December 1981, at p. 59.
3. "Science and the Citizen," *Scientific American,* May 1981, p.92.
4. Cited in *Scientific American,* op. cit.
5. For instance, see Edgar Ulsamer, "In Focus," *Air Force Magazine,* September 1979, p. 24.
6. *Department of Defense Annual Report Fiscal Year 1981*, by Harold Brown, Secretary of Defense, 29 January 1980, p. 80.
7. Clarence A. Robinson, Jr., "Soviet SALT Violations Feared," *Aviation Week & Space Technology*, 22 September 1980, pp. 14–15.
8. For a more in-depth treatment of the six measures of strategic power see Schneider, Barry R. and Leader, Stefan; "The United States-Soviet Arms Race, SALT, and Nuclear Proliferation," published in the *Congressional Record,* (Senate; Vol. 121, No. 87; June 5, 1975), pp. S9835-S9841. (Hereafter referred to as Schneider and Leader.)
9. Speech by John Newhouse at the University of California in Los Angeles (January 29, 1975), cited in Schneider and Leader, op. cit.
10. Griswold, Lawrence; "MIRVs, MARVs, Megatons, and Microminiaturization," *Sea Power,* (July 1975), p. 19.
11. Schneider and Leader, op. cit.
12. Clarence A. Robinson, Jr., "SALT May Allow 3 New Soviet Missiles," *Aviation Week & Space Technology*, 25 June 1979, pp. 21–22.
13. *United States Military Posture for FY 1979*, by Chairman of the Joint Chiefs of Staff General George S. Brown, 20 January 1978, p. 28.
14. Defense Secretary Harold Brown on ABC—Issues and Answers. Cited in *Selected Statements* (published by the Air Force for Department of Defense officials), 1 November 1980, p. 49.
15. *Offensive Missles: Stockholm Paper 5*, (Stockholm International Peace Research Institute, Stockholm, Sweden; 1974), p. 16. Another excellent

discussion of lethality is Kosta Tsipis, "The Accuracy of Strategic Missiles," *Scientific American*, July 1975, pp. 14–23.

16. *Offensive Missiles*, op. cit., p. 18.
17. Ibid.
18. For example, see "Washington Roundup," *Aviation Week & Space Technology*, 27 March 1978, p. 13.
19. For an Air Force presentation on how operational CEPs are extrapolated see *Hearings on Military Posture for Fiscal Year 1979*, before the House Armed Services Committee, 24 February 1978, Part 3, Book 1, pp. 312–318.
20. Cited in Desmond Ball, *Deja Vu: The Return to Counterforce in the Nixon Administration*, December 1974, pp. 19–20.
21. *Fiscal Year 1977 Authorization for Military Procurement, Research and Development, and Active Duty, Selected Reserve and Civilian Personnel Strengths*, hearings before the Senate Armed Services Committee, 5 February 1976, Part 4, p. 2096.
22. *Hearings on Military Posture and HR 2790*, before the House Armed Services Committee, 26 March 1981, Part 2, p. 760.
23. *Fiscal Year 1975 Authorization for Military Procurement, Research and Development, and Active Duty, Selected Reserve and Civilian Personnel Strengths*, hearings before the Senate Armed Services Committee, 5 February 1974, Part 1, p. 65.
24. *United States Military Posture for FY 1978*, by Chairman of the Joint Chiefs of Staff, General George S. Brown, 20 January 1977, p. 12.
25. *Fiscal Year 1975 Authorization*, op. cit., 2 April 1974, Part 6, pp. 3399–3400.
26. Edgar Ulsamer, "In Focus," *Air Force Magazine*, June 1979, p. 24.
27. *Aviation Week & Space Technology*, 21 April 1980, p. 148.
28. Clarence Robinson, "ICBM Survivability Aid Studied," *Aviation Week & Space Technology*, 25 February 1980, pp. 16–18.
29. *Aviation Week & Space Technology*, 3 March 1980, p. 26.
30. *Department of Defense Appropriations Fiscal Year 1979*, hearings before the Senate Appropriation Committee, 27 February 1978, Part 5, p. 200.

TRIDENT: THE ULTIMATE FIRST STRIKE WEAPON

My sanity it seems, is in the hands
Of those who control the doomsday machines.
(Don't sneeze when your finger's on the button)
This silent terror,
Big brother to Poseidon and Polaris,
Can blow up 408 cities
Accurately!

Gillian Hope
New Zealand

Submarine-launched ballistic missiles would be among the first, if not the very first, weapons used in a limited nuclear exchange during some future crisis. It has long been known that 400 Poseidon warheads are aimed at theatre targets. Early in 1976 former Defense Secretary Donald Rumsfeld confirmed that strategic submarine-launched missiles are, in fact, targeted for limited nuclear war: "Considerable capabilities for preplanned strikes against a variety of targets in the theatre is currently provided by US and allied nuclear-armed tactical aircraft, US and FRG Pershing missiles, the UK Polaris force, and *Poseidon reentry vehicles* currently committed to [the Supreme Allied Commander in Europe] for use in preplanned strikes in theatre-wide nuclear war."[1] (emphasis added) That declaration blurs the distinction between tactical and strategic weapons in order to support the Pentagon's announced doctrine of selectivity and flexibility; later called the "countervailing strategy" codified by the Carter Administration's Presidential Directive-59 and more recently emerging as the Reagan Administration's "strategy for a protracted nuclear war."

The charcteristics that make SLBMs likely to be the first weapons used in limited nuclear war are the same that make them the most probable choice to initiate a strategic first strike. First, the location of the submarine which launches them is much less certain to the Soviets than the US silo-based missiles. Soviet radar would have to provide surveillance in all directions from which a SLBM might possibly come. It is possible that they would not even detect a SLBM until it was too late. That would mean that Soviet land-based missiles would be destroyed before they could be launched. Likewise, communications centers could be annihilated before they could send the launch command to Soviet missile-carrying submarines.

The second very important advantage of SLBMs over land-based ICBMs in destroying land targets is their shorter flight time. That is made possible by the shorter range from which they can be fired. Whereas ICBMs take about thirty minutes to get from one continent to another, SLBMs travel from the submarine to their target in as little as ten to fifteen minutes. This pares down warning time from 25 minutes for an incoming attack by land-based ICBMs to as little as five minutes for a SLBM attack. Because it takes some time to launch a missile after receiving a warning of attack, the offensive use of SLBMs could reduce the margin for reaction to zero.

When we consider the destruction of early warning systems, communications centers, and other critical targets located along the Soviet coastline, the SLBM's short flight time would allow practically zero warning, to say nothing of time to react. Such an attack can be accomplished by flying the missile on what is known as a "depressed trajectory." (See Figure 3-1) The much shorter flight path allowed by "depressed trajectories" means considerably shorter flight time.

Because of the decided advantage of SLBMs in a first strike it is important that they be very accurate and that the submarines remain undetected. Trident is the US Navy's newest attempt to bring greater accuracy and elusiveness to the sea-based leg of the strategic triad. This effort began with the Strat-X study conducted for the Pentagon in 1966–67 by the Institute of Defense Analysis. By 1968 the Underwater Long-range Missile System (ULMS) emerged as the Navy's new strategic weapon. ULMS later became known as Trident.* In September 1971 the Navy was directed by then Deputy Secretary of Defense David Packard to go into full scale development of Trident. The announcement that Trident would operate in the Pacific with its home port at Bangor,

*The trident is the three-pronged spear carried by Poseidon, god of the sea in Greek mythology.

Figure 3-1
SLBM Trajectories

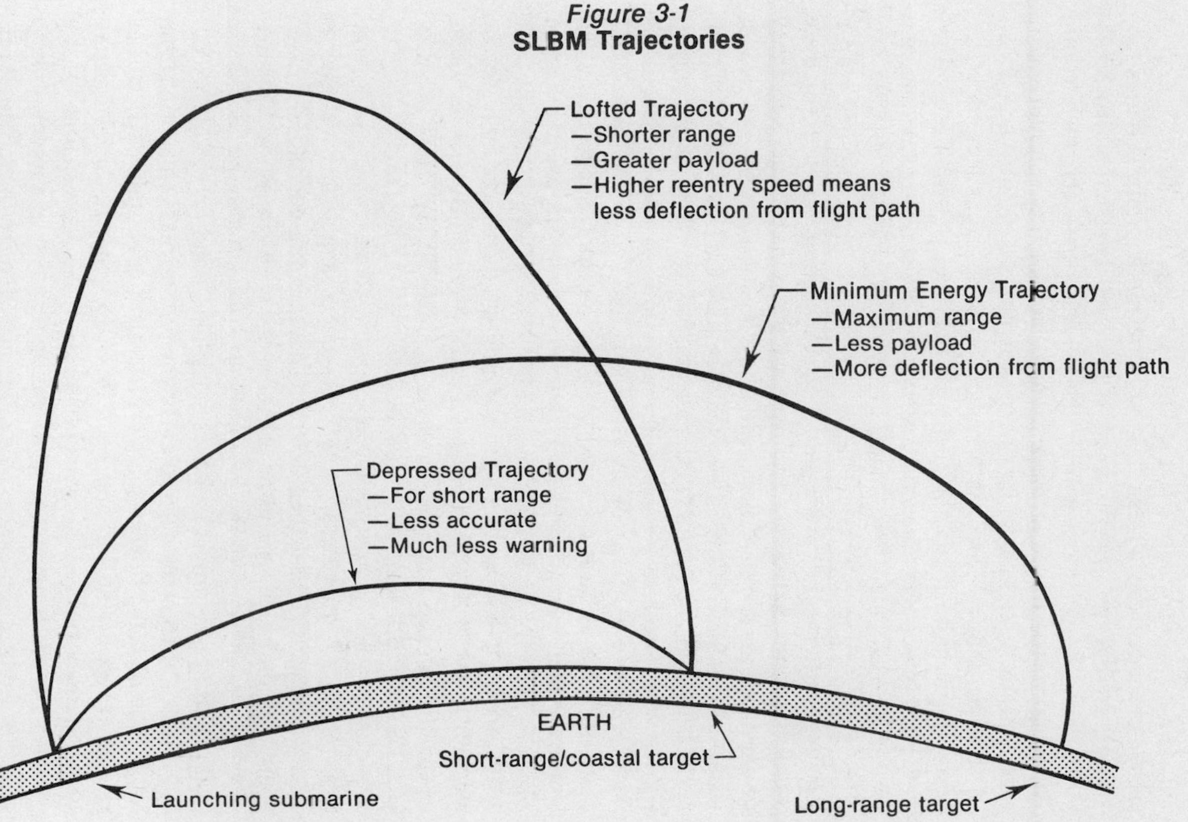

Washington—along Hood Canal in Puget Sound—came in February 1973. During the following year the first submarine was financed.

There are many facets to the Trident Weapons system. The most visible programs are a new fleet of some undetermined number of submarines and two generations of submarine-launched ballistic missiles (SLBMs). In addition, the Navy has plans for such exotic technology as maneuvering warheads and a new type of communication system which will penetrate the ocean to depths of several hundred feet. As shall be shown, public information on the various aspects of the Trident system has been clouded by official secrecy and deception.

After a strong bureaucratic struggle between the strategic and nuclear propulsion factions of the Navy, the Trident submarine was defined as a huge boat that could carry many large missiles with a considerable number of warheads.[2] The Poseidon submarines which are presently operational in the fleet displace 8,250 tons of water when they are submerged. They are just a little heavier than the Navy's newest destroyers. At 18,700 tons, Trident subs will be over double that weight and heavier than the fleet's latest nuclear strike cruisers. As for length, Trident will stretch to 560 feet—almost as long as two football fields placed end-to-end. Each of these behemoths will carry twenty-four missiles which is half again as many as Poseidon subs contain. In addition to that, each missile can be almost twice as big as the Poseidon missile.

Since the beginning of the Trident program the alleged ability of the new sub to avoid detection has been an important justification for its construction. "The name of the game is survivability," boasted Rear Admiral R.Y. Kaufman at the Senate hearings on the Trident budget.[3] One quality of a submarine closely related to its capacity to avoid detection is its "quietness," but Pentagon officials have refused to specify quietness goals in their Selected Acquisition Report to Congress. Noting the omission, the General Accounting Office pressed for that information. The Trident Program Office restated that the radiated noise levels would be significantly lower than Polaris and Poseidon subs but they didn't comment on the problem of cavitation noises emanating from the turbulent water flow around Trident's massive hulk as it pushes through the ocean at greater speeds than any other missile-launching submarine ever built. That may be the reason the Navy claimed that a quietness goal does not lend itself to a meaningful measurement—which means they either don't know how or are afraid to predict it. Moreover, they asserted, quietness characteristics cannot be accurately determined until *after* the first submarine is operational. That, they explained, is why it isn't in the report. It is interesting to note, however, that Electric Boat Division of General Dynamics, builder of the Trident subs, has assessed the difficulty of obtaining this nebulous goal as "substantial."[4]

Other serious design problems arising from attempts to employ new steel alloys in the construction of the sub have pushed the program far over budget. As more alloys are mixed with steel to give it higher strength there are penalties to pay in other areas such as its ability to be bent or welded. That is true of the new alloy developed for modern submarines. In October 1976 approximately 100 weld cracks were found in the *USS Ohio,* the first Trident ship. Subsequent close examination of two sister ships revealed similar cracking. Apparently this pushed the delivery date for the first submarine from December 1977 to April 1978 with a corresponding slip in its operational date. In August 1977 the Navy announced another six month delay in the *USS Ohio;* to October 1978. This time the slip in schedule was attributed to construction personnel and production problems.[5] It then made a series of slips to April 1979, November 1980, January 1981, June, August and October. The first Trident ship, the *USS Ohio,* was finally commissioned on November 11, 1981 and went on its first patrol in late 1982. Meanwhile, the cost of each sub has jumped from $723-million to $1.2-billion. The original 1974 estimate was $576.4-million.[6] As the admirals explain, they've had troubles aplenty with people, plans, production, materials and scheduling.[7]

Since the inception of the Trident submarine program the size of the planned fleet has been obfuscated. For the first several years of the program the Navy consistently implied that it was only planning for ten ships. But Congressman Floyd Hicks of Washington state apparently became suspicious early in 1975 and caused the House Armed Services Committee to press for a more specific answer on the actual number anticipated. Vice Admiral Frank Price, Jr., Deputy Chief of Naval Operations at the time, replied: "Right now, Mr. Chairman, our program is for ten submarines. And that is the program at this point in time."[8] But those carefully chosen words conveniently reserved the option for a future change and that is exactly what happened. In 1976 the Navy announced that it would need an eleventh sub.[9] (Advanced procurement contracts for the tenth and eleventh Tridents were awarded to Electric Boat Division of General Dynamics in March 1982.[10]) Plans for the twelfth and thirteenth followed n 1977.[11] Requirements for a fourteenth were outlined in early 1978.[12]

Pentagon charts once showed plans to build thirty Trident submarines (720 launch tubes) by 1998.[13] Now however, reflecting the construction problems described above, these charts show 28 Trident submarines (672 launch tubes) by the year 2000.[14] (See Figure 3-2) That is less than the previously planned 720 but still more than the 656 SLBM launchers that were available up until 1979 prior to retirement of the older Polaris boats. Furthermore, the total number of Trident subs could still rise to thirty, or even more, after the turn of the century.

Figure 3-2
SLBM Launcher Levels[14]

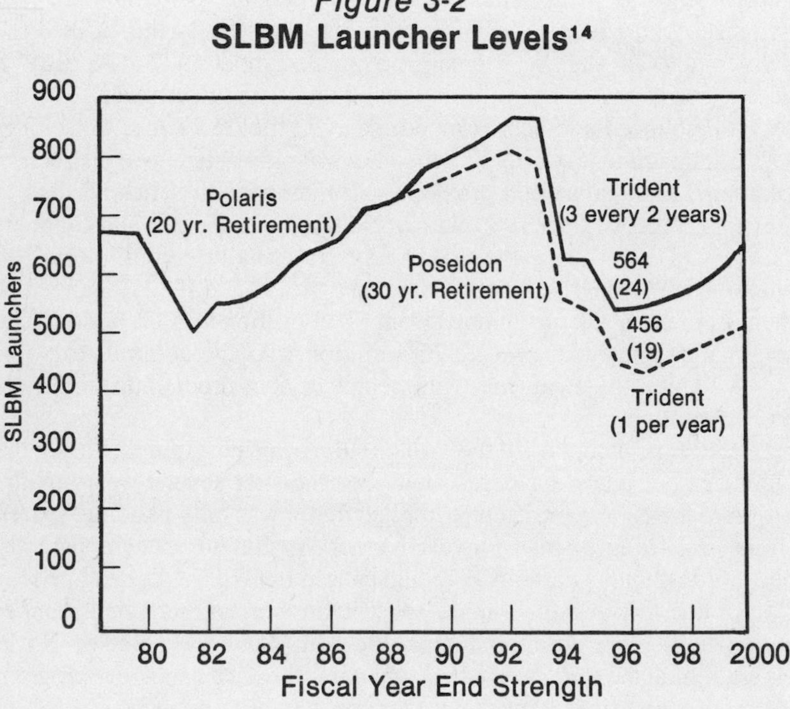

Figure 3-2 shows one curve for the desired delivery rate of 3 every 2 years and another for a slower rate of one per year. The chart is based on a June 1981 delivery date for the first Trident submarine, which wasn't delivered until five months later, so there may be need for some slight adjustment on that account. Nevertheless, the Reagan Administration's plan through fiscal year 1985 is to pump in an additional $2.6-billion to overcome Trident construction problems and speed up the schedule.

The Navy chart depicted in Figure 3-2 indicates a perceived shortage of launchers around 1997 when the last Poseidon sub reaches its 30-year service life.* In that year, there will be a low of 564 launchers available on 24 Trident ships† —with the possibility of only 456 launchers on 19 Trident subs if the slower delivery schedule is necessary. We must keep in mind, however, that by that date the Trident-2 missile is scheduled to be in the Trident submarines. When considering the number of missiles per sub, the number of targets each missile can attack, and the at-sea readiness of each submarine, the worst case low of 19 Trident ships could attack 306 more targets than the old pre-1979 fleet of 41 Polaris/Poseidon boats—4,213 vs. 3,907. The breakdown is shown in Figure 3-3.

Furthermore, because of their greater precision, the Trident system can attack harder targets. Moreover, because of Trident's longer range, many of the submarines not at sea could still conceivably attack targets.

During Congressional hearings Vice Admiral John G. Williams, Jr., Deputy Chief of Naval Operations for Submarine Warfare, referred to the 1981 dip to 496 launch tubes for SLBMs. This was caused by retirement of the ten Polaris submarines. Admiral Williams pointed out that because they were backfitting Trident-1 missiles into twelve Poseidon subs and increasing the number of warheads on Poseidon missiles, that the damage potential increased.[17] The 1997 dip is surrounded by similar circumstances. With the introduction of the Trident-2 missile the overall capabilities will take a huge upturn.

As mentioned above, the Navy chose Bangor, Washington as the support complex for Trident. One reason offered for that choice was that deploying Trident on the West Coast would dilute Soviet anti-submarine warfare capabilities by opening another ocean for surveillance. In

---

*Early in the Trident program, Poseidon submarines were presented as only having a 20-year service life. As Trident schedules slipped, Poseidon's life was extended to 25 years. Then, as Trident problems continued, Poseidon usefulness was stretched to 30 years. Even that is described by one Deputy Chief of Naval Operations as "presently planned."[15] It is quite possible that some Poseidon subs could be stretched to an even longer life. The limiting factor is not safety. It is the availability or unavailability of more technologically advanced equipment.[16]

†There appears to be a typographical error on this Pentagon chart. 24 submarines at 24 launch tubes each would equal 576 launchers, not 564.

addition, the longer range Trident missiles would be "on target" even while the submarine is tied to the dock in Puget Sound. The Navy conveniently avoided mentioning that eleven Polaris/Poseidon subs have for many years operated in the Pacific with their home port at Pearl Harbor and forward-based at Guam. The Pacific is by no means a new area of operation for ballistic missile submarines. More to the point, however, the Pacific does provide the only easy and assured access to the Indian Ocean which is becoming more and more of an operational area for the US fleet.

Figure 3-3
Maximum Readiness of SLBM Warheads

Submarine (also quantity)	Missiles per submarine	Max targets each missile can attack	Total targets possible for all subs	At-sea readiness of subs	Total targets ready to be attacked
10 Polaris	16	1	160	55%	88
31 Poseidon	16	14	6,944	55%	3,819
	Total for Polaris and Poseidon:				3,907
19 Trident	24	14	6,384	66%	4,213

Assumes each missile carries full load of warheads

Navy officials also claimed that choosing a single base in the United States is saving tax dollars. A passage from a Trident Project Office pamphlet reads:

> . . . The Trident missile makes it possible for the submarine to "be on station" as soon as it leaves port in the continental United States. This allows the requisite Trident support to be consolidated at a single US base, eliminating the need for costly overseas bases or the construction of submarine tenders to support the Trident fleet. . .[18]

That sounds like good news for the taxpayer. However, the Navy's desire to lease anchorages and strategic weapons storage sites in the Palauan Islands lends credibility to the claim that Trident will be forward-based.[19] These bases are being sought under the Compact of Free

Association that the United States is trying to negotiate with the People of Micronesia, of which Palau is a part.[20] Common sense dictates that Trident submarines will need a forward base. The entire system is justified by the premise that the longer range missiles will give the submarines ten times more ocean area to hide in. To fully utilize that larger area the submarines will operate as far south as the equator in the Pacific and Indian Oceans. It would be neither feasible nor logical that the subs would make the long voyage back to home port near Seattle every time they change crews, need supplies and servicing, or have to replace defective missiles. They would be certain to have a forward base somewhere.

Having established the need for a forward base, the next question is where would it be located. Certain considerations point to Palau as the choice spot:*

1. Palau is geographically centered in the lower Pacific where many Trident subs will patrol. Subic Bay in the Philippines and Guam are the only other suitable naval facilities close to that area. Guam is farther north and Subic only opens west into the China Sea.
2. Palau's Malakal Harbor is the only existing or proposed naval station in the Southwest Pacific which has immediate access to deep water. The sub can dive as soon as it casts away from the dock or a tender ship to become less vulnerable in an emergency.
3. Palau is the only Southwest Pacific port where the submarine commander would have a choice of two exits to preclude being bottled up in port. The second exit, however, would require blasting another channel through the barrier reef which protects Palau's vital underwater resources.
4. Current Pentagon policy is to disperse forces so they cannot be so easily destroyed by an enemy nuclear attack. Guam and Subic are heavily concentrated with military forces and would be poor candidates for a Trident port.
5. Palau is in line with the deep water Sunda and Lombok Straits of Indonesia through which Trident could pass submerged into the Indian Ocean. The wider Strait of Malacca is too shallow for that.

*The Palauan Islands are the western-most cluster of the Caroline group in Micronesia. They are located approximately seven degrees above the equator and 500 miles east of the Philippines.

6. Probably the most attractive qualification is that Palau is little known to the rest of the world and there are less than 15,000 people there to offer resistance. With the growing global opposition to military bases this would be an important consideration.

As early as 1973 the Pentagon produced maps indicating that Trident would operate down to the equator in both the Pacific and Indian Oceans.[21] The Navy's keen interest in Indian Ocean operations for Trident, and a base on the island of Diego Garcia* was brought out in a 1979 Library of Congress report:

> The United States also has a potential strategic nuclear objective in the Indian Ocean region, that of deploying, when necesary or convenient, ballistic missile submarines (SSBNs) targeted on the Soviet Union. This objective is seldom discussed by US officials and in fact the public position of the US Government is that the Navy does not regularly operate SSBNs in the Indian Ocean. The official position would appear to be generally borne out by range and capabilities of the Polaris type boats now normally operated from Guam. . . . With the inception of the Trident system, with the longer range Trident-1 missile, operations in the Indian Ocean could become feasible.
>
> . . . The base can also—and this is the main point of contention—facilitate a larger permanent naval presence, including the basing of carriers and SLBMs. . . .
>
> Conceivably, Diego Garcia could be used as a deployment point for tactical air units, as a base for a permanent surface naval force, or as a support facility for SSBNs. . . .[22]

Proof that this was not just a theoretical study, but is being actively considered, came in the *Fiscal Year 1983 Arms Control Impact Statements*—the first ones submitted to Congress by the Reagan Administration:

> The increased operating room provided by the Indian Ocean might be of future use to US SSBN/SLBM forces and might become necessary if there were a major Soviet ASW breakthrough that imperiled the US ballistic missile submarine force or a Soviet abrogation of the ABM Treaty and major new efforts to build ABMs. . . .[23]

---

*Diego Garcia is an island fairly well centered in the Indian Ocean and approximately 1,200 miles south of the tip of India. It is leased from Britain and exclusively occupied by the US military.

In later chapters we will see that Soviet anti-submarine warfare (ASW) efforts are focused near their homeland and that it is the United States that is close to abrogating the ABM Treaty. Nevertheless, the intention of putting Trident in the Indian Ocean is evidenced by these official documents.

The early claim that Trident subs would operate out of a single US base has also been proved false by events on the Atlantic seaboard. In early 1977 the Defense Department announced that studies were in progress for East Coast basing of Trident submarines and Poseidon submarines backfitted with the Trident-1 missile. That investigation was ostensibly justified because Spain would not renew the Navy's lease on a forward base for US missile-launching submarines at Rota beyond July 1979. Of course the Rota base was for shorter-range Polaris and Poseidon weapons and was never advertised as intended for Trident. But the East Coast base study actually fits into the unfolding Navy plan for a wider deployment of the Trident fleet. Former Defense Secretary Rumsfeld said:

> . . . The submarine base under construction at Bangor, Washington as currently programmed can support only ten Trident submarines. Consequently, as the program proceeds beyond ten submarines, a decision must be made either to expand the Bangor facility or to construct Trident submarine support facilities on the East Coast. The military ocean terminal at King's Bay, Georgia, currently maintained in an inactive status by the Army, has been identified as the preferred location for possible construction of an alternative East Coast refit site.[24]

It is now general knowledge that King's Bay is the support facility for the Poseidon submarines equipped with Trident-1 missiles. There is recent testimony that the first Trident submarine is scheduled to arrive there in 1990.[25] As circumstances are shaping up it can be expected that there will eventually be four Trident bases—Bangor, King's Bay, Palau and Diego Garcia—which will strategically ring the globe and provide ready access to every major ocean.

While the Navy claims that the longer range Trident missiles will give the submarine more ocean to hide in, there is another side to the coin to be considered. The submarines could use the full area of ocean available to it but upon command could be brought in to form a close ring around the USSR. One of the chief advantages of SLBMs in a counterforce strategy is their short flight time when they are positioned close to their targets. This allows the "time urgent" targets—as missile silos are called—to be destroyed before they serve their function. Also, the SLBMs can be fired very fast. One aerospace journal reports that a Poseidon sub can launch all 16 of its missiles in less than 15 minutes.[26] Thus, given the Pentagon's interest in destroying missiles in silos, it seems logical that the submarines would remain fairly close to their targets while their longer range allows them to remain on-target as they return to port.

As stated earlier, the Navy plans two generations of Trident missiles. Lockheed Missiles and Space Company in Sunnyvale, California was awarded a production contract for the Trident-1 in August 1974. Trident-1 is the same size as the Poseidon missile—34 feet long and 74 inches diameter. It was originally supposed to have weighed 70,000 pounds, a ton heavier than Poseidon, but that grew to 73,000 pounds. The Trident-1 reportedly can carry a full load of eight 100-kiloton reentry bodies a distance of 4,000 nautical miles. If weight is reduced by removing some of those reentry bodies it will have even greater range. Another goal of Trident-1 is that it be as precise at the 4,000 nautical mile range as the Poseidon missile is at 2,000 nautical miles. The stellar inertial guidance (SIG) system is the key to that accuracy.

In addition to placement of the missiles in the Trident submarines, twelve Poseidon boats have been reworked to carry Trident-1. Originally only ten had been scheduled for refitting. The first one—the USS Francis Scott Key—was sent to sea on October 20, 1979. Navy officials have always held the option open to refit an additional twelve Poseidon subs to carry Trident-1s and the Reagan Administration has included a Poseidon refitting program in its defense plan. That will cost another $2.1 billion by the time it is finished in 1983. So far, however, there has been no public announcement that the actual conversions are in process.

The Trident-1 missile actually had its origin in a plan to create a longer-range Poseidon missile for existing submarines; using existing or easily developed technologies. The plan was developed by the EXPO Task Force at Lockheed in 1971—EXPO is a contraction of EXtended-range POseidon. I was part of that project. The EXPO missile was given the Navy designation of C-4. The Navy later decided not to go ahead with EXPO because it would create an uncertain delay in new submarine construction. But the C-4 was quickly revived once the submarine program was safely underway. Now called Trident-1, and still designated C-4, it is a direct outgrowth of the EXPO study. That is how the

Figure 3-4
Trident-1 Missile Launch

Source: U.S. Department of Defense

Navy got both the backfit program into existing submarines and the new Trident ship construction program; and how Lockheed received contracts to develop two missiles.

To achieve a greater range for Trident-1 when it is no bigger than Poseidon and even slightly heavier requires more rocket motor fuel. In effect, it requires a third booster motor and that means sacrificing payload space. The central space under the nose cone is used for a small solid propellant motor. On Poseidon this space was occupied by four warheads. Even at that, however, it would be impossible to hold the weight to 70,000 pounds without other weight saving actions. For that reason Trident-1 takes advantage of lighter composite structural materials, micro miniaturization of electronics, and light weight motor cases combined with a new high energy propellant. But this has led to trouble. The Trident-1 development program has left in its wake a trail of monumental failures.[27]

Trident difficulties started in May 1974 when a second stage test motor blew up at a Utah test facility. The Navy and Lockheed initiated a panic program to isolate the problem which was later attributed to putting the new high energy propellant into lightweight motor cases. The new propellant apparently became pourous after ignition causing it to burn more fiercely and build up pressure until the motor case exploded. Contrary to previous experience, this porosity developed after ignition and, consequently, could not be detected during inspection.

Six motors which duplicated the known conditions on that ill-fated Utah motor were selected and test fired. Two exploded. Based on these tests the Navy claimed it had a handle on the problem. But knowing the cause of a problem and finding the solution are two different things. If the motor cases were made stronger that would add weight. Reverting to the older, less efficient propellant would mean losing thrust. Both spell a reduction in range and a subsequent deterioration of Trident survivability.

Lockheed has also encountered electronic problems with the Trident-1. Efforts to save weight by combining semiconductor technologies not normally used together led to serious problems with four of the thirteen basic flight control circuits. Navy spokesmen have claimed that these malfunctions have been overcome in most of the circuits and that they remain cautiously optimistic about the rest. Nevertheless, the problems are profound and reverting to conventional circuits would mean becoming more vulnerable to radiation damage and increasing the weight.

About the time the Navy was beginning to develop confidence in their rocket motors, a first stage test motor blew up at China Lake Naval Weapons Center in California, only a month before the already delayed first flight test was to take place. Although the Pentagon announced that it was "not a completely unexpected detonation," it did result in another flight postponement. Finally, on January 18, 1977, over a year later than originally planned, the first Trident missile lifted off the pad at Cape Canaveral, Florida. The exact details of that first flight vehicle are a guarded secret but it had been predicted that it would be at least twenty percent overweight. It is quite probable that that was the case and that payload was reduced to achieve the reported range. In the final analysis we may find that, by removing the four center warheads on Poseidon and substituting a similar third stage motor, Poseidon's range could be increased to equal the actual range of the operational Trident-1.

Although the Navy claimed a good understanding of their propellant problems, officials at the Florida test range were not so confident. An explosion of the powerful Trident motor on the launch pad could cause damage to the nearby town of Cape Canaveral under certain temperature inversion and wind conditions. For that reason the Trident launches were governed by the most stringent weather criteria. Seven of the first eight test flights were delayed because of weather conditions.[28]

The first ten test flights of Trident-1 reportedly went well with only one partial failure of the guidance programming. Flight number eleven was a catastrophic failure. The second stage motor blew up in flight. Navy reports claim that the insulation on the forward motor dome was reduced in thickness to save weight and that caused the dome to overheat. It seems that weight savings not achieved by motor case and electronics technologies have been tried unsuccessfully in other areas. This could be a clue as to why the production missiles ended up weighing 3,000 pounds more.

The flight eleven failure caused another delay in the development program as well as delaying the first launch of a Trident-1 from a submarine, which was originally scheduled for late 1978. The seventeenth and nineteenth tests—the latter being the first underwater launch from a submarine on April 10, 1979—were reportedly blown-up intentionally after launch.

Although Trident-1 has now become operational I am not convinced that problems with the new Class-7 propellant have been resolved. A precedent may be found with Poseidon missiles which had a massive retrofit program after becoming operational. That was not widely publicized, however. In addition, the LX-09 conventional explosive trigger in Poseidon warheads has been discovered to be extremely sensitive to impact. The missiles have to be handled very gently. Trident-1 could very easily follow Poseidon's pattern. Problems become more evident in production runs than in the carefully checked test models. In the more distant future, these problems will be magnified when the Class-7 propellant is used in Trident-2 and MX missiles.

The Navy tried unsuccessfully to obtain the first *official* funding to study concepts for the Trident-2 missile (also known as D-5) in fiscal years 1976 and 1977. Finally a budget of $5-million was obtained in 1978 for conceptual studies. It was increased gradually every year. Advanced (preliminary) development began in fiscal year 1981 and it is planned to go into full scale development and testing during fiscal 1984. Initial operational capability for the Trident-2 has been scheduled for 1989 with the provision that it could be stepped up to 1988 provided the funds are available. The Reagan Administration's guidance document for fighting a protracted nuclear war, drafted by Defense Secretary Caspar Weinberger, directs that deployment of the Trident-2 missile begin in 1988.[29]

Trident-2's range goal is 4,230 nautical miles with a full load of bombs. Its size will stretch to a 42-foot length and swell to 82 inches diameter. It will weigh 126,000 pounds and only fit into the new submarines.

To highlight the destructive potential of Trident-2 let us look at its prospective payload. One of the warhead "mixes" being considered is fourteen hydrogen bombs of 150 kilotons each.[30] Another is eight 300-kiloton bombs.[31] Each can be sent to a different target. Trident-2's 1988 operational date will allow it to use the Navstar global positioning system—a constellation of navigation satellites—to deliver those warheads within 300 feet of their targets.* But exploding the equivalent of fifteen Hiroshima bombs within rock-throwing distance of missile silos is not the end of Pentagon ambitions. It is also developing maneuvering reentry vehicles (MARVs) which will whittle that miss distance to just a few feet. That means the warheads can be smaller and more of them can be put on each missile. My best estimate is that Trident-2 will be able to carry about seventeen MARVs with an explosive force between 75 and 100 kilotons. Any of these mixes add up to tremendous kill power.

---

*Navstar will be described in more detail in chapter 4.

Lockheed Missiles and Space Company began looking at a simple maneuvering reentry vehicle in 1968. Like most defense contractors, Lockheed had an *independent development fund* which originated from the Department of Defense. Although the company is accountable to the Defense Department for how it spends these funds it has wide discretion on how they can be used to enhance the company's competitive position. It was with these funds that the 1968 studies were begun. This rudimentary MARV was called the special reentry body or SRB. It had a bent nose and a flat spot on one side at the rear to cause it to fly at a slight upward angle when it enters the earth's atmosphere. This *angle of attack* as it is called, creates aerodynamic lifting to allow the SRB to maneuver similar to an airplane although wings are not needed because of the tremendous speed it is traveling.

Maneuvering is accomplished by a weight inside the SRB which can be shifted from side to side. When the weight is centered the SRB is equally balanced and it flies straight. But when the weight is moved either to the right or left, the center of gravity shifts causing the SRB to veer in that direction. This is similar to steering a surfboard by shifting body weight. The time and distance of this weight shifting can be carefully planned to cause various maneuvers. At first the Pentagon claimed that maneuvering warheads were needed to dodge enemy interceptor missiles. But as it was with MIRVs, the real aim was to increase counterforce accuracy.

In 1970, I was given design responsibility for the first concept studies of the Mark-500 MARV which the Navy wanted for the Trident-1 missile. At the time the Navy's interest in MARVs was a guarded secret. The Mark-500 was essentially a continuation of the SRB. Like the SRB, the Mark-500 was rationalized as a counter to Soviet interceptor missiles. But from secret reports it could be determined that the Navy had a specific interest in developing a degree of accuracy adequate to destroy hard targets

The "evasion of interceptors" rationalization was undercut when the Anti-Ballistic Missile (ABM) Treaty was signed in 1972 putting severe limits on the number of interceptor missiles allowed the Soviet Union and the United States. The treaty restricted each country to only two ABM sites; each site having no more than 100 ABM launchers which can only fire one interceptor with a single warhead. That means that each country can have no more than 200 interceptors—hardly a significant number considering the thousands of offensive warheads deployed on each side. Nevertheless, in the wake of the ABM Treaty, work on the Mark-500 was only temporarily deemphasized.

In that same year, 1972, Lockheed was awarded a development contract for Trident-1 missiles. This award was granted without the customary competitive bidding and it caused some questions in Congress. To placate the lawmakers, the Navy made it a stipulation of the contract that sizeable portions of the work would be spread around to subcontractors. It was under these conditions that further development of the Mark-500 passed to General Electric.

Most people think of GE as a maker of light bulbs and refrigerators but it is also well entrenched in defense work. Besides manufacturing jet engines GE also makes the MIRVs for Minuteman-3 missiles. GE has also been looking at maneuvering reentry bodies under study contracts from Advanced Ballistic Reentry Systems (ABRES),* an all-service research program administered by the Air Force. Unlike the Mark-500, the ABRES MARV was not controlled by a crooked nose and shifting weights but rather by twin flaps on the underneath side. When they were moved in the same direction, the MARV pitched—that is, it flew up and down. Working the flaps scissor fashion made the body roll and fly to the side. An interaction of the two movements allowed very fine control of maneuvers. That particular study of the early 1970s was known as ACE, an acronym for Advanced Control Experiment.

Congressman Les Aspin blew the whistle on the Navy in January 1974 when he announced publicly that a MARV was planned for Trident. The Pentagon immediately tried to smooth things over by saying that "there is no plan to deploy a MARV on target *at this time*."[32] (Emphasis added.) It went on to claim that the Mark-500 program was only developing maneuvering technology to have on hand just in case the Russians should cancel the ABM Treaty. During the following month, then Defense Secretary James Schlesinger reaffirmed that the Mark-500 was only intended to evade enemy interceptors.

And so the evasion justification was resurrected. But it hit more rough going in 1974 when Richard Nixon and Leonid Brezhnev signed a protocol to the ABM Treaty which further restricted interceptors to 100 at only one site. In reality, the Soviets had never increased its ABMs

---

*In early 1982, ABRES had a name change to Advanced Strategic Missile Systems (ASMS). However, since it was known as ABRES during the time about which I am writing, I will continue to use that name in this chapter.

above the 64 Galosh stationed around Moscow during the 1960s. These events made development of the Mark-500 even less sensible if its true purpose was to evade interceptors. Furthermore, a MARV cannot maneuver until it gets down to about 200,000 feet altitude leaving about ten seconds for the defenders to identify it as a warhead and to aim and fire their interceptors. Even existing (nonmaneuvering) MIRVs are practically invulnerable at that late time.

The Navy does not give up easily, however. Early in 1974 Vice Admiral R.Y. Kaufman announced to Congress that the Mark-500 was intended for the purpose of penetrating enemy defenses. Furthermore, he announced, "we are making a name change . . . We are going to call it 'Evader' so that it is very clear to everyone . . . that the MARV development we have launched into is designed to evade interceptors."[33] Since that announcement the Mark-500 has flown five times on Minuteman test missiles over the Pacific and several times on Trident-1 test missiles over the Atlantic. A Mark-500 was on the ill-fated eleventh Trident-1 flight which blew up. These tests gather information on the behavior of materials, heat absorption, aerodynamics, and load distribution during maneuvers; along with checking the ability of the shifting weights roll control system to function properly. This same data is needed to develop a precision MARV which would home-in on its target. The Navy is interested in such a MARV for its SLBMs.[34]

To find the remaining technology for a precision MARV one need only turn to the ABRES program. In addition to the flap control system, ABRES is also deeply involved with sensors that would allow a maneuvering warhead to "see" its target and make fine tune course corrections to achieve a direct hit. This highly accurate and very intelligent MARV was called the Precision Guided Reentry Vehicle (PGRV). By scanning the target area as it approaches, and comparing what it sees with an electronic map stored in its computer, the PGRV will significantly improve the hard target kill capability of strategic warheads.

The Air Force awarded two competitive contracts for eight-month studies of the PGRV concept in March of 1975. General Electric and McDonnell Douglas were selected. Neither of them were novices at the manuvering game. GE had built MARVs with flap controls that were tested on four different Atlas missile flights. McDonnell Douglas, likewise, had tested its MARV concepts on two Atlas flights.

As late as February of 1976 the Defense Department was saying that the Mark-500's purpose was to outmaneuver Soviet anti-ballistic missile interceptors and that the ABRES activity was aimed toward target sensing and homing. Director of Defense Research and Engineering at the time, Dr. Malcom Currie, told the House Armed Services Committee: "We have the Mark-500 . . . we hope it will discourage the Soviets from deploying their ABM developments . . . Another type of MARV is the terminally homing MARV and has the goal of high accuracy."[35] Later in that same month Rear Admiral Albert Kelln, Trident Program Coordinator, also asserted that the Mark-500 was a hedge against possible cancellation of the ABM Treaty.

In a matter of a few weeks the Pentagon had changed the tack of its argument. In March, Navy officials told the Senate that the Mark-500 was meant to outrun simple interceptors such as upgraded surface-to-air missiles (SAMs) originally designed to shoot down aircraft.[36] For some time the Pentagon has been claiming that Soviet SAMs were being improved for ABM use. The basis of the allegation was that SAMs had been tested above 100,000 feet where conventional planes cannot fly. Yet to raise this as evidence of SAMs being used in an ABM role is an incredible supposition. Anti-aircraft missiles intended to strike airplanes cruising at not much more than mach-2 could not be easily adapted for use against warheads traveling at mach-20.* Furthermore, even existing MIRVs are virtually invulnerable below 200,000 feet which is the highest altitude at which MARVs can maneuver. It is more likely that SAMs are being improved to contend with the Lockheed-built SR-71 spy plane—the successor to the U-2. Rated as the fastest plane ever built, the SR-71 could conceivably attain unprecedented altitudes to outclimb ordinary SAMs. Nevertheless, former chairman of the Joint Chiefs of Staff, the late General George S. Brown, undercut these allegations in his 1978 posture statement. He pointed out that: "There is no present indication that the USSR has adapted its extensive surface-to-air (SAM) network to ABM defense, nor that it is currently suitable for that role."[37]

What has happened to the ABRES program's PGRV with the downgrading of the Mark-500? Its name has also been changed—to the Advanced Maneuvering Reentry Vehicle or AMARV. Its advertised function is now to evade ballistic missile interceptors without sacrificing accuracy. In other words, to go through certain evasive maneuvers and then get precisely back on target. According to John B. Walsh, then deputy director of Defense Research and Engineering, the Mark-500 is a

---

*Mach numbers denote speed in multiples, or fractions, of the speed of sound. Mach-2 is twice the speed of sound, mach-0.5 is half the speed of sound, etc

typical example of a MARV designed to outrun upgraded SAMs. But, he continued, advanced maneuvers are required to dodge ABM interceptors and that is the reason for AMARV.[38] Does this mean there is no more interest in a target homing MARV? Not really. Let us look closer at the program.

Phase-1 of the ABRES vehicle program, the eight-month study by General Electric and McDonnell Douglas, has been completed. Phase-2 saw McDonnell Douglas winning the competition to build three AMARV prototypes. ABRES started flight testing them in February 1980. The third phase of the ABRES maneuvering program, however, is not so well known. It includes the development of radar-based sensors capable of "seeking a target." If these sensors were installed in the prototype AMARVs, those vehicles would have the target homing capability needed for first strike precision. Mr. Walsh explained: "The guidance and control technology of an evader can be used for an accuracy MARV with the addition of a terminal sensor. Once the terminal sensor has been added, the vehicle can maneuver for either accuracy or evasion."[39] The destabilizing effect of developing such a precise warhead was pointed up in the President's *Fiscal Year 1979 Arms Control Impact Statements:*

> . . . If deployed in sufficient numbers, PGRVs would threaten a large share of the Soviet retaliatory forces, and could be perceived by the Soviets as indicating a US intention to develop a total first strike capability against their ICBM force. . . .
> US deployment of large numbers of systems, such as PGRVs, which would (censored) and could thus provide additional incentives for the Soviets to take countering action. . . . Any of these choices could have results which would run counter to objectives of US arms control policy. . . .[40]

As if this situation were not destabilizing enough, there are indications that MARVs, themselves, may be equipped to receive fixes from the Navstar satellite navigation constellation. That being true, the warhead accuracy would then be within 30 feet of the target *without even having to sense the target.* The President's report reads:

> If difficult technical problems were solved, Navstar GPS might make a significant contribution to the Navy's SLBM capabilities. This technology could then be applied to the Trident-1 and -2 missiles currently in development and possibly incorporated into the design of a new maneuvering reentry vehicle (MARV). . .[41]

and,

> . . . [Navstar] improvements could be applied to ballistic missiles and possibly incorporated into the design of maneuvering reentry vehicles (MARVs) . . .[42]

Clearly, MARVs, especially with the help of Navstar, will be a strong stride toward a destabilizing first strike counterforce capability.

The relative power of US SLBM systems, both existing and projected, can best be appreciated by comparing them to Soviet systems. The Delta submarine with its SS-N-8/18 missiles has been proferred as the counterpart of Trident. The only aspect of that Soviet system which is in any way compatible, however, is the 4,000+ nautical mile range of the missiles. (See Figure 2-2) This range is a few hundred nautical miles greater than Trident-1's full-load range. But it is less than Trident-1's reduced-payload range. There is no point, however, of flying a missile that far to destroy a counterforce target if it can't hit close enough to accomplish that feat.

The SS-N-8 has allegedly been fitted with a stellar inertial guidance system but reports indicate that SIG has failed to improve the missile's accuracy.[43] Even against the soft targets, which are the only ones it is capable of destroying, the SS-N-8's destructive potential is limited by the fact that it carries a single warhead.

The SS-N-18 is the successor to the SS-N-8 SLBM. Like the SS-N-8 it also burns liquid fuel and is essentially the same range. Along with a very slight increase in accuracy, the main improvement seems to be the new missile's payload of three MIRVs. Another new missile, originally thought to be the follow-on for the SS-N-6s in Yankee submarines, is the SS-N-17. It is the first Soviet SLBM to use solid fuel and it must have been a failure. Only one Yankee sub has been outfitted with SS-N-17s and that was several years ago. All of these missiles are described in Figures 2-3 and 2-4.

The first Delta submarine, the Delta-1 class, could only carry twelve missiles. About sixteen of these boats were built. The Delta-2 class subs are essentially identical to Delta-1s except they have been stretched to accommodate sixteen SLBMs. Four Delta-2s are believed to be operational. Both the Delta-1s and Delta-2s carry SS-N-8 missiles.

The newest Delta class—the Delta-3—is basically an adaptation of the Delta design to accommodate the new SS-N-18 missiles. Besides new construction, it appears that some Delta-2 boats have been converted to carry the new missiles—much as Polaris subs were converted to carry Poseidon missiles and then Trident-1s.

The most worrisome charcteristics of the SS-N-8/18 missiles is their range. One reason the Soviets seem interested in longer range SLBMs is to keep their submarines closer to home and in less danger from US anti-submarine warfare (ASW) technology. (US efforts to overcome that advantage will be discussed in the ASW chapter.) The Delta submarines operating out of Murmansk can remain in the Barents Sea. When Soviet subs were required to pass through the Greenland-Iceland-UK gap to get into the Atlantic or through the Bering Strait into the Pacific, to get within range of their targets, they were easily picked up by underwater sonar and tracked. Now the Delta boats are a little harder to keep track of.

The Soviet Union launched a new class of ballistic missile-firing submarine—the 25,000-ton Typhoon—in September 1980.[44] It is considerably bigger than the Trident sub's 18,700-ton displacement but it does not carry as many missiles—only 20 as compared to 24 for Trident. The gargantuan size of this ship for carrying only 20 missiles is most likely another example of the crude Soviet technology.

SS-NX-20 SLBMs are being developed for the Typhoon submarine. They were first tested in December 1981. As mentioned in chapter 2, there have been serious development problems with this new solid propellant missile and it may be the pacing item in Typhoon becoming operational. It is not possible at this time to compare this trouble-plagued missile with the Trident SLBMs.

As far as the counterforce capability of submarine-launched ballistic missiles is concerned, Figure 2-4 illustrates that no existing SLBM—either US or Soviet—can even remotely be considered a hard-target-kill weapon. Reports on the SS-NX-20 do not lead one to believe that it will have any substantial counter-silo capability. Quite the contrary is true, however, of the US Trident-2 missile now in development and the improved-accuracy Trident-1. Figure 3-5 depicts the expected counterforce capability of these weapons for various warhead mixes and using in-flight navigation fixes from Navstar satellites.

Figure 3-5 illustrates that two Trident-2 missiles loaded with eight 300-kiloton MIRVs and cross targeted would have a 90 percent chance of destroying eight silos (7 silos killed). If those same two missiles were loaded with fourteen 150-kiloton reentry vehicles each they would have 88 percent probability of destroying 14 silos (12 silos killed—5 more

Figure 3-5

Counterforce Capability of US Trident-2 Missile and Trident-1 Improved-Accuracy Missile

Missile and Warhead mix	Explosive yield of warhead (megatons) Y	Accuracy of reentry vehicle (Naut. Mi.) CEP	Lethality per reentry vehicle K	Reliability of missile (%) r	Probability of silo kill per reentry vehicle (%) SSP_k	Probability of silo kill for 2-on-1 cross targeting (%) CTP_k
Trident-1** 8 MIRVs 100 KT each	0.1	0.05	86	80	64	82
Trident-2 8 MIRVs 300 KT each	0.3	0.05	125*	80	78	90
Trident-2 14 MIRVs 150 KT each	0.15	0.05	113	80	74	88
Trident-2 17 MARVs 75 KT each	0.075	0.015	125*	80	78	90

*Use maximum cutoff value for lethality, K_{max} = 125 **Improved-accuracy

KT = kiloton CEP = Circular Error Probability

Assumptions:

Missile reliability (r) = 80 percent Silo hardness (H) = 3,000 p.s.i. overpressure

Missile in-flight navigation fixes from Navstar satellites

than with the bigger bombs). There seems to be no advantage to putting 300-kiloton bombs on the Trident-2 except that those warheads have already been developed as the Mark-12A (actually 335 kilotons yield) for Minuteman-3 and possibly MX.

With a little more expense these two cross targeted missiles could be loaded with seventeen 75-kiloton MARVs each to achieve a 90 percent chance of killing 17 silos (15 silos destroyed).

Looking at the improved-accuracy Trident-1, two of these missiles loaded according to Figure 3-5 would have an 82 percent change of destroying 8 silos (6 silos killed). That's not as good as Trident-2 but it is with a cheaper missile. Maybe even more important, this would give existing retrofitted Poseidon submarines a first strike capability.

If the information in Figure 3-5 were to be used for planning a first strike against the USSR, it would require 2,796 warheads for 2-on-1 cross targeting of the Soviet Union's 1,398 ICBM silos. The number of the various missiles and Trident submarines needed is shown in Figure 3-6.

The least desirable mix illustrated in Figure 3-6 is the Trident-1 improved-accuracy missile. It would require considerably more submarines than the last two cases and leave many more surviving Soviet ICBMs. Remember, however, that this is the only system that could be deployed in Poseidon submarines. It would require 22 Poseidon boats to accomplish the same destruction. That could be an important consideration in the Reagan Administration's plan to retrofit an additional twelve Poseidon subs with Trident-1 missiles.

Taking the last case in Figure 3-6—17 MARVs per missile—it would only require seven Trident submarines to wipe out all but 140 of the Soviet Union's land-based strategic missiles. The flight time for each missile would only be about fifteen minutes or less in a depressed trajectory if the sub was patrolling close enough. Nuclear detonation detectors which are now being installed on US spacecraft could feed damage assessment into a host computer to determine which silos had survived. (These detectors will be discussed in a later chapter.) In the confusion following such a massive attack it would probably be possible to launch a second salvo before Soviet commanders could regroup enough to fire their remaining ICBMs. That second salvo would require one more submarine load of missiles and would destroy all but fourteen of the remaining silos. A second salvo wouldn't be necessary, however, once the US deploys the ballistic missile defense system currently under development. Whatever quantity of missiles escaped destruction could

Figure 3-6
Trident-2 and Improved-Accuracy Trident-1 Targeting of Soviet Missile Silos

Warheads per missile n	Number of warheads required N = 2 • 1,398	Number of Trident missiles req'd M = N ÷ n	Number of Trident submarines req'd S = M ÷ 24	Number of surviving Soviet missiles
Trident-1* 8 MIRVs (100 kiloton)	2,796	350	15	252
Trident-2 8 MIRVs (300 kiloton)	2,796	350	15	140
Trident-2 14 MIRVs (150 kiloton)	2,796	200	9	168
Trident-2 17 MARVs (75 kiloton)	2,796	165	7	140

*Improved-accuracy

Parameters:
1,398 Soviet missile silos total. 2-on-1 cross targeting for each silo. Data per Figure 3.5

be intercepted on their way to their targets. (Ballistic missile defense will be discussed in a later chapter.)

There is another potential advantage to having many small but very accurate warheads on a missile. The lethality and probability-of-kill equations used in this exercise do not take into consideration the effect of radiation in disabling the opponent's silo-based ICBMs. When pinpointing becomes very precise, radiation may become the determining factor. A super accurate MARV with an enhanced radiation warhead (neutron bomb) could well become the most deadly first strike weapon. It may not be necessary to blast a missile out of the silo to disable it. An enemy missile is no threat if its electronics and fuzing systems are burned out.

Regardless of the exact configuration, Trident is shaping up to be a very lethal weapon. A few years ago Norman Cousins pointed out in a *Saturday Review* editorial that, next to the leaders of the Soviet Union and the United States, a Trident submarine commander is the third most powerful man in the world. He controls more destructive power than the military establishments of Britain, Italy, Spain, Brazil, Argentina, West Germany, Japan, the Philippines, India and Pakistan all put together.[45] Put another way, each Trident submarine commander will have at his fingertips an explosive force equal to 2,000 Hiroshimas.

As former President Carter said in his arms control impact report:

> . . . the potential impact of the Trident-2 missile on strategic stability is less clear and may be negative, due to the significant hard target kill capability it may have. . . . this hard target capability could stimulate negative effects on Soviet reactions, which, in turn, could lead to instabilities in the strategic balance and complicate future strategic arms limitation efforts.
>
> . . . the Trident-2 SLBM . . . also could be perceived as a first strike weapon with a significant hard target kill potential against time-urgent targets. . . .
>
> . . . Leonid Brezhnev has . . . announced that if the United States continues to deploy Trident, the Soviets will deploy a comparable system, Typhoon. . . .[46]

Clearly, Trident is a dangerous weapon to bring into existence. Trident will be the ultimate first strike weapon.

NOTES

1. *Annual Defense Department Report FY 1977*, by Secretary of Defense Donald H. Rumsfeld, 27 January 1976, p. 106.
2. For a thorough discussion of Trident's bureaucratic origins see John Steinbruner and Barry Carter, "Organizational and Political Dimensions of Strategic Posture: The Problems of Reform," *Daedalus: Journal of the American Academy of Arts and Sciences* (Harvard University Press; Summer 1975), pp. 131–154.
3. *Fiscal Year 1974 Authorization for Military Procurement, Research and Development, Construction Authorization for the Safeguard ABM, and Active Duty and Selected Reserve Strengths*, hearings before the Senate Armed Services Committee, 22 May 1973, Part 5, p. 3582.
4. *US General Accounting Office Staff Study: Trident and SSBN-X Systems*, February 1975, pp. 5, 6, 8, 9 and 30.
5. UPI dispatch, "Trident Sub Delivery Delay of Six Months," *San Jose Mercury*, 13 August 1977.
6. *Department of Defense Appropriations for 1979*, hearings before the House Appropriations Committee, 16 February 1978, Part 1, p. 706.
7. AP dispatch, "Cost Overrun, Delay Plague Trident Sub," *San Jose Mercury*, 30 November 1977. Also, "Navy's Trident Sub: One More Massive Miscalculation," *US News and World Report*, 12 December 1977.
8. *Hearings on Military Posture and HR 3689*, before the House Armed Services Committee, 10 March 1975, Part 3, p. 3443.
9. *Hearings on Military Posture and HR 11500*, before the House Armed Services Committee, 18 February 1976, Part 4, p.57
10. UPI dispatch, "Two More Trident Subs Likely," *Watsonville Register-Pajaronian*, 19 March 1982.
11. *Hearings on Military Posture and HR 5068*, before the House Armed Services Committee, 8 February 1977, Part 4, p. 186.
12. *Department of Defense Appropriations for 1979*, op. cit., 16 February 1978, Part 1, p. 706.
13. *Department of Defense Annual Report Fiscal Year 1979*, by Harold Brown, Secretary of Defense, 2 February 1978, p. 112.
14. *Hearings on Military Posture and HR 2970*, before the House Armed Services Committee, 5 March 1981, Part 3, p. 156.
15. *Department of Defense Authorization for Appropriations for Fiscal Year 1981*, hearings before the Senate Armed Services Committee, 20 February 1980, Part 2, p. 563.
16. Ibid, p. 561.
17. *Hearings on Military Posture and HR 2970*, op. cit.

18. *Trident System,* published by the Trident System Project Office, Department of the Navy, Washington, D.C., November 1974.
19. Robert C. Aldridge, "A Hideout for Trident," *The Progressive,* January 1977, p. 11.
20. See Robert C. Aldridge, "Jaws III," *The Progressive,* May 1982, pp. 34-37.
21. *Fiscal Year 1974 Authorization for Military Procurement . . .,* op. cit., p. 3589.
22. *United States Foreign Policy Objectives and Overseas Military Installations,* prepared for the Senate Foreign Relations Committee by the Congressional Research Service of the Library of Congress, April 1979, pp. 93 & 102.
23. *Fiscal Year 1983 Arms Control Impact Statements,* March 1982, pp. 56–57.
24. *Annual Defense Department Report FY 1978,* by Secretary of Defense Donald Rumsfeld, 17 January 1977, pp. 131–132.
25. *Military Construction Appropriations for 1981,* hearings before the House Appropriations Committee, 13 March 1980, Part 5, p. 128.
26. "Survivability Key to Trident Program," *Aviation Week & Space Technology,* 16 June 1980, p. 106.
27. For a fuller discussion of Trident missile failure see Robert C. Aldridge, "The Trident Fiasco: Obstacles on the Way to Doomsday," *The Nation,* 16 August 1975, pp. 115–116.
28. See "Weather Chief Problems in Trident Tests," *Aviation Week & Space Technology,* 31 October 1977, pp. 46-47.
29. See Richard Halloran, "Pentagon Draws Up First Strategy for Fighting a Long Nuclear War," *New York Times,* 30 May 1982, p.1.
30. *The Military Balance 1979/80,* published by the International Institute for Strategic Studies, London, England.
31. Speech by Deputy Assistant Secretary of Defense, Dr. Thomas A. Brown, at the "Defense Issues Forum" convened in Santa Cruz, CA by Congressman Leon Panetta.
32. UPI dispatch in *San Jose Mercury,* 20 January 1974.
33. *Fiscal Year 1975 Authorization for Military Procurement, Research and Development and Active Duty, Selected Reserves and Civilian Personnel Strengths,* hearings before the Senate Armed Services Committee, 23 April 1974, Part 7, p. 3766.
34. *Fiscal Year 1976 and July-August 1977 Transition Period Authorization for Military Procurement, Research and Development, and Active Duty, Selected Reserve, and Civilian Personnel Strengths,* hearings before the Senate Armed Services Committee, 14 April 1975, Part 10, p. 5315.
35. *Hearings on Military Posture and HR 11500,* op. cit., Part 5, p.78

36. *Fiscal Year 1977 Authorization for Military Procurement, Research and Development, and Active Duty, Selected Reserve and Civilian Personnel Strengths,* hearings before the Senate Armed Services Committee, 19 March 1976, Part 11, p. 6268.
37. *United States Military Posture for FY 1978,* by Chairman of the Joint Chiefs of Staff General George S. Brown, 20 January 1977, p. 24.
38. *Fiscal Year 1977 Authorizations,* op. cit., 19 March 1976, Part 11, p. 6268.
39. Ibid, p. 6530.
40. *Fiscal Year 1979 Arms Control Impact Statements,* June 1978, pp. 56 & 58.
41. Ibid, p. 110.
42. *Fiscal Year 1980 Arms Control Impact Statements,* March 1979, p. 125.
43. *World Armaments and Disarmament: SIPRI Yearbook 1974,* M.I.T. Press, Cambridge, Massachusetts, 1974, p. 110.
44. *Hearings on Military Posture and HR 2970,* before the House Armed Services Committee, 26 February 1981, Part 3, pp. 6-7.
45. Norman Cousins, "The Third Most Powerful Man In The World," *Saturday Review* editorial, 17 April 1976, p. 4.
46. *Fiscal Year 1979 Arms Control Impact Statements,* op. cit., pp. 40–41.

MISSILE-X: RESEARCH AND DEVELOPMENT FOR DOOMSDAY

Dead things will come from underground and by their fierce movements will send numberless human beings out of the world.

—Leonardo da Vinci

"We need the MX missile," pleaded Defense Secretary Caspar Weinberger as he kicked off the Townes Committee investigation in the Spring of 1981, "please tell us where we should put it."[1] That appeal highlighted the preposterous dilemma of having a new missile in development without knowing how to deploy it. But the Townes study couldn't come up with the answer either so on October 2, 1981 Ronald Reagan announced he was going to temporarily store the new missiles in old silos while he thinks about permanent basing for another three years.

Missile-Experimental, more commonly called Missile-X or just plain MX, evolved from the Strat-X study begun in 1967. It was conceived as a mobile intercontinental ballistic missile (ICBM) to supplement the fixed silo-based Minuteman and Titan missiles. Development of MX began in 1972 but over $120-million was spent prior to that time looking at various schemes for missile mobility.

Defense officials contend that Minuteman and Titan missiles could be vulnerable by the mid-1980s and, therefore, mobile missiles are needed. Before he resigned as Defense Secretary in 1977, Donald Rumsfeld repeated that warning: "Our calculations indicate that by the early 1980s there *could* be a substantial reduction in the number of surviving ICBMs should the Soviets apply sufficient numbers of their forces against the US ICBM force in a first strike."[2] (Emphasis added.) Based on this hypothetical set of circumstances he asked for $294-million to put MX into full scale development during fiscal year 1978. That request included funding for all the testing to make the weapon operational by 1983—two years ahead of previous plans. But when the Carter Administration took office later in that same month it postponed full-scale development for at least a year and cut the fiscal 1978 budget for MX by more than half. Then, in late June of 1977, funds for the B-1 bomber were blocked.

Less than a month after President Carter stopped production of the B-1 pressure began building to speed development of MX. Advocates claimed the huge new missile was needed to compensate for the nuclear clout that was lost with the B-1. In the vanguard of MX promotion was Paul Nitze, then policy chairman of the ultra conservative Committee on the Present Danger.* Nitze told the press that MX's fate "may well be the next important issue" in the arms control debate. He contended that MX was vital to maintain "rough equivalence" with the Soviet Union in nuclear weapons.[3] At that time President Carter voiced hopes that neither the United States nor the Soviet Union would deploy mobile missiles.

Nevertheless, in October 1977, apparently influenced by the mounting pressure in favor of MX, then Defense Secretary Harold Brown announced his approval of the Air Force's $245-million request to put MX into full scale development during fiscal year 1979. They were set back once again, however, when Jimmy Carter again cut their request for mobile missile funds for fiscal 1979. The National Security Council (a White House Agency) had advised against full scale development on the grounds that MX could upset the military balance between Russia and the United States and thus thwart progress in negotiating a limit on strategic arms. President Carter apparently wanted to obtain an agreement on SALT-2 during his first years in office—a feat his predecessor had failed to accomplish. The Office of Management and Budget (another White House agency) also favored delaying MX until research had better defined the basing mode.

Basing studies for MX have been going-on for well over a decade. In 1974 they covered a wide spectrum of possible "basing modes"—from road and rail mobility to hard capsules, shelter bases and trenches;

---

*A group formed by 141 leaders of the military-industrial-academic complex to promote a hard line toward communism.

even extending to waterproof missile pods on the bottoms of ponds and reservoirs as well as missiles in blimps and dirigibles. Air mobility in large transport planes was also considered a viable option. A demonstration launch of a Minuteman missile from a C-5A airplane over the Pacific Ocean took place in 1974.

In October 1976 the Air force was directed to make a detailed study of the buried trench concept. The possibility of storing missiles in semi-hard shelters was also investigated but it was not the preferred option. For about a year and a half these two basing modes received the most attention. It was hoped that one of them would be chosen by 1979, or 1980 at the latest.

The *buried trench* method would consist of numerous trenches, one for each missile, and would be between five and twenty-five miles long. The typical length would be about thirteen miles. For the 300 missiles projected at the time, that would mean almost 4,000 miles of trenches—more than the distance across the United States.

Each trench (42 feet wide and 21 feet deep) would contain a concrete tunnel fourteen feet wide on the inside with a flat floor for the missile's Transporter/Launcher vehicle to move on. This has been likened to a subway train. The concrete roof of the tunnel would be made of keystones which take a tremendous weight from the top but would require little effort to push up through when being erected to fire a missile. The entire tunnel would then be covered with at least five feet of earth. The Pentagon planned to construct these covered trenches in the southwest United States where there is an abundance of desert area and where there would be less resistance due to environmental impact. The Air Force investigated six regions in the area encompassing Arizona, California, Colorado, Kansas, Nebraska, Nevada, New Mexico, Oklahoma, Texas and Utah. At that time there wasn't much public opposition except that one state governor said he wouldn't want to see large areas of land closed to hunters.

A later and more popular variation of the trench concept was the *hybrid trench*. Rather than hardening the entire trench to the 200 p.s.i. previously intended, there would be one main buried trench of minimum hardness from which 20-25 hardened spurs would break off. An opponent would not know which of those spurs the missile was hiding in. This idea, of course, would be somewhat cheaper to realize.

One missile in its cannister would lay horizontally in each trench. It would travel at random from one point to another, or from one spur to another, on its Transporter/Launcher vehicle. The vehicle would be equipped with liquid springs to dampen out ground shock from nearby nuclear explosions. On each end of the Transporter/Launcher would be large blast plugs to block off the tunnel. (Only one would be needed for a spur.) These would prevent the blast and radiation from a nuclear explosion in another part of the tunnel from damaging the missile or its launching equipment. These plugs would move with the Transporter/Launcher which, being remotely controlled and computer programmed, would not require a crew in the tunnel. Since the exact location of the missile is not known to the Soviets they would have to use many warheads to be certain one MX is destroyed.

To fire MX the Transporter/Launcher would raise the muzzle of the launch cannister to an angle of 50-55 degrees. In so doing the cannister would break up through the trench cover, pushing debris out of the way as it does so. The missile would then be ejected from the cannister after which, with split second timing, the first stage rocket motor would light-up and be on its way. The entire operation sounds very smooth but it doesn't take into account the huge amounts of debris that might be piled on the trench from a nearby nuclear explosion. It might not be possible to erect the launch cannister. That, however, would not be a problem if Missile-X were used in a first strike.

Semi-hard shelters (earth-covered concrete bunkers) was the other basing alternative. Acording to this plan there would be many more shelters than missiles placed in various locations around the south-western United States. The missiles in their launch cannisters would be stored horizontally on the Missile Launch Vehicle to be randomly shuffled from one shelter to another every so often. Since not all shelters would house missiles it would be a "missile shell game," as one Air Force colonel called it, for the Soviets to guess which shelter to shoot at.

To launch Missile-X from a shelter the Missile Launch Vehicle would merely drive out of the shelter, erect the launch cannister to a near-vertical position and fire the missile. Of course, again, this procedure would be complicated if debris from a nuclear explosion had fallen around the shelter. Nevertheless, as with the trench concept, there would be no rubble difficulties if these weapons were used in a preemptive first strike. We shall soon see that the missile's characteristics point more toward that role than to a deterrent role.

Shelter basing has the advantages of being less expensive and of posing very few uncertainties regarding state-of-the-art. The trench concept, on the other hand, poses some major problems that must be addressed. Nevertheless, the fewer personnel involved and the fact that the missiles can be shuffled without exposing them to observation makes the trench idea more reliable in hiding the weapon.

In early 1978 a privately organized Massachusetts Institute of Technology study team released a report showing that trench and shelter basing, even when hardened to 200-300 p.s.i., would be just as vulnerable as the present Minuteman missiles in their improved silos.[4] Following this, a new study was started by the Pentagon and in May of 1978 another plan, vertical shelters, emerged as the favorite scheme.

At first *vertical shelters* were referred to as "MAP," an acronym for *multiple aim point*—meaning the Russians would have to aim at many points to destroy one missile. This concept consists of building 20-29 vertical shelters or silos for each missile—only one of which would actually contain the weapon. Each silo would be hardened to withstand 600-1200 p.s.i. overpressure. Periodically a service vehicle would drive over each silo, raise its storage cannister to a vertical position, and either load or unload a dummy missile, or load or unload a real missile, or do nothing at all. The point of this shell game being that the Soviets would not be able to determine which silo held the true missiles.

Later the vertical shelters concept was assigned the acronym MPS (for multiple protective shelters) and the number of MX missiles to be built was reduced to 200. The Defense Department was quick to point out, however, that if the Soviets deployed enough warheads to target all the shelters, then the number of missiles and shelters could be easily increased.

Air Force studies revealed that a 200-missile MPS system, protected by a modern anti-ballistic missile defense system, could withstand an attack by 20,000 Soviet warheads and still have half of the MX missiles remaining. This prediction, alone, seems to be enough to discredit the viability of a mobile MX system because after 20,000 hydrogen bombs explode in the United States one should ask what else would survive besides 100 MXs. Fallout patterns and quantities of ash from the 1980 eruption of Mt. St. Helens in Washington should lend some insight to the radioactive proliferation which would ensue.

Probably due to the cost of vertical shelters, the equation of silos with launchers in arms control philosophy, and the length of time required to move a missile from one silo to another, studies of a simpler and more flexible basing method were pursued. In July 1979 a new concept emerged combining the advantages of both hybrid trenches and shelters. It was termed the "racetrack system" because the closed loop roadway that it employed resembled a racetrack.

Figure 4-1
Loop Road for 1 Missile with 23 Shelters

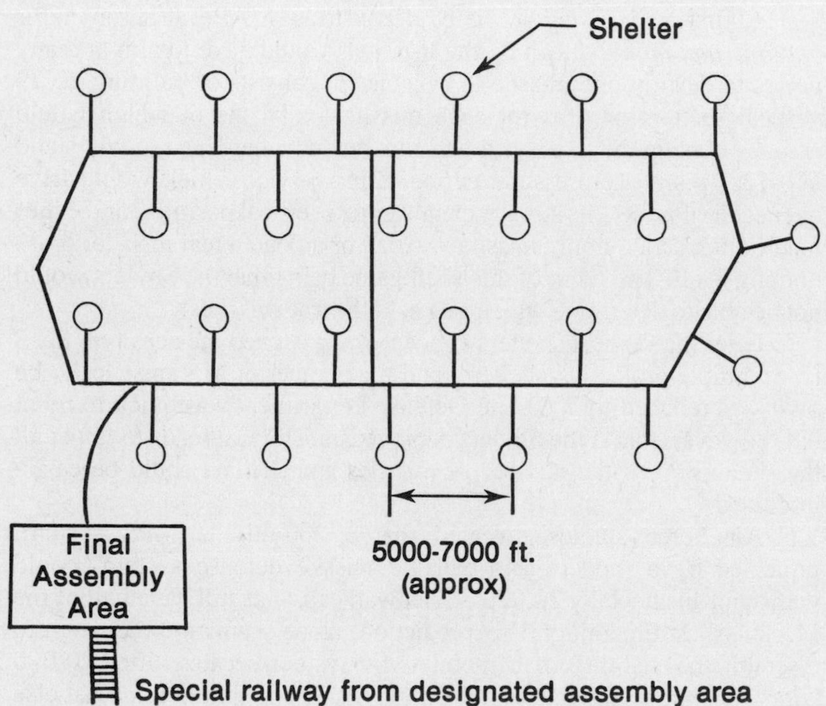

Source:
Department of Defense Annual Report Fiscal Year 1981, by Harold Brown, Secretary of Defense (January 29, 1980) p. 129.

The *racetrack system* envisages 200 of these closed loop roads (one for each missile) with each having 23 spurs leading to shelters spaced approximately 7,000 feet apart and hardened to 600 p.s.i. (Figure 4-1) The missile, carried horizontally in its launch cannister on a transporter-erector-launcher (TEL) vehicle, can move from shelter to shelter hidden by a shield vehicle which straddles the TEL. The shield vehicle masks against satellite sensing devices and would periodically move from shelter to shelter. Ocasionally the TEL and missile would move with the shield to change shelters. It would take about 12 hours to relocate the entire MX force in this way as compared to two days for the vertical shelter concept. It takes about one hour just to lower a missile into a vertical shelter. During alert all TELs would be in a shelter. If tracking sensors could determine that a Soviet warhead was heading for the occupied shelter the TEL could "dash" to another shelter before the bomb arrives. The vehicle could move between 15 and 30 miles per hour.

Another option is for the missiles to be in constant motion on the racetrack during alert and dash for a shelter when warning of attack is received. This would not require a shield vehicle because the shelter would be picked after enemy missiles are launched—Soviet commanders would not know beforehand which shelters would eventually hide the missiles. The TEL could erect the cannister and fire the missiles either from inside the shelter (breaking through the roof as in the trench concept) or out on the roadway. Periodically opening panels in the shelter roof would allow verification of the number of missiles by the Soviets for arms control verification purposes. Reduced costs and the dash technique apparently made the racetrack more appealing to the administration than vertical shelters (silos). In September 1979 President Carter announced that horizontal shelters with quick dash capabilities was the preferred basing mode, although he directed that it should be called "sheltered road mobile system" rather than "racetrack."

Polls taken in July 1979 indicated that 63 percent of the people in the chosen location for the 200 racetracks—the Great Basin of Utah and Nevada—supported the basing of MX on racetracks in their states. By February 1980 that support had dropped to 39 percent. During that same period opposition rose from 25 to 37 percent and those undecided rose from 12 to 24 percent.

In March 1980, Governors Scott Matheson (Utah) and Robert List (Nevada) jointly assailed deployment of MX in their states. Their main objections focused on the impact of the MX project on the water supply, grazing and pasture land, and the area's fragile ecostructure, as well as the violation of the sacred lands of the Shoshone Indians and the inability of the area to absorb a large influx of people.

Faced with a swelling tide of opposition, it became obvious to military planners and the Administration that something had to be adjusted. On May 6, 1980 Defense Secretary Harold Brown announced that the closed loop racetrack was out and that a new linear concept had become the prime option. The same number of missiles and shelters (200 and 4,600 respectively) were still considered but the spurs to those shelters would now branch off of existing county roads. During alert the missile could be moved to a central area where, upon warning, it could dash to any shelter. A grid of existing roads would accommodate the MX force. This would allegedly use less land and eliminate the need for additional road construction. It would not, however, alleviate some of the other concerns.

A new shelter design was also adopted—the so-called "loading dock" concept. Rather than having a complete TEL drive into the shelter, the transporter would drive up to a loading-dock-type opening and only the erector-launcher system, containing the missile, would slide into the shelter on tracks. During routine reshuffling the transporter would also visit the other shelters so a spy satellite wouldn't know in which shelter the missile had been deposited. The transporter would also provide the necessary shielding. This concept would eliminate the shield vehicle and make the shelters smaller since they do not have to accomodate the transporter.

When the missile was to be launched the erector-launcher would telescope out of the shelter, erect the launch cannister, and fire the missile. Although the linear system is less expensive, once the missile is installed in a shelter it would not be able to dash to another within the flight time of a Soviet ICBM.

It is doubtful whether this basing change, obviously motivated by the political climate, would appease the growing opposition to MX in Utah and Nevada. The Great Basin Alliance, a grass roots movement, was becoming a formidable obstacle to the Pentagon. There was also the question of whether existing county roads would support the missile in its launcher-erector loaded on a shielded transporter. Nevertheless, the adjustment in basing plans seemed to have temporarily mitigated opposition and allowed the missile to go into full-scale development.

Although the linear system/loading dock concept was the prime basing mode for the last year of the Carter Administration, the third option for basing the MX—air mobility—had enjoyed popularity among some strategic planners as late as 1978-1979. Toward the end of 1978 it was reported that members of the White House Office of Science and Technology along with the National Security Council were advocating air mobility.[5] They seemed to be supported by the Jason Committee—a secret panel of 40 U.S. scientists who advise the Secretary of Defense—which had also been studying ICBM basing.

In early 1979, two air-mobility schemes were getting attention. One would extract the missile from the tail of an aircraft with a parachute similar to the 1974 launch of a Minuteman-1 from a C-5A transport over the Pacific. The other scheme was called land-and-launch—the plane would land, the missile transporter would roll out, erect the cannister and fire the missile. To enhance survivability these aircraft might have to remain on a continuous air alert with a certain percentage of the aircraft airborne at all times. But that would be tremendously expensive. Other possibilities such as "strip alert"—with the aircraft ready to take-off upon warning of attack—might provide a more suitable solution.

In early 1979 the Air Force was ordered to look into using medium sized short-takeoff-and-land transports—the McDonnell Douglas YC-14 and the Boeing YC-15—for air-launching ICBMs. Other studies involved using the Boeing 747 airliner and Lockheed's C-5A transport. These wide-bodied jets could easily carry two MXs while the YC-14/15 could carry only one. The YC-14/15s however, seemed to be preferred because of their versatility in getting in and out of small airports. Nevertheless, they would have to be enlarged somewhat and equipped with four engines.

The Air Force study envisioned about eight main operating bases with roughly a dozen smaller facilities assigned to each. The smaller bases would accomodate two aircraft. All would be in the upper Midwest. During alert the aircraft would become airborne or be shuttled among some 4,500 small airports. The danger of having 180-200 aircraft, each carrying a strategic nuclear missile, flying around the U.S. was not explored in public accounts of the study.

With the Pentagon considering air and land basing modes it shouldn't be surprising that they also looked into the possibility of underwater basing. Seagoing ICBMs was an area which has received considerable media exposure. Installing silos on container ships with protective armor was simplest but would not meet the elusiveness criteria. Vertical floating capsules was another concept. The missile-containing capsules would be stored on seagoing vessels and heaved overboard upon warning. The missiles could then be remotely launched if needed. Should the crisis pass, the capsules would, hopefully, be recovered. This system, known as *Hydra,* after the mythological nine-headed monster which rose from the water and grew two new heads for every one cut off, was actually tested during the early 1960s.

Most renowned of seagoing schemes was the *Shallow Underwater Missile* or SUM. In this case an ICBM in a cannister would be strapped to each side of a small diesel-powered submarine. These subs would move about in the shallow coastal waters where they could be protected from enemy anti-submarine forces. The subs would have to surface to fire their missiles. The persuading argument against this type of basing was that barrage bombing with large nuclear weapons in shallow water would destroy the subs en masse.

Two other mobile missile systems which sparked special attention—more from their uniqueness than their utility—were the Cruise Ballistic Missile and the possibility of holding ICBMs in parking orbits.

Scale models of a *Cruise Ballistic Missile* airframe were actually tested in a wind tunnel. Wings and tail of this structure, holding an ICBM, would be folded up to fit in the launcher. On warning it would be popped out of the tube to cruise by remote control at about 20,000 feet. If not necessary to fire the missile the vehicle would be landed at an airport. Technological difficulties and safety were probably the main considerations that killed this scheme.

Putting ICBMs in *Parking Orbit* upon warning of attack was also proposed. The missiles would be held there until ready to fire. A separate rocket motor would be required for maneuvering. How the missile would be recovered if further use is not desired, however, is less clear. This concept would also violate the Outer Space Treaty.

These ancillary basing proposals seemed to be more of a thorn-in-the-side than anything else for Pentagon and Administration officials. For one thing, many of the proposals relinquished tight control over the missiles. Furthermore, most of these ideas focused on using existing Minuteman missiles rather than MX. This annoyance was compounded when Air Force Chief of Staff, General Lew Allen, Jr., stated that modifying Minuteman-3 for launch from a mobile cannister would require only about two years.[6] Then a Library of Congress study commissioned by Senator Mark Hatfield demonstrated that the Air Force had overestimated the cost of making Minuteman mobile by $10-12 billion.[7] Furthermore, a General Accounting Office report showed that the $33-billion estimated cost for MX in 1978 dollars will rise to

$56-billion from inflation alone, and probably higher due to uncertainties not yet resolved.[8]

On October 2, 1981 Ronald Reagan scuttled the multiple shelter basing system and decreased the talking-figure quantity of MX missiles to 100. He said the first forty would be temporarily placed in existing but hardened Titan and Minuteman silos. Then he outlined a 3-year plan for studying more permanent basing schemes. They are:

Air mobility.
Deep underground basing.
Silos protected by a ballistic missile defense system.

Reagan immediately got a blast from Congress saying three years was too long and that MX funding would be cut until the decision was made. Internal discontent was also forthcoming from the Air Force because it had favored the cancelled MPS basing.

Reagan moved-up his 3-year deadline to June 1982 and started the study. In spite of Senate Armed Services Committee opposition a continuous patrol aircraft named *Big Bird* (not to be confused with the US spy satellite) was investigated. It would be able to stay aloft for two days and launch MX from the air. It was abandoned in March 1982—three months early—because of lack of Congressional enthusiasm.

Deep basing studies were also undertaken by Lawrence Livermore National Laboratory in California. The plan was to put 100 MX missiles in holes between 2,500 and 3,500 feet deep. It was generally agreed that this would protect the missiles but there were many schedule and technical problems—not the least of which was how to extricate the missiles so they could be fired.

The interim plan of putting 40 MX missiles in existing silos was also unsuccessful. The requirement for superhardening those silos was dropped when White House officials had to agree with Congressional critics that it just "wasn't worth the money."[9] At about the same time a February 1982 Congressional Budget Office report concluded that "Placing MX missiles in existing silos not hardened for increased survivability, will not narrow the 'window of vulnerability'."[10] In addition the GAO report assessed the long term options as follows:

> "—Air mobile basing has previously been assessed by DOD as too costly to acquire, operate and maintain. It also has some postattack endurance limitations.

"—Deep underground basing has previously been assessed by DOD as having a slow reaction time and potentially vulnerable communications system.

"—Ballistic missile defense of fixed sites has previously been assessed by DOD as not within the (time) specified by the President's program."[11]

By late March of 1982 Ronald Reagan's full menu of options from the previous October had been scrapped. A *Washington Post* staff writer reported: "Some officials say that the overriding quest for secrecy among the handful of top White House and Pentagon leaders who knew what the final MX decision would be prevented a full airing of final technical details before they were announced publicly, and thus contributed to the subsequent reversals."[12]

Nevertheless, faced with a complete wipeout of proposed basing options and the imminent denial of MX funds, Reagan Administration officials started grabbing for straws. In mid-April they announced *Dense Pack,* which employs the fratricide concept. The theory is that by packing the missile silos close together the first Soviet warhead to explode would destroy one MX but it would also create the ionized atmosphere, dust and debris to destroy other incoming Soviet warheads. Then, the rationale goes, when MX is launched it will rise slower and not be affected.

I cannot see how a "fratricide environment" can be created that would effect a very hard, incoming enemy warhead and not the missile that it is supposed to protect. It is true that the tremendous speed of an incoming warhead passing through such an environment would generate a higher electromagnetic pulse (EMP) in its circuitry, but when a missile blasts-off it isn't exactly dragging its feet. It is also more vulnerable and more difficult to shield from EMP than a warhead. In addition, no one knows enough about fratricide to reliably predict what will happen, let alone try to incorporate this effect into a system design. Once Dense Pack is constructed—which would take six to eight years—its survivability would hinge on the rate of Soviet advances and no one knows when the Soviets will find protection from fratricide. Retired Admiral Stansfield Turner, former director of the CIA, says Dense Pack is "truly a Maginot Line concept . . . Why is it not obvious that MX is the wrong missile?"[13]

We will soon see that MX is exactly what the Pentagon wants. At the time of this writing there is a line rush to get MX on the fiscal 1983 budget list. Criticism of Dense Pack is still mounting, however, and the picture may change by the time this book is published. But the pattern will remain constant.

Before leaving the mobility aspect of MX—the element on which justification for this new missile rests—I want to once more emphasize the inaccuracy of the premises which have led to its development. The key to the whole MX program is that Minuteman missiles will soon be able to be destroyed in a Soviet first strike. But the likelihood of that first strike happening should also be weighed. In the past, several high ranking Defense Department officials have been questioned along these lines. Former Defense Secretary Harold Brown was asked during House hearings if the Soviets having the capability to threaten Minuteman and Titan silos would give them the perception they have an advantage over the US sufficient to risk a first strike nuclear attack. His reply was:

> I think it gives them the perception they have an advantage. I don't think it gives them the perception that they can risk a first strike nuclear attack, not on the basis of vulnerability of Minuteman alone.
>
> The reason for that is that we continue to have our submarine-launched ballistic missiles and bombers with cruise missiles that can strike back . . . .[14]

In a statement to the Senate, former Under Secretary of Defense for Research and Engineering, Dr. William J. Perry, made similar testimony:

> Finally, whatever he does to our ICBM force, if he were to destroy 100 percent of them, he still has to accomodate the bomber and submarine forces. So he must consider that the very act of striking the continental United States with the several thousand warheads that would be necessary to destroy the ICBM force, would surely trigger retaliation.[15]

During recent Senate Foreign Affairs Committee hearings, Senator Alan Cranston asked General Russell E. Dougherty, former chief-of-staff Allied Command in Europe and former commander-in-chief of the Strategic Air Command, if he could conceive of any circumstances, under present conditions and in terms of strategic capabilities on both sides, where the Soviets would feel they successfully could launch a first strike against the US. The heart of General Dougherty's reply was:

> The total nuclear attack which has been postulated which is required to knock out all of our land-based missiles is very far fetched. In fact, it is so remote it is difficult for me to conceive of . . . .[16]

Finally, a National Intelligence Estimate compiled by the CIA and released during the first half of 1980 is reported to have contained information not too supportive of the MX program. According to *Air Force Magazine:* "The recently released 11-38 NIE is strongly biased toward net-assessment information that is damaging to MX."[17] The magazine pointed out that it sparked a protest from the Defense Department because the CIA diluted the National Intelligence Estimate with net-assessment information.

The entire MX program is founded on deception and slanted information. Even the survivability requirement that the missile's mobility is meant to address is unnecessary. From the meager information that can be gleaned from public documents a reasonable case can be constructed to allay any fears of a Soviet first strike against our land-based missile silos. Yet the successful promotion of this fear is making the MX system a reality. This point is critical to the public's understanding of how this remarkably expensive and dangerous system is moving from the drawing boards to the production line.

There is steady and strong pressure to get MX into regular production. I've gone into considerable detail to illustrate the futile groping for an acceptable mobile basing system that will justify deployment of MX. It's been well over a decade and hundreds of millions of dollars have been spent since MX basing studies first began. Yet the Pentagon is no closer now than they were ten years ago. For reasons of public relations the number of missiles has been repeatedly reduced; from 300 to 200 to 100. Hoping to get a foot in the door, a figure of forty has been proferred for initial deployment. But once the decision to commence production is made we can be certain that the numbers will again rise.

The basing debate has overshadowed discussion of the characteristics of the missile; what it will do and what impact it will have on global stability. There is a second ingredient to MX which has no relation to mobility or survivability. It is this ingredient—accuracy—that is so dangerous. It is the sinister pursuit of this quality that lies behind the vigorous efforts to get MX into production.

Figure 4-2
Missile-X

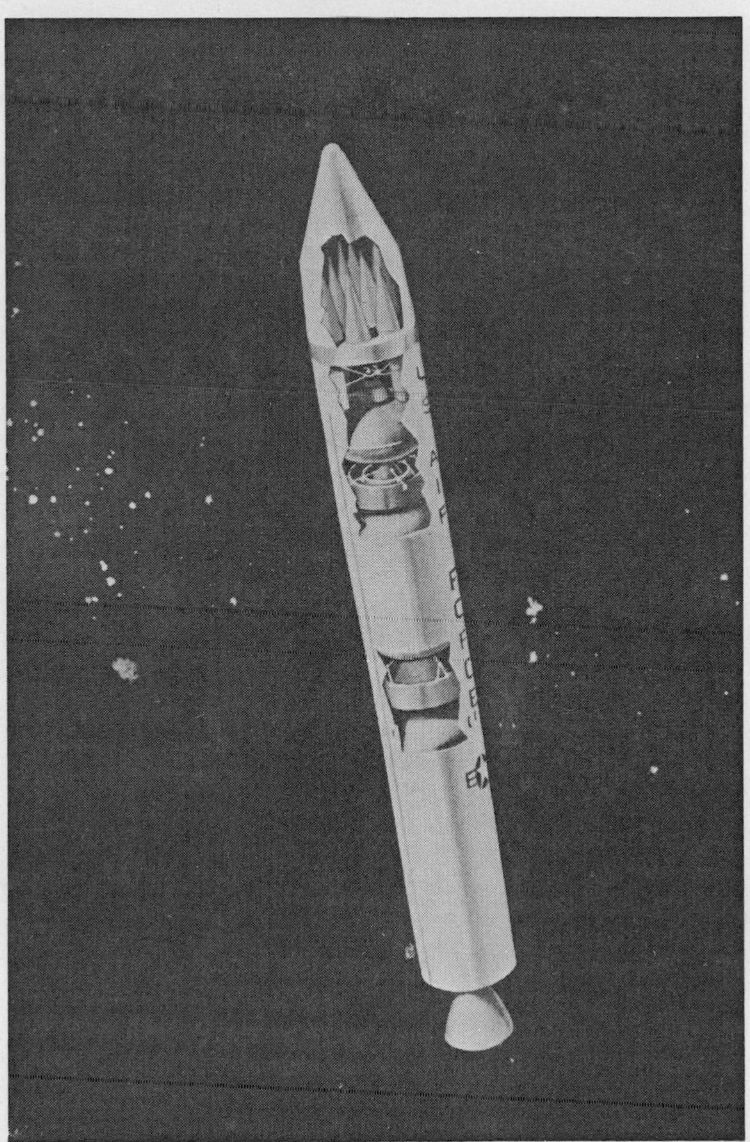

Source: U.S. Department of Defense

Pentagon spokesmen describe MX as an advanced, large throw-weight, MIRVed ICBM which should be capable of fulfilling US military requirements into the 21st century. It was originally proposed as a three stage, solid propellant missile but the Air Force has added a fourth liquid-fueled stage. For the first three stages the Pentagon at first planned to use the same high energy propellant and light weight motor cases that gave the Navy so much trouble in the Trident-1 program. Later reports, however, indicate that the first and second stage motors will use Minuteman-3 propellant. Only the third stage will use the high energy Class 7 propellant. The fourth stage will have liquid hypergolic propellant and will be used to maneuver the bus into position for dropping the various MIRVs and MARVs off for their targets.

MX will be 92 inches diameter, 72 feet long and will weigh 95 tons (190,000 pounds)—over twice the weight of Minuteman-3. It will deliver a payload in excess of 4½ tons over a range of at least 7,000 nautical miles. Although the weapon has been promoted and justified because of its survivability—its capacity to ride out a Soviet first strike—it will be capable of a degree of accuracy that will place it in the vanguard of a US first strike. Survivability could be achieved without increasing accuracy—presuming that the true rationale for this weapon is purely defensive.

To help obtain the accuracy needed for a first strike capability, MX will have a new guidance package called the Advanced Inertial Reference Sphere. Weighing only 115 pounds this package will be physically smaller than the Minuteman-3 guidance system (about the size of a basketball) but it will compute five to six times as fast. Using only inertial measurements of the missile's acceleration, roll, pitch, yaw and lateral motion this new guidance capsule will provide a midcourse positioning within 100 feet for dropping off the MIRVs. That will give a target CEP no greater than 600 feet—some experts say as small as 400 feet. Pentagon officials have also testified that MX will be designed to use Navstar fixes to insure high accuracy.[18] That will bring the CEP down to 300 feet. Then, with MARVs the CEP can be further diminished to less than 100 feet.

I have mentioned Navstar in previous chapters and since it is so important to warhead accuracy it might be appropriate to digress momentarily for a better description. Navstar (see figure 4-3) has been described as "one of the most important and far reaching programs in the Department of Defense."[19] Former Director of Defense Research and

Engineering, Dr. Malcolm Currie, explained that Navstar will enhance missile delivery, blind bombing, enroute navigation, artillery fire, troop movements and rendezvous.[20] New generations of inertial guidance packages which give missiles a 600-foot CEP are accurate enough for some points of aim but the really hard targets—the concrete and steel missile silos and the underground command posts—would require fairly large bombs at that miss distance. It is much more efficient in terms of missile payload, however, to increase accuracy, use a greater number of smaller bombs, and destroy more targets. That is where Navstar enters the picture. It is expected to provide a CEP of 300 feet even without the use of maneuvering warheads.

Development of Navstar began in 1964 when the Naval Research Laboratory (NRL) conceived the idea of "direct ranging" which they called *Timation*. It was based on the principle that if the velocity of two points and the time needed for a radio signal to travel between these points are known then the distance between these points can be determined. The strategic implication of this principle becomes clear if we conceive of one of these points as a missile in flight and the other as a satellite with a precisely known position. If there are several of these satellites, the distance of the missile from each can be calculated and, by solving the resulting geometry on a computer, the precise location of the missile relative to the earth's surface can be determined. Going even a step farther, by taking these readings at several points in time the trajectory of the warhead relative to the target, and also the velocity, can be plotted. It can be seen how this type of navigation fix would be tremendously helpful in meticulous warhead placing.

Timing radio waves with precision is not an easy thing to do. It requires an extremely accurate timer that can remain synchronized for long periods of time in space. In 1967, NRL launched Timation-1, a satellite carrying a precision quartz crystal oscillator (quartz clock) for testing the concept. In that same year the Air Force apparently caught the scent and launched into a parallel and often conflicitng program. This was the same year in which the strategic exercise study (Strat-X) was initiated to look for more aggressive strategic weapons.

Timation-2 was placed in orbit by NRL in 1969. It also used a quartz clock. But it was not until four years later, in May of 1973, that the Defense Department gathered these fragmented Navy and Air Force programs together under one project office named *Navstar*.

Figure 4-3
Navstar Satellite

Source: U.S. Department of Defense

Although the Air Force muscled its way into the management seat, the Navy retained responsibility for developing the clock and that, of course, was the real challenge.

The first *Navigation Technology Satellite* (NTS-1, formerly called Timation-3 and also manufactured by NRL) was launched into orbit in July 1974 with two rubidium vapor clocks on board. This was the first spacecraft to test atomic clocks although a quartz clock was also carried along for back-up purposes. Rubidium clocks are ten times more accurate than quartz but they still need to be reset daily to maintain the precision needed for Navstar. NTS-1 has since started tumbling in space due to a stabilization problem.

Let us now look for a moment at what is expected of Navstar. The satellites are solar powered to continuously transmit navigation signals on two jam-resistant frequencies. Each satellite will be in a 12,500-mile high cirular orbit which will cross the equator at an angle of 63 degrees to circle the earth every twelve hours. All signals will come from the satellites so the user of those signals will not have to reveal his location during clandestine operations. While these signals can be coded to prevent hostile forces from using them, the number of friendly users will be unlimited. They are expected to exceed 27,000 including all four branches of the military services. User equipment will range from sophisticated computers down to 10-20 pound backpacks.

Originally, twenty-four satellites were planned for the constellation—eight equally spaced in each of three orbital planes. (Figure 4-4) They will provide position fixes within 33 feet in all three dimensions, velocity (speed within 0.55 feet/second and direction), and time synchronization to a fraction of a microsecond for user clocks*—the latter being vital for timing radio waves. Navstar will give global coverage in all kinds of weather and will replace existing Transit satellites as well as other navigation systems whose accuracy is too crude for weapons delivery.

Phase 1 of Navstar development—the demonstration and validation phase—extended into the latter half of 1979. NTS-2 was launched on June 23, 1977. Also built by NRL, it was the predecessor of four prototype Naustas satellites built by Rockwell International. NTS-2 carried two cesium beam atomic clocks into orbit along with two backup quartz clocks. Cesium clocks are expected to give ten times the accuracy of rubidium and are the planned instrument for the operational system.

---

*A microsecond is one-millionth of a second.

They will be able to go three to four days, if necessary, without being reset.

The Rockwell-built Navstar-1 was launched on February 27, 1978 and Navstar-2 followed on May 13th. Navstar-3 was scheduled for launch in August but was delayed until October 6th because of cracks found in the device which keeps the spacecraft right-side-up relative to the surface of the earth. On December 10, 1978 Navstar-4 was put into orbit to complete the compliment for this phase. All four Navstar prototypes have three rubidium clocks and a quartz clock. In addition, Navstar-4 carried a cesium clock.

Toward the end of phase-1 there were several impressive tests. Using Navstar, a marine landing craft was guided to within 75 feet of its intended landing point. An F-4 fighter plane made a rendezvous with a C-141 transport playing the role of a tanker. Another C-141 made two cargo drops from 1,000 feet altitude and both landed within 70 feet of the intended drop point. These satellites were also used in conjuction with Trident-1 test flights to enhance the Navy's fleet ballistic missile accuracy improvement program.

Not all was success, however. The atomic clocks did not perform as hoped. After only two months in space one of the rubidium clocks on Navstar-1 went bad. Since then the others have also gone out. By early 1980, two of the rubidium clocks on Navstar-2 had failed with the third acting abnormally. One clock on Navstar-3 was also acting abnormally by this time and the cesium clock on Navstar-4 had failed. These difficulties certainly played a part in the delay of predicted full operational capability from 1984 until 1987.

Notwithstanding the atomic clock difficulties, the Navstar program went into full scale development in August 1979. Navstar-5 was launched on February 9, 1980 to replace Navstar-1 which was no longer operating. It also had three improved rubidium clocks and one improved cesium clock. On the following April 26th, Navstar-6 went into orbit. Navstar-7's rocket booster crashed shortly after lift-off on December 18, 1981. As of this writing the Air Force is considering stepping up the launch date for Navastar-8 due to the December failure.

Eleven development (Block-1) Navstar satellites have been built and more are in production. Besides refining global positioning technology they have been used to support the Trident Improved Accuracy Program. These 1,000-pound spacecraft designed for a 5-year life are lifted into orbit by Atlas missiles. Starting with Navstar-8 they will carry nuclear detection system (NUDETS) sensors to spot nuclear

Figure 4-4

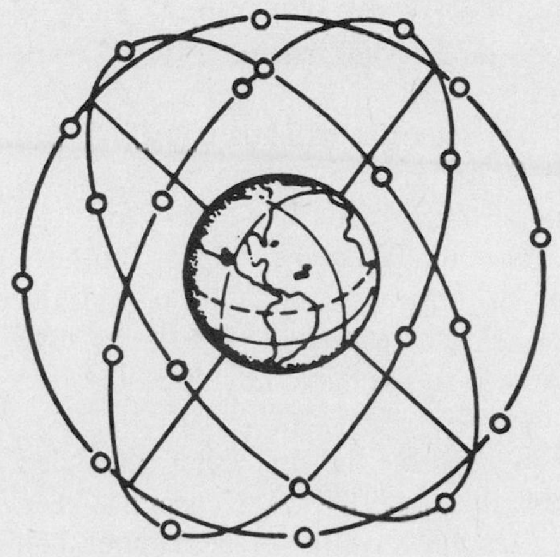

Orbital Configuration
- 24 Satellites*
- 3 Circular Orbits**
- 12 Hour Periods

*Anticipated full compliment
**Later changed to 6 orbit planes.

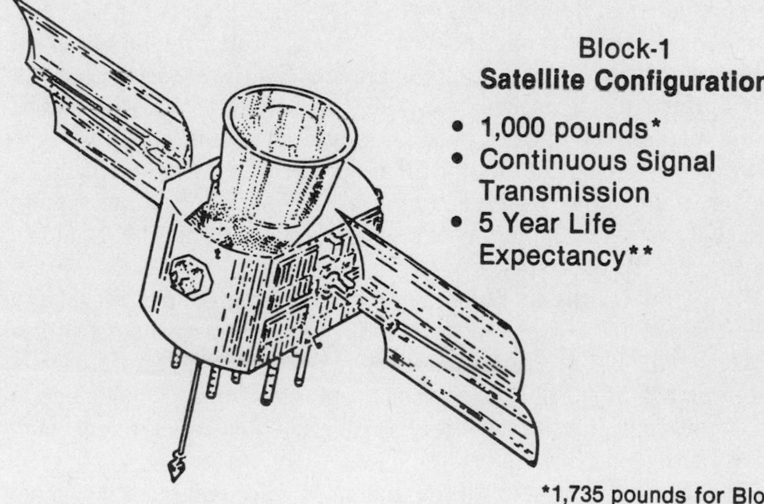

Block-1
Satellite Configuration
- 1,000 pounds*
- Continuous Signal Transmission
- 5 Year Life Expectancy**

*1,735 pounds for Block-2
**7½ years for Block-2

Navstar System

Source:
Status of the Navstar Global Positioning System, Report to Congress by the Comptroller General of the United States, (March 2, 1977), p. 3.

explosions. These, along with NUDETS sensors on early warning satellites and the 70,000-mile-high Vela satellites, are intended to provide damage assessment both in the US and USSR in the event of nuclear war. An Integrated Operational NUDETS System (IONS) will be on operational satellites.

The production phase for Navstar satellites will begin in 1982, and for the user equipment in 1984. The Air Force is preparing to order a block of 28 Navstars (Block-2) for operational use. These spacecraft will be a third larger and weigh 1,735 pounds. They are supposed to have increased survivability, nuclear hardening, and compatibility with the space shuttle. Block-2 Navstars will have a 7½-year design life, will be equipped with IONS, and will carry 2 rubidium clocks and 2 cesium clocks.

Initial operational capability with 12 satellites in orbit is scheduled for 1985. The definition of full operation by 1987, however, has been changed. It will consist of 18 satellites in six orbital planes (rather than three planes) plus three spare satellites in orbit. This arrangement can guarantee a signal from four satellites 99.5 percent of the time. During the other 0.5 percent the positional accuracy will be degraded from 33 feet to 53 feet in all three dimensions.

It seems evident to me, however, that the full compliment of 24 satellites will be operational shortly thereafter. *Air Force Magazine*, for instance, refers to "at least eighteen satellites" in orbit.[21] It will then be possible for a missile to "lock onto" at least four satellites at all times to achieve the expected 300-foot CEP mentioned in previous chapters. However, if a maneuvering reentry vehicle (MARV) were equipped to receive Navstar fixes all the way to the target the resulting CEP would be more on the order of 30 feet.

The Army facility in Yuma, Arizona has been the control facility and test range for Navstar development. The final control facility, however, will be at Vandenberg Air Base in California. Daily corrections will be given each Navstar from this station. Vandenberg is also one of four Navstar monitoring stations—the other three being Alaska, Hawaii and Guam.

The Navstar program office has also discussed adding three earth-synchronous satellites to provide higher resistance to interference in places like Europe, where an intense jamming environment exists. Those 22,000-mile-high spacecraft would be able to transmit signals 100 times more powerful than the regular Navstar vehicles and would, therefore, be less vulnerable to electronic countermeasures.

The Navy is also looking at a hydrogen maser clock which, it claims, will be 10 to 100 times more stable than even cesium clocks. That represents a loss of one second every 33 years at the upper expectation. These clocks would only have to be reset every 2-3 weeks to meet Navstar standards. The biggest drawback to their use is their size and they are difficult to miniaturize.

President Carter pointed out in his *Fiscal Year 1980 Arms Control Impact Statements* that if Navstar receivers were added to missiles, "then significant improvements in US missile accuracy could result; this development might warrant analysis of its potential arms control impact."[22] He added quickly that there were no *approved* plans to add Navstar receivers to US strategic missiles. He reported a similar warning the following year:

> Missile in-flight guidance also could be substantially improved through the use of Navstar data, if missiles were equipped with receivers for GPS (global positioning system) positioning and velocity updates. However, difficult technical problems would have to be solved before Navstar GPS data could be used for in-flight guidance. Although these are *presently no approved* plans to add GPS receivers to US strategic missiles, conceptual studies are underway as part of the Navstar GPS research and development role.[23] (emphasis mine)

As already noted, the MX's guidance system has been designed to be compatible with receiving Navstar in-flight navigation updates, but this has occurred *without* an evaluation of its impact on arms control. In the Reagan Administration's fiscal 1982 and 1983 arms control impact statements Navstar items are merely listed with a comment that nothing has changed to cause re-evaluation. The issue has in effect been dodged.

Our assessment of the MX would not be complete without a look at the warheads which this missile could carry to its distant targets. Perhaps the prime candidate warhead for the MX is the Mark-12A which was discussed in previous chapters. The Mark-12A is made by replacing the center section of the old Mark-12 with a new bomb of double yield but no added weight. MX can reportedly carry twelve of the Mark-12As but the unratified SALT-2 treaty limits ICBMs to ten. This warhead is completely developed and tested, and is now operational on Minuteman-3 missiles.

Another candidate warhead for the MX presently in full-scale development is known as the Advanced Ballistic Reentry Vehicle

(ABRV). At the time of this writing there is a controversy over whether the ABRV will replace the Mark-12A as the "baseline warhead" for MX. The ABRV, with a yield between 450-500 kilotons, would, if anything, make MX more lethal.* One of these warheads is to be on the sixth MX flight test. Eleven ABRVs can fit on MX but there is doubt that it will be ready in time for initial deployment. ABRVs may be retrofitted at a later date.*

MX may eventually be loaded with maneuvering reentry vehicles—either target-homing MARVs or those which use Navstar fixes all the way to their targets. Precision MARVs allow the use of smaller bombs which, again, means more of them can be put on one missile. I estimate that about twenty MARVs with a yield between 75 and 100 kilotons each could be loaded on MX. That certainly fits into the category of a precision weapon with a lot of silo-killing capability.

President Carter ordered MX into full scale development in June 1979. The first flight test is scheduled for early 1983, possibly in January, from Vandenberg Air Base in California. Initial operational capability for ten missiles with one launch control center is set for late 1986.

MX will have a functional reliability of at least 80 percent. With any warhead mix it might carry, the calculated lethality (K) per reentry vehicle will exceed 125. Therefore, when figuring the probability of destroying missile silos (3,000 p.s.i. hardness) the cutoff value of lethality (K_{max} = 125) would be used. That means the single shot kill probability (SSP_k) would be 78 percent and the cross-targeted 2-on-1 probability of kill (CTP_k) will be 90 percent.

If we compare that to the Soviet missiles in Figure 2-4 we see that one warhead from MX has slightly better kill power against silos than an SS-18, Mod-1 or Mod-3 missile. If MX carries ten MIRVs, that means each MX equals 10 SS-18s, each equipped with a 25-megaton warhead—even though the SS-18s may have 75 times the megatonnage. A similar comparison applies to the single-warhead SS-19s. That is the power of accuracy over yield.

If all 308 SS-18s and all 362 SS-19s were of the single warhead type, they could only destroy 291 US silos. Reagan's quota of 100 MXs with 10 MIRVs each will be able to destroy 450 Soviet silos. The original figure of 300 MXs would threaten 90 percent of the USSR's ICBMs.

---

*Since this text was written the ABRV—now designed the Mark-21 RV—has become the prime warhead for MX.

One might argue that the SS-18, Mod-2 or Mod-4 missiles, with ten MIRVs each, might be deadlier. Two warheads from different missiles cross-targeted on a silo only have a 49 percent chance of killing it (CTP_k = 49). Because of fratricide it would be impractical to send enough SS-18 MIRVs to a given silo to have any confidence that it would be destroyed. The SS-18, Mod-2s and Mod-4s just don't have the capability to attack silos. Likewise with the MIRVed SS-19s. MIRVed SS-18s or SS-19s could only destroy about half of US silos. Again, 300 MX could wipe out 90 percent of Soviet silos.

I have often been criticized for comparing future US missiles with existing Soviet missiles. (I made a comparison of existing missiles in Chapter 2.) The facts are that there are no future Russian ICBMs with which to make comparisons. For many years Pentagon officials have alluded to a new fifth generation of Soviet ICBMs being in development and warning that "Flight testing of one or two of these missiles could begin at any time, with the others following in the early 1980s."[24] That was in 1978 and it hasn't happened yet. There have been allegations of new types of rocket motors being test fired and new types of silos being constructed at test sites. Those were one-time reports a couple years ago and I have seen no follow up information. It seems to me, judging from all the modifications ("Mod" numbers, as shown in Figures 2-2 and 2-4) to SS-17s, SS-18s, and SS-19s, that most of the so-called Soviet activity on fifth generation ICBMs has really been to improve the fourth generation family. These are all there are to compare with.

The fact that 300 MX missiles could threaten 90 percent of the Soviet silo-based ICBMs has frightening implications. That could be why former Under Secretary of Defense for Research and Engineering, Dr. William Perry, said four years ago: "The reason we are holding back on [MX] has to do with, No. 1, our uncertainty about basing and, No. 2, there is some significant debate in the country as to whether it is appropriate for the United States to deploy a missile which has those capabilities."[25] But MX is now in full scale development. The Pentagon and the Administration are determined to deploy this weapon, ostensibly for second strike counterforce. A Congressional Budget Office paper elaborated on MX's prompt counterforce capability:

> The MX ICBM and the Trident-2 submarine-launched missile, both highly accurate ballistic missiles planned for future deployment in survivable basing systems, would provide a "prompt" counterforce capability, one that would provide the

> means to retaliate against reserve Soviet ICBMs within minutes of a Soviet first strike. Such prompt counterforce capability *would give the Soviets little time to launch a second-round attack* before the arrival of counterattacking US missiles.[26] (Emphasis added)

Another CBO paper noted how such a second strike counterforce capability would also have the potential for a disarming first strike against Soviet land targets:

> . . . It would be virtually impossible to deploy a force of MX ICBMs large enough to provide a significant second-strike retaliatory capability yet small enough to avoid posing a counterforce threat to the Soviet silo-based ICBM force.[27]

Mobility plays a part in destabilizing arms control negotiations because it hampers verification, but it is the pinpoint accuracy of missiles now in development which will cause instability during times of international crisis. It can be argued, however, that making the ICBM force mobile would eliminate the need for a second strike counterforce capability because by overcoming the vulnerability of ICBMs the mobile basing mode undercuts the possibility of a successful Soviet first strike. Therefore, a hard target kill capability is not required for mobile missiles.[28]

Some argue that silo-killing missiles are needed to destroy Soviet silos before they can be reloaded. But as the CBO paper notes: "Preventing the Soviets from reloading their ICBM silos would probably not require missiles with high accuracy and powerful warheads, since reloading equipment and operations would be vulnerable to less accurate and less powerful warheads."[29]

It seems apparent that military planners and government officials recognize the destabilizing aspect of MX with its first strike counterforce potential. In 1977, then Defense Secretary Brown highlighted the risk of having such a weapon:

> Before I leave the subject of land-based ballistic missiles, I would like to turn to another matter of perceptions—how the Soviets might perceive the threat to them of a US preemptive strike. They may calculate that a first strike would result in a (missile) ratio adverse to them, just as we calculate that a Soviet first strike would result in a ratio more adverse to us. To the extent that this is so, either side will, during the next decade, have a so-called "advantage" in firing first . . . .[30]

What Secretary Brown was saying in his roundabout way is that (1) the US would have a military advantage in being able to shoot first but (2) in developing that capability we risk the chance that the Soviets might fire first in desperation before they lose all their missiles. MX is a very visible program and there is no doubt that the Soviets recognize its first strike potential. That "perception," as Secretary Brown called it, might prompt the Soviets to embark on a course of action more drastic than what they would otherwise consider.

When he was Research and Development Chairman of the Senate Armed Services Committee, former Senator Thomas J. McIntyre sounded the warning in more forthright language. He noted that because the MX could destroy the Soviet ICBM force—which contains three-quarters of all Soviet strategic warheads—in thirty minutes, the Soviets might feel a military need to strike first. "In a period of crisis," he explained, "the Soviets would be faced with the choice of either using their missiles or losing them." That "would put a hair trigger on nuclear war."[31]

President Carter's words in his arms control impact statements on MX are probably the most potent as well as being very cogent:

> . . . With the MX deployed in substantial numbers, in addition to Minuteman, the US would have acquired a capability to destroy most of the Soviet silo-based ICBM force in a first strike. Such a prospect could be of considerable concern to Soviet leaders since a significantly greater percentage of Soviet strategic weapons (about 75 percent for the USSR versus about 25 percent for US) is in its ICBM force, despite the fact that some [deleted] percent of the Soviets' deployed strategic weapons could survive.[32]
>
> . . . under extreme crisis conditions, Soviet leaders, concerned that war was imminent, and fearing for the survivability of their ICBMs if the United States struck first, nonetheless might perceive pressures to strike first themselves. Such a situation, of course, would be unstable.[33]

The Reaganized *Fiscal Year 1983 Arms Control Impact Statements* are not as explicit on MX. They pose the problem but omit the ramifications:

> The initial deployment of less than 50 MXs . . . will not represent a threat to the entire force of Soviet ICBMs, which now total 1400.*

*A footnote at the bottom of the ACIS page reads: "At a maximum, assuming ten RV's per missile, deployment of 50 MX missiles will add only 500 highly accurate RV's to the US total, and if some MXs displace Minuteman-3s the increase of RVs will be reduced below 500 because the latter have up to 3 RVs. By the usual rule of thumb of 2 RVs per silo, 500 additional RVs would threaten only 250 more Soviet ICBMs."[35]

> The effect of the MX program on stability will depend in very large part upon Soviet interpretation of its implications for the vulnerability of their strategic forces overall, and Soviet perceptions could be heavily influenced by the fact that they have about three-quarters of their strategic warheads deployed in silo-based ICBMs, while we have only about one-quarter of our strategic warheads so deployed.
>
> Although the ultimate Soviet response to the MX will to a large extent depend upon the outcome of our future basing decisions, the basic question in the meantime is whether the Soviets interpret our overall strategic program as representing primarily an escalation of the threat to their strategic forces or recognize the new program's clear emphasis on retaliatory capability. If the Soviets recognize the retaliatory aspects of the US program, they should find opportunities for enhancing their security through arms control.[34]

The deceptive implications of that official statement are startling. Confining itself to initial deployment of less than 50 MXs, it does not address the full impact of the MX program and thereby fails to fulfill the intent of Section 36 of the Arms Control and Disarmament Act which mandates the annual ACIS by the president. The footnote appears to be a further distraction.

The most blatant omission, however, appears in the last paragraph. After posing two ways the MX program can be perceived, the statement only deals with the impact of the one most favorable to the Administration's position. Failure to address the consequences if the Soviets perceive MX as an escalation of the threat to their strategic forces is sidestepping a sensitive issue. Coming from an Administration obsessed with secrecy this statement is disturbing. It is a preview of the lack of candor we can expect in the future.

In this chapter I have highlighted two hazards: the actual danger from MX as a weapon, and the danger epitomized by the way MX has been promoted. The former concerns the nature of the missile. It might actually cause the nuclear war government officials tell us it is needed to prevent. The latter has to do with public deception and coverup of information. These are the practices which have allowed MX to reach full scale development and to approach production. People have been deceived by a threat fabricated to create a need for MX—a "vulnerability gap," so to speak. But at the same time the actual threat created by the first strike nature of MX is being covered up.

The consequences of these two dangers are twofold. One threatens our physical health and well being. The other endangers our self-determination and freedom in a democratic society. Clearly, MX is an unhealthy device. Former Research and Development Chairman, Senator Thomas McIntyre, expressed it well when he said that besides being "hideously expensive," MX is a "disastrous mistake."[36] We should correct that mistake quickly.

NOTES

1. Cited by Jim Gibney, "Defense Chief Remains Mum On MX Sites," *Denver Post*, 28 May 1981, p. 1.
2. *Annual Defense Department Report Fiscal Year 1978*, by Secretary of Defense Donald H. Rumsfeld, 17 January 1977, p. 122.
3. Washington Post Service dispatch, "Pressure Mounting for 'Super Missile'," *San Jose Mercury*, 7 July 1977.
4. Richard Burt, "M.I.T. Team Is Critical of Proposal To Base Mobile Missiles In Tunnels," *New York Times*, 25 March 1978, p. 8. Also see Robert Cook, "New US Super-Missile Called Major Mistake," *Boston Globe*, 23 March 1978, p. 1.
5. Edgar Ulsamer, "In Focus," *Air Force Magazine*, November 1978, p. 16.
6. Cited by Edgar Ulsamer, "In Focus" *Air Force Magazine*, March 1979, p. 20.
7. Cited in "Savings Overestimated on MX, Study Finds," *San Jose Mercury*, 6 June 1979.
8. *The MX Weapon System—A Program With Cost And Schedule Uncertainties*, report to Congress by the Comptroller General of the United States, General Accounting Office, 29 February 1980, p. i.
9. Cited by Steven R. Weisman, "Reagan Abandons Plans To Reinforce First 40 MX Silos," *New York Times*, 12 February 1982, p. 1.
10. "Issues Concerning The Survivability And Capability of the ICBM Force," General Accounting Office letter report to Defense Secretary Caspar Weinburger (MASAD-82-21), 25 February 1982, Enclosure I
11. Ibid.
12. Michael Getler, "President Scrapping 2d MX Idea," *Washington Post*, 11 February 1982, p. 1.
13. Stansfield Turner," 'Dense Pack': It's the Planning That's Dense," *Los Angeles Times*, 21 May 1982, p. 7B.
14. *Military Construction Appropriations for 1981*, hearings before the House Appropriations Committee, 25 March 1980, Part 5, p. 150.

15. *Department of Defense Authorization for Appropriations for Fiscal Year 1981*, hearings before the Senate Armed Services Committee, 12 March 1980, Part 5, p. 2864.
16. Cited in "Deterrence is Everybody's Business," *Air Force Magazine*, January 1982, p. 36.
17. Edgar Ulsamer, "In Focus," *Air Force Magazine*, July 1980, p. 20.
18. *Department of Defense Appropriations for 1981*, hearings before the House Appropriations Committee, 30 April 1980, Part 3, p. 895.
19. *Hearings on Military Posture and HR 11500, Fiscal Year 1977*, before the House Armed Services Committee, 10 February 1976, Part 1, p. 1334.
20. Ibid, p. 1333
21. Captain Phil Lacombe, "The Air Force Satellite System," *Air Force Magazine*, June 1982, p. 52.
22. *Fiscal Year 1980 Arms Control Impact Statements*, March 1979, p. 129.
23. *Fiscal Year 1981 Arms Control Impact Statements*, May 1980, pp. 416-417.
24. *Department of Defense Annual Report Fiscal Year 1979*, by Harold Brown, Secretary of Defense, 2 February 1978, p. 50.
25. *Department of Defense Appropriations Fiscal Year 1979*, Senate Appropriations Committee, 27 February 1978, Part 5, p. 199.
26. *Counterforce Issues for the US Strategic Nuclear Forces*, Congressional Budget Office background paper, January 1978, p. 50.
27. *Planning US Strategic Nuclear Forces for the 1980s*, Congressional Budget Office budget issue paper, June 1978, p. xv.
28. *The MX Missile and Multiple Protective Structure Basing: Long Term Budgetary Implications*, Congressional Budget Office budget issue paper for fiscal year 1980, June 1979, p. 105.
29. Ibid, footnote 3.
30. *Department of Defense Appropriations for 1978*, hearings before the Defense Subcommittee of the House Appropriations Committee, 15 September 1977, Part 7, p. 146.
31. "MX Development Termed 'Disasterous Mistake'," *Aviation Week & Space Technology*, 17 October 1977, p. 16.
32. *Fiscal Year 1981 Arms Control Impact Statements*, op. cit., p. 65.
33. *Fiscal Year 1979 Arms Control Impact Statements*, June 1978, p. 21.
34. *Fiscal Year 1983 Arms Control Impact Statements*, March 1982, pp. 23-24.
35. Ibid., p. 23.
36. "MX Development Termed 'Disasterous Mistake'," op. cit.

PENETRATING BOMBERS AND CRUISE MISSILES

The leading governments mouth phrases about disarmament, but they have not yet decided that disarmament is both practical and essential for the survival of mankind. They will only decide when a worldwide tide of public opinion makes them understand that the peoples are ready for this great revolution in the conduct of international affairs.

—Lord Philip J. Noel-Baker
British Nobel Laureate

The final portion of the strategic triad is the air wing—or, as former Defense Secretary Brown called it, "the air-breathing leg." Traditionally this leg has been composed of heavy intercontinental bombers, also called penetrating bombers because they must penetrate enemy defenses to fly right to their target. At present the strategic bomber force consists of B-52s and four B-1 bomber prototypes which have been in development for many years. During that time a nationwide debate has taken place on the ability of a bomber to penetrate Soviet air defenses. The Soviet Union has dozens of surveillance radars and hundreds of ground radars around its entire periphery and into its interior. It has deployed 2,600 interceptor aircraft and more than 12,000 surface-to-air missile (SAM) launchers capable of being reloaded and fired repeatedly. Soviet anti-bomber defenses have been described by military experts as the most sophisticated in the world. The USSR is still investing a large portion of its military budget in this area and the systems are being constantly improved.

In February 1976 a Brookings Institution study concluded that there was no military advantage to deploying the B-1 fleet. Besides urging against producing such an expensive aircraft the study took issue with the whole concept of a penetrating bomber.[1] Pentagon plans at that time were to build 244 B-1s.

During his election campaign Jimmy Carter took a stand against the B-1 bomber saying: "The B-1 is an example of a proposed system which should not be funded and would be wasteful of taxpayer dollars."[2] In the following year Carter made the Presidential decision that the B-1 would not go into production. It looked like the new bomber was dead with only four prototypes built.

Probably the main reason for President Carter's rejection of the B-1 was that it, like Trident, had been plagued with a long history of cost overruns and technical failures. A secret General Accounting Office (GAO) study noted that cost estimates for the bomber were "continually increasing" and that the planned cost of the program "could be exceeded by several billion dollars." The GAO, which is the investigative arm of Congress, also recommended a closer look at the static test results of the B-1's airframe because some engineers had "expressed concern" over the adequacy of the test program.[3]

Cost escalations have become a predictable occurence with all weapons systems and are unique to the Department of Defense in their magnitude. In comparing the B-1's development with that of the commercial 747 jetliner one Congressional critic noted: "We know what it costs to produce a 747 today. It has been in production for seven years. 747 production will continue under *the watchful eye of the commercial marketplace which, unlike the Department of Defense, is absolutely unforgiving of 'cost growth.'* Government purchases of 747 basic aircraft will benefit from the cost-control pressures of concurrent commercial production; the B-1 offers no such insurance."[4] (Emphasis added.)

Equally predictable is the gradual deterioration in the weapon's projected performance. Such reevaluations are usually presented as the result of cost cutting measures but are more often due to the contractor's inability to meet the promises made when the job was up for bid. The B-1's most obvious shortfall was its inability to fly faster than mach-1.6 without developing serious vibrations. But there have been other degradations which are not so widely known. In January 1975 the Air Force made "engineering trade-offs," a euphemism for quality cuts, ostensibly to offset about $127-million in cost overruns. The list of eight degradations included termination of the crew escape module that was supposed to save $70-million. Another was lowering the requirements for engine infrared suppression which was a countermeasure to prevent heat-homing anti-aircraft missiles from finding the airplane. Congressman Les Aspin pointed out that these changes would result in a slower, heavier, shorter range and less safe airplane.[5]

We should also review some of the test results that gave rise to the GAO's concern. In May 1976 a five-inch long crack was discovered in a tail section assembly which was undergoing load cycling to test for fatigue failure. A spokesman for Rockwell International, prime contractor for the B-1, immediately downplayed the failure by stating: "The section was built to be tested, not flown."[6] That rationale, if accepted, would completely invalidate the purpose of proof testing. Test specimens are supposed to undergo the same stringent inspection as operational hardware. I have observed that industry actually gives them a closer inspection to preclude this type of embarassing failure. Had the tail section passed the fatigue test it would have been counted toward certifying the design. Apparently what Rockwell International would like to do is discard the bad test results and only count the good ones.

Another example occurred in August of that same year when a crack spread completely across a longeron in the body section where the wing attaches. Air Force officials immediately announced that the crack was not due to fatigue but was the fault of the test procedure. Rather than correcting the procedure, they pointed out that "the longeron *had been reinforced* and testing has now resumed."[7] (Emphasis added.) There is a hole in this type of experimental design that several billions of dollars could easily fall through. If a test procedure fails to simulate flight conditions then it should be corrected, but the test specimen should never be jury-rigged to pass a test. These two examples substantiate the GAO's concern about testing methods.

After Carter's announcement about stopping the B-1, the Senate immediately scratched fiscal year 1978 funding for the program. But the move was hotly debated in the House and the motion to terminate funding passed by a meager three-vote margin. Debate continued into the following year on whether to go ahead and build the fifth and sixth aircraft since $462-million had already been appropriated in fiscal 1977 for that purpose. Rockwell International and the Pentagon, of course, lobbied heavily, using the threat of unemployment to keep their foot in the door. Nevertheless, after a sharp debate between Senate and House conferees, airplanes #5 and #6 were cancelled and all funds rescinded.

Two-and-a-half months after President Carter shot down the B-1, Defense Secretary Harold Brown presented the House Appropriations

Committee with a list of bomber alternatives which, oddly enough, still included the B-1. They were:[8]

The B-1 bomber.

A stretched-out version of the FB-111 fighter bomber, designated FB-111H

A rebuilt and upgraded B-52 for a penetrating bomber, designated B-52X.

Reworking some or all of the B-52 bombers to be cruise missile carriers.

Converting existing commercial or military wide-bodied jet transports to carry cruise missiles.

A new penetrating bomber designed B-X.

While Secretary Brown immediately pointed out that most of these options had fallen by the wayside, the Air Force was still keeping all of them open. Three members of the House Armed Services Committee—Representatives Bob Carr, Thomas Downey and Patricia Schroeder—took a dissenting view of this activity. They called attention to the fact that "the B-1 was rejected, not because it was a defective airplane, but because the penetrating bomber concept was judged defective." They went on to illustrate that the other penetrating bomber studies shared all the conceptual defects of the B-1 bomber and suggested that: " if the first team could not make the grade, it makes no sense to try to go it with the second team."[9]

In response to a request from Congressman Carr for clarification of the administration's position President Carter made clear that he too was keeping the options open for a new penetrating bomber: "While I hope that it will not be necessry to produce a new aircraft . . . I believe we must ensure against the possibility, however remote, that we might have to produce a new penetrating bomber."[10] In this manner he retracted with one hand what support he had given to B-1 foes with the other.

Congress, also, seemed to agree that a penetrating bomber option should be maintained but the two houses were far apart on what it should be. In September 1977 the Senate Armed Services committee recommended a $20-million budget for fiscal year 1978 to study the stretched FB-111 concept. The House, on the other hand, leaned toward the B-1.

Although the FB-111 was promoted as a tactical aircraft, particularly in connection with SALT negotiations, sixty-eight of these craft were assigned to the Strategic Air Command. The Air Force proposal was to modify two of these existing bombers by stretching them out twelve feet so they could hold more equipment and bombs, equip them with the more powerful B-1 engines, install B-1 electronics that could confuse detection and throw anti-aircraft missiles off course, and make some accompanying wing and tail modifications. Revised in that manner the FB-111H, as it would be called, would perform comparably to the B-1 in everything except payload—it would only have about half the nuclear weapons capacity. The first of these two modified aircraft would be ready to fly in two years; the second six months later.

After successful testing, the Air Force proposal called for converting another sixty-five of the existing planes while at the same time reopening the General Dynamics Corporation production line to turn out another hundred of the brand new "H" models. The projected cost of this new fleet of 167 medium bombers was in the neighborhood of $7-billion. However, Defense Secretary Brown admitted that that number was only chosen for illustrative purposes and did not represent the final quantity that might be needed for a FB-111H force.[11] A technical advantage of these airplanes is that, being medium bombers, they would not be counted against the US quota of heavy bombers in any future SALT-type agreement now that US negotiators have conceded that the Soviet Backfire bomber is not a strategic weapons carrier.

The FB-111H was not a new concept. Strategic Air Command officials had been discussing its design with General Dynamics for almost three years prior to their 1977 proposal. In addition, General Dynamics had racked-up about 800 hours of wind tunnel testing on the "H" configuration scale models at a cost of $10-million—reportedly out of their "discretionary funds."

After the Senate Committee voted against the B-1 in favor of the FB-111H, members of the House Appropriations committee cried "foul." They claimed they had been misled by the Carter Administration regarding the future of penetrating bombers. Had they been aware of the Administration's plans to proceed with some form of penetrating bomber, they insisted, they would never have approved the B-1's cancellation. The House rejected the Senate-proposed FB-111H study budget and started pushing hard to restore funds for the fifth and sixth B-1 planes.

This House-Senate deadlock was immediately sent to a joint conference to work out a compromise. At first it was believed that the conferees had approved the FB-111H proposal but a late October 1977 decision rejected that option because of adamant House opposition. The conferees agreed, however, that the deletion of FB-111H funds was done "without prejudice" to the program and that they would consider any official request for the current fiscal year or next for more funds.[12] In early 1978, however, Dr. William Perry, Under Secretary of Defense for Research and Engineering at the time, told the Senate Appropriations Committee: "I don't anticipate any recommendations on the FB-111H in fiscal year 1978. We might have some recommendations for it in 1979."[13]

In late 1979 Air Force officials revived the idea of modifying the FB-111 but according to different specifications and under a new designation—the FB-111B/C. To produce it entailed stretching out and reengining the 66 FB-111 fighter-bombers then assigned to the Strategic Air Command along with another 89 tactical F-111D fighters. The first ones could be operational by 1983 with all converted by 1985. They would, with one in-flight refueling, have the same range as B-52 bombers. Strategic Air Commander, General Richard Ellis, stated: "In my opinion, the best near-term solution to the penetrating bomber problem is to modify our existing FB-111s and F-111s into more effective aircraft."[14] He was still voicing that opinion as late as 1981 with continuing support from the Senate Armed Services Committee. Meanwhile, the fourth B-1 prototype made its last scheduled flight on April 30, 1981.

Even before the B-1 was cancelled in June 1977 there were extensive modifications planned for existing B-52s. Planning proceeded despite announcements that the B-1 was to be a replacement for those "aging" airplanes. In an article reporting 1976 statements by then Strategic Air Commander General Russell E. Dougherty, *Aviation Week and Space Technology* magazine stated: "Even with delivery of 241 B-1 bombers by 1986, SAC will retain about 300 B-52s in the inventory beyond the year 2000, arming them with standoff missiles for greater survivability."[15]

Many modifications have already been completed on the B-52 fleet and they will continue into the mid-1980s. A rotary missile rack has been installed in one bomb bay of the "G" and "H" models (to carry short-range attack missiles, or SRAMs) along with low-light-level television and infrared sensors to see the target better. The so-called "Phase-6 Mod" improved the B-52s' resistance to enemy radar and ability to detect anti-aircraft missiles.

When he was Secretary of Defense, Donald Rumsfeld suggested that the 172 B-52G models would be modified to be cruise missile carriers and that the primary role of the B-52 in the future would be to carry cruise missiles. Nevertheless, additional major reworking of the B-52s, planned before the cancellation of the B-1 in 1977, seemed to be aimed at maintaining and enhancing their penetration capability. The modifications, scheduled to be completed by 1983, "could add fifteen years" to the B-52's life.[16] They will be equipped with control systems operated by terrain-following radars which will allow planes to follow ground contours and avoid obstacles to sneak past enemy defenses at altitudes as low as 300-400 feet. Such ground-skimming capabilities are not necessary for a plane destined to be a "cruise missile carrier." These capabilities are more suited to a penetrating bomber.

Other B-52 bomber improvements, besides equipping certain models to carry cruise missiles, include:

—Overhauling the navigation and weapons delivery systems.

—Identifying any structural areas that may need special inspection or attention in future years.

—Nuclear hardening and thermal blast protection.

—Improving defensive electronic countermeasures systems.

—Possible ways of saving fuel.

—An effort to identify other improvements needed to keep the B-52s in service as long as the Air Force deems necessary.

It seems certain that we can figure on B-52s being around for a long time. Initial durability tests on B-52G and B-52H models indicate those aircraft will remain structurally sound until the year 2010.

In addition to pressing for the FB-111 study, the Senate Armed Services Committee voted in September 1977 to appropriate $5-million to investigate a new penetrating bomber which they called B-X. Although the proposal was soundly defeated by the House-Senate conference in late October 1977, Defense Under Secretary William J. Perry announced the following month that his office planned to contract with the aerospace industry to study the role of penetrating bombers in the US strategic triad. Following completion of that study in 1978, Dr. Perry requested another $10-million for a detailed look and preliminary design analysis during 1979 of specified approaches identified in the 1978 study.

Meanwhile, the Air Force did some investigating on its own. By early 1978 it had completed an exercise called SABER PENETRATOR

VII aimed at "addressing strategic bomber weapons mix alternatives for the mid-1980s."[17] But the commander-in-chief of the Strategic Air Command, General Richard H. Ellis, said the $10-million requested by Dr. Perry only financed the first phase of the penetrating bomber study. He said the study would cover a completely different aircraft involving new technology. "It might turn out to be the B-2 if anything ever develops from it," he explained, "but it would be many steps beyond the B-1."[18]

Although Dr. Perry originally claimed his study would center on the direction the B-1 research and development program would take, it was announced at about the same time that the National Aeronautics and Space Administration had awarded Lockheed a $270,000 grant to study a hypersonic jet transport that would burn liquid hydrogen as a fuel. While this was ostensibly a civilian program, financed from money appropriated for civilian use, it was reported that the Air Force was also interested.[19]

Studies contracted by the Defense Department in fiscal years 1978 and 1979 generated a number of new ideas, including a flying wing similar to the NASA design and an aircraft which folds its wings and flies like a rocket ship. Fiscal year 1980 and 1981 programs were aimed at refining these concepts and defining future aircraft characteristics such as payload, speed, range and other performance parameters. Eschewing the controversial "penetrating bomber" nametag, the new vehicle was referred to as the long-range combat aircraft (LRCA). The guideline for future bomber planning was that the low-level penetrators were outmoded. Emphasis swung back to the other extreme of high-and-fast operations which had lain dormant since the B-70 was cancelled. This new bomber was to be designed to fly higher and faster than the B-70—4,000 miles per hour at 120,000 feet—and to defend itself with laser weapons capable of shooting down 20-30 hypersonic interceptor missiles.

In the last days of the Carter Administration, the latter half of 1980, another aspect of the new bomber activity "leaked" into the news. Known as the "stealth" technology, it is supposed to allow an aircraft or missile to sneak furtively through enemy radar to reach its target. Lockheed has been the forerunner in making airplanes less detectable by radar. Besides using nonmetallic structural materials that are transparent to radar—that is, will let the beam pass through and beyond rather than bounce back—coating-type materials are being developed to absorb the radar beam. These innovations are supplemented by special shaping and contouring that will deflect the beam to the side rather than reflect it back to its source.

The Germans started working on stealth-type techniques to hide U-boat periscopes during World War II. Efforts to reduce radar visibility have been going on ever since. Stealth is the most recent activity. Although the alleged "leak" caused an uproar and was decried as a serious security breach, public information regarding stealth work has been in existence for some time.* It dates back to before the Carter Administration and Lockheed, reportedly, has been conducting flight tests since 1978.[20] Northrop, General Dynamics and Boeing are also getting involved, the latter two on cruise missile applications.

When President Carter put the B-1 bomber on the shelf in 1977, he gave the go-ahead to a new family of weapons. They are cruise missiles and I will describe them in this chapter because one variety is now becoming the primary weapon for strategic bombers. To put the picture in better perspective it would be more proper to say that intercontinental bombers are now being modified and designed to be cruise missile carriers.

Cruise missiles cross all lines between strategic and tactical weapons. They blur the distinction between conventional and nuclear weaponry. Anti-ship tactical versions with conventional warheads look identical to the nuclear land-attack weapons from the outside. Some land attack versions are for theater targets while others are for strategic use. Soviet negotiators at arms control parleys have good reason to be wary of this new weapon because all of its nuances are still not revealed. What meets the public eye is only the beginning of Pentagon ambitions and Kremlin worries.

A *cruise* missile is like a small jet airplane which is flown by sensors and an automatic pilot, rather than a human being. It can be programmed to fly a certain route at various altitudes. Having an "air breathing" jet engine, it must fly low in the atmosphere where it can scoop up air to mix with its fuel for combustion. This is in contrast to a *ballistic* missile which carries its own oxidizer as well as fuel, and thus can fly hundreds of miles above the earth. Also, a cruise missile uses wings to hold it up and those are only useful in the lower atmosphere.

---

*See *Aviation Week and Space Technology*, 19 January 1976, p. 16. Also *Jane's All The World's Aircraft 1977-78.*

Cruise missiles are not a new idea. Germany's V-2 "buzz bomb" of World War II renown was a cruise missile. Shortly thereafter the US Navy put its version, called Regulus, on submarines. The sub had to surface while the crew ran out on deck to fire the missile. The sailors would then scramble back down the hatch as the sub dove. Surfacing in that manner, of course, was risky business and defeated the submarine's advantage of elusiveness. When hypersonic ballistic missiles capable of being launched from underwater entered the picture, Regulus was abandoned.

After the US developed the technology to miniaturize everything from nuclear warheads to jet engines and electronics, Pentagon strategists and corporate salesmen again became fascinated with cruise missiles. At first the development effort focused on two types: the Air Force's *air-launched cruise missile* (ALCM) and the Navy's *sea-launched cruise missile* (SLCM). They were both designed to use the same 200 kiloton warhead originally developed for SRAM-Bs to be used on the B-1.

Also common to both the air-launched and sea-launched versions is a small fanjet engine (12 inches diameter by 36.9 inches long) weighing only 144 pounds. Although they are not put together in exactly the same shape, the navigation system components are the same on both missiles. These components include an inertial guidance package which controls a small automatic pilot and is periodically updated by a sensor system called TERCOM (*terrain contour matching*). The entire package does not exceed a cubic foot in volume and weighs less than 100 pounds.

TERCOM is the eye of the cruise missile. It follows a mapped target route with deadly accuracy giving the cruise missile almost 100 percent kill capability. TERCOM also watches the ground below so the missile can fly extremely low.

Prior to being launched, the appropriate target route is plugged into the cruise missile's navigation package. It is, of course, computerized. TERCOM then compares what it "sees" with the digital map. When a discrepancy between where the missile is and where it should be is noted, TERCOM sends corrective instructions to the guidance package. The automatic pilot then makes the course change.

To provide the map of the computerized target route that is programmed into the missile's computer is the responsibility of the Defense Mapping Agency (DMA). Much of the mapping is done by satellite-borne devices and DMA has been working since 1975 to collect all the required data. This effort supported inclusion of ALCMs into the SIOP (single integrated operational plan).

Because the cruise missile is so small it can be adapted to a great number of mobile carrier vehicles. When approaching its target it is difficult for radar to see the low flying cruise but even if that happens it looks like a seagull on the scope. According to former Defense Secretary Harold Brown the cruise missile "would probably be the best weapon against hardened targets, except time-urgent targets because it would take eight hours to get there, but at (censored) feet accuracy *it has the highest kill probability against hard targets of any of our forces*."[21] (Emphasis added.) These are some of the reasons the cruise missile is so attractive to the Pentagon as a counterforce weapon.

But I do not share the opinion that the cruise is impotent against time-urgent targets. There are two ways in which cruise missiles can enhance a first strike capability against missile silos. First, if the Soviets should resort to reloading silos the cruise could destroy those silos before reloading could be accomplished. But second and even more important, because the cruise goes in low and slow it may be able to avoid the fratricide effect from an electromagnetic pulse that would be generated in a high speed warhead reentering through an ionosphere charged by a previous nuclear explosion. While enemy missiles are held down in their silos by a high altitude burst—incapable of being launched without suffering from the effects of electromagnetic pulse—they are also safe from a direct hit by incoming warheads for the same reason. Under some circumstances the cruise may be the only weapon capable of delivering a direct hit in such an environment precisely because of its "low and slow" flight profile. That is why it's dangerous to shrug off the cruise missile because it's so slow.

Development of the sea-launched cruise missile began in 1972. The Air Force initiated its air-launched cruise missile program the following year. The first prototype, known as the ALCM-A, was 168 inches long with a 25-inch noncircular cross section. Its shape and size were designed to be interchangeable with the SRAMs on the rotary racks in the weapons bays of both the B-52 and the B-1 bombers. Each rack holds eight missiles. The B-52 "G" and "H" models have had one rack installed plus twelve ALCMs on underwing pylons bringing their total missile capacity to twenty. The B-1 was originally designed with three internal rotary racks capable of accommodating twenty-four missiles. The FB-111B/C would be able to carry four missiles internally and ten to fourteen externally, depending on the amount of fuel it needs.

ALCM-As were designed to fly 650 nautical miles in the so-called "high-low profile."* The high part of the profile is flown during the first portion of the missile's flight pattern when it is far enough from enemy territory to be relatively safe. Jet engines achieve better range at the higher altitudes but an aircraft or cruise missile can be easily detected and destroyed up there. Since these missiles are subsonic—that is, they fly slower than the speed of sound—their survival depends more than ever on their ability to avoid detection. The slower they go the easier it is to target them with an anti-aircraft missile. For that reason, as they approach hostile territory, cruise missiles drop to a low altitude and sacrifice fuel for safety.

The "high-low-flight" scenario for an ALCM begins when the missile is released from the bomber at about 45,000 feet. Within two seconds the wings and tail unfold and the fanjet engine starts up. To obtain the best fuel efficiency the missile cruises at mach-0.55 (slightly above half the speed of sound—330-380 miles per hour, depending on altitude) most of the way; dropping to a mere 100 feet above the ground as it approaches enemy radar. It skims the surface in that fashion, following the hills and valleys until it gets within fifty miles of its target. Then it drops still lower, a scant fifty feet off the ground, while speeding up to mach-0.7 for the final dash. (See Figure 5-1)

The Navy's sea-launched cruise missile (SLCM) is more commonly called *Tomahawk*. Tomahawk has now grown to a whole family of cruise missile variants which shall be discussed throughout this chapter. There are three Tomahawk SLCMs. They are all 219 inches long and 20.4 inches diameter. They have all been specifically designed to be launched from the torpedo tubes of US nuclear-powered submarines.

Three types of Tomahawk SLCMs are now in the final stages of development. (See table 5-4) The nuclear-armed Tomahawk land-attack missile (TLAM/N) will be able to fly 2,100 nautical miles in a "high-low" profile using a concentrated fuel known as "TH-Dimer." Dimer is about fifteen percent hotter than conventional jet fuel and allows more propulsive energy to be stored in a smaller volume. But research chemists are looking at even better fuels such as "Shelldyne-H" which would add more range to the missile's flight. TLAM/N is scheduled to start becoming operational in 1984.

---

*The ALCM-As designed to be carried on wing pylons could carry an extra 400 pounds of fuel in a belly tank to stretch their range to 1,200 nautical miles.

The initial part of Tomahawk's "high-low" flight profile is slightly different than that of the ALCM. Since it is launched at sea level or below, it needs a 27-inch long rocket motor to get it started and boost it to altitude. After being ejected from a submarine launch tube or a surface ship launch cannister, the rocket motor ignites and its nozzle steers the missile skyward. In the case of being launched from a submarine, the booster motor actually ignites underwater and tips the missile up to broach the surface. As the rocket continues to push the missile upward, a protective fairing comes off to allow tail fins to unfold. When the booster motor burns out it also falls away. The wings then unfold and the fanjet engine takes over to power the climb to about 20,000 feet. From that point the flight pattern is approximately the same as its air-launched counterpart.

Figure 5-1
Land Attack Cruise Missile Mission Profile

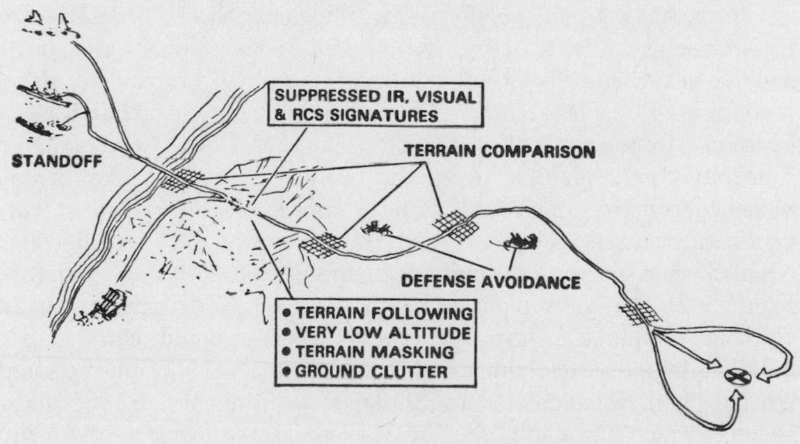

Source:
Department of Defense Authorization for Appropriations for Fiscal Year 1979, Senate Armed Services Committee (February 21, 1978) p. 1053.

If the distance from the launch point to the target is not over 1,500 nautical miles the Tomahawk can stay low all the way. In that case the rocket motor will terminate its thrust and fall off shortly after the missile leaves the water. The fanjet engine then takes over as wings and tail unfold.

A conventional-armed Tomahawk land-attack missile (TLAM/C) will be operational in September 1985. It will carry 60-80 submunitions or a conventional unitary bomb to attack targets 700 nautical miles away. While navigating to its target it will use TERCOM. But to zero-in for dispensing the submunitions it will use a sensor to match the target area with a 35-millimeter film picture of stationary targets (such as airfields) or to sense moving targets (such as tanks). Any number of different types of submunitions could be installed. For airfields each submunition would have two charges—one to penetrate the runway and the other to blast a huge crater. The second charges would be timed to go off at various long-term intervals so the enemy couldn't rush right out and repair the damage. For targeting armored vehicles the new fire-and-forget precision guided anti-tank munitions that are now in development could be used. There would be appropriate submunitions for other missions as well including anti-personnel, anti-radar, demolition of concrete structures, etc.

A tactical anti-ship version of the Tomahawk SLCM is designed to fly 300 nautical miles to deliver its 980-pound conventional warhead. Its deployment schedule is 1983 for submarines and 1984 for surface ships. It is powered by a less efficient but cheaper turbojet engine and uses a modified Harpoon missile guidance package. All of these versions of Tomahawk look identical from the outside. Moreover, they are all launched from the same vessels with the same launchers. As far as treaty verification purposes are concerned, there is no way to be certain which is which when counting the number of strategic SLCMs deployed. (See Figure 5-2) The Navy plans to put SLCMs on 30 destroyers and 22 cruisers. Eventually, however, every warship could carry cruise missiles. Initially each ship will carry 32 Tomahawks in four armored box launchers which erect to a slight angle for firing. But in 1985 a new launcher which stores and fires SLCMs vertically will squeeze more into the allotted space. The number of missiles on each ship can then be increased to 60. More recent plans have included restoring some mothballed battleships to carry cruise missiles. Using vertical launchers instead of gun turrets these battlewagons will be able to carry 320 Tomahawks each.

At least 90 fast attack submarines will also be equipped with cruise missiles. The early model attack subs will carry eight SLCMs in their torpedo room to fire through their torpedo tubes. But since these boats are limited to only 22 torpedo-size weapons, having cruise missiles will reduce their capability for other missions. That is why the new *Los Angeles* class subs will be modified by installing twelve vertical SLCM launchers in their ballast compartment, which is forward of the conning tower and outside the pressure hull. A new class of attack sub slated for delivery starting in 1989 will be built with these 12 launch tubes in place.

Another option once considered was to put cruise missiles in the obsolete Polaris ballistic missile-launching submarines—five in each of the 16 Polaris launch tubes for a total of 80 per submarine. However, it seems that this idea is not being pursued. Nevertheless, the US Navy plans on deploying over 4,000 SLCMs within the next decade.

Figure 5-2
Tomahawk Cruise Missile Variants

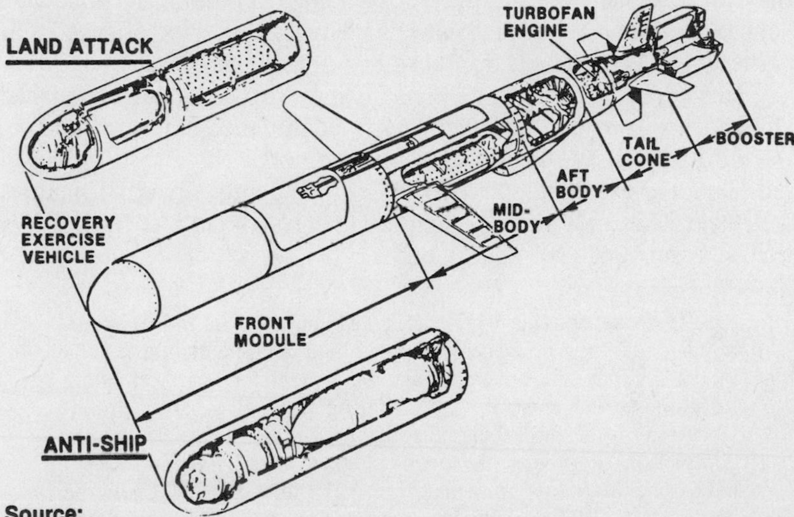

Source:
Department of Defense Authorization for Appropriations for Fiscal Year 1979, Senate Armed Services Committee (February 21, 1978) p. 1051.

Always ready to expand its sphere of operations, the Navy once conceived an air-launched variant of its Tomahawk SLCM. Ostensibly for use on carrier-based aircraft, this navy design was actually in direct competition with Air Force efforts to develop a bomber-launched strategic cruise missile. Since it is dropped from an airplane the booster rocket is not needed. And since the air-launched variant burns the less concentrated jet fuel its range is cut to 1,600 nautical miles; but that is still over twice the range of ALCM-A. This variant was called the Tomahawk ALCM, or TALCM.

The Air Force responded to this blatant invasion of its territory by stretching its cruise prototype to 250 inches. This new configuration, termed ALCM-B, accommodated enough additional fuel to allow a range of 1,500 nautical miles and new electronic countermeasures to make it less vulnerable to detection and interception. The wingspan was also increased slightly. This ALCM-B would fit modified rotary racks and reworked wing pylons of the B-52 but it would not go through the bomb bay doorways of the B-1 as originally designed.

Ten competitive "flyoffs" between the Boeing-built ALCM-B and General Dynamics' TALCM took place during late 1979 and early 1980. They were launched over the Pacific and overflew California and Nevada to their target area in Utah. Each manufacturer experienced four crashes raising complaints from residents of those three states.

In March 1980 the Air Force/Boeing ALCM-B was announced winner of the competition. Boeing received initial contracts to build the 3,418 ALCMs then planned. Twenty additional flight tests began in mid-1980 and extended over two years. Apparently severe difficulties were experienced because an unclassified digest of a secret GAO report dated February 26, 1982 concluded:

> It is questionable whether ALCM can meet its initial operational capability in December 1982 and it appears the risk is increasing that initial operational capability may not be met with a fully operational missile. The initial operational capability milestone seems to have been the driving force in the premature completion of other milestones and has raised concern. GAO believes that unless this matter is resolved, ALCM could be deployed in significant numbers with operational limitations which may require costly modifications.[22]

At the time of this writing it looks like December 1982 is still the target date for initial operation of one squadron of B-52Gs (16 aircraft) equipped to carry twelve ALCMs each under their wings.[23] SAC's 416th Bomb Wing at Griffiss Air Base in New York will be the first to receive ALCMs. All 172 B-52Gs are being fitted to carry cruise missiles on external wing pylons. 151 of these will be loaded and ready to go at all times. President Reagan also announced in his October 1981 statement that the 96 B-52Hs will also be modified to carry 20 ALCMs—12 externally and 8 internally on a new rotary rack. It now looks like only the B-52H aircraft will have the internal ALCM capability.[24] There will always be the option, however, to add that feature to the "G" models.

B-52 bombers are not the only aircraft that have been studied as cruise missile carriers. Wide-bodied jetliners and transports could also be converted to perform that task. The Air Force once considered purchasing 60 of these reworked airplanes along with another 4,320 ALCMs plus spares.[25] Needless to say, the manufacturers of wide-bodied aircraft started scurrying for the business. Boeing presented a plan to carry 70-90 ALCMs in its 747 jumbo jet.[26] Lockheed came up with a scheme whereby 72 ALCMs could be loaded on its C-5A transport.[27] Lockheed's L-1011 jetliner and its YC-14 medium transport were also studied. McDonnell Douglas made proposals for its DC-10 and YC-15 airplanes.[28] But for the present at least, converted transports have fallen by the wayside since they were outlawed in the SALT-2 agreement.

Not wanting to be left out of the market, Rockwell International proposed a B-1 design to carry thirty ALCM weapons—sixteen of them internally on two rotary racks, eight under the wings, and another six beneath the fuselage.[29] Early in 1980 the Air Force announced its intention to start developing the B-1 as a cruise missile carrier commencing in fiscal year 1982.[30] As early as June 1980 there were reports that a B-1 prototype would be modified during 1981 to carry ALCMs, followed by a flight test program beginning in late 1981 or 1982.[31] If the testing started on schedule it was not reported but it should be noted that these intentions date back to before the Reagan Administration. A year later, in June 1981, the *Wall Street Journal* announced that the future of the B-1 looked so promising that Rockwell International was going ahead with planning and would start ordering long-leadtime parts in October.[32]

Rockwell International planners must have had some insight because it was in that month, October 1981, that President Reagan announced his decision to build 100 B-1 bombers and have the first ones operational in 1986. The B-1B, as it was then designated, is now designed to carry up to 22 ALCMs—14 externally and 8 internally, plus 8 SRAMs. If no cruise missiles are loaded internally the three bomb bays will accommodate 24 SRAMs. But a moveable partition between two of the bays allows expansion for the longer ALCMs. It looks like the total inventory will go way beyond the 3,418 ALCMs planned. (See Figure 5-4 for ALCM-B tabulation.)

During the mid-1970s another bomber-launched weapon called the *advanced strategic air-launched missile* (ASALM) entered the concept formulation stage. It was envisioned to skim the ground for long distances at supersonic speed. It had tail fins like a rocket, but because of its speed did not need wings to stay aloft. ASALM was proposed as a weapon to knock down other aircraft designed to detect and destroy cruise missiles, destroy anti-aircraft missile sites on the ground which threaten cruise missiles and bombers, and penetrate long distances to demolish strategic targets. Having the same accuracy as other cruise missiles, ASALM would definitely be a hard target killer. It would use the TERCOM guidance system but would probably also employ some more advanced scheme of "area correlation."

Figure 5-3
Asalm Rocket-Ramjet Engine

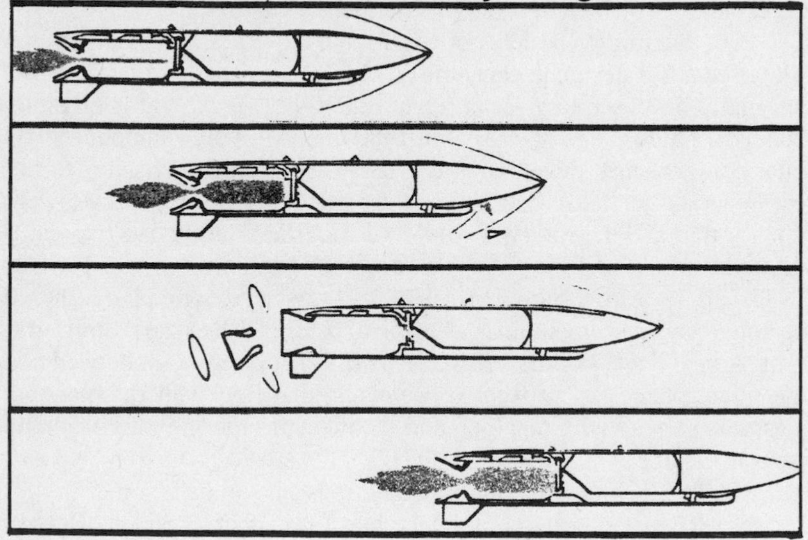

Source:
***Hearings on Military Posture and HR10929*, House Armed Services Committee (February 24, 1978) p. 294.**

In November 1977 the ASALM program was speeded up by two years and put into the early stages of development. It was supposed to go into full scale development in November 1981 with the first missile becoming operational in 1985.[33]

The technology that opened the door for ASALM is the integral rocket/ramjet engine—integral to the extent that a solid rocket-fuel motor casing also serves as a ramjet combustion chamber. When ASALM is launched from an aircraft the rocket motor will ignite and propel the missile to supersonic speed where the ramjet can take over to maintain that speed. After the rocket burns out, the nozzle liner will fall out leaving a more efficient shape for the ramjet nozzle. Air ducts and fuel metering orifices will then open as the ramjet starts up. (See Figure 5-3) The new Shelldyne-H will be the fuel used for the ramjet and a greater volume can be carried because of the 30-40 percent space saving made possible by integrating the engines. Hotter fuel and more of it makes it possible to use the simpler, cheaper and faster ramjet engine instead of the more efficient fanjet.

Information concerning ASALM seemed to fade out about mid-1981. That was about the same time the stealth technology "leak" was getting a lot of attention. In the previous year the Defense Advanced Research Projects Agency (DARPA) had initiated a 5-year program to investigate reducing the radar visibility of cruise missiles. The study also looked into advanced fuels for greater range and sophisticated avionics to evade or spoof enemy interceptor missiles. Among the concepts studied was a hypersonic cruise missile which could penetrate enemy territory at altitudes above 100,000 feet while traveling many times the speed of sound. That would require a supersonic combustion ramjet engine called a SCRAMJET. It would most likely use liquid hydrogen or what is known as a slurry fuel. Later it might use a solid ramjet fuel and the development of "hard hydrogen"—a sort of hydrogen coal—seems to be a "door-opener" for that approach.[34] The weight saved by eliminating fuel tanks, lines, valves and metering devices would increase the missile's effectiveness and range. This advanced cruise missile is believed to be the size of ALCM-B with a 2,600 nautical mile range and an initial operational date in 1987.

It seems that the supersonic, tree-skimming ASALM program may have been redirected to support the emerging strategy of penetrating enemy territory high and fast.

The Defense Department has approved production, starting in 1982, of a *Stealth ALCM*.[35] Lockheed won the contract over General Dynamics and Boeing for the first 500 missiles. This weapon will approach the Soviet Union at higher altitudes to further confound the

Russian effort to counter all cruise missile threats. It will have an autonomous all-weather guidance system using passive sensors to follow the terrain—thereby reducing the risk of detection associated with the Tercom radar altimeter. Delivery of the first Lockheed stealth cruise missile is expected in 1984.

The Stealth bomber is also on its way. In October 1981, President Reagan announced intentions to build 132 of them with the first ones becoming operational in the early 1990s. Under Secretary of Defense Richard D. De Lauer later pinned the year down to 1991.[36] Northrop has the contract for this aircraft which is more formally known as the *advanced technology bomber* (ATB). It will somewhat resemble the flying wing Northrop built in the 1940s. Ten days after Reagan's October 2nd announcement it was reported that the Northrop stealth will fly for the first time in late 1984.[37]

Some critics say the Pentagon is downplaying stealth to keep the B-1B in work—they claim stealth could be available sooner with more funding. It is also pointed out that CIA data says the B-52 will be able to penetrate Soviet defenses until 1990 and, therefore, we don't need the B-1B in the interim.

Others look at the flip side of the coin. They say the B-1B has 90 percent the penetration capability of stealth and therefore stealth is not needed so soon. Apparently the B-1B uses some stealth technology and these critics feel the B-1B should receive more attention. So the arguments go—there are ample reasons from both sides why we only need one new bomber in development. But the facts are strikingly clear that we have two.

When the General Dynamics Tomahawk lost the ALCM decathlon flyoff it was far from the end of that missile. The versatile Tomahawk family is experiencing prolific growth. Besides the SLCM described above, it has also been selected as the prototype for the ground-launched cruise missile (GLCM). This weapon is essentially identical to the Navy's nuclear land-attack Tomahawk (TLAM/N) model—rocket booster and all—except that it is fired from a four-tube mobile transporter-erector-launcher (TEL) vehicle. Ironically, GLCM development has been put under Air Force auspices but will, nevertheless, fall under the purview of the Joint Cruise Missile Program Office managed by the Navy.

On December 12, 1979 NATO defense and foreign ministers agreed to deploy 464 GLCMs in five European countries by 1988, along with 102 new Pershing-2 IRBMs in Germany by 1985. The first 160 would go to England—80 at the Greenham Common Royal Air Force (RAF) base by December 1983 and another 80 later at RAF-Molesworth. Italy would get 112 at Comiso in southern Sicily beginning in 1984. The remainder would go to Germany (96), Holland (48), and Belgium (48).

With their 1,600 nautical mile range GLCMs could reach all Warsaw Pact countries from England. But it, along with the 1,000-plus mile range Pershing-2s, would pose a direct threat to forty percent of the Soviet population and most of the USSR's industry from anywhere in Western Europe. It could also be able to attack counterforce targets anywhere in Russia that lay west of the Ural Mountains. Although GLCMs and Pershing-2s are presented to the public as theater weapons, their actual capability has obvious strategic value.

It was shortly after the ALCM contract went to Boeing that the Defense Department accelerated development of the medium-range air-to-surface missile (MRASM)—a program which had started in 1979. DOD mandated that the General Dynamics Tomahawk design be the baseline. The MRASM will be an extremely accurate weapon of about 300 nautical miles range for both Air Force and Navy use.

The Air Force design is 232 inches long—13 inches longer than the basic Tomahawk—and is expected to become operational in 1984 or 1985. It will use a small turbojet engine, have TERCOM navigation updates to its inertial guidance system while enroute to the target, and scene-matching area-correlation for the final delivery of the payload. The B-52 will be the prime carrier, being able to carry up to twenty in the same fashion as ALCMs. The F-16 fighter is also being considered as a MRASM carrier and it could carry up to four, but more than two would restrict its combat maneuverability. This Air Force version of the MRASM is currently being designed to carry 60 bomblets to attack airfields—runways, operating bases, aircraft shelters, and maintenance/supply/storage facilities. It could easily be converted, however, to carry submunitions of a different type, or even a unitary warhead, to attack other land targets. It is already being discussed as a carrier and dispenser vehicle for the new fire-and-forget anti-tank submunitions.

The Navy's land-attack MRASM, also expected to be operational in 1984 or 1985, will be 192 inches long—27 inches shorter than the basic Tomahawk because of space restrictions on aircraft carrier elevators. The primary delivery vehicle will be the A-6 aircraft which can carry four missiles under its wings. The turbojet engine, TERCOM, and scene-matching features will be the same as those on the Air Force version. The Navy is presently designing a unitary (single) warhead for penetrating concrete structures but the missile's payload could easily be altered to carry various types of submunitions.

The Navy is also working on an anti-ship MRASM identical to its present land-attack design except space has been allowed for substituting the new imaging infrared guidance system being developed for the Harpoon missile. That system will not be available until 1985. Since it is the pacing item, the anti-ship MRASM will not become operational until that year or later. When deployed, however, this missile will have a dual rol against those ships or land targets that could be attacked by unitary warheads. The three MRASM concepts are shown in Figure 5-4.

Another potential member of the Tomahawk family is the *Army ground-launched missile*. Three missile-launching cannisters could be carried on the Army's standard ten-ton truck. We can safely assume that the payload would be various conventional submunitions to attack a variety of land targets, such as tanks. Against mobile targets a cruise missile would be able to attack, reevaluate, attack again, etc. (Figure 5-4).

The final new member of the Tomahawk family that I shall discuss is the Anti-Submarine Warfare Stand-Off Weapon (ASW/SOW). It is intended to replace ASROC and SUBROC which will be discussed in the next chapter. ASW/SOW would be fired from a submarine's torpedo tube or from a surface ship's launcher. The missile would fly to the vicinity of an enemy submarine which could presumably be as far as 300 miles away. There it would drop a REmotely-Guided Autonomous Lightweight (REGAL) torpedo by parachute. When the torpedo enters the water an acoustic array, having a small computer and sonar transmitter, would separate and sink to a preset depth. The torpedo would propel itself in a slow search pattern until the array picks up the submarine. Then the torpedo would be directed in for the kill. ASW/SOW is expected to be operational by the mid-1980s. (See Figure 5-4)

One other cruise missile program that merits mention is the proposed *intercontinental cruise missile*. It is envisioned as having several stages that will drop off as they consume their capacity of fuel. Proposals for a feasibility study were requested during fiscal year 1979.[38] Contracts for those feasibility studies were awarded to Vought and General Dynamics in late 1981.[39] The Defense Department seems to have decided that launching a massive cruise missile force in response to a Soviet nuclear strike is a feasible concept.

Figure 5-4
US Cruise Missile Programs

Missile	Length (Inches)	Diameter (Inches)	Engine	Guidance Package	Warhead	Range (Naut. Mi.)	Initial Operational Date	Comments
TLAM/N (SLCM) Land-attack	219	20.4	Miniature fanjet***	TERCOM	200 kiloton nuclear	2,100*	1984	Length does not include 27-inch long rocket motor.
TLAM/C (SCLM) Land-attack	219	20.4	Miniature fanjet***	TERCOM + scene matching	Conventional bombs or submunitions	700	Sept. 1985	Length does not include 27-inch long rocket motor.
SLCM Anti-ship tactical	219	20.4	Small turbo-jet***	Modified Harpoon	980-pound conventional unitary	300	Fall 1983 for subs, 1984 for surface ships	Length does not include 27-inch long rocket motor.
ALCM-B	250	25 non-circular	Miniature fanjet	TERCOM	200 kiloton nuclear	1,500****	Dec. 1982	
Stealth ALCM	250	25 non-circular	SCRAMJET	Autonomous all-weather passive	Nuclear	2,600	1987	
GLCM	219	20.4	Miniature fanjet***	TERCOM	Selectable yield nuclear	1,600****	Dec. 1983	Length does not include 27-inch long rocket motor.
MRASM (Air Force) Land-attack	232	20.4	Small turbojet	TERCOM + scene matching	Conventional submunitions	300	1984 or 1985	Adaptable to unitary warhead.

Figure 5-4 (continued)
US Cruise Missile Programs

Missile	Length (inches)	Diameter (inches)	Engine	Guidance Package	Warhead	Range (Naut. Mi.)	Initial Operational Date	Comments
MRASM (Navy) Land-attack	192	20.4	Small turbojet	TERCOM + scene matching	Concrete penetrating unitary	300	1984 or 1985	Adaptable to conventional submunitions.
MRASM (Navy) Anti-ship	192	20.4	Small turbojet	Imaging infrared	Conventional unitary	300	Possibly 1985	Could also attack land targets.
Army ground-launched missile	**	20.4	**	Depending on target	Conventional submunitions or unitary	**	**	Would need rocket motor to boost to speed and altitude.
ASW/SOW	192	20.4	Small turbo-jet***	Autonomous homing	REGAL torpedo	**	mid-1980s	Torpedo receives navigation directions from acoustic array.
Intercontinental cruise missile	**	**	**	**	Nuclear	**	**	Multi-stage.

ALCM = air-launched cruise missile ASW/SOW = anti-submarine warfare stand-off weapon GLCM = ground-launched cruise missile
MRASM = medium-range air-to-surface missile REGAL = remotely-guided autonomous lightweight (torpedo) TERCOM = terrain contour matching
TLAM = Tomahawk land-attack missile SCRAMJET = supersonic combustion ramjet SLCM = sea-launched missile

*1,400 nautical mile range if it stays low all the time. **Information not available. ***Uses a rocket motor to boost missile to speed and altitude.
****This advertised range probably doesn't take advantage of the high-low flight profile or concentrated fuels.

Note:
According to a recent issue of *Aviation Week & Space Technology* (23 August 1982, p. 13), Defense Secretary Caspar Weinberger presented a plan to Congress and the White House to eventually procure 1,500 Stealth cruise missiles to replace the ALCM-B. This is reported to be the first part of an overall $63-billion plan for 30,000 tactical and strategic cruise missiles of all types.

This long discourse on cruise missiles has covered a lot of territory and has wandered into the area of tactical nuclear weapons. It illustrates the diminishing distinction between tactical and strategic, conventional and nuclear warfare. Cruise missiles were one of the main obstacles in SALT-2 negotiations since at least 1975. It is easy to see why the Soviets are concerned about this prolific new weapon. They could never be certain which missiles are nuclear and which conventional. They could never know what ships, aircraft and submarines are carrying cruise missiles or how many. President Carter pointed out this verification problem to Congress:

> Cruise missiles represent a class of weapons which raises potentially troublesome verification problems. The physical characteristics of the cruise missile contribute substantially to these difficulties. Compared to ballistic missiles, cruise missiles are smaller, fly lower, have small radar and infrared signatures, and use small, simpler and less easily identifiable launchers and support facilities. Cruise missiles can be launched from a wide variety of air, sea and land platforms. Another complicating feature is that cruise missiles of similar size and external configuration may have significantly different range capabilities, nuclear or conventional payloads, guidance systems and missions.[40]

Furthermore, President Carter noted that " . . . because [the cruise missile] introduces a new type of nuclear weapon into the US inventory, it may be perceived as inconsistent with the US commitment to the NPT."[41] NPT stands for the Non-Proliferation Treaty which is binding on the United States. Clearly, cruise missiles violate existing treaties and undercut the prospect for working out future arms control agreements.

Another reason the Soviets are concerned about cruise missiles is because they can approach the Soviet Union from so many directions that defending against them would be economically prohibitive. It is reported that defense against 3,000 cruise missiles would require an investment of tens of billions of dollars.[42] That requirement could be doubled by the introduction of a new type of cruise missile, such as a stealth version with a high and fast approach.

While the Soviets also have cruise missiles, they are of a completely different vintage than US weapons. Until recently they only had one—the SS-N-3 Shaddock—that could go farther than 70 miles. There were once about 342 Shaddocks with their single nuclear warhead but that number has been reduced somewhat. About half are in submarines and the rest are in surface ships. These 42-foot-long missiles have a range of only 240 miles and are suitable only for anti-ship missions. Even then they need an airplane to provide mid-course guidance updates and the submarine has to surface and raise its external launch tubes in order to fire the missiles.

In 1979 the Soviets started replacing some Shaddocks with the SS-N-12s—a missile with two warheads and a 300 nautical mile range; obviously still only a tactical anti-ship weapon. There must have been a problem with the SS-N-12 because by mid-1981—two years after becoming operational—there were only 56 deployed, and that only represented an increase of eight missiles from the year before.[43]

In 1980 the Soviet SS-N-19 cruise missile became operational on the new Oscar submarine and Kirov aircraft carrier. Although these new weapons are supersonic, and can be launched from underwater in the case of Oscar, they still have only a 300 nautical mile range. *Air Force Magazine* reports they were developed to assure reliable kill probabilities against aircraft carriers.[44] They cannot be construed to be a strategic weapon or in a class with the US ALCM/SLCM/GLCM designs. By mid-1981 there had been only 40 SS-N-19s deployed.[45]

In the area of strategic bombers, Pentagon public relations officers have been referring to a new Soviet bomber for many years. In early 1979 it was reported that the Soviets were developing two new bombers—one of which was comparable to the "US-cancelled Rockwell B-1," and was expected to become operational in 1982.[46] The other was reported to be a carrier for cruise missiles with an operational date in 1983.[47]

As the years went by, however, there was no evidence of bomber flight tests or of air-launched cruise missile tests by the Soviets. Then, on November 25, 1981, a US spy satellite photographed a new bomber on the apron at the Remenskoye flight test center in the USSR. This Russian "roll-out" of a new bomber occurred the month after Ronald Reagan's announcement that the US was reactivating the B-1 program and planned to build at least 100 of those aircraft. A February 1982 report says the aircraft is a prototype and has not been flight tested: "It is probable that the Soviets wanted the US to 'see' the aircraft at this time since it was displayed in a way that, according to US experts, would have made it next to impossible for US spy satellites to miss observing it."[48] There seems to be reasonable evidence that this Soviet bomber rollout is a response to the US decision to build the B-1B and Stealth bombers. I believe we are witnessing another escalation of the arms race.

There is one pattern in the last three chapters that should be noticed. Although there are competing weapons systems, and inter-service rivalry flourishes, all of the weapons involved eventually reach production. Even when one weapon is first presented as a replacement for an "aging" or "obsolete" system, the new one usually ends up complementing the old, rather than replacing it. MX is now going to supplement Minuteman. The Navy has programs for both the Trident-1 and the Trident-2 missiles. Tridents are being backfitted into existing Poseidon subs as well as the new Trident ships. The Air Force still has its B-52s with highly sophisticated modifications as well as the B-1B and Stealth bombers. The General Dynamics Tomahawk cruise missile is making inroads into every conceivable category while Boeing has ALCMs in production and Lockheed has cornered a Stealth ALCM contract. The Military-Industrial-Complex is quite adept at having its cake and eating it too—a pattern that the American public needs to become aware of.

Now let us move on into other aspects of a First Strike capability. In the next chapter we'll look into anti-submarine warfare.

Notes

1. AP dispatch, "B-1 Bomber Shot Down By Study," *San Jose Mercury,* 4 November 1976.
2. UPI dispatch, "Carter Faces Decision On B-1," *Watsonville Register Pajaronian,* 4 November 1976.
3. UPI dispatch, "B-1s Cost, Safety Doubted By GAO," *San Jose Mercury-News,* 6 March 1977. Also see UPI dispatch, "Cost of B-1 Bomber Fleet Still Climbing," *San Jose Mercury,* 23 June 1977, just a few days before Carter announced his decision against the B-1.
4. *Department of Defense Supplemental Appropriations Act, 1978;* a House Armed Services Committee report with dissenting views, 20 September 1977, p. 26.
5. UPI dispatch, "Quality Cuts In Bomber Under Fire," *San Jose Mercury,* 13 January 1975. Also see Fitzgerald, Markoff, Walke and Woodmansee; *Rockwell International: Where Business Gets Down To The Science Of War,* (Philadelphia, American Friends Service Committee; 1975) pp. 4-21.
6. AP dispatch, "Small Crack Found In Tail Of Bomber," *Des Moines Register,* 6 May 1976. Also, "Crack In B-1 Horizontal Stabilizer," *Aviation Week and Space Technology,* 10 May 1976, p. 21.
7. *Aviation Week and Space Technology,* 6 September 1976, p. 41.
8. *Department of Defense Appropriations for 1978,* hearings before the

Defense Subcommittee of the House Appropriations Committee, 15 & 20 September 1977, Part 7, p. 147.

9. *Department of Defense Supplemental Appropriations Act, 1978;* op. cit., p. 20.
10. Cited by Eugene Kozicharow, "House Debates FB-111H Study Funding," *Aviation Week and Space Technology,* 17 October 1977, p. 21.
11. *Department of Defense Appropriations for 1978,* op. cit., Appendix to Part 7, p. 178.
12. Cited in *Arms Control Today,* published by the Arms Control Association, 11 DuPont Circle NW, Washington, D.C. 20009; November 1977.
13. *Department of Defense Appropriations Fiscal Year 1979,* hearings before the Senate Appropriations Committee, 27 February 1978, Part 5, p. 204.
14. Cited by Clarence A. Robinson, Jr., "USAF Commands Push Stretching 155 F-111s," *Aviation Week and Space Technology,* 24 September 1979, p. 17
15. *Aviation Week and Space Technology,* 10 May 1976, p. 28.
16. *Aviation Week and Space Technology,* 23 February 1976, pp. 56-57.
17. *Department of Defense Authorization for Appropriations for Fiscal Year 1979,* hearings before the Senate Armed Services Committee, 21 February 1978, Part 2, p. 1100.
18. Howard Silber, "Pentagon Study Aims At Bomber Advances," *Omaha World Herald,* 28 May 1978, p. 1.
19. AP dispatch, "Hydrogen Aircraft Study Funded," *San Jose Mercury,* 7 November 1977, p. 8. Also see *Aviation Week and Space Technology,* 14 November 1977, p. 54.
20. *Atlanta Constitution,* 11 September 1980, p. 1
21. *Department of Defense Appropriations for 1978,* op. cit., Part 7, p. 193.
22. "Air-Launched Cruise Missile Shows Promise But Problems Could Result in Operational Limitations," unclassified digest furnished in lieu of a secret GAO report, C-MASAD-82-13, 26 February 1982, p. iii.
23. *Fiscal Year 1983 Arms Control Impact Statements,* March 1982, p. 68.
24. Ibid, pp. 67 & 73.
25. *Fiscal Year 1980 Arms Control Impact Statements,* March 1979, p. 31, Table 5.
26. Richard G. O'Lone, "Boeing Proposes 747 As Missile Launcher," *Aviation Week and Space Technology,* 5 September 1977, pp. 17-18.
27. Slava W. Harlamor, "C-5 Cruise Missile Launcher Tested," *Aviation Week and Space Technology,* 9 January 1978, pp. 40-47.
28. *Aviation Week and Space Technology,* 12 June 1978, pp. 56-57.
29. Donald E. Fink, "Rockwell Designers Define New Derivative of B-1" *Aviation Week and Space Technology,* 10 October 1977, pp. 22-24.

30. *Aviation Week and Space Technology,* 3 March 1980, p. 36.
31. *Aviation Week and Space Technology,* 16 June 1980, p. 139.
32. *Wall Street Journal* 3 June 1981, p. 5.
33. *Hearings on Military Posture and HR 10929, Fiscal Year 1979* before the House Armed Services Committee, 24 February, 1978, Part 3, Book 1, pp. 293-299.
34. William P. Schlitz, "Aerospace World: News, Views and Comments," *Air Force Magazine,* March 1979 pp. 29 & 33; and May 1, 1979, pp. 36 & 39. Also see New York Times News Service dispatch by Malcolm W. Browne, "'Hard' Hydrogen Created," *San Francisco Chronicle,* 3 March 1979, p. 1.
35. *Air Force Times,* 14 June 1982, p. 23.
36. *Washington Post,* 13 March 1982, p. 8.
37. *Aviation Week and Space Technology,* 12 October 1981, p 17.
38. *Aviation Week and Space Technology,* 21 August 1978, p. 9.
39. *Aviation Week and Space Technology,* 30 November 1981, p. 133
40. *Fiscal Year 1979 Arms Control Impact Statements,* June 1978, p. 69.
41. Ibid, p. 64.
42. Under Secretary of Defense Dr. William J. Perry and Cruise Missile Program Office Manager Rear Admiral Walter Locke. Cited in *Aviation Week and Space Technology,* 12 June 1978, p. 20.
43. *The Military Balance 1980/81* and *The Military Balance 1981/82,* International Institute for Strategic Studies, London, England.
44. *Air Force Magazine,* July 1980, p. 19.
45. *The Military Balance 1980/81,* op. cit.
46. *Aviation Week and Space Technology,* 19 February 1979, p. 14.
47. Ibid, p. 15.
48. *Air Force Magazine,* February 1982, p. 21.

ANTI-SUBMARINE WARFARE

Out there
Somewhere
In the ocean
Lurks a dark, primeval shape
Gliding smoothly through the water
Stiff-finned
Vicious

—*Gillian Hope*
New Zealand

The role of anti-submarine warfare (ASW) in a first strike strategy is to destroy all hostile missile-launching submarines at sea—those in port could be annihilated with strategic missiles. Most people believe submarines are invulnerable. That is still true for US subs but not for those of the Soviet Union. I started investigating ASW in 1976—searching out the sensors, weapons and carriers that the US Navy has or soon will have. The outcome of that first study unnerved me. It indicated that, if all the programs in progress came to a successful conclusion, the United States, by the early 1980s, would be able to locate and track every Soviet missile-launching submarine in the ocean. From there it would not be difficult to destroy those vessels on command. Developments in the meantime tend to substantiate that prediction.

Navy expenditures for ASW development jumped from $3 billion a year during the early part of the 1970s to somewhere between $4- and $6½-billion by 1978.[1] The Navy's fiscal 1979 budget contained approximately $7.4-billion for ASW.[2] Frost & Sullivan, a market research firm in New York, has forecast that US spending for ASW will total $46.2-billion during the six-year period ending with fiscal 1983.[3] All of this does not include unknown amounts buried in the budgets of such agencies as the Department of Energy, the National Aeronautics and Space Administration, the National Oceanic and Atmospheric Administration, and the National Science Foundation. ASW has become a big thing in Pentagon circles. It is also a big market for business. ASW is no longer geared solely toward the protection of convoys in shipping lanes. It has now assumed a more aggressive posture suited to the Pentagon's emerging first strike capability.

Our discussion of the place of US anti-submarine warfare activities in such a strategy must begin with an assessment of how many Soviet submarines would have to be instantaneously destroyed to sap the Soviet Union's SLBM capability. In his fiscal year 1983 posture statement, General David C. Jones, then Chairman of the Joint Chiefs of Staff, said the Soviet Union has 70 modern nuclear-powered ballistic missile-launching submarines of which 62 would be accountable under SALT–2.[4] There are another 15 diesel-powered submarines which carry ballistic missiles. These latter poke along at ten miles per hour submerged and have to surface every night to recharge their batteries, and are so easy to track that they are not counted in SALT quotas. Even if the total Soviet missile launching force becomes significantly larger by the latter 1980s it will still pose no real challenge to the US anti-sub capability currently under development.

The anti-submarine warfare system can be divided into three basic groups: sensors, weapons, and carriers. *Sensors* will be described first. Just as the name implies, sensors are the devices by which anti-submarine forces "see" and "hear" what is happening beneath the waves. They not only detect submarines but pinpoint their location and determine if they are friend or foe. The sensing function (or surveillance) is divided into two regimes: escort and open-ocean.

Escort surveillance is supposed to be a defensive activity to protect ships, convoys and task forces from hostile submarines. It is ostensibly confined to a limited ocean area of about sixty miles radius around the ships. The sensors used are specifically designed for short-range detection so that a hostile sub in the area can be pinpointed and destroyed. Sensors are now so precise that they can even determine the class of submarine.

Open-ocean surveillance uses different types of sensors to determine, within a sixty-mile radius of error, the position of all submarines in the ocean. These two types of sensing systems would work hand-in-glove during a preemptive first strike. Open-ocean surveillance would detect all the Soviet submarines and put escort surveillance forces on their tail which, in turn, would set them up for the kill.

Throughout the history of submarines, sound propagation has been the basis of underwater detection because radio and radar do not penetrate water to any significant depth. The device used to listen underwater is called *sonar* (an acronym for SOund Navigation And Ranging). To fully appreciate how it works one must understand that sound behaves differently in water than in air. It will travel much farther and much faster than in the atmosphere. Other features of underwater sound propagation, however, pose special problems for detection systems. Sound bends as it passes through various ocean temperatures and water densities, much as light does when it shines through a lens. And as the visible light spectrum can be separated into a rainbow, so can sound be scattered in the ocean. In addition, sound echoes and bounces from the ocean floor, coastlines, the surface, and the warmer layers of water near the surface (called the thermal layers). This causes it to divert into many paths and ricocheting patterns. Further complicating undersea listening are the ships, storms, underwater volcanoes, and sea creatures. All of these add to the clamor beneath the waves. The ocean is far from being a quiet place and the challenge to ASW sensing is to pull the sounds of submarines out of this voluminous discord.

There are two types of sonar: active and passive. Active sonars emit beeps which echo from submarines and other underwater objects in a manner comparable to the way radar bounces back from bodies in the atmosphere. Active sonars, of course, reveal their positions by the sound probe they emit and can be destroyed if they are not protected. They are not the type of sensor suitable to clandestine operations. Passive sonars, on the other hand, are ideally suited to such a role because they are simply listening devices.

The mainstay of the Navy's open-ocean sensing system is SOSUS (SOund SUrveillance System)—a system of passive underwater listening devices which are permanently fixed on the continental shelves of the United States and friendly countries. The information picked up by SOSUS listening devices—called hydrophones—travel through underwater cables to shore stations.* SOSUS dates back to the 1960s but it has

*It is reported that Soviet "fishing trawlers" hover over the suspected locations of these cables trying to snag and sever them. Whatever the reason, it does appear that they do need frequent attention because the US has a fleet of cable repair ships (designated T-ARC) which are civilian-operated under the Military Sealift Command.

undergone continuous improvements. The Navy has invested well over a billion dollars in SOSUS and, although its original mission has changed, it still remains an effective and important system.

Even though SOSUS is a passive system, the general locations of some installations are known. There is a sonar chain between Greenland and Scotland which keeps tabs on every Russian submarine passing from the Arctic Ocean into the Atlantic. Another chain extends from the northern tip of Norway to Bear Island in the Arctic. Farther south in the Atlantic is the Azores Fixed Acoustic Range which monitors submarine traffic through the Strait of Gibralter and other surrounding waters. In the Pacific area, another array is deployed parallel to the Kamchatka Peninsula. There are many more similar installations throughout the world.

SOSUS can spot a sub anywhere in the ocean when conditions are favorable and pinpoint it within a sixty-mile radius. It can also interact with ASW aircraft and escort surveillance ships. But conditions are frequently not favorable and there are limits to the sensitivity of SOSUS. For that reason the Navy has two additional systems to enhance open-ocean ASW—the *SURveillance Towed Array Sensor System* (SURTASS) and, currently under development, the *Rapidly Deployable Sensor System* (RDSS). It is my impression that they will use a new sonar which focuses on the cavitation noises generated by the turbulent flow of water around large and fast submarines, as opposed to detecting engine noises and other sounds that originate from within the vessels.

SURTASS went into service in 1980. These arrays are pulled around the ocean by slow tuna-clipper-type boats and have sensors tuned for long distance sound detection. Data is relayed from the towing ship through a communications satellite to the shore station where it is processed and analyzed. SURTASS provides a geographic mobility which SOSUS does not have. There will eventually be 18 of these arrays complete with their towing ships (designated T-AGOS and AGOS).

RDSS arrays are buoys with passive sensors that can be readily deployed by aircraft, surface ships, or submarines in selected areas during times of crisis. This system, originally called moored arrays, was supposed to have gone into the final stages of development in 1977. But development was halted prior to that time. This delay may have been prompted by a breakthrough in sonar sensing technology by the Defense Advanced Research Projects Agency (DARPA). Deployment is now scheduled for the late 1980s. Assistant Navy Secretary Gerald A. Cann recently called RDSS a system "flexible to the needs of the operational users so that surveillance can be provided where and when needed. (Deleted.) RDSS will provide a long life, moored capability with excellent detection capabilities (deleted)."[5] I believe this system will have particular application in the Barents Sea where the Soviet Delta submarines tend to patrol. That is the location of greatest challenge to US ASW efforts.

The Defense Advanced Research Projects Agency was formed in 1958, in reaction to Sputnik, to anticipate technological trends and stay ahead of the Russians. ASW is an important focus of DARPA research and, from looking at DARPA studies, we can fully appreciate the Pentagon's interest in this important element of a disarming first strike. The three basic questions defining DARPA anti-submarine warfare research are:[6]

1. Is a new class of undersea surveillance system possible that could locate submerged submarines at great range with sufficient accuracy to target them?
2. What are the limits of ocean hearing?
3. Can the oceans really be made transparent?

DARPA first became interested in underwater sonic sensing during an exercise in which an existing towed array was pulled around the ocean. It found out that sound patterns in the ocean were more consistent than previously believed and that it was possible to predict sound travel from one time to another. Even though most conditions which affect sound propagation are constantly changing, they do remain the same for short periods of time. Therefore, by working in a series of "shorter time slices," sound travel in the ocean could be forecast much more accurately than previously thought.

Follow-up DARPA exercises took place in 1973 under the rubric of the *Long-Range Propagation Project*. These consisted of making measurements at sea aimed at developing a computer program to predict background noises. The following year, at the Eighth International Acoustics Congress in London, a representative of Bell Laboratories described a model computer program which could predict sonar patterns. This model could integrate known oceanographic information (bottom contours and coastlines) with up-to-date sea state, tide, and current conditions to predict background noises.[7] With the help of this program ambient noise could be cancelled out so that submarine sounds can be located.

As mentioned earlier, the choppiness of the ocean's surface, the thermal layers, and bottom contours all cause sound to be scattered and bent. This has an influence on how long it takes sound to travel from its source to its sensor, and how many echoes will shadow the original sound. The effects of coastlines and bottom topography are relatively simple to program on the computer because they do not change. Sea states, ice packs and ocean traffic, on the other hand, are constantly changing. This type of information would have to be continuously updated in half-mile intervals over the ocean surface. That would undoubtedly require satellite observation. Nevertheless, once acquired, it takes only two minutes of computer running time to reduce this profusion of data to a prediction of sound travel over a 10,000-mile range. It is believed that the Navy's current computer model, used in conjunction with ocean-wide surveillance sensors, would be able to pinpoint a sub well within the sixty-mile radius where escort surveillance forces can take over.

In early 1975 DARPA launched a new program, *Project Seaguard*, whose goal was to optimize acoustic sensing and processing to permit detection and tracking of very quiet submarines with maximum accuracy. By focusing on the water cavitation noises that occur around submarines as they push their way through the ocean, DARPA is addressing the inherent weakness of nuclear-powered submarines which depend heavily on speed. Especially vulnerable to this type of acoustic sensing are the larger ships which are now under construction. Furthermore, in 1977 more stringent requirements were imposed on the submarine laser satellite communications system under development, "as an adaptation of performance projected for Project Seafarer."[8] (Project Seafarer communications system will be discussed in chapter 9.) This could also have a bearing on why RDSS full-scale development was delayed and why RDSS will not be operational until the late 1980s. It may depend on some sort of laser satellite communications signal as part of its covert operations. DARPA's fiscal year 1983 report states that a fully deployed system of submarine laser communications satellites (SLCSATs) would, among other things, "control a broad variety of pre-placed underwater assets, such as minefields and acoustic arrays."[9] A tactical capability will be operationally tested during fiscal years 1984 and 1985.[10]

Being able to predict and cancel out background noises would mark a major leap in sonar technology. Project Seaguard will do that by using various arrangements of mobile and fixed arrays in locations where they can triangulate on specific areas, eliminate blind spots, and analyze signals almost instantaneously. The processing capability needed to simultaneously update all ocean sound patterns, process data from all sensors, and isolate and classify submarine noises far exceeds the capacity of conventional computers. To do the job DARPA has developed the *Illiac–4*—one of the world's most powerful computers. It does the work of sixty-four large computers operating simultaneously. The volume of data which can be processed in a short time is tremendous. The Illiac–4 is located at NASA's Ames Research Center in California, immediately adjacent to Moffett Naval Air Station where the Navy's Acoustic Research Center is situated. The computer is not, however, nuclear survivable—probably not even conventional warfare survivable. It would be safe only until the outbreak of hostilities. Its military importance would apply only to a US first strike.

Dr. George Heilmeier, former director of DARPA, explained in 1976 that the chief goal of Project Seaguard is to develop a surveillance system capable of providing appropriate commanders with timely and accurate information on the operation, location, identification and specific movements of all hostile submarines. Dr. Heilmeier's injection of the Russian threat was probably meant to mollify the ominous implications of Project Seaguard. He said: "If a majority of our submarines were to be kept under surveillance at all times, the vulnerability to preemptive attack would significantly reduce the deterrent effectiveness of our fleet ballistic missile forces."[11] But the outcome of Project Seaguard will allow the US Navy to track Soviet submarines all of the time. It is the Russian missile-launching subs that will cease to be a deterrent to a US first strike.

The effort to predict ocean background noise was originally to be augmented by the information gathering activities of a new series of spacecraft known as *Seasat*. A constellation of six Seasats, equipped with existing sensors, were to have been operational by 1985. But the program, with only one satellite launched, was beset with failures and cancelled in 1978. Following the pattern of Congressional mandates that existing satellites be used to their capacity for additional functions, it now appears that ocean surveillance, meteorological, and other types of spacecraft will carry the sensors to update ASW computers.

The sensors required for this task include various types of radar, passive microwave detectors, and infrared sensors. They will measure wind (velocity and direction), waves (height, shape and length), precise sea surface topography (due to currents, tides and storms), and depressions in the ocean's surface due to gravitational forces. In addition, the sensors will monitor surface temperature, current patterns, ice packs, and ocean traffic. They will provide the spectrum of information needed to update sound travel patterns over 95 percent of the earth's surface every six hours—a small enough slice of time to allow the Navy to keep every Russian sub under surveillance.

Once ocean-wide surveillance has located an enemy submarine within the prescribed radius, the burden falls upon *escort surveillance* to zero-in on the boat for the kill. The oldest escort ASW sensors are sonars mounted below the water line in ships and submarines. These *hull-mounted sonars* are huge devices containing thousands of individual sensors—both active and passive—which operate over various ranges. The active mode may not be appropriate for covert missions but it is effective during noisy operations such as high speed task force maneuvers. It is also the most sensitive and precise.

To supplement hull-mounted sonars the Navy has developed *escort towed arrays* which are pulled behind the ships. Although the arrays of sensors now in use improve the ability to detect and locate submarines, they are cumbersome devices. Also, if towed too fast the noise they generate tends to mask the sounds of submarines; and they add drag to prevent the towing ship from reaching top speed. A new model of escort towed array with better hydrodynamic design became operational in 1980.

Despite advances in hull-mounted sonars and escort towed arrays, if a submarine is below the thermal layers of water its sound will bounce back down, rendering it immune to detection from the surface. To overcome that problem the US Navy now has a *variable depth sonar*. It is towed at the end of a 600–foot cable and has controllable vanes to make it dive below the thermal layers.

Another family of escort sonar, the *sonobuoys*, is used by ASW patrol planes and helicopters to pinpoint submarines. They are hydrophones (microphones used to pick up underwater sounds) which are dropped into the water by the aircraft. They come in a wide selection of types: directional and omnidirectional, passive and active, short-range and long-range. Passive sonobuoy cannisters are approximately five inches in diameter and a yard long but a new dwarf type allows three to be put in a single cannister that size. Active sonobuoys are slightly larger and are used to pinpoint the submarine for attack after it has been found and identified. The sonobuoy antenna floats on the surface of the ocean to transmit acoustic information back to the aircraft while a probe sinks as deep as 800 feet to get below the thermal layers.

Before concluding this discussion of escort sensors several nonacoustic devices should be mentioned. In addition to the usual *radar* which is quick to spot an antenna poking above the water, and *passive radiation receivers* which pick up and classify signals from other vessels, ASW aircraft also use *infrared sensors* to measure ocean surface temperature differences in the order of hundredths of a degree. Local variations that do not conform to the general pattern, as determined by satellite observations, could be caused by a submarine churning up the thermal layers or, conceivably, by the hotter water released from the cooling system of the submarine's reactor. In addition, biological tracks of dying micro-organisms in the submarine's wake can also be a telltale sign. The bigger the submarine, the more likely a hydrodynamic disturbance or biological track can be detected.

ASW airplanes and helicopters also use a device called the *magnetic anomaly detector* to spot deviations from the earth's magnetic field. A large steel submarine would, of course, cause a considerable variation in the lines of magnetic flux. Scripps Institute of Oceanography has developed instruments which have made it possible to chart the total magnetic field at sea. A map of that field can be stored digitally in a computer to compare with what the detector picks up so that anomalies can be isolated. Those anomalies are in turn compared with known magnetic "signatures" of various submarines which are also stored in the computer's memory. In that fashion the final identification is accomplished. Present magnetic anomaly detectors, however, have a short range and, although remarkably effective in guiding aircraft into position for the kill, they are only useful for final pinpointing and identification.

There is evidence, however, that new strides in magnetic sensing are taking place. When Assistant Secretary of the Navy for Research and Development H. Tyler Marcy testified on magnetic detectors in early 1976, he said:

> We do have one thing which is being carried forward right now which is kind of exciting in this area, and that is a result of really new technology, the use of (censored) magnetic detectors. Our new magnetic anomaly detectors have an intrinsic design factor which is like an order of magnitude [ten times] better than those we have used heretofore. And we expect that that will translate into an operational effectiveness of magnetic detection

> (censored) that we encountered. And that is going forward from one of our research programs into active experimentation in the next period.[12]

More recently, in his fiscal year 1979 posture statement as Undersecretary of Defense for Research and Engineering, Dr. William Perry described a new "magnetic gradiometer." He said: "By employing magnetic field detectors with considerably improved sensitivity, the Navy has demonstrated a new magnetometer that can measure magnetic field gradients for submarine detection."[13] Soon after that, new "superconducting magnetic sensors" for future airborne sub hunters were described in a classified briefing at the Naval Coastal Systems Laboratory in Panama City, Florida.[14] Of course the details of that "classified" presentation are not available to the general public—only to the industry representatives who make a business of constructing such weapons systems.

All of the escort ASW sensors which we have been discussing are intricately interconnected through a network of shore, ship and aircraft computers. In addition to sonic "signatures" (characteristics) of submarines, these computers' memories also store radar and magnetic signatures of both friendly and hostile vessels along with a host of other significant data. Reference systems to tell where any sensor is relative to others have been developed to enhance the precise pinpointing of submarines. Television-type screens display the sensed information while "data links" interconnect computer activities between aircraft, ships and shore stations.

New advances in laser optics are also being applied to ASW. *ORICS* (Optical Ranging, Identification and Communications System) is a laser system used not only to find hostile subs but to communicate with friendly ones.* It operates in the blue-green wavelength of the visible light spectrum. That seems to be the tuning that allows maximum penetration of seawater. An ASW helicopter tested ORICS off the Florida Keys in late 1976 and was reportedly successful in locating a submarine.

The development of ORICS has sparked speculation on the use of lasers for open-ocean surveillance. In the mid-1960s DARPA conducted

---

*A laser can be simply described as a concentrated beam of coherent light that requires considerable energy to get started. The word *laser* is an acronym for Light Amplification by Stimulated Emission of Radiation.

a study called *Deep Look* to address some basic obstacles to light travel through the ocean. Its goal was to define the practical limits to underwater imaging and then demonstrate a rudimentary system that would perform near those limits. DARPA discovered that the depth of ocean penetration of the laser developed was limited mainly by the power of the beam.

On July 23, 1972 the first *Landsat* earth resources satellite was put in orbit. Ostensibly a tool to help solve the world's food and energy problems by estimating how much wheat, barley, corn and rice is growing around the globe, Landsat also photographed scenes of military interest such as the Chinese missile launch complex at Shuang-Cheng-Tzu and the Soviet bases at Kapustin Yar and Plesetsk.

Skylab was launched the following year and was subsequently occupied by three different space crews. Both Landsat and Skylab viewed the earth's surface with a variety of color frequencies and some of their photographs show the ocean bottom in shallow waters near the coast. These pictures were made using a laser scanner operating close to the blue-green wavelength that gives maximum seawater penetration.

In 1976, I received a letter from a colleague working in the satellite communications field that noted the new advances in laser photography of the ocean floor. I will quote several passages: ". . . refinement of tracking has given the Navy another fine tune focusing capability for precision control of short duration (2 week) laser camera orbital satellites. Camera angle (side looking) . . . was the breakthrough that scored the success of the Navy mission to photograph the ocean floor. It's real. It exists. I have seen the photographs . . . The laser photo that I saw was tuned to the frequency spectrum of seawater. As such it simply nulled out seawater, leaving exposed the ocean floor . . ." The letter went on to explain that given the ability to photograph the ocean bottom, it would also be possible to detect a submarine.

That letter ties in with a statement made by former Under Secretary of Defense William Perry in early 1980. He said that research into nonacoustic means of detecting submarines includes methods of remotely measuring ocean depths and determining the presence of objects under the surface.[15]

The placement of infrared sensors on spacecraft or high-flying aircraft capable of spotting the thermal wake of submarines may provide another means of tracking submarines. According to *Air Force Magazine*, space-borne infrared sensors can tell the difference between submarines in port that have their reactors in a standby mode and those that are running up their reactors to get under way.[16] Defense analyst Norman Freedman of the Hudson Institute predicts: "Probably the ultimate in remote ASW surveillance system will, in time, be satellite-based and employ some type of nonacoustic sensor. Nonacoustic sensors, such as those which home in on the thermal wake of a submarine, have been on the drawing boards for a long time."[17] DARPA's fiscal year 1983 report said that it had an intensive effort aimed at "submarine detection based on observable changes in the ocean environment caused by recent passage of a target."[18]

As can be seen, sensor development has taken sinister leaps since its proof test on the automated battlefields of Southeast Asia. They have now been refined for use in homing maneuvering warheads, as the eyes for navigating and targeting various weapons, and in many other applications to be discussed in later chapters. Anti-submarine warfare has reaped its share of this technology. The main obstacle to simultaneously sinking all Soviet missile-carrying submarines is the ability to find them, identify them, and shadow them. Sensors in development will soon make this possible. Let's take a look at a likely scenario for such a search and destroy mission.

After a Soviet submarine has been detected and identified by open-ocean surveillance, a patrol aircraft, ship or attack sub is sent to pinpoint it and stay on its tail. Should hostilities erupt between the two superpowers, US anti-submarine warfare forces would then be set up for the kill. Weapons for that purpose are abundant.

When thinking of sinking submarines, the first weapons that usually come to mind are torpedoes and depth charges. The Navy has two species of torpedoes for use against submerged boats—the classical type launched from underwater by submarines and a smaller version which can be dropped from aircraft or fired from surface ships. The two principal submarine-launched ASW torpedoes are designated the *Mark–45* and the *Mark–48*. The Mark–45 is more commonly called ASTOR (an acronym for Anti-Submarine Torpedo). Weighing 2,400 pounds and packing a nuclear warhead, it can dive deep and fast over a range of ten miles. It is an older torpedo, though, and is being replaced by the Mark–48.

The 3,600–pound Mark–48, half again the weight of ASTOR, is rapidly becoming the submarine's principal weapon for sinking other subs. It has a conventional warhead and the flexibility of also being an anti-surface ship weapon. It finds its way to the target by "homing in" on the sound of the ship or submarine. A total procurement of 2,800 Mark–48s was reached in 1979.

A *Mark–48 Advanced Capability* (ADCAP) modification program was started in 1980 to update the acoustic homing and control electronics so the torpedo can go farther and dive deeper. ADCAP will start becoming part of the fleet's inventory in 1986.

The main ship-launched and aircraft-launched torpedo is the lightweight *Mark–46*. About 3,000 are now in service. The Mark–46 weighs only 580 pounds and can dive as deep as 2,500 feet. Its range is twenty miles and it can travel at speeds in excess of fifty miles per hour. If it misses the submarine on the first pass it can turn around for another try. It, also, has a nonnuclear warhead.

An improved version of the Mark–46 started becoming operational in 1980 as the *Near-Term Improvement Program* (NEARTIP). This program was begun in 1978 to develop kits to modify existing torpedoes so they are more resistant to enemy countermeasures that try to spoof its acoustic homing device. NEARTIP will also endow the torpedoes with the ability to identify their target from a longer distance.

Development of an *Advanced Light Weight Torpedo* (ALWT) is also underway. It will improve on NEARTIP modifications and, in addition, be faster, deeper diving, and have a longer range. It will also have a more powerful warhead—still conventional. It will also employ the REGAL technology (described in Chapter 5 under the ASW/SOW cruise missile) that integrates an acoustic sensing array and a small computer into the weapon. The ALWT may also have a new means of delivery because the Navy is reported to be experimenting with remotely piloted drone aircraft to carry torpedoes. Such a system would allow ships to reach enemy submarines from greater distances without jeopardizing expensive aircraft and their crews.

Two other major anti-submarine weapons are depth bombs and mines. Today's depth bombs are a far cry from the World War II vintage "ash cans" that were thrown overboard with Y-guns from the poopdeck of destroyers. The two principal ones are the *Mark–57* and the *Mark–101*. Both are nuclear and can be dropped from anti-submarine patrol planes or helicopters. There are also applications where they are delivered by rockets which shall be discussed below.

Mines are receiving increased attention from the Navy. The intense effort to mine Haiphong Harbor during the waning days of direct US involvement in Vietnam served as proof test for the offensive use of mines. In the words of Dr. William Perry, former Undersecretary of

Defense for Research and Engineering: "Often thought of as a defensive weapon, the mine can actually be a highly effective instrument of offensive sea power . . ."[19] Today we have mines for various water depths as well as mobile mines.

CAPTOR (enCAPsulated TORpedo) is an acronym for a deep water anti-submarine smart mine. It is reported to be useful to a depth of 2,500 feet. This weapon, now in production and expected to reach a rate of 600 per year by 1984, consists of a Mark–46 torpedo fit into an 11–foot long mine casing with acoustic sensors and a miniature computer. CAPTOR listens to the ocean traffic passing by and, when the sound heard matches the sonic signature of a hostile submarine, the Mark–46 is released. CAPTOR then floats a code buoy to the surface to send a cryptic message reporting time of release and the serial number of the mine.

The purpose of CAPTOR is to bottle up the Soviet submarine fleet. According to *Jane's Weapons Systems*, US operational plans include sowing CAPTOR mines in the narrow seas between Greenland and Britain to attack Soviet subs as they pass to and from their operational stations.[20] Intelligence documents reportedly indicate that a mere 500 CAPTORs would fully seed that passage.[21] Dr. Perry summed up the projected significance of this mine: "CAPTOR will kill more submarines per dollar than any other ASW system."[22]

The US Navy has not yet been successful, in spite of several tries, in developing a mine for medium water depths such as on the continental shelves. It is currently investigating a variant of CAPTOR for use in some of these areas. It is also investigating other alternatives including a cooperative mine development program with the British Navy.

Quickstrike is a family of mines designed for shallow areas of the ocean such as parts of the North Sea and along the skirts of the Norwegian Sea area. Two models are bottom mines converted from Air Force demolition bombs.* A third member of that family—a 2,000 pound mine—is a completely new development effort.

The Submarine-Launched Mobile Mine (SLMM) is a self-propelled weapon which can be released from a submarine's torpedo tube about five miles from where it is to be planted.† It then propels itself to the desired location and sinks to the bottom to listen for its prey. The

---

*Quickstrike Mark-62 is a converted Mark-82 bomb and is in production. Quickstrike Mark-64 is in or close to production as a modified Mark-84 bomb. The new-development Quickstrike is designated Mark-65.

†SLMM is a converted Mark-37 torpedo.

SLMM can be aimed into waters too shallow for a submarine to safely enter and too dangerous for ships or aircraft. It is especially designed to seed areas during covert operations. It is now in production.

Last in the family of anti-submarine weapons are the ASW missiles—or stand-off weapons. *ASROC* (Anti-Submarine ROCket) is probably the oldest. Weighing half a ton, it can be launched either day or night in any weather from surface ships. Its warhead is either a nuclear depth bomb or, on later versions, a Mark–46 torpedo. These are boosted on their way by a rocket motor which drops off when it burns out. The torpedo or depth bomb continues on in a ballistic arc. Before falling into the water the torpedo is slowed by a parachute and is activated when it contacts the water. If the warhead is a nuclear depth bomb it will explode at a prescribed depth. ASROC has a range of six miles and is the primary ASW stand-off weapon for frigates, destroyers and some cruisers.

SUBROC (SUBmarine ROCket) is the current ASW stand-off weapon for submarines. Four to six of these four-ton missiles are usually carried on each of the Navy's attack submarines. When an enemy sub is within SUBROC's thirty-mile range, the flight trajectory is calculated by the attack sub's computer and fed into the missile before it is launched. SUBROC is then ejected from the torpedo tube and the rocket motor ignites. A swivel nozzle tips the nose up causing it to broach the surface. The rocket then accelerates the missile toward its target and separates when it burns out. The nuclear depth bomb continues coasting toward the hostile submarine, reenters the water, and explodes at a prescribed depth. SUBROC's booster motor is the forerunner of the rocket used to boost Tomahawk cruise missiles to altitude.

A replacement for the obsolete ASROC and SUBROC ASW rockets is the Tomahawk cruise missile variant called the Anti-Submarine Warfare Stand-Off Weapon (ASW/SOW). It was described in Chapter 5 and will have the advanced lightweight torpedo with the REGAL technology for a weapon. Being a cruise missile it will have the advantage of being able to release a sonobuoy pattern, to pinpoint the sub's location and confirm that it is hostile, before releasing the torpedo.

The third and final portion of the ASW suite are the variety of vehicles which carry the sensors and fire the weapons. They can be divided into three categories—*airborne, subsurface* and *surface*—and will be discussed in that order.

Anti-submarine patrol aircraft operate from both land and ships. The *P–3 Orion* is the land-based ASW airplane. With four turboprop engines and a crew of twelve, it can fly 1,400 nautical miles to its station, patrol for four hours, and then return to its base without refueling.[23] With in-flight refueling Orion can remain four hours on station 2,400 nautical miles from its base.[24] The US Navy now operates over 300 of these airplanes which take turns following Russia's missile-carrying submarines around the oceans of the world.

Orion carries a full compliment of ASW sensors: radar, passive microwave receiver, infrared sensor, magnetic anomoly detector, and many sonobuoys. There are 52 loaded sonobuoy launch tubes in the bottom of the aircraft plus extra buoys on board.

Orion's ASW weapons inventory includes eight Mark–46 torpedoes and eight Mark–57 nuclear depth bombs. Two Mark–101 nuclear depth bombs can be substituted for four of the torpedoes and, if desired, the airplane can also carry six mines weighing up to 2,000 pounds each. The latest addition is the Harpoon missile which will give Orion added clout against submarines which surface to launch cruise missiles.

All of these sensors and weapons, plus navigation instruments and automatic pilot, are digitally interconnected and highly automated. When the sensors pick up a submarine it is instantly pinpointed and classified. The computer plots the desired flight path and steers the airplane to the next point where the submarine can again be contacted. If the sub is hostile, the computer selects and fires a torpedo or depth bomb. Then a camera controlled by the computer photographs the results with each sequential picture identified according to time. Of course the pilot and crew can override the computer but this description gives you an idea of how systematically the killing of a submarine can be executed. Even the Orion's patrol flight plan is recorded on a cassette tape and inserted into the computer prior to takeoff. Orion is expected to remain in service into the 1990s and by the turn of the decade all of the planes will be the latest P–3C model.

The Navy would like people to believe that Orion is only meant to enhance escort ASW activities. In 1978, however, then Defense Secretary Brown acknowledged that the P–3 is "well suited for vectored intercept missions in conjunction with undersea surveillance systems."[25] That means it can take directions from ocean-wide surveillance arrays to be guided to the vicinity of a Soviet submarine. Navy studies show that Orion P–3s, in conjunction with undersea surveillance sensors, would make the largest contribution to US anti-submarine warfare capabilities prior to and during a major conflict with the Soviets.[26] Secretary Brown said this combination would be the most effective rapid-response system to ocean-wide ASW, particularly prior to hostilities.[27]

Now to move on to the carrier-based anti-submarine planes which are also combing the oceans. Twelve of the fleet's aircraft carriers have a squadron of ten *S–3A Viking* ASW airplanes assigned to them and they can be shuttled from carrier to carrier as the need arises. The full complement of 187 Vikings was attained in 1978 but the Navy is considering starting production again in 1986 or 1987 to complement new aircraft carriers. In addition, existing Vikings are being improved to an S–3B configuration. The first of these updates are scheduled for service in 1985.

Viking is a twin-engine, four-seat jet which can patrol for seven hours—longer if refueled in flight. It carries essentially the same sensors and weapons as Orion but not as many because it is smaller. The S–3B model will have improved sensors and will be equipped with harpoon missiles. Vikings also have an automatic landing system whereby the carrier's radar can control the plane's automatic pilot. They are just one step away from a pilotless aircraft.

The third type of aircraft used in anti-submarine warfare is the helicopter. One variety is known as the *Light Airborne Multipurpose System* (LAMPS). LAMPS helicopters operate off of frigates, destroyers, and cruisers. Their purpose is to extend the reach of those surface ships in their ASW role. The present LAMPS–1 force consists of about 98 *SH–2 Seasprite* helicopters. They carry sonobuoys, radar, and a passive microwave receiver as well as a magnetic anomoly detector and two Mark–46 torpedoes. They can spend an hour on station at a distance of forty miles from their ship. To increase that time or range they would have to substitute extra fuel tanks for one or both torpedoes.

The limitation in range, endurance and sensor processing of the Seasprites will be overcome by LAMPS–3—the *SH–60B Seahawk* helicopters—which will start becoming operational in fiscal year 1984. The Navy presently plans to buy 204 Seahawks.* They will weigh 19,000 pounds each—half again as much as the Seasprite—and will be able to stay on station for two hours at a distance of 100 miles from their ship. Besides carrying two Mark–46 or ALWT torpedoes they will also be equipped with more sensitive instruments and an improved data link

*LAMPS-3 helicopters were originally presented as a replacement for LAMPS-1. But now, as has happened with so many other weapons systems, the new will be used to supplement the old.

for interconnecting computer operations with its ship or other ASW aircraft. By 1984 the Navy hopes to have 154 ships capable of carrying LAMPS helicopters. The newest ones will be able to accommodate two or more of these aircraft.

Another type of ASW helicopter is the *SH–3 Sea King* which operates from aircraft carriers. Each carrier has six Sea Kings which carry Mark–46 torpedoes and Mark–57 depth bombs. Sea Kings now have improved navigation systems, improved power-plants, and on-board acoustic processing of sonobuoy information. Development has started on a LAMPS–3 derivative to replace the Sea Kings. Procurement is planned for fiscal 1986.

The ASW aircraft of the future may be *V/STOL*—Vertical/Short Take-Off and Land airplanes. V/STOL, which have been studied for use in the 1990s, can land and hover like a helicopter but also fly like a jet. They will provide what the military calls a quick reaction and kill capability against hostile subs. The Marines are now using V/STOLs—Britain's "Harriers"—but not for ASW. Twenty-three US companies responded, however, to the Navy's request for quotations and information on what would be required to build a US V/STOL airplane.

The first generation of the Navy V/STOL, designated Type–A, is in development. Designed to travel at subsonic speeds it could start becoming operational in the 1990s to replace (supplement?) the carrier-based Vikings. A subsonic Type–B will follow but it is not slated for anti-submarine work. Still farther down the line, a Type-C may become available to replace the LAMPS helicopters some time after the year 2000.

The Navy could invest over a billion dollars in V/STOL work by 1992, which is an indication that this concept is not being taken lightly. As Vice Admiral Forrest S. Petersen once said as commander of the Naval Air Systems Command: V/STOL is "one of the biggest technical jumps undertaken by the command in recent years."[28]

To complete the record a brief mention should be made of B–52 bombers. The range of that aircraft makes them well suited for ocean surveillance. Since 1975, SAC B–52 crews have been trained in that area and have performed that mission. In addition, B–52s are certified to lay acoustic and magnetic mines and can do that job accurately. It is presumed they could also put the rapidly deployable surveillance system buoys into position.

Turning now to subsurface anti-sub platforms, we need only consider *attack submarines*. Although the strategic ballistic missile submarines also have sonar and torpedoes, they are mainly carried for defensive purposes. It is the attack subs which are designed to hunt and kill other submarines. By mid–1982 the US Navy had 91 nuclear-powered attack subs.* The most modern of these are of the Los Angeles class of which 39 have been ordered and 17 commissioned. During the five-year period ending with fiscal year 1987 the Pentagon plans to order another 17. The goal is to eventually have at least 100 nuclear-powered hunter-killer attack submarines.

Hunter-killer submarines use a very intricate hull-mounted sonar in their nose and a special towed array. Of course they do not require a variable depth sonar because they are already below the thermal layers. The attack sub's ASW weapons are torpedoes and SUBROC missiles but they can also lay mines and will be able to place acoustic sensor buoys in clandestine locations for area surveillance. Attack submarines can either operate as part of a carrier task force or work alone to conduct search operations. One of their striking advantages is their ability to enter hostile waters that are untenable for other ASW forces. Because of their unique capacity for covert operations the nuclear-powered attack sub has often been called the most effective element of the varied ASW forces. Attack subs are planned for conducting offensive operations in heavily defended waters near or in Soviet territory.[29] A former crewman of a fast attack submarine explained to me how they entered the Barents Sea and got close enough to a Soviet Delta missile-launching sub to photograph its keel without being detected.

In terms of surface ships, virtually every naval vessel is equipped with sonar. About a hundred frigates, destroyers and cruisers carry Seasprite helicopters and, as mentioned above, all operational aircraft carriers have Viking airplanes along with Sea King helicopters. These forces are not inclusive because profound improvements are taking place.

The Perry class of *guided missile frigate* went into production in the early 1970s. Frigates are the smallest type of warship and have the advantage of being simple and cheap to build. Fifty of the Perry class were originally planned but then the prospects jumped to around seventy. There are 12 in the FY '83–'87 five-year defense plan. Having a speed of 32 miles per hour, these frigates use a hull-mounted sonar supplemented by a tactical towed array and a variable

*Including ex-Polaris ballistic missile submarines converted to attack subs.

depth sonar. Their weapons include Mark–46 torpedoes and they can operate two ASW helicopters.

By mid–1982 the Navy had 84 destroyers and 27 cruisers with more under construction. The FY '83–'87 five-year ship-building plan requests authorization for another 7 destroyers and 18 cruisers. These ships also use hull-mounted sonars supplemented by a tactical towed array and a variable depth sonar. Besides torpedoes they can also launch ASROC and, eventually, the ASW/SOW. Many of these ships can carry two to four LAMPS helicopters and the later designs will accommodate the Type-A V/STOL.

Before completing our survey of the conventional ASW craft, mention should be made of the glorified tugboats that tow SURTASS sensor arrays around the ocean at 4 miles per hour. Designated T-AGOS and AGOS, these ships will stay on station 90 days at a time and be able to travel 3,000 nautical miles (in addition to the 90–day watch) at a transit speed of 13 miles per hour. The first of an estimated fleet of 18 of these vessels was requested in fiscal year 1979.

Beyond these conventional craft the Navy is considering several exotic models for possible deployment in the future. These include the *Surface Effect Ship* (SES) and the *Advanced Hydrofoil*. SES is the fastest vehicle that can be envisioned operating on the ocean's surface. It rides an air cushion over the top of the water rather than having to push its way through. Two 100–ton SESs have already been built and successfully tested. One of them has established the Navy speed record of 103.3 miles per hour. The Navy has also fired missiles from these vessels while they were clipping along at seventy miles per hour.

On December 9, 1976, the Navy awarded a contract to build a frigate-size SES that was expected to be operational in the late 1980s and be capable of speeds between 70 and 80 miles per hour. In early 1980, however, the SES program was cancelled by Congress. Development still proceeds, however, under the Army program for a SES amphibious landing barge.

One serious disadvantage of conventional ships is that with a top speed of 30–35 miles per hour they cannot outpace nuclear subs. If they slow up to take a good sonar reading the sub is soon out of reach. The SES, however, opens new avenues to submarine pursuit. It can race quickly in the suspected direction of the enemy sub and then occasionally stop dead in the water for eight or nine minutes to lower a powerful sonar below the thermal layers. Then the SES can reel in the sonar and make a high-speed dash in pursuit until it has to stop again to take another precise reading. This "sprint and drift" tactic, as it is called, would not only be useful for chasing hostile subs but also would allow the SES to keep up with a fast moving task force while performing routine escort surveillance.

Hydrofoils are another means of skimming swiftly over the water. The first 235–ton patrol hydrofoil was launched on November 9, 1975. Patrol hydrofoils are a NATO project and were not originally intended for ASW work although the Navy seems to have reevaluated their capability in that role.

However, the Navy is also eager to develop *Advanced Hydrofoils* that will weigh in the neighborhood of a thousand tons (about a third the size of a frigate) and travel 45–55 miles per hour. While the hydrofoil is not as speedy as the SES it would be capable of the "sprint and drift" tactic and would be able to operate in rougher seas.

Although a severe storm may churn several thousand square miles of ocean area, a few feet below the surface the water is relatively calm. Hydrofoils take advantage of that phenomenon. In its conventional operation the Advanced Hydrofoil ship would sit in the water like any other. But when high speed travel is needed the foils would be lowered fore and aft and the ship would pick up speed until the hull lifts out of the water and the vessel is "foilborne." The foils do not skim the top of the water but rather remain a few feet below the surface where the water is calmer. In this fashion they support the ship's weight while racing through the water, in much the same way that airplane wings support an aircraft. This technique will allow the Advanced Hydrofoil to traverse rougher seas than the SES which rides like a bubble over the surface.

In comparing US and Soviet anti-submarine activity, what is immediately apparent is that the Soviets tend to concentrate their efforts closer to their own territory and shipping lanes. They apparently have no open-ocean ASW forces.[30] Meanwhile, the US has a commanding lead in ASW capabilities because it possesses a significant technological advantage in ASW sensors, ASW weapons, and submarine quieting.[31] Former Defense Secretary Brown noted that although Russian subs are becoming quieter and harder to detect, "our Navy has maintained and, in some cases, even widened our technological lead."[32] The Soviets even lag the US in the more traditional acoustic sensing technology.[33] Finally, because of its two-ocean coastline which provides easy access to sea lanes, and its large network of overseas bases and allies, the US enjoys a decided geographical advantage.[34]

Proponents for continued and increased arms production have circulated reports of the new Soviet "Alpha" submarine with its titanium alloy hull which allegedly can outrun and outdive the best US submarines. Former Defense Secretary Harold Brown affirmed that the Alpha boat can probably operate at greater depths and is faster than other Soviet subs but is noisy by US standards.[35] He went on to say that its mission is not clear but that it will probably fulfill the same function as Soviet Victor class SSNs.* In this regard he said:

> The Soviets continue their efforts to develop an anti-submarine warfare capability both against alliance SSBNs and in protection of their own SSBNs. However, the performance of their ASW forces is improving only gradually, and remains substantially below that of comparable US forces. The Victor class nuclear-powered attack submarine (SSN) remains the most capable Soviet ASW platform. At present, neither it nor other currently deployed Soviet ASW platforms constitute a significant threat to our SSBNs.[36]

Clearly, as with other Soviet systems, the Alpha sub is being overplayed by weapons advocates to justify their position. The final clincher to illustrate Soviet ASW inferiority comes from Admiral Hyman G. Rickover, commonly known as the father of the nuclear navy:

> Admiral Hyman G. Rickover is quoted as saying that despite the 1,500 sixty-day patrols that have been carried out by the 41 US Polaris [and Poseidon] submarines since they were begun in 1960, *the Soviet Union has yet to detect even one of them*. He told Congress that the SLBM subs are probably the greatest means the US has to deter war. The Navy has claimed, on the other hand, that it can keep track of Soviet SLBM submarines thanks to electronic surveillance and the noisiness of Soviet craft.[37] (emphasis mine)

More recently, in March 1982, Vice Admiral N.R. Thunman, Deputy Chief of Naval Operations for Submarine Warfare, told Congress:

> Turning now to the program that has the highest priority in the Navy, our strategic submarine program. Through 1981 we have conducted more than 2,000 strategic deterrent patrols, and I am pleased to report that our fleet ballistic missile submarine today is

*SSN is the Navy designation for a nuclear-powered attack submarine.

> just as secure and invulnerable as it was when [the] *George Washington* went to sea in 1960.[38]

This US advantage is further enhanced by NATO, ANZUS and Asian allies who also have elaborate ASW forces. Rear Admiral John Grove of Britain's Ministry of Defense, for instance, claims that his country detects every Soviet submarine in the area and that the Soviets detect no British subs.[39]

To be able to keep track of Soviet submarines the US Navy engages in a wide range of ASW activities which not only upgrade the various elements but systematically and coherently integrate them. It is this "achievement of mutually reinforcing relationships among the individual elements, rather than the incremental improvements to particular programs, that accounts for the rapid overall increase in ASW effectiveness."[40] In this regard, ASW programs are fulfilling the goal laid out over a decade and a half ago by then Secretary of Defense Robert McNamara:

> Our principal active defense capability against submarine-launched missiles lies in our system for detecting, tracking, and destroying the submarines before they can launch their missiles.[41]

McNamara's aspiration in that statement is synonymous with a first strike capability against Soviet submarines and illustrates the qualitative difference between US and USSR anti-submarine warfare. The open-ocean ability to locate and track subsurface craft has aggressive connotations because if that can be accomplished those submarines could be summarily destroyed at the appropriate signal. The implication of such a US capability was raised by a US Library of Congress report:

> . . .If the United States achieves a disarming first strike capability against Soviet ICBMs, and also develops an ASW capability that together with attacks on Naval facilities could practically negate the Soviet SSBN force, then the strategic balance as it has come to be broadly defined and accepted would no longer be stable.[42]

That report then goes on to warn that in this regard "*current trends in US ASW programs should fall under close scrutiny*."[43] (emphasis added) In spite of that warning, US anti-submarine warfare development programs continue unabated. It is obvious that America is not providing the scrutiny prescribed. But how do the Soviets view this activity?

President Reagan's *Arms Control Impact Statements* provide a clue—saying that "Soviet perceptions of the potential success of the US ASW development programs could . . . lead to their taking political and/or military actions which could be destabilizing in a political or a strategic military sense."[44]

What is the significance of this "potential success?" What actions might the Soviets take? How would they be destabilizing? These are questions Americans should be asking. And then they should be pressing to remove the problem.

Notes

1. James Coates, "Oceans Bristling With Deadly Weapons," *Chicago Tribune*, 4 December 1977, p. 21. Also see "The High Stakes Business of Antisub Warfare," *Business Week*, 8 May 1978, p. 50B.
2. *Department of Defense Appropriations for 1979*, hearings before the House Appropriations Committee, 15 March 1978, Part 6, p. 97.
3. "Scoop & Scuttle," *Sea Power*, August 1979, p. 4.
4. *United States Military Posture For Fiscal Year 1983*, prepared by the Organization of the Joint Chiefs of Staff, p. 107.
5. *Department of Defense Appropriations, Fiscal Year 1982*, hearings before the Senate Appropriations Committee, 30 April 1981, Part 4, p. 589.
6. *Hearings on Military Posture and HR 11500, Fiscal Year 1977*, before the House Armed Services Committee, 1 March 1976, Part 5, p. 1138.
7. See Hussain Farooq, "No Place To Hide," *New Scientist*, 15 August 1974.
8. *Department of Defense Authorization for Appropriations for Fiscal Year 1981*, hearings before the Senate Armed Services Committee, 5 March 1980, Part 5, pp. 2741-2742.
9. *Fiscal Year 1983 Research and Development Program; A Summary Description*, 30 March 1982, pp. III-16 & III-17.
10. Ibid, p. III-17.
11. *Hearings on Military Posture and HR 11500*, op. cit., 1 March 1976, Part 5, p. 1164.
12. *Fiscal Year 1977 Authorization for Military Procurement, Research and Development, and Active Duty, Selected Reserve and Civilian Personnel Strengths*, hearings before the Senate Armed Services Committee, 2 February 1976, Part 6, p. 3321.
13. *The Fiscal Year 1979 Department of Defense Program for Research,*

Development and Acquisition, a statement by William J. Perry, Under Secretary of Defense for Research and Engineering, 1 February 1978, p. VIII-24.

14. *Aviation Week and Space Technology*, 6 March 1978, p. 53.
15. *The Fiscal Year 1981 Department of Defense Program For Research, Development and Acquisition*, a statement by William J. Perry, Under Secretary of Defense for Research and Engineering, 1 February 1980, p. V-9.
16. *Air Force Magazine*, August 1979, p. 20.
17. Norman Freedman, "The Navy's RDT&E Program," *Sea Power*, April 1980, p. 52.
18. *Fiscal year 1983 Research and Development Program*, op. cit., p. III-29.
19. *The Fiscal Year 1979 Department of Defense Program for Research, Development and Acquisition*, op. cit., p. VI-87.
20. *Jane's Weapons Systems*, 1974-75.
21. James Coates, "Oceans Bristling With Deadly Weapons," op. cit., p. 21.
22. *The Fiscal Year 1979 Department of Defense Program for Research, Development and Acquisition*, op. cit., p. VI-87.
23. *Department of Defense Annual Report Fiscal Year 1979*, by Harold Brown, Secretary of Defense, 2 February 1978, p. 180.
24. Ibid.
25. Cited in "The High Stakes Business of Antisub Warfare," op. cit. Also, *Evaluation of Fiscal Year 1979 Arms Control Impact Statements: Toward More Informed Congressional Participation in National Security Policy-making*, a report prepared by the Congressional Research Service of the Library of Congress, 3 January 1979, pp. 110-111.
26. *Department of Defense Annual Report Fiscal Year 1981*, by Harold Brown, Secretary of Defense, 29 January 1980, p. 176.
27. *Department of Defense Annual Report Fiscal Year 1982*, by Harold Brown, Secretary of Defense, 19 January 1981, p. 159.
28. Clarence A. Robinson, Jr., "Navy Goals Keyed To Readiness," *Aviation Week and Space Technology*, 31 January 1977, p. 35.
29. *Evaluation of Fiscal Year 1979 Arms Control Impact Statements*, op. cit. p. 115.
30. Ibid, p. 104.
31. Ibid, p. 107.
32. Cited by Joel S. Wit, "Advances in Antisubmarine Warfare," *Scientific American*, February 1981, p. 35.
33. *Fiscal Year 1981 Arms Control Impact Statements*, May 1980, p. 359.
34. *Evaluation of Fiscal Year 1979 Arms Control Impact Statements*, op. cit., p. 107.
35. *Department of Defense Annual Report Fiscal year 1981*, op. cit., p. 103.

36. Ibid, p. 82.
37. *National Defense,* publication of the American Defense Preparedness Association, July-August 1978.
38. *Hearings on Military Posture and HR 5968, Fiscal Year 1983,* before the House Armed Service Committee, 11 March 1982, Part 4, p.232.
39. Cited in "British Say Soviet Lags In Sub Detection," *Baltimore Sun*, 31 December 1980, p. 4.
40. *Evaluation of Fiscal Year 1979 Arms Control Impact Statements*, op. cit., p. 112.
41. *Military Posture and HR 9637*, hearings before the House Armed Services Committee, 1964, pp. 7018-7019.
42. *Evaluation of Fiscal Year 1979 Arms Control Impact Statements*, op. cit., p. 119.
43. Ibid.
44. *Fiscal year 1982 Arms Control Impact Statements*, February 1981, p. 362.

MISSILE AND BOMBER DEFENSE

There is only one good, knowledge, and one evil, ignorance.

—*Socrates*

Engineers have a rigid rule which guides their work. It is generally called Murphy's Law and, simply stated, it says: "If something can go wrong, it will!" Although one may exercise extreme care in design to insure against every conceivable malfunction, the odds are that the first time a mechanism or system is used it won't work properly. That is why all development programs include extensive test plans. Murphy's Law also applies to the first strike machinery which cannot be tested until it is actually used. The most likely consequence of some failure would be that a few Soviet missiles would be left undamaged and able to retaliate against the United States. To prevent damage to American cities those weapons would have to be shot down before they arrive. Pentagon planners have not overlooked that need—defense against ballistic missiles and bombers figures prominently in their weapons programs. Before he resigned in 1977, Defense Secretary Donald Rumsfeld asserted: "I believe it is time to give US strategic defense programs increased priority."[1]

During the early years of the nuclear age, bombers were the only strategic delivery system. Consequently, during the 1950s both superpowers started developing systems to warn of and intercept bomber attacks. The United States and Canada set up the *Distant Early Warning Line* (DEWLINE) radars along the 70th Parallel and the *Pinetree Line* in mid-Canada. F-101 and F-106 interceptors were deployed to attack any Soviet bombers detected.

As ballistic missiles started becoming nuclear weapons carriers in the early 1960s, the USSR ceased to maintain a large heavy bomber fleet. Consequently there was not too much need for the American air defense system. When James Schlesinger was Defense Secretary in 1974 he deemphasized defense against bombers and the Air Force's interceptors assigned to North American defense dwindled to 273 aircraft. Also, the Army's elaborate network of anti-aircraft missile batteries in the US declined to 12 in Florida and 3 in Alaska.

In early 1976 Donald Rumsfeld reaffirmed that an elaborate bomber defense without a comparable missile defense, in a time of massive missile threats, would not be sound use of resources. By the end of that same year, however, Air Force spokesmen had introduced a new $2½-billion program to modernize their anti-bomber network. The fiscal year 1978 budget proposal included $30-million as the initial funding for a six-year plan in which 170 new interceptor fighters would be bought to replace the old anti-bomber aircraft. The new F-15 fighter is shaping up as the most likely candidate and the first of these new interceptors was operational in 1980. The Air Force would like 320 of these airplanes for anti-bomber and anti-cruise missile defense—since cruise missiles are air-breathing and fly in the atmosphere they are defended against in the same manner as bombers. In addition, many tactical Air Force fighter planes based in the US can supplement the continental defense interceptors.

The North American air defense radar network now consists of 83 radar sites—24 in Canada, 14 in Alaska (12 Air Force and 2 jointly used with the Federal Aviation Administration), and 46 around the periphery of the United States all jointly used with the FAA. These radars are being improved to provide for more sensitivity, longer range, lower coverage, greater automation, and less maintenance. DEWLINE radars are being updated by the *SEEK FROST* program and Air Force radars in Alaska are being replaced by *SEEK IGLOO*—a system with a 200-mile range. Defense authorities say these improvements are necessary to enhance detection of low flying aircraft over the northern bomber approaches to the United States. Full operation is expected in 1984.

Related to the foregoing programs is development of *over-the-horizon radar* that will bend its beam through the ionosphere to see over the horizon where line-of-site is not possible. They will be based in the US, one on each coast, and are supposed to give warning of bombers or cruise missiles while they are still 500-1,800 miles from the US coastline. They will not function properly in the auroral zones of the Arctic atmosphere, however, and that is the reason for the deployment of SEEK FROST and SEEK IGLOO. The first over-the-horizon site is at Bingham, Maine. When all of these programs are completed they will combine to form the North American Surveillance System.

To provide surveillance for enemy bombers in the radar gaps between Greenland, Iceland and Britain, the Air Force used to operate ten EC-121 radar surveillance planes. By 1982 that function had been completely taken over by seven of the new E-3A *AWACS* (Airborne Warning And Control System) aircraft with their long-range look-down radar to overcome the limitations of ground-based radars in detecting low-flying bombers and cruise missiles. The first AWACS started flying this mission in January 1979.

It is obvious that radar is presently the central element in defending against hostile bombers and cruise missiles. But it can be easily jammed or destroyed by special missiles which home in on its beam. It would be much more desirable to use passive sensors to detect bombers and cruise missiles because these do not reveal their position by emitting a signal. The Defense Advanced Research Projects Agency (DARPA) is currently working on a multi-million dollar passive sensor, code named *Teal Ruby*, which will focus on that portion of the infrared spectrum most prominent in jet engine exhaust gases. Teal Ruby will be the forerunner of a modern network of satellites capable of spotting and tracking aircraft from space. A spacecraft containing this 580-pound sensor will be put into orbit by the space shuttle some time in 1983. It will take up about half of the shuttle's payload bay.

Teal Ruby will use a mosaic of about a quarter of a million individual sensors with integral processing capability. A good analogy of how mosaic sensors work is provided by the frog's eye which stares, unblinking, and does not move as the human eye does. It has many receptors which pick up a wide field of vision and is well described in the following mosaic sensor advertisement by Grumman Aerospace Corporation:

> The staring approach. A mosaic of thousands of tiny receptors in the frog's eye can detect and track an object in flight and transmit the information to his data processing system (his brain) which then

> determines target class by signature and provides trajectory information to his intercept system (his tongue) while he continues to watch for other threats.[2]

Each of the infrared detectors in Teal Ruby, by staring at a given point, absorb a greater concentration of light than does a scanning sensor which revolves about an axis. This provides greater sensitivity. But all of the 250,000 detectors together provide a composite picture of the entire area under surveillance and anything that moves is quickly noted. If an aircraft is detected, a silicon chip processor sends the information through a computer data-link to the central computer system for identification. (Mosaic sensors and processors will be discussed in more detail later in this chapter.)

Since infrared detectors are sensitive to "heat signatures" it is sometimes possible for them to "see" aircraft hours after they have flown a certain route. They can, in a sense, look back in time. This capability is significant in tracking bombers and cruise missiles.

It also appears that the Air Force is studying the development of millimeter-wave radars on space platforms to augment infrared sensors. These would be able to spot aircraft when conditions are not favorable for infrared—such as through smoke and haze.

Now let us turn to defense against ballistic missiles—once called anti-ballistic missile (ABM) but now more commonly referred to as ballistic missile defense (BMD). As anti-submarine warfare involves both ocean-wide and escort surveillance, ballistic missile defense is also distinguished by two concepts—*area defense* and *point defense*. *Area defense* means the ability to defend a large portion of the United States and, thus, is usually associated with protecting cities. A "thin" or "light" area defense means defending the entire country against a small attack as from China (which has very few intercontinental missiles) or an accidental launch from the Soviet Union—*or*, from retaliation by a few surviving Soviet missiles after a US first strike.

Point defense, on the other hand, involves defending a specific geographic point such as a complex of missile silos. As can be seen, area defense against ballistic missiles would be associated more with preventing retaliation against US cities after a US attack on Russia. Point defense is more applicable to protecting US missiles from a potential aggressor so those missiles would be able to retaliate—and thus deter that aggressor from attempting an attack in the first place. Seen in that light, area defense has offensive connotations while point defense fits better into a deterrent strategy. Recognizing that distinction is essential to understanding the trend in anti-ballistic missile (ABM) weaponry that is taking place.

Before examining current ballistic missile defense programs we should review the history of ABM development. The first full-scale work on missile interceptors was the Nike-Zeus program initiated in the early 1960s. Nike-Zeus, like its successors, had a nuclear warhead. It was later abandoned in favor of Nike-X but neither of these weapons could cope with a full-scale missile attack. Recognizing this, President Johnson authorized only a *thin area defense* of the US, ostensibly to counter the emerging "Chinese threat" or to intercept an accidental launch from the Soviet Union.

When Robert McNamara, Defense Secretary at the time, announced on September 8, 1967 that President Johnson had approved the ABM system called *Sentinel*, he touched off what historians will long refer to as the "Great ABM Debate." McNamara postulated that the purpose of Sentinel was to counter a "Chinese threat" expected to emerge in the 1970s. That threat, of course, never did materialize. He ruled out the possibility of defending large areas against a large-scale Soviet attack but left open the possibility that Minuteman missile silos might be protected from a wholesale Soviet assault.

Contrary to expectations, Sentinel sparked protest from the cities being defended rather than those left out. Critics claimed that it was impossible to defend soft targets. ABM defense became the major political issue during the last months of the Johnson Administration and the Sentinel system was never deployed.

After Richard Nixon took office in 1969 he renamed the proposed ABM system *Safeguard* and authorized twelve sites to defend ICBM silos, with a combination of 100 Spartan and Sprint interceptors in each. With this deemphasis from light area defense to point defense the ABM controversy moved to a new pitch. Three aspects of the strategic picture were interacting at that time: ABMs, MIRVs, and the SALT-1 negotiations. Of the three, ABMs were the most pressing. ABM critics were not mollified by Nixon's modification because it involved no more than a change in deployment strategy.

Opponents charged that protection for twelve sites could not stop a Soviet onslaught and that the system was much too expensive for the obscure Chinese threat. The weak point of the system, they pointed out, was the radar which could be destroyed by a small overpressure from a blast or blacked out by nuclear explosives. Besides that, they claimed, the whole thing was too complicated to even work in trial runs let alone under stress of attack.

Along with these functional difficulties, the opposition pointed to Safeguard's political implications. First, due solely to defects in the system, the effort would escalate to still more sites. Also, deployment of Safeguard would touch off another reaction by the Soviets—they would start developing MIRVs and penetration aids as the US did when Russia began installing its Galosh ABM system around Moscow a few years earlier.*

Proponents for ABM deployment argued that it was the least destabilizing reply to the developing situation and that the time lag between development and deployment dictated an immediate decision to protect against a preemptive strike by 1975. This threat, too, never did materialize. Other response options such as building more Minuteman and Poseidon strategic missiles, they contended, would be interpreted by the Soviets as seeking a more aggressive stance. At the other extreme, passive measures like making the silos harder (which the US later did anyway) were denounced as ineffective.

After a bitter debate in the Senate, phase-1 of Nixon's Safeguard system was authorized by a one-vote margin on August 6, 1969. It included four sites; located in Missouri, Wyoming, North Dakota and Montana.

Meanwhile, after many years of negotiation the first Strategic Arms Limitation Talks (SALT-1) resulted in agreement in several areas. Probably the most significant document to come out of those negotiations was the *ABM Treaty* which was signed on May 26, 1972 and became effective the following October 3rd.[3] It was a bilateral agreement between the US and USSR which put restraints on defense against ballistic missiles. By doing so it appeared to enhance the ability of deterrent weapons to retaliate and thus initiated what became known as the strategy of *mutual assured destruction*—better known as the MAD policy.

The key to understanding the ABM Treaty is its definition of *system* and *components*. An ABM system, for purposes of the treaty, is composed of three components: *interceptors*, *launchers* and *radar*. The treaty does not restrict other important components such as computers and communications networks. An ABM system is further defined as "a

---

*The Soviets never did install more than 64 Galosh ABM launchers. In recent years half of them have been dismantled.

system to counter strategic missiles or their elements in flight trajectory." This provision ruled out a preemptive attack to destroy missiles in their silos. ABM systems can only be brought into play after the offensive missiles have been launched.

The treaty allows each country to have two ABM sites not exceeding a circular area of 185 miles in diameter each. The two sites must be no closer than 800 miles to each other and must lie within the country's boundaries. One site can be centered about an ICBM complex to defend some of the retaliatory missiles and the other must be placed to defend the national capital.

Each of these two sites is allowed only 100 missile launchers which cannot be rapidly reloaded. Furthermore, each interceptor may carry only one warhead—MIRVs are prohibited on ABMs. This adds up to each country being able to fire only 200 interceptors against the thousands of warheads deployed. Such restrictions were aimed at insuring that a few retaliatory missiles would survive and be able to destroy their soft city targets, thereby deterring a first strike by the opponent. These constraints, along with radar restrictions, are the main points which preclude area defense and thus help to insure that the MAD policy will still work.

Radar restrictions are not the same for both sites. Around the capital the radars must be confined within six circular areas of about two-miles diameter. Other than that there are no restrictions. For the ICBM site there may be two large and eighteen small radars. The power and size are specified and they must all lie within the boundaries of the site. The US Safeguard site only had the two large radars—called the *perimeter acquisition radar* (PAR) with its 116-foot diameter phased array antenna for long range, and the *missile site radar* (MSR) for closer in. All other radars of sufficient power to detect and track ballistic missiles, except for certain prescribed allowances at test ranges and for early warning radars, are illegal. Future early warning radars, however, must be constructed within each country's boundaries and must face outward so they cannot be readily used in conjunction with the ABM system. This, admittedly, is a hazy restriction because early warning radars do provide some tracking capability.

The treaty also stipulates other significant bans on future ABM systems which could be substituted for one or more of the existing systems. Deployment of exotic weapons, such as killer lasers, to replace interceptors is outlawed. So is the deployment of any type of sensor other than radar. The key word here is deployment—development and testing of these kinds of components are allowed.

The treaty is more restrictive regarding ABM basing. Even development and testing of air-based, space-based, sea-based and mobile land-based systems or components is a violation of the treaty. For instance, testing a satellite-based laser or infrared sensor for ABM use is forbidden. These restrictions make even a thin area defense from the two specified sites impossible even should technological advances make it technologically feasible.

The ABM Treaty was modified by a protocol in 1974 to eliminate one of the sites. Either country was allowed to dismantle the remaining site, and move it to the alternative location, but that option may be exercised only once. The original treaty, of course, allows modifications or replacements within existing sites without declaring types of components as long as they remain within the guidelines of the treaty.

After the treaty went into effect in 1972 the US stopped work on its ABM site around Malmstrom Air Force Base in Montana. The only remaining site under construction was at Grand Forks, North Dakota and it became operational in October 1974. Early in 1975, however, after spending $5.7-billion on its construction, Congress ordered the Grand Forks site closed. Safeguard was terminated.

Why this abrupt change in direction took place is not clear. It could be that the United States was exercising its once-only option to change sites—or intended to at the time. As one Defense Department official commented, after the North Dakota site was dismantled "we would be free under the constraints of the treaty to build another site of quite a different character . . ."[4] We'll see soon what that "different character" amounts to, and how it affects the future of the ABM Treaty. For now let us look into today's ballistic missile warning systems.

There are currently three basic networks to warn of ballistic missile attack: the *Ballistic Missile Early Warning System* (BMEWS) to watch for Soviet ICBMs coming over the North Pole, the *PAVE PAWS* radars which look for submarine-launched ballistic missiles, and the *early warning satellites*. As with sensors that warn of enemy bombers and cruise missiles, these ballistic missile warning devices also feed into and are controlled by the North American Aerospace Defense Command's (NORAD) combat operations center 1,400 feet deep in a granite cavern in Cheyenne Mountain, Colorado.

BMEWS (pronounced Bee-mews) consists of three radar sites located in Alaska, Greenland and Britain. Each site contains various combinations of detection and tracking radars along with a missile impact predictor and a site control room. An upgrade program currently under way will make BMEWS more effective in determining how many MIRVs are released from each missile and what their targets are. The missile impact predictor portion of the modernization is to be completed in 1982. Replacement by upgraded detection and tracking radars will start going operational by about 1984.

In addition to BMEWS improvements, the new phased-array *Perimeter Acquisition Radar* (PAR) at the now defunct North Dakota ABM site has been turned over to the Air Force for missile warning. (Phased-array radars work similarly to the staring approach. Rather than having a revolving dish, an array of sensors are electronically swept at a very fast rate to provide a composite computerized television-type picture. The panorama for each face of the antenna takes in a third of a circle—120 degrees—horizontally and extends from horizon to almost vertical.) Conversion of the PAR was completed in 1981 to focus its beam energy in a northward direction only. Focusing in this manner increases its range from 1,700 to 2,500 nautical miles. Besides spotting ICBMs coming over the pole, it will also detect missiles launched from submarines in the Hudson Bay and Arctic Ocean regions. Being a thousand miles south of BMEWS makes the PAR better for counting MIRVs and telling where they are going to hit, but less effective for early warning.

Originally there were seven scanning-dish radars, for detecting submarine-launched ballistic missiles (SLBMs), situated in Maine, North Carolina, Florida, Texas, Oregon, and two in California. They have been replaced by *PAVE PAWS* phased-array radars—one at Otis Air National Guard Base in Massachusetts to cover the Atlantic and the other at Beale AFB in California to scan the Pacific. Besides complementing early warning satellites in detecting and tracking SLBMs, PAVE PAWS will also be used by NORAD to keep tabs on satellites in space. Each PAVE PAWS facility has two sloping 72-foot-diameter array faces—each containing 3,500 elements. This combination gives each site 3,000-mile-range coverage with a picture 240 degrees (two-thirds of a circle) across and extending in a vertical direction from horizon to zenith. The Massachusetts facility became operational in April 1979 and the one in California about a year later.

Two additional PAVE PAWS sites have been approved and are expected to be operational in 1984. One is at Robins Air Force Base,

Georgia and the other at Goodfellow Air Force Base in Texas. Besides watching for SLBMs they, also, will support NORAD spacetracking activities.

Another huge phased-array radar at Eglin Air Force Base in Florida that was originally built to track satellites spends twenty-percent of its time watching for SLBM launches from the southern oceans. There have been reports that the allotment of time for BMD use has been increased.

Turning now to early warning satellites; there are presently three in geosynchronous orbit (each orbit taking the same time as one revolution of the earth so that the satellite appears to hover over one spot on the equator). The satellite over the Indian Ocean looks for ICBM launches from Russia. Two others over the Pacific and Atlantic Oceans watch for SLBMs. These spacecraft can track missiles only when their rocket motors are burning, however, because after "burn-out" the infrared signal is too weak for the sensors used. But when the satellite's 2,000 infrared detectors are tuned to that rocket exhaust spectrum it is easy to distinguish a missile launch from the background infrared radiation of the earth and other sources.

The longer term improvements for ballistic missile early warning are even more exotic. DARPA has a program called *High Altitude Large Optics* or HALO which includes Teal Ruby. It is not as saintly a program as the name would imply. HALO will eventually be a space platform with an optical structure up to a hundred feet across which will consist of approximately ten-million detectors including mosaics of different frequencies and, most likely, low-light-level television, phased-array radar, and laser-radar. About six space shuttle loads will be required to put HALO into orbit—the shuttle is essential to assembling this space platform. HALO will be a multi-mission surveillance system satisfying many tactical and strategic needs during the late 1980s and 1990s; including ballistic missile, bomber and cruise missile warning and tracking as well as satellite detection, classification and tracking.

Dr. George H. Heilmeier, former director of DARPA, has made note of two technologies that HALO will incorporate: mosaic infrared sensors with integral data processing capability and adaptive optics. Regarding the first, the full size sensor on HALO will have millions of detector cells with built in data processing capability that will ease the need for an elaborate data-link with a central computer. Some of these, like the Teal Ruby sensors, will be tuned to medium-wavelength infrared sources to detect jet engine exhaust wakes and rocket motor plumes. Teal Ruby detectors would see ICBM and SLBM launches as well as bombers and cruise missiles. Other detectors will be tuned to long-wavelength infrared frequencies and will be efficient for tracking "cooler" objects through space, such as missiles or warheads after their rocket motors burn out—or satellites.

These mosaic sensors will use a telescope to magnify target images. The telescopes will be equipped with filters to cancel out radiation from known sources or different frequencies. Both MWIR and LWIR detectors operate on bands that do not have good atmospheric penetration capabilities so they will be relatively immune to being blinded by land-based lasers. Nevertheless, the ability to track missiles and warheads after their booster motors burn out will violate the ABM Treaty because the sensors are other than radar and they are based in space.

The other breakthrough mentioned by Dr. Heilmeier is *adaptive optics*. It will be used in telescopes that look through the turbulent atmosphere—either up at satellites or down at missile launches. Ordinarily it is not possible to get a good image through the atmosphere because of air turbulence. That is why stars appear to twinkle. But adaptive optics will correct for that effect. It can be analogized to a mirror that bends to compensate for each distortion.

Several test programs—past, present and planned—appear to be leading up to an operational HALO system late in this decade. The first fully-integrated test of mosaic detectors in a telescope equipped with filters was conducted at DARPA's 60-inch telescope facility on Maui, Hawaii in 1978. A self-compensating imaging system to overcome atmospheric turbulence was tested there in 1979.

During 1978 and 1979, in a program called *Hi-CAMP* (High-resolution Calibrated Airborne Measurements Program), mosaic sensors were tested on a high-flying U-2 spy plane belonging to the National Aeronautics and Space Administration. These were the first field demonstrations of mosaics in the focal plane of an infrared telescope where large numbers of detectors were used.

Another 1978-79 program, the *Balloon Altitude Mosaic Measurement* (BAMM), was started in September 1978. On two different occasions a large balloon lifted mosaic sensors to high altitudes from Hollaman Air Force Base in New Mexico. Then the testing moved to Keesler Air Force Base in Mississippi so the sensors could make both land and sea interface measurements. Balloons kept the sensors aloft at about 100,000 feet for up to 11 hours.

In December 1978 the Army started launching its *designating optical tracker* (DOT) vehicle from Kwajalein Atoll. DOT flies in a ballistic arc, lifting LWIR sensors to the edge of the atmosphere to track targets launched from Vandenberg Air Force Base in California. It is then recovered with a parachute. DOT is not entirely a test concept, however. It could be an operational vehicle to put survivable sensors up at the last instant to discriminate between decoys and the actual warheads.

The fourth space shuttle flight during June-July 1982 carried its first military payload—a cyrogenic infrared sensor directly applicable to future space surveillance systems.

Teal Ruby, as mentioned earlier, is to be launched in 1983. It will be in an approximate 400-nautical mile high circular orbit with an expected lifespan of 18 months.

All of these tests lead up to the *Advanced Sensor Demonstration* of the HALO detector array technology scheduled for the mid-1980s. This array will have a very large mosaic area, spectral filters and a substantial amount of on-board data processing. The satellite carrying this array will be put in geosynchronous orbit. After that, of course, comes HALO in the latter 1980s.

This ambitious early warning and tracking activity certainly implies that the military must be developing the weapons to shoot down hostile missiles once they are spotted. That is indeed true. Under the auspices of the Army work started at Kwajalein Atoll in 1977 toward a flight test program for ballistic missile defense scheduled for the early 1980s. Kwajalein is the terminal end of the Pacific Missile Range. Test flights from Vandenberg Air Force Base in California can be used as targets of opportunity for BMD. Under certain circumstances, however, flights are launched from Vandenberg specifically for BMD purposes.

The BMD program now being pursued is called a "layered defense." At present it consists of an exoatmospheric layer (above the atmosphere—above 300,000 feet) and an endoatmospheric or terminal layer (low in the atmosphere). The program to develop the upper layer is called the *Homing Overlay Experiment* (HOE). A series of four tests is planned to start on Kwajalein in late 1982. The goal is for the exoatmospheric layer to intercept 96 percent of enemy warheads. Space-based mosaic infrared sensors, possibly with the help of the Designating Optical Tracker (DOT) vehicle, will do the tracking to calculate intercept trajectory. Interceptor missiles are then launched and each of them dispense several small nonnuclear warheads known as *HIT*—for Homing Interceptor Technology. These warheads are less than a foot long, about seven inches diameter, and weigh in the neighborhood of 14 pounds—slightly larger than a gallon pickle jar. They incorporate a LWIR seeker to home on their target, a guidance system, a right-side-up sensing device, and solid propellant rocket motors for maneuvering in space.

The HIT vehicle will destroy its target upon impact at a relative speed of 27,000 miles per hour. It may also dispense a screen of metal rods to increase its kill radius. Any one of the rods that collide with the approaching enemy warhead at that speed would penetrate to the vital innards and rip them apart.*

A nonnuclear interceptor has many advantages. First of all, it could be launched sooner because the NORAD commander would, theoretically, not have to wait for a presidential release order. That means enemy missiles or warheads could be intercepted earlier in their flight. In addition, the problems associated with nuclear explosives—radar blackout or distortion, interceptor fratricide, perturbed environment—are not introduced. Putting more than one warhead on each ballistic missile interceptor would, however, violate the ABM Treaty.

Homing Interceptor Technology was once considered a form of light area defense because the intercept would take place midcourse in the hostile missile's flight. At that point it would be just as easy to intercept a retaliatory missile after a US first strike, thereby making that strike unanswerable, as it would be to shoot down a missile aimed at the US in a first strike. For that reason area defense is contrary to the intent of the ABM Treaty and Congress ordered all work along that line terminated. Nevertheless, HIT development continues.

The terminal defense system under development is called *Low-Altitude Defense System* or LoADS. The purpose of this lower of the two-tiered system is to intercept the 4 percent of enemy warheads that penetrate the exoatmospheric layer. Ground based radars would be used to calculate the intercept trajectory while the weapon used would be a gun-launched hypervelocity interceptor. It would destroy enemy warheads below 50,000 feet—probably as low as 6,000-8,000 feet—with a small nuclear bomb of about 2-kilotons yield. This highly maneuverable interceptor would use a millimeter-wave radar seeker to home-in on its

---

*A variation of HIT which appears to be the prime concept for BMD is the Lockheed-built nonnuculear kill mechanism which unfolds like an umbrella with metal slugs attached to the ribs. There is also an alternate Honeywell design which spits out concentric circles of metal cubes to provide a larger kill radius.

target. At that low altitude, the booster tank fragments—which is the only type of penetration aid the Soviets have used—would have burned up and the seeker would have no trouble locking onto the real target. The biggest challenge, however, is to get the interceptor launched only ten seconds after initial detection of the hostile warhead—there is only a fifteen second interval available.

The LoADS program is ostensibly justified to protect MX missiles, however they may be based. If MX is mobile, LoADS would be too—and developing a mobile ballistic missile defense system is another violation of the ABM Treaty.

There is a third less notorious layer to the ballistic missile defense network being developed. If interceptors were based close enough to the Soviet Union they could destroy a missile before it started spewing MIRVs. The Pentagon seems to be interested in that type of missile intercept. In a prepared report to a Senate committee Major General Robert C. Marshall made note of a fiscal year 1977 Boost Phase Measurements Program that would investigate "techniques for detecting and discriminating SLBM threats in the boost phase . . ."[5]

Destroying ballistic missiles immediately after they are launched would be a much cleaner kill than trying to shoot down a skyful of MIRVs bearing down on their targets at Mach-20. It would be like smashing all the eggs in one basket. Also, disabling a missile before the booster motors finish accelerating will cause the fragments and radioactive debris to fall short of the target—possibly into the ocean or onto the enemy's homeland.

More recently, in early 1982, the Heritage Foundation proposed a space-based ABM system which would be comprised of 18,000-20,000 small interceptors on 450 orbiting battle stations. Each interceptor would use the HIT warhead and would weigh less than 100 pounds. It did not discuss how target assignments would be made to prevent duplicate attacks on some ICBMs and missing others.

Pentagon ambitions to shoot down Russian missiles during their powered flight phase are not new. In the late 1960s the *Ballistic Missile Boost Intercept* (BAMBI) program conceptualized the idea of launching interceptors from a low-orbit satellite to knock down the ballistic missiles shortly after they are launched. Because that would have required a vast number of satellites it did not appear too feasible. But the idea of stationing ABMs close to Soviet launch points gained adherents and it wasn't long before all three branches of the military jumped into the act. The Army suggested schemes for deploying its Nike-X interceptors in foreign countries close to the Soviet Union. The Air Force proposed having C-5A transports loaded with ABMs loitering within range of enemy silos. And the Navy came up with the concept of sea-based ABM interceptors on surface ships. The latter was the most touted, apparently because it allowed greater flexibility and could be kept more secretive. It would also work as well for shooting down SLBMs as it would against ICBMs.

In December 1975 a Honolulu, Hawaii researcher named Tony Hodges released a forty-five page *Warning Document* in which he alleged that the Navy had started seabed missile emplacements in 1968.[6] This document resulted from months of study and it postulated that some of these emplacements could be as deep as three miles.

On November 11, 1975, according to his report, Hodges had an interview with Dr. John P. Craven, Dean of Marine Studies at the University of Hawaii and former chief scientist for the Navy's Special Projects Office (since renamed the Strategic Systems Project Office). Craven was heavily involved with the Navy's Polaris and Poseidon submarine-launched missile development and its deep submersible program. According to Hodges, Craven claimed he could develop an underwater system in four years and that silos in the seabed would not be necessary—it would only be required to dump capsules off the back of a destroyer. Craven seemed somewhat upset, Hodges believed, when an electronic ABM system at sea was mentioned.

Hodges' report also pointed out that Rear Admiral George H. Miller (ret.) has long been an advocate of ABMs at sea. Admiral Miller was considered one of the Pentagon's foremost long-range strategic analysts and was the first director of the Naval Operations Strategic Offensive and Defensive Systems Office. Admiral Miller wrote in the July 1975 issue of *Sea Power* that "Use of the seas for defense of the United States, against nonnuclear as well as nuclear attack, would permit interception of incoming attacks before they get too close to US territory."[7]

Following up on Tony Hodges' *Warning Document*, Michael Drosnin exhibited an excellent job of investigative reporting in an article called "Desktop."[8] Desktop was the code name for a super-secret Navy project believed to be associated with missiles based in the seabed. Drosnin reports one naval witness as stating that an underwater ABM system was started before 1970 and was under construction until at least 1971.

The Desktop article also quotes Professor Craven as confirming that sea floor missiles were considered and found technically feasible; and that encapsulated missiles designed to surface and fire were tested in the early 1960s. Rear Admiral David M. Cooney, speaking as the Navy's Chief of Information, is reported to have confirmed that "missiles in or on the seabed were things considered in various modes in the past."[9] We can see that sea-based ABMs are not a wild dream. Encapsulated ABM interceptors equipped with HIT warheads could be distributed close to Soviet territory in much the same manner as CAPTOR mines and moored sonar buoys are deployed. They would surface at a given acoustic or extreme low frequency (ELF) signal and, once on the surface, be targeted electronically and fired by satellite. Russian retaliatory missiles would then be destroyed before they could dispatch their MIRVs.

All of these weapons and sensors, of course, depend on the ability to process vast quantities of data instantaneously. Even the 64-element Illiac-4 would not do the job. Consequently, the Army is developing the *Parallel Element Processing Ensemble*(PEPE) comprising from 300 to 900 minicomputers working concurrently and feeding into a master computer. About 12-million instructions per second are required to track 200 targets and 30-million instructions per second are routine for ballistic missile defense. PEPE will be able to operate at a whopping 800-million instructions per second rate.

Dr. George Heilmeier, former director of DARPA, has pointed out that a defense against ballistic missiles that is based solely on interceptors can easily be saturated by a large number of warheads. The limits of defensive interceptors has motivated research and development of *directed energy weapons* including high-energy lasers and sub-atomic particle beams. Referring to these weapons Dr. Heilmeier asked Congress in 1977 to ponder the consequences of a leak-proof defense—one that could not be overcome by projected numbers of hostile missiles.[10]

The most prominent of the directed energy weapons is the *high energy laser*—more commonly called the *killer laser*. Lasers are highly concentrated beams of coherent light. The name is an acronym for Light Amplification by Stimulated Emission of Radiation. The stronger the stimulating force, the more concentrated the beam and the more destructive it is to physical substances. Focusing sunlight with a magnifying glass is a crude example of how concentrated light affects matter. In the area affected, the energy applied by a killer laser surpasses that of a nuclear explosion.

In 1960 the first laser beam was fired and two years later DARPA was looking for military applications. The discovery of the flowing-gas laser in 1968 opened the door for high energy (killer) lasers and by 1970 there were three types: gas dynamics, chemical and electrical discharge. A demonstration at China Lake, California in 1975 proved that killer lasers could cause structural damage to an airplane. In 1978 a laser prototype was tested against much smaller and faster anti-tank missiles with a reported high rate of success.

After the 1975 test DARPA reoriented its stepped-up laser program toward small, pulsing chemical lasers with ultraprecise aiming and tracking devices for deployment in space. Chemical lasers are particularly suited for space because they require no external energy source, take advantage of the low temperature to simplify cooling, and release the highly toxic byproducts where they are unlikely to cause harm. In addition, the vacuum of space allows the beam to travel several thousand miles without being scattered. Thus, the unique properties of a laser—the ability to precisely concentrate vast amounts of energy at extreme distances with the speed of light—can be fully exploited. Defense officials are optimistic that they can put a killer laser in space before the end of the 1980s. DARPA's present high-energy laser program has three technology goals:

> *Alpha*: To develop and demonstrate a 4-meter (13.1-foot) diameter beam chemical laser suitable for use in space.
>
> *Talon Gold*: To develop the low-power pointing and tracking laser which can locate the target and aim the killer laser. It employs almost the same technology used to point NASA's space-based infrared astronomy telescope. The goal is to aim the killer laser to within 0.2 microradians.*
>
> *LODE*: (Large Optics Demonstration Experiment) To develop a huge mirror—13.1 feet in diameter—of very strong, lightweight glass to steer and control the killer laser beam. It would have to be manufactured in sections and assembled in space. Optics for an operational killer laser would be up to 50 feet in diameter.

Another potential space-based killer laser which has attracted some

---

*A microradian is the angular distance which spans one centimeter at ten kilometers distance.

interest is the X-ray laser. It is pumped by a small nuclear explosion—possibly using laser fusion technology. Many laser rods emanate from the pumping chamber to aim as many laser beams. When each rod has acquired a target the nuclear detonation takes place and they are all zapped at once. The targets are destroyed by shock waves generated when they are struck by the laser energy. It has been proposed that X-ray lasers might supplement the pulsing chemical lasers on a space battle station.

Death rays made up of subatomic particles such as protons or neutrons are another type of directed energy weapon which the Pentagon has studied off and on since 1960. These beams are analogous to a lightning bolt and have an advantage over terrestrial lasers in bad weather. They are almost as fast as a laser and more destructive. If the target is close enough the beam will detonate the high explosive trigger of the nuclear bomb. At a longer distance it can disrupt the electronics. The Army started development of a proton beam in 1977 to zap out incoming warheads.

Beams using charged particles such as protons or electrons, however, are deflected by the earth's magnetic field and would not be very accurate over long distances in space. To overcome that problem the Army is now pursuing research on a neutral particle beam which can be mounted in space to destroy ballistic missiles in flight. Originally called *Sipapu* (an American Indian word meaning "sacred fire") but later renamed *White Horse* to avoid ethnic offense, this neutrally-charged beam will not be affected by the earth's pull. For ballistic missile defense applications White Horse would need a compact nuclear reactor in space to provide the necessary power and that, also, is in development.

Most of this directed energy work had been kept very quiet until it was smoked out recently by allegations that the Russians were near a breakthrough in such weapons. It is true that Soviet scientists are also pursuing research on directed energy weapons and there is even widespread belief they may put a laser in orbit during this decade. But it would be a showcase flight and would not pose any significant threat to the US. General Lew Allen, as Air Force Chief of Staff, told the House Appropriations subcommittee on defense that he was "skeptical" about Soviet space-based lasers posing a threat any time soon.[11] Lt. Gen. Kelly Burke, Air Force research director, told the House Armed Services Committee that there is no need for the US to embark on a crash effort to develop space-based lasers.[12] He said that any early Soviet laser weapons would be very costly and relatively crude and would not be able to knock down US missiles and satellites.[13] Furthermore, Secretary of Defense Harold Brown noted in his fiscal 1981 posture statement that: "Although the Soviets may be investigating the application of high energy lasers and even charged particle beams . . . severe technical obstacles remain in the way of converting this technology into a weapon system that would have any practical capability against missiles."[14]

Throughout this chapter I have highlighted various aspects of BMD programs which conflict with the ABM Treaty: sensors and weapons in space or at sea, mobile BMD systems, other-than-radar sensors, multiple warheads on interceptors, area defense, and exotic directed energy weapons. Regarding the latter, the Fiscal Year 1983 Arms Control Impact Statements warn that their future ABM potential "could create a conflict with the obligations assumed by the US under the provisions of the ABM Treaty."[15]

Regarding BMD as a whole, the FY '83 ACIS claims the current year's programs are consistent with the ABM Treaty but that they will be closely monitored to assure continued compliance. The ACIS takes note of the treaty review coming up in October 1982 and makes the observation that there are provisions for withdrawal.[16] That, of course, would relieve the pressure concerning future violations and seems to be what the Administration is counting on. Reports indicate a pervasive feeling within the arms control community and the Defense Department that the treaty will not survive the next review in its present form.[17] The committee on National Security, headed by Paul Warnke, chief arms control negotiator in the Carter Administration, reports that President Reagan has hinted at renunciation of the treaty and warns that such action will paralyze all arms control negotiations.[18] Clearly, US ballistic missile defense activities are counter-productive as far as stopping the arms race is concerned.

There is, however, an even more dangerous aspect of BMD—it is moving the world toward a more unstable nuclear standoff. Being able to defend the United States sounds like a defensive, therefore good, program to pursue. With regard to the strategic balance, however, that is far from being the case. If it is possible for the US to intercept all Soviet bombers and missiles while the Soviets cannot defend against a US attack, the US gains the freedom to attack with impunity. The Congressional Research Service of the Library of Congress warns of how ballistic missile defense will likely abrade international relations:

> Prospective developments in BMD will raise significant

questions for arms control and defense policy in the near and intermediate-near future. . . .

. . . Furthermore, many of the more attractive defense concepts such as midcourse interception would inherently provide a capability for a nationwide defense that could be used to protect cities as well as the silo-based missile force.

Advanced weapons systems such as high energy lasers and charged-particle beams in the long term and nonnuclear homing intercept technology warheads in the near term, could pose significant arms control problems. . . . In particular, the United States is considering homing intercept and space-based laser technology for satellite inspection and defense programs. The overlap between technology envisioned for antisatellite and satellite defense systems and the space-based ABM systems could create difficult verification problems. . . .

. . . Thus after years of relative quiescence, BMD policy is again likely to command substantial attention in the near future.[19]

An old axiom says that the best defense is a good offense. In this case the reverse is true— a "good" offense is guaranteed by a leak-proof ballistic missile and bomber defense. It is possible to defend ourselves so well that the Pentagon will feel no restraint against taking the offensive. BMD is doing just that. By supplementing silo-killing strategic missiles and anti-submarine warfare forces it is moving the United States toward the capability for a disarming first strike.

NOTES

1. *Annual Defense Department Report FY 1978*, by Secretary of Defense Donald H. Rumsfeld, 17 January 1977, p. 140.
2. Grumman Aerospace Corporation advertisement in *Aviation Week and Space Technology*.
3. For a more complete discussion of the ABM Treaty see *SALT: the Moscow Agreements and Beyond*, edited by Mason Willrich and John B. Rhinelander, (NY, Free Press; 1974), Chapter 5.
4. *Fiscal Year 1977 Authorization for Military Procurement, Research and Development, and Active Duty, Selected Reserve and Civilian Personnel Strengths*, Senate Armed Services Committee, 30 March 1976, Part 12, p. 6735.
5. Ibid, p. 6691.

6. Tony Hodges, *A Warning Concerning Probable Violations by the USA and the USSR of the 1971 Seabed Arms Control Treaty*, December 1975, published by the author.
7. George H. Miller, "To Provide for the Common Defense," *Sea Power*, July 1975, pp. 15-16.
8. Michael Drosnin, "Desktop," *New Times*, 2 April 1976, pp. 21-35.
9. Ibid.
10. *Defense Advanced Research Projects Agency Fiscal Year 1978 Program for Research and Development*, by Dr. George H. Heilmeier, Director, February 1977, p. I-5.
11. Cited by George Wilson, "AF Leaders Skeptical of Laser Threat," *Washington Post*, 10 March 1982, p. 7.
12. Ibid.
13. Cited by Walter S. Mossberg, "Soviet Could Build Laser Weapon to Kill Satellites in 5 Years, Pentagon Aide Says," *Wall Street Journal*, 11 February 1981, p. 6.
14. *Department of Defense Annual Report Fiscal Year 1981*, by Harold Brown, Secretary of Defense, 29 January 1980, p. 82.
15. *Fiscal Year 1983 Arms Control Impact Statements*, March 1982, p. 321.
16. Ibid, pp. 139-142.
17. Cited by Clarence A. Robinson, Jr., "Emphasis Grows on Nuclear Defense," *Aviation Week and Space Technology*, 8 March 1982, p. 27.
18. Cited in "Missile Pact in Peril, Panel Warns," *Christian Science Monitor*, 1 July 1981, p. 2.
19. *Evaluation of Fiscal Year 1979 Arms Control Impact Statements: Toward More Informed Congressional Participation in National Security Policy-making*, a report prepared for the House Committee on Internal Relations by the Congressional Research Service of the Library of Congress, 3 January 1979, pp. 101-102.

SPACE WARFARE

Ponder the consequences
of a space associated system
that could protect our own
satellite resources
while possessing the capability
to destroy enemy satellites
in a surgical and timely manner.
—*Dr. George H. Heilmeier,*
former director of DARPA

During my lifetime I have watched the growth of the public enchantment with outer space—from Buck Rogers of the late 1930s to Star Wars of today. Kids and adults alike revel in the flights of fancy and the actual aerospace projects that have carried their imaginations into this ethereal realm. The Pentagon and the Kremlin also share this affinity to space but their fascination is grounded in a more pragmatic and deadly purpose. They seem intent on making Star Wars a reality. Over 75 percent of the current use of space is for military purposes and that proportion is increasing. The arms race has expanded into space. Virtually all military operations—from spying to communication—depend on satellites. And these celestial outposts are becoming a focus for hostilities.

Destroying satellites in orbit is very similar to intercepting ballistic missiles or MIRVs while they are coasting through space. The sensors and weapons used in one can be applied toward the other. The main difference is that some satellites are at a much higher altitude—in what is called *deep space*. The reader has already seen the importance of satellites to the military systems which enhance a first strike. Almost every one of these weapons or sensors depends in some way on spacecraft for communications, navigation, verification, early warning, or spying. Satellites are likewise important to the Soviet Union's strategic missile force and destroying them reduces the retaliation which could follow a first strike by the US. Without early warning satellites there would be fewer Soviet missiles launched before they are destroyed. Without communications satellites the command to launch ICBMs would be complicated and it would be more difficult to order submarines to fire their missiles. Loss of navigation satellites could cause some of the latest Soviet missiles to be less accurate if they should survive to retaliate. Aside from some sensation-oriented media reports, the satellite aspect of the arms race has received essentially no public attention. Nevertheless, space warfare figures prominently in the Pentagon's emerging first strike capability.

The first requirement for eradicating Soviet satellites is the ability to predict where they will be at any point in time. Again, as in the case of antisubmarine warfare and ballistic missile defense, sensors emerge as the most visible component of the aggressive weapons systems. First, let's review space tracking history and then take a look at what is planned for the future.

The campaign to militarize space was first led by Lyndon B. Johnson when he was Senate Majority Leader in the late 1950s. At that time the United States was making plans for the International Geophysical Year scheduled for 1957-58. Preparation for tracking satellites which were intended to be launched during that time began in 1955. *Minitrack* was a low accuracy, economical system developed by the US Navy to follow the spacecraft by their radio beacons. It was first used to keep tabs on Sputnik. *Moonwatch* was another which consisted of a network of volunteers with telescopes and stop watches. In addition, a network of twelve Baker-Nunn cameras was set up around the world.

In December 1958 the newly-formed Defense Advanced Research Projects Agency (DARPA) initiated the Spacetrack program which was transferred to the Air Force a few months later. In 1959 the National Space Surveillance Control Center was set up in Bedford, Massachusetts to plot satellite orbits from data supplied from over a hundred tracking stations. By October 1959 the Air Force, DARPA, and the Navy were working together to develop a space tracking network which eventually became known as the *Space Detection and Tracking System* (SPADATS). It became operational under the North American Aerospace Defense Command (NORAD) in July 1961. One of its main missions is to detect, identify and track all objects in space—including space junk. It identifies hostile satellites, constantly updating their orbital characteristics so they can be instantly targeted should that be necessary.

SPADATS was first established with its headquarters in Colorado Springs but the data processing facilities remained at Bedford until the underground NORAD headquarters was completed in 1966. SPADATS headquarters is now located at the Space Defense Operations Center which is part of NORAD's Combat Operations Center buried under 1,400 feet of granite rock in Cheyenne Mountain, Colorado. The Combat Operations Center is the nerve center for all surveillance and weapons systems controlled by NORAD. Besides SPADATS it also monitors the bomber detection and warning systems, ballistic missile early warning, and the SLBM detection and warning systems. Interceptor aircraft are also directed from Cheyenne Mountain which can be sealed with nuclear blast proof doors and contains enough supplies to maintain operations for thirty days. It is linked by nuclear-survivable communications with all NORAD commands as well as the Strategic Air Command, the Pentagon, the White House, civilian defense agencies, and other key governmental units.

The Space Defense Operations Center is housed in a three-story building inside one of Cheyenne Mountain's giant caverns and it is mounted on helical springs to withstand the shock of a direct nuclear blast. It contains a computer which catalogs all of the four-thousand-some artificial objects in orbit (expected to exceed 10,000 by 1985) and continually updates their orbital parameters. Data processing for the computer handles approximately 10,500 data inputs daily from SPADATS sensors all over the globe. But even with the kind of survivability offered by Cheyenne Mountain, NORAD still has an alternate Space Defense Center at Eglin Air Force Base in Florida.

Besides the Air Force's Spacetrack network, SPADATS now consists of numerous cooperating sensors. In addition to the Navy's space surveillance radio fence across the southern United States there are six tracking radars on the Eastern Test Range extending out into the Atlantic Ocean from Cape Canaveral, Florida and another five tracking radars over the Pacific Missile Range between Vandenburg Air Force Base, California and the Kwajalein Atoll. The US Air Force satellite control system tracking radars and the NASA tracking network also contribute to SPADATS as do approximately a dozen Baker-Nunn cameras operated by the Smithsonian Astrophysical Observatory. Many other miscellaneous radars and numerous civilian sensors such as astronomy telescopes complete the network. The new PAVE PAWS phased array radars for SLBM detection will also devote a portion of their operation to space surveillance. Other sensors, alleged to contribute to the Space Defense Center, remain less prominent: the ballistic missile early warning radars, the former Safeguard perimeter acquisition radar, over-the-horizon radars, the Air Force satellite control system telemetry receivers, and the National Security Agency listening posts.

The Air Force *Spacetrack* network, however, remains the backbone of SPADATS. Of its various sensors, the most significant are the two huge phased array radars which can scan 120 degrees of sky from horizon to zenith in millionths of a second. One, at Eglin Air Force Base in Florida, has a southward facing panel as high as a thirteen story building and a city block long. A second, called Cobra Dane and located on Shemya Island in the Aleutian group, is even more modern and sensitive and is used to track satellites in polar orbit, to observe Soviet missile tests and to perform ballistic missile early warning functions. In addition to phased array radars, Spacetrack also has tracking and early-warning-type radars strewn about the globe.

Spacetrack also incorporates a number of Baker-Nunn cameras operated around the world by US and Canadian Air Force personnel. Baker-Nunn cameras are presently the most sensitive and precise satellite tracking instruments. Whereas radars can only reach out about 3,000 miles into space, the Baker-Nunns can photograph light reflected off a dinner plate 25,000 miles away. They are well suited to accurately determine orbital parameters but they lack the scanning ability to detect new objects in space. Their use is limited to identifying and tracking objects that are already known to be in orbit and they are usable only in good weather and during the hours of darkness when the satellites being observed are illuminated by the sun.

Many SPADATS sensor systems are being improved. Spacetrack low altitude radars are being modernized to provide information on new satellites during their initial orbit. Small scale models of a new phased array radar concept were tested in 1978. DARPA is experimenting with millimeter radar and laser radar in addition to the conventional microwave radar in an attempt to extend the detection range and upgrade the space-object identification function. Focusing two radars of different frequencies from different locations on satellites gives a stereoscopic image which, with the aid of a computerized library of radar signatures, allows instant classification. The Navy's space surveillance fence is also being given a longer range capability.

In Cheyenne Mountain, the Space Defense Operations Center is being enhanced with a Space Computation Center featuring increased space object cataloging. In addition, the Air Force has developed a satellite attack warning system which will feed tracking information from SPADATS and other sources into a new computer program to generate a second-by-second display of all hostile satellites. From this it can be determined when an American satellite is threatened by a killer so an alarm can be sent to the appropriate commands.

But these improvements will not extend coverage beyond the 3,000 mile radar limit and there will still be gaps in that coverage. With the increasing number of higher altitude geosynchronous satellites being orbited by the Soviet Union there is a need to extend detection capabilities out to about 25,000 miles while minimizing the gaps. There are both short-term and long-term modifications planned for surveillance systems that aim to accomplish these goals.

The near term improvement for Spacetrack is the *Ground-based Electro-Optical Deep Space Surveillance* (GEODSS) system which will scan like a radar with the sensitivity and range of a Baker-Nunn camera (the ability to spot a one-foot diameter object at 25,000 miles altitude). It will eventually replace the Baker-Nunn cameras in the Spacetrack network. GEODSS will use low-light-level television to give nearly instantaneous visual observations, as compared with the time lag needed to develop camera film. The GEODSS video sensor is combined with a technology known as fiber optics for rapid scanning, which is computer-aided to discover any new object not filed in its catalog or not moving with the star field. Orbital parameters will be calculated automatically for immediate transmission to the Space Defense Operation Center computer. While adding the capability of detecting objects at geosynchronous altitude (about 1,500 human-made objects at those heights expected by 1985), GEODSS is still limited to certain hours of darkness in good weather. It will be able to track up to 200 objects per night.

DARPA has been developing GEODSS for some time at its Cloudcroft, New Mexico and Maui, Hawaii facilities. Five sites are planned for the final system and they will be about evenly distributed around the globe and near the equator. New Mexico was the first one fully operational in April 1981. The other four sites will be (1) near Taegu, South Korea; (2) Maui, Hawaii; (3) somewhere in the eastern Atlantic region, possibly in North Africa; and (4) in the Middle East/Indian Ocean area, originally planned for Iran but now likely to be on the island of Diego Garcia.

Each site will have three telescopes. Two 40-inch telescopes will observe at high altitudes and a 15-inch telescope will perform low-altitude surveillance. All five sites are scheduled to be in operation by the mid-1980s.

Eventually the video sensor in GEODSS will be replaced by *Teal Amber*—a mosaic sensor operating in the visible light wavelength and having integral data processing capability. Teal Amber will be a staring sensor and will provide greater sensitivity, a wider field of view, and a greater search rate than low-light-level television. It will also use adaptive optics to remove the distortion caused by atmospheric turbulence. Tested during fiscal year 1981, Teal Amber is likely to be retrofitted into GEODSS sometime around the middle-1980s.

To eventually overcome handicaps and gaps associated with a ground-based tracking system, the Air Force has a longer term improvement known as the *Spacetrack Enhancement Program*.

Initial funding was requested during fiscal year 1978 to start design of a prototype space-based long-wavelength infrared (LWIR) mosaic sensor for real-time detection and tracking of objects against a "cool" space background.

While space tracking appears to have a logical role in the peaceful use of space, it takes on a more sinister appearance in light of other first strike technologies—and in the context of anti-satellite weapons which are also being developed. A full-scale satellite war would be a likely prelude to World War III because of the military role being fulfilled by spacecraft. In the last chapter we discussed the killer laser, a form of death ray that could systematically zap out enemy space vehicles. That type of laser could be used against satellites in several ways. It could blind the spacecraft's horizon sensors so that it starts tumbling helplessly in orbit. Or it could cause actual physical damage which would prevent the satellite from performing its mission. Satellite-borne and ground-based killer lasers will certainly figure prominently in future space wars. This fact was confirmed by President Carter in November 1977 when he told Georgia Congressmen that America is developing laser beams which can destroy other satellites.[1] Dr. Robert Fossum, director of DARPA, subsequently pointed out that space-based killer lasers are receiving prime attention:

> . . . Since [last year] we have broadened the examination of

> the capabilities of this technology and have concluded that lasers have unique and high pay-off potential in some space applications . . . The DARPA high energy laser program is concentrating on the development of efficient infrared chemical and visible electrical laser technologies as well as precise pointing systems . . .[2]

Space-based lasers do not exhaust Air Force ambitions, however. In 1983 it plans to make two ground-based lasers operational for anti-satellite missions.[3] One installation will be at Kirtland Air Force Base in New Mexico and the other facility at China Lake, California for destroying low-orbit satellites.

The Air Force is also looking into the other prominent form of directed energy weapon—subatomic particle beams—at its Kirtland Air Force Base weapons laboratory. Besides charged particle beams to defend ground installations and aircraft from attack, the Air Force's interest also extends to neutral particle beams for anti-satellite applications in space. An anti-satellite version of the Army's White Horse beam would be possible with existing power sources—a reactor in space would not be necessary.

In spite of these advanced programs currently underway, when the subject of shooting down satellites in space is brought up our thoughts tend to jump to sensational media accounts of Soviet killer spacecraft that can track down and destroy US orbiting vehicles. But on looking deeper one can see that those accounts are strongly biased to justify a "reaction" by the US. Although the Pentagon's precise preparations for space warfare are still very secret, there are many aspects which are available in public documents. The most obvious of these is the placement of alarm systems on US satellites that would sound off if another spacecraft approaches or attacks. The Air Force has even considered giving some of the key satellites some maneuverability in orbit to evade an attack as well as equipping them with some sort of device to fire upon attacking satellites.

Other passive measures include radiation hardening of vulnerable components in case of a nuclear explosion in space. Although such detonations are prohibited by the Outer Space Treaty, if a violation did occur the instantaneous gamma and neutron radiation would cripple an unprotected satellite. The Air Force's Special Weapons Center is now conducting a program that exposes experimental satellites to radiation as well as the related electro-magnetic pulse—a very high electric pulse generated in unshielded electronic systems by nuclear explosions which short out or burn up circuitry.

Still other purely defensive measures include detectors in spy and early warning satellites that would identify high intensity infrared radiation and trigger a cover for their optical sensors before they are blinded. Also, using self-contained nuclear power aboard spacecraft instead of fragile solar arrays, and installing precision gyros in place of optical horizon sensors to keep the satellite upright are other passive techniques. Even decoys that can be ejected from a satellite to mislead a killer have been considered.

There seems to be another US plan for backup communications satellites to take over in the case the primary spacecraft are immobilized, but information in this area is more obscure. It apparently consists of a group of so-called dark satellites with self-contained nuclear-power sources hiding out in deep space. Some Pentagon officials are reported to have hinted that such a system already exists. Dark satellites are either coated black to prevent light reflection or have a system of mirrors to camouflage them in sunlight. Communications satellites of this sort would remain on standby while loitering 70,000 miles or higher above the earth—at least three times the altitude of geosynchronous satellites and well out of range of even such instruments as Baker-Nunn cameras or GEODSS. Even after they started operating in time of crisis they would still remain invisible.

One should note that these extremely high orbits are not beyond the reach of present technology. On April 8, 1970 the US placed two Vela satellites in 67,000-mile high orbits to watch for nuclear explosions from space. On March 14, 1976 two Navy Solrad spacecraft were orbited 75,000 miles above the earth for the announced purpose of monitoring solar radiation. Any of these could easily be backup communications satellites.

Finally, reconstitutable satellites are being prepared to reestablish various communications, reconnaissance, and other types of functions that may be lost because of spacecraft destroyed. These small space vehicles would be hidden around the country and oceans in silos and submarines, and launched during wartime when their particular function is needed.

Aside from killer lasers and particle beams the foregoing defenses could still be interpreted as justifiable responses to a possible Soviet threat. However, one should look farther back into history to see just how strong the Pentagon's interest in satellite warfare has been and exactly how threatening Soviet anti-satellite capabilities are. As early as 1959 DARPA began studying a manned, maneuverable anti-satellite space vehicle. By 1960 the US was deeply involved with applying spacework to military needs. The *Discoverer* series of spacecraft was testing space surveillance sensors. SAMOS (reconnaissance), Transit (navigation), and MIDAS (early warning) satellites were in the advanced stages of development. As the end of aircraft reconnaissance was signaled when Gary Powers and his U-2 spy plane were shot out of Soviet skies, the development of SAMOS was accelerated.

Also in 1960, the Army's director of Air Defense and Special Weapons predicted that the Soviets would have a bombardment-from-orbit satellite by 1965—a vehicle mentioned as a possibility in a Soviet pre-Sputnik article. At the same time, the Air Force Ballistic Missile Division announced that the Russians would develop a satellite interceptor capability (on which the Pentagon, itself, had already started studies) in time to shoot down the first MIDAS satellites when they became operational in 1963. For psychological effect, however, the US anti-satellite vehicle was called *SAINT* (an acronym for satellite interceptor) while the alleged Soviet counterpart was referred to as a killer satellite.

A January 1961 conference on SPADATS is reported to have planned for the type of detection and tracking needed to shoot down Soviet satellites. Four half-scale models of the SAINT vehicle were allegedly under construction in 1961 with test intercepts planned for 1962. SAINT was designed to be either piloted or remote controlled. What actually happened regarding those tests, however, remains obscure because in February 1962 a news blackout was lowered on all military satellites and it has lasted until this day.

SAINT was abandoned because of cost and technical problems but orbital intercepts were transferred to the Air Force's *Manned Orbital Laboratory*—also later cancelled by President John Kennedy because America's space programs had too much of a military flavor. Nevertheless, earth orbit rendezvous in the Apollo program were allegedly connected to SAINT studies. Today the Soviets claim the US space shuttle is an anti-satellite spacecraft.

Hostile satellites can also be disabled by a missile fired from below. A *direct ascent* satellite intercept study was reported in progress in 1959. During 1960-62, several contracts were awarded to study nonnuclear kill techniques using target-homing warheads. They included blinding a satellite with a maser beam (Project Blackeye), blinding satellites with paint to cover their optical windows, and deploying a cloud of metal pellets to collide with the satellite at tremendous speed.

The Army proposed giving their Nike Zeus ABMs the ability to knock down satellites in 1961 and the following year Defense Secretary McNamara directed them to be prepared for tests which began in May 1963. Also, in 1962 the Air Force Space Systems Division began investigating a target-homing guidance concept for satellite interceptors which eventually led to the *homing interceptor technology* (HIT) described in the previous chapter. The Air Force then developed the thrust augmented Thor missile which had extra booster rockets strapped on to obtain a greater range. It was successfully tested in 1964. It was tested again in 1966 using a Burner-2 upper stage which had better maneuverability for intercepting satellites. The precision with which the Burner-2 could position itself led to speculation that it might also be capable of satellite rendezvous and inspection.

As Director of Defense Research and Engineering in 1963 and early 1964, Dr. Harold Brown (who later became President Carter's Secretary of Defense) alluded to these satellite intercept programs. In a 1964 press conference Robert McNamara announced that for certain trial launches of Nike Zeus and Thor missiles, SPADATS monitored the target orbits—a tacit admission that those missiles were tested as anti-satellite weapons. By 1964 the ground-launched Thor and Nike Zeus weapons had the limited capability to intercept certain satellites in low orbit over specific geographic areas.

McNamara told the Senate Armed Services Committee in 1967 that: "As described in previous years, we have a capability to intercept and destroy hostile satellites within certain ranges . . . "[4] By 1968 it is believed that the Nike Zeus system located on Kwajalein Atoll was inactive. The Thor system armed with nuclear warheads, on the other hand, was maintained on five-minute alert until 1975. Today it is believed to be maintained in a status where it can be reactivated within six months.

Another program that was not officially mentioned by the Pentagon also reached the development stage in 1964. The Navy used a modified Polaris submarine-launched missile called *Early Spring* to place a screen of metal pellets in a satellite's path. This nonnuclear technique of destroying spacecraft with impact energy was also tried on the Air Force program which used the Thor missiles on Johnston Island. It included terminal homing that was precise enough to allow substitution of a burst of metal pellets for the nuclear warhead.

By 1969 the US Air Force was exploring a direct-ascent anti-satellite concept which dispensed numerous five-pound powered projectiles from a ground-launched booster into the path of an oncoming satellite. Each of these projectiles had small rocket motors to correct course and an infrared seeker to home-in on the target.

In 1975 the Air Force proposed a miniature space interceptor as part of its four-year effort to develop anti-satellite technology. Using a long-wavelength infrared sensor it would seek and then collide with its target satellite. In November 1977 the Air Force approved a $58.7-million contract for a ground-launched, direct ascent, nonnuclear anti-satellite system that will destroy its target with collision energy. Presently, plans to achieve an anti-satellite capability against low-orbit spacecraft involve putting this HIT warhead on a combination SRAM/-Altair-3 booster rocket which will in turn be launched from an F-15 fighter plane. Space tests of this system were believed to have been started in 1982.

A direct-ascent anti-satellite interceptor such as HIT is not classed as a killer satellite because it does not actually go into orbit. That is why military spokesmen can say the US is not developing a killer satellite. It is, however, developing a satellite killer which will eventually be able to reach spacecraft in high geosynchronous orbits. That is more than even the most generous estimates can attribute to Soviet capabilities. By the late 1980s the Pentagon expects to have HIT vehicles deployed to knock out those 24,000-mile-high satellites. Minuteman or Trident-1 missile boosters would be used for that mission.

In spite of the US Air Force's claim that the Soviets would have an anti-satellite capability by 1963, the USSR didn't even start testing such a system until 1968. In October of that year the Soviets began their first series of co-orbital intercepts that ended in December 1971. It involved seven attempted intercepts which achieved only slight success.

These Soviet intercept tests entailed putting a target satellite in orbit and a few days later launching an interceptor. Sometimes one target was used for two intercepts. The interceptors were planned to either match the target's orbit or achieve a highly elliptical orbit with a quick swoop past the target. More recent tests involve the interceptor popping up from a lower orbit into the path of the target. The only method of killing which the Soviets have demonstrated so far is with conventional explosives which scatter shrapnel-like pellets to destroy or disable the target. Intercepts have varied from between 150 and 600 miles altitude with most of them occurring at about the middle of that range. That would only threaten US spy satellites and transit navigation spacecraft.

Figure 8-1

Current Series of Soviet Satellite Intercept Tests

Target and Date Launched	Interceptor and Date Launched	Comments
Cosmos 803 February 12, 1976	Cosmos 804 February 16, 1976	Interceptor passed within 96 miles of target on fifth orbit. Not close enough to have damaged target had it exploded. Failure.
"	Cosmos 814 April 13, 1976	Interceptor passed within one kilometer of target. Reentered atmosphere and burned up after first orbit. Possible success.
Cosmos 839 July 9, 1976	Cosmos 843 July 21, 1976	Interceptor failed to achieve intercept altitude. Reentered atmosphere and burned up during first orbit. Failure.
Cosmos 880 December 9, 1976	Cosmos 886 December 27, 1976	Interceptor passed within one kilometer of target, moved to a higher altitude and exploded. Possible success.
Cosmos 909 May 19, 1977	Cosmos 910 May 23, 1977	Interceptor failed to achieve intercept altitude. This appears to be a duplicate of the July 1976 test. Failure.
"	Cosmos 918 June 16, 1977	Interceptor attempted to change orbit before one revolution about the earth but reentered atmosphere. Apparently a duplicate of the July 1976 attempted pop-up test. Did not pass close enough to target to damage it with fragmentation. Failure.

Figure 8-1 (continued)
Current Series of Soviet Satellite Intercept Tests

Target and Date Launched	Interceptor and Date Launched	Comments
Cosmos 959 October 21, 1977	Cosmos 961 October 26, 1977	Interceptor first attained a low orbit and then, reportedly, popped-up into a higher orbit and within one kilometer of the target. Possible success.
Cosmos 967 December 13, 1977	Cosmos 970 December 21, 1977	Interceptor used pop-up technique but did not pass close enough to target to damage with fragmentation. Commanded to explode in space. Failure.
"	Cosmos 1,009 May 19, 1978	Interceptor passed within one kilometer of target on second orbit. Possible success.
Cosmos 1,171 April 3, 1980	Cosmos 1,174 April 18, 1980	Intercept attempted during first orbit but missed target by 8 kilometers. Failure.
Cosmos 1,241 January 21, 1981	Cosmos 1,243 February 2, 1981	Passed within 8 kilometers of target on second orbit. Possible success.
"	Cosmos 1,258 March 14, 1981	Passed within 8 kilometers of target on second orbit. Possible success.
Cosmos 1,375 June 6, 1982	Cosmos 1,379 June 18, 1982	Passed within 8 kilometers of target but exploded too early due to fusing malfunction. Failure.

Note:
Killer must pass within 8 kilometers of target to be close enough to destroy it with shrapnel.

A second series of intermittent tests commenced in February 1976 and is still in progress. The individual tests in this series are summarized in Figure 8-1. Half of the current series were failures, chiefly because they did not pass close enough to the target to kill it with fragmentation.

There is speculation that much of the Soviet anti-satellite effort is aimed at what they see as a Chinese threat. Only 2½ months prior to the beginning of the current USSR test series China had launched its fourth satellite (China-4)—the first to exhibit characteristics of a military spy craft. China-4 was also the first to eject a recoverable capsule. China-5 and China-6 were launched early in 1976 just prior to the first Soviet killer satellite test of the present series. The Cosmos 880/886 test which took place in December 1976 only followed by a few days the launching of China-7—the second Chinese reconnaissance spacecraft which also ejected a capsule. In January 1978, about a month after the Cosmos 967/970 test, China-8 was launched and it also exhibited spy satellite characteristics including the release of a reentry module.

According to Owen Wilkes, a New Zealand researcher who has done extensive studies on space warfare for the Oslo International Peace Research Institute and the Stockholm International Peace Research Institute, there is a high degree of coincidence between the orbital characteristics of the Soviet anti-satellite tests and Chinese satellites. At the same time there is much less similarity between the Russian test parameters and American satellites.[5] He also points out that the even higher degree of similarity between killer satellite orbits and other USSR military spacecraft opens conjecture that these co-orbital intercepts may only be for defense of their own vehicles against US killers.

Another alleged Soviet anti-satellite move which received widespread and sensational media coverage was a reported attack on US spacecraft by Russian lasers. On October 18, 1975 infrared sensors were temporarily blinded on the US early warning satellite over the Indian Ocean. At the same time the infrared horizon sensors on two US Air Force data relay satellites in lower orbit were also blinded and those satellites began to tumble. Again on November 17th and 18th two other Air Force satellites had the same thing happen with their horizon sensors. The energy level of the infrared radiation that caused this problem was estimated to be at least ten times the intensity of an ICBM launch.

An immediate cry went up that Soviet ground-based lasers were being used to intentionally blind those spacecraft. Articles on the subject kept popping up for over a year. Meanwhile, only two months after the first incident, a Defense Department investigation had proved that was not the case. On December 15th the Pentagon told Congress that they had eliminated initial concerns that lasers were being used. Instead, they said, the blinding was caused by several large fires along Soviet natural gas pipelines which were local in nature and did not reduce the satellite's ability to provide early warning of ballistic missile launches. But this admission received only fine print coverage.

In summary, Soviet anti-satellite capabilities have been greatly exaggerated by Pentagon spokespeople. The USSR's twenty intercept attempts reflect a poor success rate. Meanwhile, for over two decades the Pentagon has been perfecting the direct ascent technique of destroying orbiting vehicles. At the same time it is pursuing killer laser and particle beam development for use against satellites. It is the US that is ahead with these weapons which fit neatly into its emerging first strike capability. As former White House press secretary Jody Powell pointed out, the deployment of satellite killers will increase the chances of a first strike in space.[6]

Today's enchantment with Star Wars is not confined to the movie houses and video arcades. Pentagon war rooms are preparing for the real thing. Space could well be the battleground of the future but we cannot deceive ourselves that the fighting will be confined there. The war that starts in space will likely engulf this planet in nuclear fire.[7]

NOTES

1. "New Laser Weapon Being Developed," *Watsonville Register-Pajaronian*, 5 November 1977.

2. *Defense Advanced Research Projects Agency Fiscal Year 1979 Research and Development Report*, statement by Dr. Robert R. Fossum, Director, 9 March 1978, p. I-3.

3. Robinson, Clarence A., Jr; "US Pushes Development of Beam Weapons," *Aviation Week and Space Technology,* 2 October 1978, p. 15.

4. Senate Committee on Appropriations, 1967, p. 68; cited in "Spacetracking and Space Warfare," *PRIO Publication S-1/77*, (Peace Research Institute, Oslo, Norway; 1977).

5. Personal Letter from Owen Wilkes. His plots of this comparison appear in Chapter 5 of *World Armaments and Disarmament: SIPRI Yearbook 1978*, (Stockholm International Peace Research Institute, Stockholm, Sweden).

6. AP Dispatch, "SALT Deal Predicted by Carter," *San Jose Mercury*, 13 November 1977.
7. Primary sources of reference for this chapter were pre-publication drafts of: Owen Wilkes and Nils Petter Gleditsch, "Optical Satellite Tracking: University Participation in Satellite War," *Journal of Peace Research 1978*, (Peace Research Institute, Oslo, Norway); "Chapter 5—The Arms Race in Space," *World Armaments and Disarmament: SIPRI Yearbook 1978*, (Stockholm International Peace Research Institute, Stockholm, Sweden); and Owen Wilkes, "Spacetracking and Space Warfare," *PRIO Publication S-1/77*, (Peace Research Institute, Oslo, Norway; 1977).

COMMAND, CONTROL AND COMMUNICATION

In the place where our old home village was destroyed, we buried the charred bones.
Now the white flowers are blooming there.
Ah! We must never allow, we must absolutely forbid, another atom bomb to fall.

—A Hiroshima peace song
by Ishiji Asada

Deep in the Pentagon behind heavy oak doors is a super secret room. Even the Joint Chiefs of Staff must submit their color-coded identification cards to the scrutiny of armed guards under ultra violet light before they can enter. Shifts of officers from all four branches of the military maintain a round-the-clock vigil in this two-story chamber. A red telephone provides a direct link to the White House. Lifting a beige phone instantly establishes contact with any US military commander anywhere in the world. One wall is covered with huge computer-fed display screens which flash the readiness of all American forces. A touch of a button will provide an item-by-item inventory of strategic weapons "on target." This is the War Room—the National Military Command Center; nerve center for the most potent military force in the world—control room for modern automated war.

The network which links the Pentagon and the National Command Authority (NCA—the President and Secretary of Defense) with the military forces is the *Command, Control* and *Communications* system, otherwise referred to as *C-cubed.* It consists of command centers, warning systems, data processing, and communications facilities as well as personnel and procedures. Like the extremely automated weapons and sensors it controls, C-cubed hinges on and revolves around computers. This, of course, is necessary to handle all of the rapidly occurring, unpredictable, and interrelated events of nuclear war—particularly the assimilation of data and coordination of forces required to initiate a first strike.

The command and control arm of C-cubed is called the *Worldwide Military Command and Control System* (WWMCCS—pronounced "Wimmex"). A prime component of Wimmex is the *National Military Command System* which is set up to execute instructions from the NCA through the channels of command and control down to the strategic and tactical forces. It makes the most use of all the sensor information regarding strike damage, attack warning, and surviving missile numbers. (Figure 9-1)

Since survivability is a top priority for Wimmex it has alternate underground and airborne command posts, redundant command and control systems, and communications networks that are protected from the atmospheric effects of nuclear explosions and intentional jamming. Besides the War Room in the Pentagon, there is an underground *Alternate National Military Command Center* near Fort Richie, Maryland and the *National Emergency Airborne Command Post*(NEACAP—pronounced "Kneecap").

The War Room has direct connections with all military information sources and is equipped for automatic distribution of incoming messages. Instantaneous access to the Wimmex computerized data file is made possible by large television-type screens which display critical information to key decision makers.

The underground Alternate National Military Command Center operates in conjunction with the Pentagon's War Room so that it can assume control instantaneously should the need arise. There are also two other hardened command posts in the United States: the NORAD headquarters in Cheyenne Mountain and the Strategic Air Command headquarters at Offutt Air Force Base in Nebraska.

In case of a direct nuclear attack on the C-cubed systems of the United States, the Pentagon assumes that the Kneecap aircraft is the only element certain to survive.* Therefore it is considered an essential

*The superior survivability of Kneecap is attributed to the fact that it is in the air. It also hinges on the plane being airborne before the attack hits. Even if it is airborne, I question that it is as invulnerable as the Air Force claims, given the massive clouds of dust that are certain to accompany a full-scale nuclear attack. A commercial jetliner's engines recently flamed-out while passing through high-altitude dust from a volcano.

Figure 9-1
Command, Control & Communication

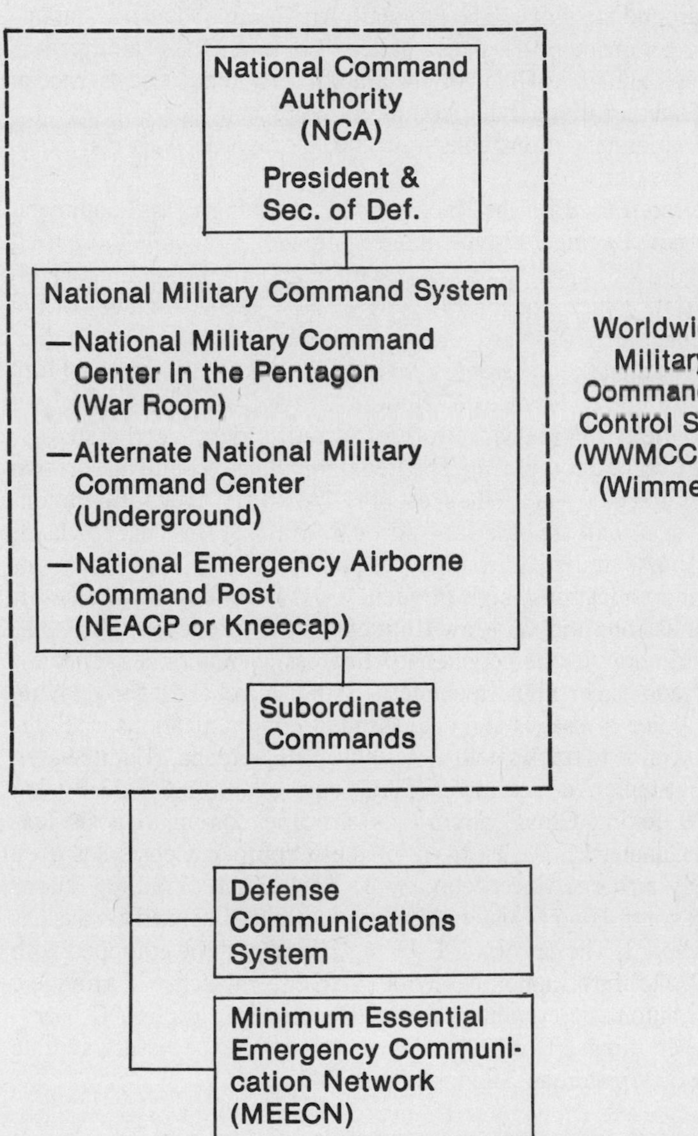

element of the national command system. It is equipped with several types of communications systems operating over a wide range of frequencies in order to send instructions to the strategic and nuclear forces all around the globe. The Strategic Air Command also maintains an airborne command post—the so-called "Looking Glass" aircraft—as do the Commanders-in-Chief of the Pacific, Atlantic, and European theatres. Together these flying command posts and special planes for submarine communications constitute the Worldwide Airborne Command Post System.

The aircraft used for the Kneecap and "Looking Glass" command posts are a new Boeing 747-type plane designated E-4 while those used for the airborne command posts of the three subordinate commanders-in-chief are the older Boeing 707-type planes. The advantages of the E-4A over the older 707-type craft range from increased communication capability and enhanced "hardness" to nuclear effects to greater mobility and a longer flight endurance of 72 hours. Three E-4As are presently in service and the Air Force has retrofitted a fourth, designated the E-4B, with better C-cubed equipment. The Pentagon plans to build at least two more E-4Bs and then retrofit the present E-4As to the "B" configuration. The Kneecap aircraft are based at Andrews Air Force Base in Maryland.

The E-4As utilize ultra-high frequency (UHF) wavebands for satellite communications, high frequency (HF) for long-range line-of-sight transmission, and very-low-frequency/low-frequency (VLF/LF) to send instructions to submerged ballistic missile submarines. The new E-4B will add super-high frequency (SHF) wavebands for relaying scrambled voice messages and data through communications satellites and it will be able to track satellites with its SHF antenna. (Figure 9-2)

The Strategic Air Command (SAC) currently employs 23 Boeing 707-type "Looking Glass" aircraft as airborne command posts (explained in Chapter 2). At least one of these command posts has been continuously airborne since February 3, 1961. Each "Looking Glass" aircraft can control two Minuteman wings (300 missiles) and always has a general aboard. The new E-4 "Looking Glass" will be equipped with the SAC Digital Information Network (SACDIN) which will provide a secure and automatic communication link connecting all SAC bases. Among other things, SACDIN will speed up the necessary remote retargeting of Minuteman-3 and the future MX.

To collect information for the C-cubed network the United States has placed three basic types of data-gathering satellites in orbit. They can be classed as *warning, reconnaissance* (spy), and *meteorological.* I touched on early warning spacecraft in an earlier chapter. Three of these satellites, equipped with arrays of infrared sensors, are in geosynchronous orbit. One, over the Indian Ocean, watches for ICBM launches from the Soviet Union. The other two, one over the Atlantic and another over the Pacific, watch for SLBM launches from those oceans. Early warning satellites also serve secondary secret functions. Satellites using mosaic infrared sensors will eventually replace the present spacecraft for missile warning as well as bomber warning and satellite tracking.

Of the numerous *spy satellites* belonging to the United States, *Big Bird* is probably the best known. The first of these 12-ton orbiting cameras was put into orbit in June 1971. Only one is in the sky at a time and it stays in a low polar orbit for four or five months. It is equipped with area surveillance and close-look visible light cameras, infrared sensors, side-looking radar, multi-spectral sensors, and a television camera with a zoom lens to see images in real time. Big Bird can also maneuver for a close look at a particular area or to take advantage of breaks in the clouds. It transmits information to a network of bases throughout the world which, in turn, relay that data to the satellite control facility in Sunnyvale, California. Capsules of film ejected from Big Bird are scooped up in mid-air over the Pacific by special aircraft based at Hickam Air Base in Hawaii.

Another type of observation satellite, designated *KH-11*, is supplanting many of the Big Bird functions. Two are always in orbit and they last as long as three years. They carry more sensors and send high resolution photos by digital image transmission rather than time-consuming film drops. These satellites are said to be able to discern golf balls on a green, license numbers on automobiles, and the "five-o'clock shadow" on a soldier's face.

One of the objectives of space observation is to detect nuclear explosions on earth. *Nuclear Detection Sensors* (NUDETS) are carried on the 70,000-mile-high *Vela* spacecraft which have detected every atmospheric nuclear test since 1973. These sensors are also being installed on the *Navstar* navigation satellites (Chapter 4). The entire system is referred to as the *Integrated Operational NUDETS System* (IONS). Besides verifying compliance with the test ban treaty IONS would function as part of the C-cubed network to determine damage to the US during nuclear attack and also to assess the damage and the silos destroyed in the Soviet Union.

Other types of US reconnaissance satellites include the vehicles which intercept various radio and radar signals. The *Rhyolite* series of spacecraft, for instance, intercept Soviet telemetry signals from missile tests. And of course many so-called civilian satellites such as Landsat (Chapter 6) also serve a reconnaissance role. Spy satellites characteristically have low-altitude polar orbits of 70-250 miles above the earth.

The four *Defense Meteorological Satellites* (DMS), which provide global weather information, also support a wide variety of military activities from strategic missions to tactical air operations and anti-submarine warfare. The DMS spacecraft are in 500-mile-high polar orbits and can photograph the earth twice in twelve hours. Their orbits are called "sun synchronous" because two always provide data in the morning and early evening, wherever they may be, while the other two are timed to take readings at noon and midnight. Visual and infrared cloud photos are transmitted to ground stations as well as to ships and mobile vans. A spare DMS satellite is available for launch on 45 days notice.

The communications arm of C-cubed—which links the various elements of Wimmex—consists of the *Defense Communications System* (DCS) and the *Minimum Essential Emergency Communication Network* (MEECN). (See Figure 9-1) The Defense Communications System is a global network which serves Wimmex as well as major intelligence, surveillance, and weapons systems by providing voice, teletype, and data transmissions. The basic components of the DCS are the *Automatic Voice Network, Automatic Secure Voice Communications,* the *Automatic Digital Network* (AUTODIN), and the *Defense Satellite Communications System* (DSCS).

The Automatic Voice Network is little more than a global telephone network and, as the name implies, the Automatic Secure Voice Communications is a more sophisticated system to allow worldwide communications relatively immune to enemy intercepts. The Automatic Digital Network enhances interaction among military computers and will soon allow dynamic sharing of communications satellite channels by a number of widely scattered earth stations.

More than 70 percent of the Pentagon's communications are routed through space. Satellites are providing an ever-widening scope of communications functions; not only for the Pentagon but for commercial users as well. Many civilian communications satellites, however, provide services for the military. The Pentagon leases channels on several commercial spacecraft as well as using satellites sponsored by Britain, NATO, and the European Space Agency.

The Pentagon's principle military satellite network is called the *Defense Satellite Communications System,* or DSCS. The DSCS constellation consists of six spacecraft in geosynchronous orbit—one each over the Indian, Western Pacific, Eastern Pacific and Atlantic Oceans plus two spares in orbit. These spacecraft use two-way super-high frequency (SHF) broadcasting to provide secure voice communication and a very fast transmission rate for data. They handle information from surveillance and warning satellites as well as performing many other functions. Existing *DSCS-2* spacecraft have a lifetime of three years and that network is expected to remain in operation until the mid-1980s. By that time it is expected that eighteen satellites will have been launched although many will have since burned out.

The first of a new generation of *DSCS-3* spacecraft that will have a ten-year lifespan and be hardened against nuclear effects is scheduled for launch in 1983. Besides providing global coverage, DSCS-3 will be able to focus transmissions to a confined area of the earth to make it spy-proof. These vehicles will also be equipped with "null steering" anti-jam features which point at the jammer and null out all reception from that line of sight. According to Lt. Gen. Lee M. Paschall, as director of the Defense Communications Agency, DSCS-3 provides a five-fold increase in controlability, a ten-fold increase in flexibility, and a hundred-to-one improvement in resistance to jamming.[1]

The *Fleet Satellite Communications* (FLTSATCOM) network consists of four spacecraft in geosynchronous orbit that provide global communications for ships, anti-submarine warfare planes, and other mobile forces including strategic Air Force communications. A fifth satellite was damaged during launch but three more are on order to fill the gap during the mid-1980s. These twenty-three channel UHF spacecraft are considered the most advanced communications satellites in orbit.

Survival of communications during a nuclear conflict is vital to the command and control function—the ability to conduct a nuclear war. For this reason there is another communications network—the Minimum Essential Emergency Communications Network (MEECN)—that is designed to survive a nuclear attack and provide at minimum a one-way flow of commands to activate strategic forces during severe jamming and nuclear effects environments. This system can be described as providing the guts of command, control and communications for nuclear war fighting.

The basic components of this network include satellite communications systems coupled with means of sending one-way messages to ballistic missile-launching submarines. Because of their alleged survivability the Kneecap airborne command posts are also considered an important part of this system. Planned improvements for the system stress survivability along with better security, interoperability, anti-jam capabilities, and the quality, accuracy and speed of message transmission. One of the most important modernization programs involves improving communications with the strategic submarine fleet.

Because regular radio waves don't penetrate into the ocean, maintaining contact with submarines poses special difficulties. Submarines can of course raise an antenna to the surface but that reveals their position. Very-low frequency (VLF) wavelengths, however, can penetrate the ocean to a depth of 30-40 feet and allow communications without compromising survivability too much. The United States uses a network of VLF stations around the world known as the *Fleet Broadcasting System* for submarine communications.

Another network, the *Loran-C* system, compliments the VLF stations by providing a pulsing low frequency (LF) signal that can penetrate water 9-12 feet and can be regulated in such a way as to send very slow one-way messages. The Northeast Atlantic Loran chain can send messages at the rate of about fifty letters per minute. A newer "Clarinet Pilgrim" system in the Central Pacific chain communicates about 400 letters per minute. Although primarily a navigation system, Loran-C adds to the redundancy of communications that makes command, control and communication survivable under extreme conditions.[2]

Because land transmitting stations are vulnerable to enemy sabotage and conventional or nuclear attack the Navy also maintains a fleet of flying broadcasting stations known as *Tacamo*—an acronym for "Take Charge And Move Out." This fleet, which presently consists of fourteen specially-equipped Lockheed C-130 transports, is an important component of MEECN. Relatively immune from attack, these aircraft can reel out a 5½-mile-long trailing antenna for VLF communications with submarines. The fleet will be increased to 18 aircraft by 1983, at which time two of these craft will always be in the air—one over the Pacific and the other over the Atlantic. The Navy is also planning to start replacing existing aircraft with a more modern plane.

Navigation for submarines presents problems similar to those associated with communications. Although US submarines have self-contained inertial guidance systems, they have to be updated periodically. One means of doing that is to get a position "fix" from one of the *Transit* navigation satellites, which are available approximately every hour and give fixes accurate to within 150-600 feet. But that requires putting an antenna on the surface for 3 to 4 minutes which risks being detected. When the *Navstar* global positioning system is operational it will provide instantaneous fixes accurate within 30 feet but will still require surfacing an antenna.

In some areas of the ocean the LF Loran-C is available which can penetrate seawater 9-12 feet and provide fixes within 250-500 feet. This is complimented by the VLF *Omega* network—eight Omega stations around the globe provide worldwide coverage with a signal that can penetrate seawater 30-40 feet. These stations transmit their signals in a prearranged sequence every ten seconds and each station has a discrete point in time when it emits its beep. The time that each station transmits relative to the others is very carefully controlled by perfectly synchronized atomic clocks. When a ship or submarine receives these signals—it can receive signals from at least three stations regardless of its location—it measures the time lag between the various beeps. By comparing the time difference between beeps at the receiver's location with the known interval between the transmitting times for the different stations, the submarine can determine its location to within 3,000 feet. A supplement to this system known as "Differential Omega" uses corrections broadcast from a nearby station of known location to improve accuracy to several hundred feet.*

The communications systems mentioned so far are cumbersome for the submarine and pose risks to its security. In addition, the communication link is completed only when the submarine has an antenna near the surface. The only available frequency for reaching submarines which are traveling at cruising speed and at operational depth is extremely-low frequency (ELF). Although ELF transmits messages at a very slow rate it would be able to reach a sub at all times and signal it to put an antenna near the surface for a Tacamo mesage. This capability is essential for orchestrating a first strike attack.† Vice Admiral R.Y. Kaufman alluded

*Even 3,000 foot accuracy will be adequate for targeting missiles in a first strike once the missile can obtain in-flight navigation updates from Navstar.

†The ELF transmitter is vulnerable to a simple pair of bolt cutters so it would only be useful prior to the beginning of hostilities, which is the time it would be needed to coordinate a first strike.

Figure 9-2
Communications/Navigation Frequencies

Frequency	Characteristics	Uses
ELF Extreme Low Frequency	Penetrates water hundreds of feet. Also penetrates earth. Slow rate of transmission. Virtually unaffected by nuclear blackouts and jamming. (Seafarer and formerly Sanguine)	Submarine communications and possibly communications with underground command posts.
VLF Very Low Frequency	Penetrates water to a depth of 30-40 feet. Highly immune to blackout and jamming. (Fleet Broadcasting System, Tacamo, Omega, NEACP)	Navigation and submarine communication. Long distance communication.
LF Low Frequency	Penetrates water to a depth of 9-12 feet. Fairly immune to blackout and jamming. (Loran, Clarinet Pilgrim, Transit satellites)	Navigation. Medium range communication.
MF Medium Frequency	(AM broadcasting)	Navigation. Medium range communication.
HF High Frequency	Cheap and portable but vulnerable. (Short wave and amateur radio; Over-the-horizon radar)	Global multi-purpose communication. Long range line-of-sight.

Figure 9-2 (continued)

Communications/Navigation Frequencies

Frequency	Characteristics	Uses
VHF Very High Frequency	(FM broadcasting and television; Radar)	Air-to-ground communications. Navigation.
UHF Ultra High Frequency	(FLTSATCOM, AFSATCOM, Transit, NEACP, microwave radar, SDS, MILSTAR)	Satellite communications. Navigation.
SHF Super High Frequency	Resistant to jamming. High data rate of transmission. Unaffected by nuclear blackout. (DSCS, AFSATCOM, NEACP, and microwave radar)	Secure voice transmission and high speed data transmission.
EHF Extreme High Frequency	Resistant to jamming (SDS, MILSTAR, millimeter wave radar)	Communications with and between satellites.

to the importance of continuous communication when he was asked back in 1973 if the deployment of Trident was in any way dependent on the ELF system:

> Yes, in that the Trident operating in the Pacific would require a capability to deliver a message to it some timely fashion. . . For example, were you to consider the Trident or any submarine in the role of retaliatory only, striking urban and industrial targets only, you would accept (censored) delay. On the other hand, were you to demand from the system response to a time-sensitive target . . . you would expect response in a matter of (censored).[3]

Figure 9-3
Submarine Communications Receiving Methods

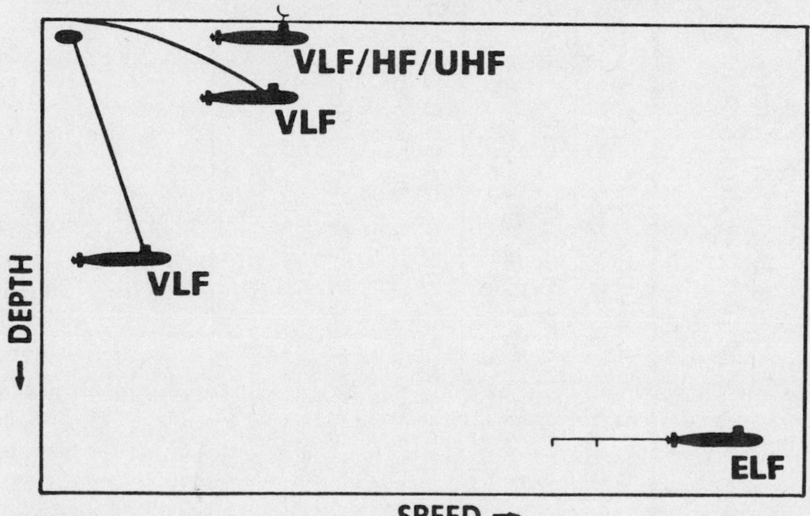

Source:
Hearings on Military Posture and HR 10929, before the House Armed Services Committee, (March 15, 1978), Part 3, Book 2, p. 1292.

In order to attack "time-urgent" counterforce targets such as missile silos it would be necessary to rally the submarine force quickly for more detailed instructions. An ELF network would provide that capability. Figure 9-3 depicts the depth and speed possible for submarines while receiving ELF as compared to other communications frequencies.

The scale for depth and speed in Figure 9-3 has been omitted from this Navy furnished chart. However, if we assume the scale of 0-35 miles per hour—the approximate speed range of nuclear-powered subs—across the bottom of the chart, it looks like the vessel could be going about 30 miles per hour while receiving ELF messages. For an antenna or antenna buoy on the surface it could only travel about ten miles per hour. With the antenna buoy 30-40 feet below the surface the speed would be cut to about five miles per hour. Figure 9-3 also shows that the sub can stay considerably deeper while receiving ELF than with the other means of delivering instructions.

The US Navy started researching ELF in 1958. One project, code-named *Pisces,* considered using the 850-mile-long powerline extending from Los Angeles to Oregon as a giant ELF transmitting antenna. In 1969 the Navy built its ELF Test Facility at Clam Lake, Wisconsin with two above-ground antennas in the form of a cross—each 14 miles long. That test facility has now been hooked into the Navy's telecommunications system and is sending messages to submerged submarines, reportedly with impressive results.

Because of its low power, however, the Wisconsin Test Facility has a restricted rate. To create an operational ELF facility the Navy proposed a deeply-buried network of antenna cables in Wisconsin. Called *Sanguine,* this system was supposed to have a good chance of surviving a nuclear attack. Public unease about the possible harmful physical and environmental effects, however, caused that site to be abandoned.

The Navy next picked Texas as a possible site but, again, popular pressure caused the site to be abandoned. With two strikes against it the Navy decided to revise its approach. First it changed the project's name to *Seafarer* to remove the undesirable stigma attached to the ill-fated Sanguine. Next it cut costs by eliminating the hardness requirement. Nevertheless, Seafarer would still be a grid consisting of 2,400 miles of antenna cable buried three to six feet deep over a 4,700 square-mile area.

The Upper Peninsula of Michigan was chosen as a likely site for Seafarer because the underlying layers of low-conductivity rock makes that portion of the US particularly suited for ELF transmission. This Laurentian Shield, as it is called, provides the geological resonance which makes the antenna effective.

On March 18, 1977, however, Governor William G. Millikan vetoed the installation of Seafarer in the state of Michigan. In a telegram to Defense Secretary Harold Brown he said: "The people of Michigan do not want Seafarer, nor do I."[4] Nevertheless, Congress granted the Navy $15-million to spend in 1978 for ELF equipment development and continued operation of the Wisconsin Test Facility. Within a year, however, President Carter sent a memorandum to Defense Secretary Brown ordering the termination of Seafarer.

The Navy quickly proposed an *Austere ELF* system in the Upper Peninsula which would comprise only 130 miles of antenna divided into three grids and buried along roadways and other rights of way. Each grid would terminate at the K.I. Sawyer Air Force Base (a SAC base) where the transmitter would be located. This proposed Michigan network would be coupled electronically with the Wisconsin facility 165 miles away by a simple leased telephone line. The Navy claimed the resulting total of 158 miles of antenna would provide almost the same global coverage as Seafarer although the transmission speed of messages would be slower.

Controversy continued and the Navy again reduced the proposed length of the antenna in Michigan—this time to 56 miles—and situated it above ground but coupled with the Wisconsin antenna. Now with a total of only 84 miles the program was renamed *Project ELF* with a planned completion date in 1985. It is generally believed, however, that this smaller scale ELF system will serve as the Pentagon's "foot-in-the-door" and that the future holds renewed attempts to construct a more ambitious project. Figure 9-4 maps the ELF coverage expected over the oceans of the world.

From Figure 9-4 we can see that communications with submarines in the Southwest Pacific and Indian Oceans is not possible with Project ELF. If, however, there were a comparable installation in Australia it would just about cover the remaining portions of the globe. As early as 1970, Bob Cooksey—a lecturer in International Relations at the Australian National University who has written extensively on US bases in Australia—presented evidence that a so-called "weather station" near Alice Springs in the Northern Territory is actually a US facility for sending ELF messages to submarines.[5] This station was reportedly modified in 1967 for that purpose—two years before the Wisconsin Test Facility was in operation. If it is in fact an ELF transmitter it would complete the global coverage for sending a rally signal to America's missile-packing submarines. (See Figure 9-5 for a summary of submarine communication and navigation systems).

The final element of the Minimum Essential Emergency Communication Network involves communications satellites. The prime mission of the *Air Force Satellite Communications* (AFSATCOM) system is to facilitate command and control over strategic bombers, silo-based missiles, airborne command posts, and Tacamo aircraft during crisis situations when jamming attempts and nuclear blackouts are severe. AFSATCOM consists of two-way transponders ("transmitter responders" tuned to pick up and relay long-range communications) on host satellites. In geosynchronous orbit, it uses 12 of the 23 UHF channels on the Fleet Satellite Communications (FLTSATCOM) spacecraft and will use SHF channels on DSCS-3. For coverage in the higher latitudes and polar regions, AFSATCOM transponders are on weather satellites.

Figure 9-4
ELF Communications Coverage

The area above the heavy line could have been reached with the 158-mile long ELF antenna formerly proposed for Wisconsin and the upper peninsula of Michigan. Timely messages would have been delivered in that region. The 84-mile antenna will cover approximately the same area at a transmission rate of one letter in five minutes—the data rate is functional to how big the system is.

Source:
Department of Defense Appropriations for 1979, hearings before the House Appropriations Committee (April 4, 1978), Part 4, p. 501.

The *Satellite Data System* (SDS) satellites form another part of AFSATCOM. They have highly eliptical orbits—25,000 miles high over the northern hemishere and swooping down to 200 miles high as they zoom around the southern hemisphere. They spend most of their time over the northern half of the globe and, being in polar orbit, provide

Figure 9-5

US Submarine Communications/Navigations Systems

System	Frequency	Ocean Penetration Depth	Accuracy	Availability
Fleet Broadcasting System	VLF	30-40 feet	N/A	Continuous. Submarine must raise antenna.
Tacamo	VLF	30-40 feet	N/A	Continuous. Submarine must raise antenna.
Loran-C/Clarinet Pilgrim	LF	9-12 feet	N/A	Continuous but not globally available. Submarine must raise antenna.
Project ELF	ELF	To submarine's operation depth	N/A	Continuous.
Transit	HF	None	150-600 feet	About every hour. Submarine must raise antenna to the surface.
Navstar	HF	None	30 feet	Continuous. Submarine must raise antenna to the surface.
Loran-C	LF	9-12 feet	250-500 feet	Continuous but not globally available. Submarine must raise antenna.
Omega	VLF	30-40 feet	200 to several thousand feet	Continous. Submarine must raise antenna.

N/A = not applicable HF = high frequency LF = low frequency VLF = very low frequency ELF = extremely low frequency better communication in the upper latitudes than do geosynchronous craft which must stay over the equator. SDS satellites have self-contained radioisotope power supplies rather than vulnerable solar arrays, and precision gyros to keep themselves right-side-up rather than relying on optical horizon sensors which can be blinded. Communications frequencies are in the UHF and EHF bands (Figure 9-2).

A more invulnerable follow-on to AFSATCOM and SDS—and possibly FLTSATCOM—is the all-service *Military Strategic-Tactical And Relay* (MILSTAR) system. Four spacecraft will be placed in geosynchronous orbit with an unspecified number of "dark satellite" spares hiding as high as 110,000 miles. Each MILSTAR will have 25 channels—15 UHF and 10 EHF—and will incorporate the latest survivability and anti-jam technology. The first of these satellites is expected to be launched in 1987.

A quick mention of futuristic communication systems is in order at this point. Both the Navy and Air Force have development programs in progress for laser communication by way of satellite. The Air Force's *Laser Satellite Communications System* first got under way in 1973 with a competitive study between Lockheed and McDonnell Douglas. McDonnell Douglas won the contract to build a laser communication system suitable for satellite use.

The Navy has also awarded contracts to McDonnell Douglas and GTE Sylvania to study the feasibility of satellite-related laser communication with submerged submarines. The laser for this purpose would operate in the blue-green portion of the visible light spectrum. For either the Air Force or the Navy system, it has been estimated that a satchel-sized laser transmitter could handle about 40,000 voice channels and 12 video channels simultaneously. The instantaneous transmission of a message combined with the narrow beam used would make this system secure from spying. An eavesdropper would have to erect sophisticated equipment within 250 feet of the intended receiving station in order to intercept the message.

This summary of command, control and communications systems should provide some insight into the complexities surrounding Pentagon war planning. Computer technology is the key link between the various C-cubed systems and between the various components of each system. The central role of computers would have a significant impact on the decision-making process leading up to a strategic first strike.*

---

*For this very reason we can conclude that the Soviets are not as near a first strike capability as the United States. Soviet inferiority in computer technology is well

Most strategists do not believe that a first strike would be launched like a "bolt out of the blue." It seems more likely that it would escalate from a crisis situation. If, for example, the US actually carried out its threat to use nuclear weapons to stop a massive conventional attack, where would things go from there? Soviet Premier Aleksei Kosygin stated that if the United States starts shooting nuclear weapons in the limited manner proposed then the Soviet Union would have no choice but to attack with its nuclear forces.[6] When that happens, tempers and emotions are certain to surge and the stage will be set to overreact with a knockout strike.

Other strategists cannot even imagine a battlefield commander requesting a limited strike when he knows it will lead to an exchange with himself as the final target. Neither can decision makers in the War Room be sure the Soviets would actually respond in a limited fashion. The upshot of these uncertainties could be that the limited-strike option would be skipped and a preemptive first strike undertaken.

Events would happen fast and with finality in these situations. Warning and surveillance systems would be shoring up data at a tremendous rate—all to be evaluated in "real time." Under such circumstances computers would usurp much of the decision making prerogative. Former director of Ballistic Missile Defense, Dr. Jacob B. Gilstein, aptly summed up the picture:

> . . . Computers are extremely important . . . No human being can enter the real time decision making loop and control the system. It has to be pre-programmed with logic so the computer can make the decision and run the game.[7]

This brings us to the question of who has control. Or does anyone, really, when the computer is running the game? When Dr. Herbert York testified before the House Subcommittee on International Security and Scientific Affairs regarding first use and responsible control of nuclear weapons, he pointed out that automatic "hair trigger" launch mechanisms and "launch-on-warning strategies" were two of his main concerns.[8] What he calls a "hair trigger" mechanism is an electronic system that upon sensing an attack would set off a signal to launch weapons without human

---

known. Recent years are replete with Soviet attempts to purchase or otherwise obtain US computer know-how. This fact is clear evidence in itself that the US is leading the way toward the ability to orchestrate a disarming first strike.

intervention. False alarms would be deadly—and they do happen. An incident like the accidental blinding of US warning satellites by gas field fires in the USSR would very likely lead to missile launches under a hair-trigger system. The perceptual limitations of warning systems can also give rise to false alerts. Only four days after the new BMEWS station in Thule, Greenland went into operation, for instance, NORAD headquarters in Cheyenne Mountain received a warning of a full scale attack. The "attack" turned out to be a radar mirage caused by reflections off the moon. Had a hair-trigger mechanism been operational this mirage would have automatically launched US nuclear weapons against the USSR.

There have been a series of similar incidents which are undoubtedly fresher in the reader's memory. During the autumn of 1979, old 1960-vintage Philco computers at NORAD were replaced by modern Honeywell, Univac and Nova models. Several weeks later, on November 9th, the computers signaled an attack by Soviet submarine-launched ballistic missiles. Because SLBMs fired from as far as a thousand miles off the US coast can reach their targets in ten minutes or less, US systems quickly prepared for retaliation. Four minutes before expected impact it was discovered that a training tape had been mistakenly inserted in the computer system.

Twice the following June, on the 3rd and 6th, NORAD computers warned of attack—this time ICBMs as well as SLBMs. Each time the alarm lasted three minutes before it was found to be false. The culprit turned out to be a 47-cent computer chip—and there are thousands of them in the C-cubed network. A subsequent report by Senators Gary Hart and Barry Goldwater revealed 147 false alerts during the 18-month period following installation of the new NORAD computers.[9] Four of those were serious enough to move the US strategic forces to a higher state of readiness. In the wake of these fiascos one can feel fortunate that, although hair-trigger systems have been suggested several times, they have never been approved. When the complexity of the situation makes them necessary, however, the story may be different.

Launch-on-Warning is almost as dangerous. Although a human being reserves the option of "pushing the button," that person still relies on warning sensors and computer logic to make an instantaneous decision. This launch-on-warning posture was alluded to in a footnote to former Secretary of State Henry Kissinger's speech before the Commonwealth Club in San Francisco on February 3, 1976.[10] There has since been considerable controversy over whether that is *de facto* evidence that the United States has such a policy. In 1977, then Defense Secretary Harold Brown was asked if the US would not launch its missiles until after it had been attacked and Soviet bombs had actually exploded on US soil. He replied: "I am not answering that question one way or the other, Mr. Chairman. I think that it is not our doctrine to do so—neither is it our doctrine that under no circumstances would we ever do so."[11] It is hard not to attach significance to such an evasive answer.

More direct answers were given in 1980 by two prominent generals. General Lew Allen, Jr., then Air Force Chief of Staff, told the House Appropriations Committee that "the United States has not foresworn the use of nuclear weapons launched under warning, and it is important that the Soviets not believe that they can rest in certainty that we would not do that."[12] On that same day, then Strategic Air Commander Richard H. Ellis was testifying before the Senate Armed Services Committee. The following dialogue took place:

> *Senator Jackson:* What can you do to improve the survivability of Minuteman? I assume, of course, you have always been looking at launch-on-warning—which I think is a very dangerous concept.
>
> *General Ellis:* Beyond the recently completed upgrade program there are no plans to improve its survivability other than the option to launch on warning, and I certainly agree with your assessment of that tactic.
>
> *Senator Jackson:* But that is what you could be forced to do in a crisis management situation?
>
> *General Ellis:* We could be forced to do that.[13]

Civilian control of the military is heralded as the guarantee that the decision to use nuclear weapons will never belong exclusively to the military. Legend has it that a little black box goes everywhere with the President of the United States and that no nuclear weapon can be launched unless he pushes a button in that box. The adequacy of this fail-safe system was challenged when Major Harold L. Hering asked how he would know that an order to fire a missile wasn't a fake. The answer this 21-year veteran of the Air Force received was an administrative discharge for "failure to demonstrate acceptable qualities of leadership."[14]

Safety devices, called "permissive action links," are reportedly attached to all nuclear weapons in silos. These devices can only be remotely opened by a code transmitted with the launch order so that a missile crew cannot arbitrarily fire the weapon. Submarines, however, have no outside controls. Instead, they have a verification code which is changed hourly. It is transmitted to the sub along with the launch order and must be verified by the submarine skipper, the executive officer, and the weapons officer. But for those three men to be able to verify the code there has to be prior knowledge of what it is and that implies someone else knows the key. It could be possible that someone in the Pentagon could usurp authority and send the command.

A 1975 Library of Congress report points out that the authority to release nuclear weapons "may be delegated to subordinate officers in the chain of command virtually without limitation."[15] The report goes on to say that because nuclear weapons can wreak unprecedented havoc it is popular belief that the President has tighter limitations on delegating authority for their use, but "we have been unable to find any constitutional or statutory basis supporting [that belief]."[16] According to the report, delegation of authority to use nuclear weapons would be secret. Nevertheless, there is substantial evidence that others than the President have access to the nuclear button.

During the 1964 presidential campaign when Senator Barry Goldwater advocated that small tactical nuclear weapons be classed as conventional,[17] it was pointed out that on October 7, 1958 General Earl E. Partridge, former NORAD commander, had told the *New York Times* that his command was authorized to launch nuclear weapons under certain circumstances without specific approval from the President.[18] Vice Admiral Gerald E. Miller, retired former deputy commander of the Joint Strategic Target Planning Staff, substantiated Partridge's statement when he told a congressional committee in 1976 that the NORAD commander "has been delegated such authority only under severe restrictions and specific conditions of attack."[19]

Admiral Miller also alluded to reports that Presidents Eisenhower and Kennedy had also delegated nuclear release authority to regional commanders but said he could not confirm them. However, Daniel Ellsberg, a former consultant to high Pentagon officials and source of the Pentagon Papers, claims he saw secret letters signed by Eisenhower authorizing overseas commanders to use nuclear weapons under certain conditions. Ellsberg said this delegation of authority remained in effect through the Kennedy Administration and, to the best of his knowledge, also under Presidents Johnson and Nixon.[20]

Ellsberg identified Admiral Harry D. Felt, then commander of the Pacific theatre, as one who had been given nuclear release authority. That authority apparently trickled farther down the chain. An Air Force major in Korea reportedly told Ellsberg he would put his dozen nuclear-armed planes in the air if he believed he was under attack. According to Ellsberg the major did concede that one of his pilots could possibly misunderstand instructions and touch off World War III.[21]

Congressman Clement Zablocki of Wisconsin was apparently troubled over Admiral Miller's testimony. He asked Deputy Assistant Secretary of Defense James Wade, Jr., for current details. Dr. Wade replied: "May I say right from the start that the subject of command and control, management, and employment of nuclear weapons is a very sensitive subject. We here in this room are not interested in providing information of this kind to those people outside this room whose interests are not compatible with our own. These matters are very sensitive. It is just inappropriate for discussion in this type of . . ."[22]

At that point the question was withdrawn "for now." Congressman Zablocki later submitted his query to be answered in writing for the record, possibly thinking the response would be secret. But Dr. Wade's answer was still unclassified: "There are highly sensitive operational plans and procedures for executing this release (of nuclear weapons) on the President's command under various emergency situations...Obviously, these plans and procedures as well as the safeguards that protect against unauthorized or accidental release of nuclear weapons are extremely sensitive and must be closely held by only a few senior civilian and military officials. For that reason I am unable to be more responsive to this question *in either classified or unclassified form*."[23] (emphasis added)

The word "sensitive," in military usage, usually implies concern regarding matters of public opinion or other political considerations rather than national security. Nevertheless, such concerns are adequate for the Pentagon to keep both the public and the Congress uninformed.*

---

*This incident is a striking example of why a Senate Special Committee on National Emergencies and Delegated Emergency Powers emphasized that it "is important that the different ways in which the President gives orders to carry out the law be understood and studied . . . " It has become evident in recent years that "many Executive directives are given without any means on the part of Congress and the public of determining whether such orders are lawful and in the spirit of our constitutional checks and balances." The special committee then warned that until Congress "grapples with these various issues directly, it will be faced with a continuing veil of secrecy and be unable to carry out its constitutional task of overseeing the Executive. The Indochina war and 'Watergate' tragically illustrate the results of such congressional inattention."[25]

The House committee appended this footnote to Dr. Wade's evasive answer: "Reply is not only inadequate on an unclassified basis but does not respond to the question which could have been supplied on a classified basis."[24]

At the time of this writing the Army has made a secret presentation to Congress entitled "AirLand Battle 2000" in which it requested pre-clearance to use tactical nuclear weapons in Europe. The Army says it expects "the battlefield of the 21st century to be dense with sophisticated combat systems whose range, lethality, and employment capabilities surpass anything known in contemporary warfare. . . . One other aspect of the future battlefield is drawn from the growing proliferation of nuclear, chemical and biological weapons coupled with the enemy's apparent permissive attitude regarding employment of those weapons. It is imperative that forces plan from the outset to fight dispersed on the conventional-nuclear-chemical-biological-electronic battlefield."[26] New Army manuals based in the "integrated battlefield" concept are reportedly about to be published.

In real life situations the requirement for a Presidential release prior to the use of nuclear weapons would be a mere formality. The parameters of any decision made by the President during a crisis situation would be set by Pentagon strategists and their battery of computers. Deputy Director of Defense Research and Engineering John Walsh explained it this way:

> The President does not participate often in command and control exercises, some Presidents never have, some a couple of times.
>
> So now you present the President with an absolutely new situation. It is no use to give him a room full of status boards and say, "Here it is boss, make a decision." It has to be boiled down to a scale—for example green, yellow and red—and he can decide by how far the needle moves, what he should do.[27]

That does not seem to be too difficult a task for the Chief Executive. The only criterion would be that he not be color blind. Such a scenario, however, reduces the Presidential decision to a mere formality and places the real responsibility right back in the War Room where the President's policy options are defined. Former DARPA Director George Heilmeier commented on how future movement of the needle might be handled:

> . . . Human limitations in formulating and communicating commands will be a central difficulty in increasingly complex command, control and communications systems. In anticipating this problem, DARPA has initiated research aimed at developing and demonstrating a new type of command system cybernetics, principally concerned with the development of a new technology for information management.[28]

Dr. Heilmeier's new command systems cybernetics has also been referred to as "machine intelligence." The goal of this research is to imbue computers with the ability to infer and deduce, as opposed to their traditional logic task of numerical processing. Such a capability approximates the type of "hair trigger" mechanism mentioned by Dr. York. We seem to be a mere step away from removing all human faculties from the decision-making function.

The fact that computers frequently break down would, of course, mean that human intervention would still be necessary. But given an information and decision-making situation geared toward the instantaneous integration of massive volumes of data, the human mind would be thrown back into the decision-making loop at points where its capabilities would be woefully inadequate. Such situations would add chaos to calamity. Nevertheless, according to Colonel Perry Nunn, once acting director for the Pentagon's office of command, control and communication, military commanders often "turn away from the computer in times of crisis because of its inefficiencies."[29]

Colonel Nunn was probably referring to the 1978 exercise called "Nifty Nugget"—the first simulated government-wide war mobilization since the real thing during World War II. It was a disaster. In addition to planning and supply shortfalls the computer system sent an army of 400,000 to the front in Europe where it was digitally annihilated. A November 1980 war game code-named "Proud Spirit" met with similar shortcomings including a "major failure of the computer-driven Worldwide Military Command and Control System (WWMCCS) that left military commanders without essential information concerning the readiness of their units for 12 hours during the height of the 'crisis' as Pentagon programmers found themselves locked out of one of their own computers."[30] A 1982 House Government Operations Committee report described Wimmex:

> . . . the existing WWMCCS management structure is so complex and fragmented that no one organization or individual has a complete overview of the program or the centralized responsibility

> for its funding, budgeting, and management. As a result the WWMCCS program:
> Is unresponsive to stated requirements;
> Is unreliable;
> Lacks economical and effective growth potential;
> Is incapable of transferring data and information efficiently;
> Makes the exploitation of [automatic data processing] technology extremely difficult and costly; and
> Impairs each command's operation backup capability.[31]

The delegation of so much of the decision-making function to automated systems and military commanders suggests that we have lost the concept of democratic processes outlined in the US Constitution. Article I of that document gives Congress the sole prerogative to declare war. Pentagon apologists would certainly argue that this provision is not suited to the character of contemporary crisis situations. Yet, it is precisely the Pentagon's drive for a first strike capability that has made the parameters of crisis so acute.

As the US approaches a first strike posture we can be certain that the USSR will strive for the same objective. Once the two superpowers face each other in a first strike standoff, with weapons systems and decision making highly automated, an international crisis, such as we have every few years, may prove disastrous. Nervous fingers will be poised over the button and the slightest miscalculation of what the other side is thinking will provide the deadly twitch. More to the point, an extraneous computer interference may slide aside the silo covers and raise submarine launch hatches. A blink of the wrong light on the display panel could, in microseconds, signal the flash of nuclear cremation. Such is the automated devastation toward which we are headed. In the following chapters I will depart from the technical aspects of a first strike posture to explore the political and economic imperatives that have led us to this perilous juncture.

NOTES

1. Lee M. Paschall, Lt. Gen. US Air Force, "The Second Generation DCS," *Air Force Magazine*, July 1978, pp. 72-75.
2. Ingvar Botnen, "The Use of Loran-C for Military Navigation and Communication," *PRIO Publication S-10/77*, (Peace Research Institute, Oslo, Norway; 1977).

3. *Fiscal Year 1974 Authorization for Military Procurement, Research and Development, Construction Authorization for the Safeguard ABM, and Active Duty and Selected Reserve Strengths*, hearings before the Senate Armed Forces Committee, 21 February 1973, Part 4, pp. 2210-2211.
4. Cited in 29 March 1977 Fact Sheet published by the Greenwood Nonviolent Community in Michigan.
5. Bob Cooksey, "Beyond Pine Gap: US Bases in Australia and New Zealand," *Dissent*, (Melbourne, Australia; Winter 1970), pp. 3-6.
6. "1974 Kennedy Leadership Address," by then Senator Walter F. Mondale, a speech at Johns Hopkins University in Baltimore, Maryland, 3 December 1974.
7. *Fiscal Year 1974 Authorization* . . . , op. cit., 8 February 1973, Part 4, p. 1900.
8. *First Use of Nuclear Weapons: Preserving Responsible Control*, hearings before the Subcommittee on International Security and Scientific Affairs of the House Committee on International Relations, 18 March 1976, pp. 58-60.
9. *Recent False Alerts From The Nation's Missile Attack Warning System*, report of Senators Gary Hart and Barry Goldwater to the Senate Armed Forces Committee, 9 October 1980, pp. 4-5.
10. *First Use of Nuclear Weapons*, op. cit., 25 March 1976, pp. 165-167.
11. *Department of Defense Appropriations for 1978*, hearings before the Defense Subcommittee of the House Appropriations Committee, 15 September 1977, Part 7, p. 155.
12. *Department of Defense Appropriations for 1981*, hearings before a subcommittee of the House Appropriations Committee, 20 February 1980, Part 2, p. 342.
13. *Department of Defense Authorization for Appropriations for Fiscal Year 1981*, hearings before the Senate Armed Forces Committee, 20 February 1980, Part 2, p. 502.
14. Phil Stanford, "Who Pushes The Button?", *Parade*, 28 March 1976.
15. *Authority to Order the Use of Nuclear Weapons*, a report prepared for the House International Relations Committee by the Congressional Research Service of the Library of Congress, 1 December 1975, p. 1.
16. Ibid, p. 3.
17. "Goldwater's Military Views," *The Nation*, 10 August 1964, p. 41; and "Our Defense," *Life*, 25 September 1964, p. 10. Cited in *Authority to Order Use of Nuclear Weapons*, op. cit., p. 2.
18. Lionel Lokas, *Hysteria 1964*, (New Rochelle, N.Y.; Arlington House, 1967), p. 47. Cited in *Authority to Order Use of Nuclear Weapons*, op. cit., p. 3.
19. *First Use of Nuclear Weapons*, op. cit., 18 March 1976, p. 49.

20. Opening address by Daniel Ellsberg at a "Whistleblowers' Conference," in Rayburn House Office Building, Washington, D.C. on 19 May 1978 which I attended. These statements were later published in the *San Jose Mercury*, p. 8F, in an article written by *Chicago Sun-Times* correspondent William Hines.
21. Ibid.
22. *First use of Nuclear Weapons*, op. cit., 25 March 1976, p. 165.
23. Ibid, p. 184.
24. Ibid.
25. *Summary of Executive orders in Times of War and National Emergency*, a working paper prepared by the Special Committee on National Emergencies and Delegated Emergency Powers, US Senate, August 1974, pp. 1 & 9.
26. Cited by Walter Pincus, "Army Would Like Authority to Use A-Weapons," *Washington Post*, 21 July 1982, p. 18.
27. *Hearings on Military Posture and HR 11500, Fiscal Year 1977*, before the House Armed Forces Committee, 20 February 1976, Part 5, p. 228.
28. *DARPA Fiscal Year 1978 Program for Research and Development*, a statement by Dr. George H. Heilmeier, Director, February 1977, p. II-57.
29. Cited by Bob Wyrick (*Newsday*), "$1-Billion Military Computer System Doesn't Work," *San Jose Mercury*, 7 July 1978, p. 16D.
30. John J. Fialka, "The Pentagon's Exercise 'Proud Spirit': Little Cause for Pride," *Parameters*, Journal of the US Army War College, March 1981, pp. 38-41.
31. *NORAD Computer Systems are Dangerously Obsolete*, Twenty-Third Report by the House Committee on Government Operations, 8 March 1982, p.9.

WHAT ABOUT THE RUSSIANS?

Today we are faced with the pre-eminent fact that, if civilization is to survive, we must cultivate the science of human relationships—the ability of all peoples, of all kinds, to live together and work together in the same world, at peace . . .

—From an undelivered speech
by Franklin D. Roosevelt
written shortly before his death.

One of the biggest obstacles to disarmament is the US public's perception of the "Soviet Threat." The fear of communism has been meticulously cultivated in America and today a mere mention of that word stirs up mass paranoia. It has proved to be a successful means of soliciting public approval for huge military spending programs, ostensibly to stay ahead of the Russians. In previous chapters I have made detailed comparisons of US and Soviet capabilities. In this chapter I'll address more pointedly the misconceptions held by the US public. The premises from which I begin are simple: while I do not condone Soviet participation in the nuclear weapons race, neither do I look upon Moscow as the spring-source of a world communist conspiracy. With a GNP that is half the size of our own, the Soviet Union is feeling the crunch of the arms race. As the Western press tirelessly points out, the Soviet people are pressuring the Kremlin for more emphasis on economic development and a better way of life. In this, and in the basic desire for survival, the American people can find common ground with their counterparts in the Soviet Union. Let us review some of the history of attempts at arms reduction and learn of opportunities which can lead us toward disarmament.

During almost four decades of the nuclear age it has been the United States which has led virtually every escalation in weapons production while the Soviet Union has, for the most part, tried to catch up. At only two points in the arms race did the Soviets have leading breakthroughs—when they launched the first intercontinental ballistic missile (ICBM) and when they put the first satellite into orbit; both in 1957. But their early accomplishments in those fields were shallow. The USSR had neither the resources nor the momentum to press ahead and they were soon surpassed by the US.

Let us move back to the beginning of the nuclear age.[1] The seed of the present arms race was planted when Albert Einstein wrote a letter to President Roosevelt about the possibility of building an atom bomb. That set the wheels in motion and on December 2, 1942 the first nuclear chain reaction was sustained at the University of Chicago. The reactor used became the first means of manufacturing plutonium for atomic bombs and was the forerunner of today's controversial power plants.

On July 16, 1945 the first atomic bomb blazed across the desert at Alamagordo, New Mexico. During the following month, on the sixth and ninth respectively, atomic bombs ripped into the Japanese cities of Hiroshima and Nagasaki. World War II ended as humanity stepped carelessly into the nuclear age.

For the few years following World War II the United States remained the sole nuclear power in the world. There was a lot of soul-searching by some leaders over how to control this formidable weapon. Some thought that atomic energy should be under international supervision and saw the United Nations as the logical overseer. A proposal to that effect, known as the Baruch Plan, was presented in June 1946. Unfortunately, it was not specific about when nuclear weapons should be destroyed—apparently because other US leaders wanted that to happen only after a certain amount of technological development had taken place. This, along with the Soviet recognition that the US essentially dominated the UN, caused Moscow to reject the proposal. In the following December the Soviets achieved their first chain reaction, almost exactly four years after the US.

The Kremlin countered with the Gromyko Plan which called for a complete ban on production and use of nuclear weapons and specified elimination of existing stockpiles within three months. The US, having the only stockpile, quickly rejected that idea and the arms race went on. The chance to stop the nuclear menance in its infancy was lost forever and the cold war set in. On August 29, 1949, again four years after the

US, the Soviets detonated their first atomic bomb near Semipalatinsk in Central Asia.

By the time the world's second nuclear power was born the US had exploded eight nuclear devices and had stockpiled several hundred. In that same year (August 1949) the North Atlantic Treaty Organization (NATO) went into effect—almost six years before the "Eastern bloc" counterpart, the Warsaw Pact, was created. As the Soviets tried to catch up the United States surged still farther ahead. Early in 1950, President Truman ordered a full scale program to develop the hydrogen bomb. The first thermonuclear reaction took place at Eniwetok Atoll in the Pacific in May of the following year. It was followed by the first significant hydrogen bomb explosion at Eniwetok on November 1, 1952 which had an explosive force of ten megatons.

Since the Eniwetok explosion took place in the atmosphere, it has been speculated that Soviet scientists were able to examine fallout particles to determine the composition of the bomb. At any rate, they were quick to develop a fusion device and they exploded their first hydrogen bomb on August 12, 1953. These events heralded the age of missiles because the increased power of hydrogen warheads compensated for the rudimentary navigation systems which were available at that time. Both the USSR and US started exploring the field.

1953 also marked the beginning of new leadership in both countries. Dwight Eisenhower became President of the United States in January. Stalin died in March and Georgi Malenkov was named Premier. Up until this time the US "containment of communism" policy was contingent on having a monopoly on nuclear weapons because the Soviet Union was vastly superior in numbers of conventional military divisions. Because the US and Western European countries gave reconstruction first priority in the immediate post-war period, they had no intentions of trying to match the Soviets' conventional forces. For that reason, US policy focused on fighting a nuclear war of whatever magnitude necessary to counter Soviet conventional superiority, rather than putting restraints on nuclear weapons. But when the USSR started making nuclear weapons operational the US escalated its nuclear doctrine to include "massive retaliation" to deter a potential nuclear attack. That remained the "announced" strategy until James Schlesinger introduced the doctrine of selectivity and flexibility—limited nuclear war—twenty years later.

The Soviet Union emerged from World War II as a major world power. Prior to 1953 its strategy was maintaining a large conventional army and establishing an Eastern European buffer zone to protect against Western Europe, and breaking the nuclear monopoly. Although Soviet development of nuclear weapons started earlier, they had not made any operational until 1953. As the Soviet strategic arsenal became more significant, however, the emphasis on conventional arms diminished. By the time Krushchev came to power in 1957 the number of Soviet army divisions had been reduced by a third.

It was during the Eisenhower Administration that the United States ringed the Soviet Union with mutual defense treaties. Besides NATO, Secretary of State John Foster Dulles negotiated the Southeast Asia Treaty Organization (SEATO, which scuttled the 1954 Geneva Accord specifying that Vietnam should not be divided), the Baghdad Pact (although the US is not a member), the Australia-New Zealand-United States (ANZUS) Treaty in the South Pacific, and bilateral ties with Japan, Taiwan, South Korea and the Philippines. It was in the midst of these negotiations that the Warsaw Pact between Russia and the Eastern European countries was signed.

Early in 1955 the Soviets announced that they would accept a modified Anglo-French disarmament plan which had been proposed the previous year and which was backed by the United States. It would have banned the use of nuclear weapons while providing for a gradual decrease of existing stockpiles, along with reduction of conventional forces. It was the first serious disarmament proposal in a decade. The United States responded by stating that it had reevaluated its position and now had some serious reservations concerning the steps proposed.

The next offer came at the Geneva summit meeting on July 21, 1955 when Eisenhower proposed his *Open Skies* policy. It specified that the US and USSR would exchange military blueprints and allow aircraft flights over each other's territory. At that time the US had a 5,000 to 1,000 lead in the number of nuclear warheads and the Soviets promptly rejected Eisenhower's proposal—apparantly to conceal their nuclear inferiority and economic weakness.

Also in 1955, the year before the Soviets started making their first strategic bombers operational, the famous *bomber gap* panic started. Although the alleged Soviet lead was later proved to be fictional, it served to justify the deployment of the US B-52 fleet which began in 1955 and continued until 1962. 1955 also marked the beginning of the Atlas and Titan ICBM programs in the US along with the American Thor and Jupiter intermediate range ballistic missiles. During mid-1956, U-2 spy plane flights were started over Russia in an attempt to penetrate

Soviet secrecy and in 1957 the Minuteman ICBM and Polaris SLBM programs commenced.

A Soviet reaction to the flurry of activity was soon forthcoming. On August 26, 1957 the USSR announced the first flight of a long-range intercontinental missile. Five weeks later, October 4th, Sputnik-1 was put into orbit. On November 3rd, Sputnik-2 was successfully launched carrying the dog, Laika. These events took place as Nikita Krushchev came into power. The Soviets seem to have felt so hopelessly outclassed in the bomber age that they were trying to transcend it into the missile age.

I had just started to work at Lockheed Missiles and Space Company when these events happened. These Soviet demonstrations brought on an atmosphere of panic as development programs were stepped-up and the 58-hour week became a way of life. My collegues and I were warned that if we were caught even discussing some topics pertaining to satellites we would be fired on the spot—even though we had been cleared for security. A remark made in jest about the Orwellian phrase "Big Brother is watching" could send the jester scurrying down the road with his or her termination pay. Lockheed was doing work on a spacecraft—undoubtedly a spy satellite—called Big Brother. Security was so tight that it was a secret that certain subjects were taboo to discuss at work.

Those were scary times in the aerospace industry. The Gaither Committee had reported to President Eisenhower that by 1959 the Soviets could launch 100 ICBMs against the United States. Various intelligence agencies predicted that within five years the Soviet ICBM inventory would soar to 1,000 or 1,500 missiles. Although the mythical *bomber gap* had evaporated we were now confronted with the famous *missile gap*.

Eisenhower ordered more U-2 spy plane flights to verify the *missile gap*. As it turned out, the Soviet missile program was really focused on shorter range weapons to be targeted against Western Europe, rather than on ICBMs. By 1961 the *missile gap* was seen to be just as illusory as the *bomber gap* but by that time it had done its work. The Polaris weapons system became operational in 1961—eight years before a comparable Soviet counterpart. The ICBM program was also accelerated and by 1964 the US inventory was over 700. Four years were to pass before the Soviets would possess a comparable ICBM force. Figure 10-1 illustrates the US and USSR buildup of both ICBMs and SLBMs. When President Kennedy discovered in 1961 that the US was leading Russia

Figure 10-1
ICBM & SLBM Buildup[2]

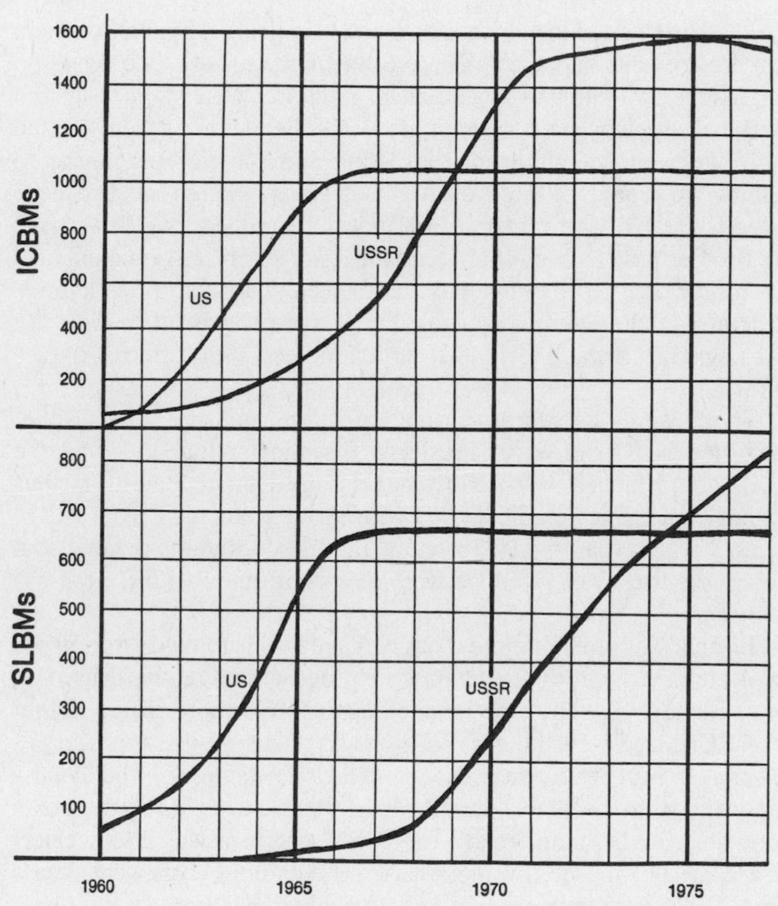

with ICBMs and bombers he discontinued the Air Force B-70 supersonic bomber program. Nevertheless, he allowed the ICBM and SLBM programs to continue.

Another attempt to close the nonexistant *missile gap* involved deploying so-called tactical US nuclear weapons on aircraft carriers and in NATO territory. This not only gave the US more weapons capable of hitting targets in the Soviet homeland but it made a coordinated attack by the USSR against both US-based ICBMs and forward-based tactical nuclear weapons very difficult.

Russia's reaction to this forward basing plan was to attempt to move intermediate-range into Cuba. A most telling indication of Soviet strategic inferiority came when the US forced Krushchev to back down and remove the Cuban missiles.

Figure 10-2
Strategic Weapons Allowed by SALT-1

	U.S.	U.S.S.R.
ICBMs	1,054	1,618
SLBMs	656*	740**
Ballistic Missile Submarines	41*	62

*If the 54 US Titan-2 ICBMs are dismantled, these figures could be raised to 710 SLBMs in 44 submarines.
**If the 210 SS-7 and SS-8 ICBMs are dismantled, this figure could be raised to 950 SLBMs.

Source:
Britannica Book of the Year 1973, (Encyclopedia Britannioa, Inc.), pp. 212-213.

This loss of face in Cuba galvanized Soviet determination to match US nuclear might. Krushchev promised that the US would never again be able to force the USSR to back down. Tremendous effort went into accelerating their ICBM buildup and beginning an SLBM force. The size of the Soviet missile force eventually surpassed the US inventory in the early seventies (Figure 10-1). But in the meantime the US had switched its emphasis from increasing the quantity to improving the quality of its strategic weapons. One of these quality improvements,

MIRVs, allowed the US to dramatically increase its number of nuclear warheads without increasing the quantity of carrier vehicles, thereby giving the US a three-to-one edge in deliverable warheads.

By 1970 a semblance of parity had been established; the Soviet lead in numbers of ICBMs was offset by a US warhead advantage. Of course there were other factors involved such as the bomber inventory and forward basing, but this rough degree of equivalence led to the first Strategic Arms Limitation Talks which culminated in the 1972 SALT-1 accords. One of those accords was the Interim Agreement on Offensive Weapons which merely froze the planned inventory of each country. Figure 10-2 depicts the numbers allowed.

Numerous cold warriors have asserted that the United States had sacrificed too much in reaching the temporary five-year agreement. Nevertheless, US negotiators had very solid justification for allowing the Soviets numerical superiority in missiles and bombers. Some of those reasons were:

1. US deployment of MIRVs gave America a three-to-one advantage in deliverable warheads.
2. Intercontinental heavy bombers were not limited by the Interim Agreement and the US had between 350 and 450. The Soviet Union had about 150.
3. The United States had tactical nuclear weapons and forward-based medium bombers which could reach the Soviet Union.
4. NATO allies (Great Britain and France) also had missiles and missile-launching submarines.
5. Forward bases in Scotland, Spain and Guam allowed US ballistic missile submarines to be "on station" up to fifty percent longer.
6. Other aspects of weapons and submarines (readiness, reliability, accuracy) favor the United States.

SALT-1 merely gave the Soviets increased numbers in some areas to compensate for their deficiencies in others, and to offset the superior American technologies. It put no restrictions at all on quality improvements which was the area of a decided US advantage. It did, however, change the emphasis of negotiations away from the concept of *disarmament* and toward the more nebulous *arms limitation*.

After seven years of frustrating negotiation SALT 2 was finally signed by Presidents Carter and Brezhnev at Vienna on June 18, 1979.

The final document did nothing to slow strategic arms development in either country. To summarize the agreement quickly, each country is restricted to:

—2,400 strategic nuclear delivery vehicles (long-range ballistic missiles and heavy bombers) initially. By the end of 1981 that number is to be reduced to 2,250. (The US had 2,283 at the time of signing and the USSR 2,504.)

—Of that total number, only 1,320 can be MIRVed missiles or bombers carrying cruise missiles. (The US had 1,049 and the USSR 752 at the time of signing.)

—Of the 1,320 only 1,200 can be MIRVed strategic missiles. That leaves 120 bombers carrying cruise missiles which can be increased if the number of MIRVed missiles is decreased accordingly.

—Of the 1,200 maximum of MIRVed missiles, not more than 820 can be ICBMs.

The fact that SALT-2 would not have slowed military plans was confirmed by President Carter on February 20, 1979: " . . . the MX missile; the Trident submarine and its missiles; air-, ground-, and sea-launched cruise missiles; cruise missile carrier aircraft; and a new penetrating bomber. These would be permitted."[3] Although it has not been ratified, both countries are abiding by its restrictions—chiefly because it did not restrict anything either country wanted to do anyway.

The Reagan Adminstration's START (STrategic Arms Reduction Talks) negotiations, in spite of their promising title, appear to be aimed at giving the Pentagon greater superiority. President Reagan's proposal for cutting ballistic missiles and their warheads by a third aims at the components where Soviet technology is strongest. But it will do nothing to stop the thousands of cruise missiles and hundreds of new bombers the US is geared up to deploy. Also, while severely paring the Soviet advantage in megatonnage the START proposal would not affect quality improvements—where the US excels.

The Soviets should be credited for some overtures on their part which could have led to meaningful arms reduction through bilateral and multilateral agreements. Although the Soviets have not led the way with unilateral initiatives, these proposals do indicate that, as former US Ambassador to the Soviet Union Averill Harriman has frequently stated, the Russians do not want nuclear war. They want peaceful competition and will be receptive to new moves to develop trade, control the spread of nuclear arms, and reduce arms budgets.[4] In December 1973 the USSR, Guinea and Nigeria proposed to the United Nations General Assembly that the nuclear powers reduce their military spending by ten percent, and use a tenth of the savings to help developing countries.[5] The savings would have amounted to between 15 and 20 billion dollars.

The UN approved that resolution with 83 in favor, 2 against and 38 abstentions—the United States and its NATO allies abstained. The UN Secretary General then set up an international group of experts to study the proposed reductions.[6] In spite of its indifference, the US did participate in that study by appointing A. S. Becker of Rand Corporation to take part. The group unanimously agreed on a report in September 1974 but the resolution was never implemented.[7] Instead, in December 1974 then US Ambassador to the UN John A. Scali threatened that the United Nations would fade into the shadow world of rhetoric if a numerical majority kept pushing through resolutions that offend an influential minority.[8]

I witnessed another indication of the Soviets' willingness to negotiate meaningful arms reduction while attending a scientific symposium on disarmament in Moscow during July 1975. Virtually all of the Soviets on the commission dealing with nuclear weapons were members of the Soviet Academy of Sciences and some were actually working on the SALT-2 negotiations in progess at the time. Although those of us from the Western countries certainly did not represent the views of our governments regarding arms control, the Soviet scientists would not support a statement coming out of the commission for worldwide publication if it weren't along the lines of Kremlin thinking. Nevertheless, one set of proposals in that statement outlined some meaningful steps toward disarmament. They were:

1. Immediate complete prohibition of underground nuclear weapons tests. (This would prevent developing new warheads.)
2. A ban on all flight tests of strategic weapons systems. (This would prevent developing new carrier vehicles.)
3. Begin negotiations for the elimination of ICBMs and bombers from each country's strategic triad, and reduction of SLBMs by 90 percent.

All participants in the commission accepted the general principle of these proposals although some stressed the need for a gradual approach and appropriate timing of each measure.[9]

There have been other overtures on the part of the USSR to negotiate a meaningful reduction in nuclear weapons. At the Twenty-Fifth Communist Party Convention in Moscow during February 1976, Soviet leader Brezhnev said that if the United States would stop the development of Trident and the B-1 bomber the Soviets would cut back on their strategic programs accordingly. Then on September 27, 1977 Soviet Foreign Minister Andrei Gromyko announced to the UN that the Soviet Union had suspended testing of its neutron bomb and was willing to join the US and Britain in a treaty to ban all underground nuclear testing. The subsequent halting of the B-1 bomber by the Carter Administration, however, was clouded by the cruise-missile step-up and the speculation about other penetrating bomber options. It did not give the appearance of good faith. The negotiations on a nuclear test ban which followed Gromyko's UN announcement appeared hopeful for a while but were later overshadowed by the debate over SALT-2. In July 1982, President Reagan announced that he does not plan on resuming negotiations for a comprehensive test ban.

The actual events which have taken place since Einstein's letter are not readily apparent to the general public. When they are mentioned they are usually slanted—particularly around the time of Pentagon budget proposals. History is replete with examples of so-called intelligence information being declassified so it can be used to make a strong pitch for more guns or ships. When a new weapon system looks technologically feasible a scenerio is fabricated to create a need for it. Then some Soviet activity is brought into focus so the public and Congress will fear another threat—or gap.

A pointed example of this is the militarization of the Indian Ocean over the objections of its littoral countries. There are numerous reasons why that body of water is important to the United States, not the least of which is that most of our oil passes through it. As a result, there is an increasing US naval buildup taking place and the island of Diego Garcia (about a thousand miles south of India) is the site of a growing military base. The Bangladesh war of 1971 gave the first excuse for a few US ships to slip in. The October 1973 Mid-East war justified still more. More recently a justification for increasing the US fleet was the allegedly significant Soviet naval presence in the area. Since the fall of the Shah in Iran and the Soviet invasion of Afghanistan, the US presence in the Indian Ocean has increased appreciably.

Let us examine how Soviet naval activities have been consistently exaggerated. During 1975-76 the US Navy's campaign to construct the Diego Garcia base hit its peak. The Soviet base in Somalia was described by then Defense Secretary Schlesinger as a "significant new facility" which could store ship-to-ship and air-to-surface missiles. He also said it could support Soviet warship and air operations. But a subsequent tour of the Somalian base by US Congressmen disclosed no evidence of such storage or that the airstrip and communications facilities were anything significant. Subsequently, in 1977, the Soviet contingent was expelled by the Somalian government. Ironically, the US now has use of this very base that had supposedly justified an increased US presence in the region.

The Soviet Navy had first appeared in the Indian Ocean in 1967 with a space tracking ship. By 1973 their military flotilla usually consisted of about twelve ships; including two oilers, two to four supply ships, and an occasional oceanographic ship. They were never particularly active except for short bursts such as during the Bangladesh and Mid-East wars and even then they were restrained by lack of shore facilities. Ten mine sweepers were temporarily brought in during 1971 and that prompted US reports that the Soviets' Indian Ocean fleet had been boosted to twenty ships.

About 1974, however, the Russian flotilla declined to not more than seven ships, the largest being a destroyer. During the height of the Diego Garcia debate in 1976, the Soviet Navy only had four combat ships in that theatre—France had eighteen and the US eight. During closed-door hearings, former CIA director William Colby admitted to the House Armed Services Committee that the Soviet presence was relatively small and inactive, and that it lacked air cover and land bases.[10]

Most, if not all, intelligence estimates concerning the Soviet threat come from the very source that wants to build the weapons to counter it—the Pentagon. As a matter of policy the Pentagon deals with worst case scenerios. That means they specify what it is *possible* for the Soviets to do rather than what they are *likely* to do. Since the Pentagon has been set up as the sole authority, and since it has a monopoly on most of the relevant information, what data trickles down to the public is slanted, fragmented, or buried so deep in an impenetrable mass of superfluos information that the key facts are lost.

To further illustrate these points I would like to discuss two prominent *gaps* that are being proferred today. First is the *dollar gap*. The Pentagon has bombarded the American public with the story that the

Soviets are outspending the US for military defense. But many factors contribute to the difficulty in comparing the military expenditures of the two countries—secrecy on both sides, military projects hidden in "civilian" agencies, different economic structures in the two countries, and capital-intensive vs labor-intensive industry are a few that come readily to mind. Nevertheless, there have been attempts to make a comparison. Studies of fiscal year 1976 serve as good examples.

According to the Soviet government, its defense budget for FY 1976 was somewhere between 27-and 30-billion roubles. Considering the exchange rate between dollars and roubles that would be around $40-billion, give or take a few billion. However, the CIA estimates Soviet expenditures for that year at about $130-billion, compared to $102.2-billion for the US. Intelligence experts say that figure is calculated by comparing what it would cost to duplicate the Soviet effort in the United States. Such a comparison would naturally boost the cost since US production lines are not geared for Soviet technology. According to Congressman Les Aspin, another study was started by the intelligence community to calculate what it would cost the Soviets in roubles to duplicate the US activity. That study was apparently never publicized but the calculated cost was predicted to be astronomical because the Soviet Union has no counterpart for US technology. As Congressman Aspin summed it up: "It would cost each country a great deal more than is actually spent to build the other fellow's armed forces."[11]

A more credible evaluation of Soviet military expenditures during fiscal year 1976 was done by the Stockholm International Peace Research Institute (SIPRI) which is an independent body established by the Swedish Parliament in 1966. Its comparison is based on the rouble/dollar purchasing power parity which shows that Soviet military spending is more like $61-billion.[12] For the Pentagon's purposes, that does not compare favorably with the $102.2-billion US expenditure. It seems clear that the higher CIA estimate is just another illustration of how evidence is juggled to create the Soviet threat.

The second major scare which confronts us today is the *counterforce gap*. We have already seen how a comparison of *all* the characteristics of weapons indicates that the US arsenal is much more aggressive. But the Pentagon consistently distorts the facts to make it look like the Russians are achieving a disarming first strike while the US is reluctantly improving its military capability purely out of self defense. Carefully chosen phrases ("*Present* plans are to build ten submarines"), deceptive wording ("We have no *announced* counterforce strategy"), and psychological terms ("killer satellites" vs "SAINT vehicles") all contribute to the deception. A further example of this technique is provided by a presentation to Congress by former Director of Defense Research and Engineering Malcolm R. Currie and his deputy, John B. Walsh.

Currie and Walsh listed general nuclear war as one of the potentialities the US is trying to deter while leaving the door open for a first strike. But Currie alleged that the only form in which first use of nuclear weapons can be destabilizing is as a disarming first strike. Such a capability, he claimed, is absurd for the US because our "open society" would not allow the secrecy needed for a disarming first strike. Currie admitted he did not pretend to understand how the Soviets think and then immediately offered an explanation of their thinking. He said they plan to go beyond nuclear equivalence by obtaining the ability to destroy America militarily while minimizing retaliation. He explained that "though we believe they do not have such an ability now, it is not forever impossible of achievement."[13]

Currie's perspective conveniently slipped back and forth between present and future tense to accomodate his preordained conclusions. When looking at the US forces he spoke in the present tense of our inability to launch a preemptive first strike in an open society. But when referring to the Soviets he alluded to what may be possible at some future date and used that as evidence that the Soviets are upsetting some perceived stability in the nuclear balance. On this basis he argued that we need even more sophisticated weapons, thereby upsetting the current balance, in order to "restore" a balance that might be upset by the Soviets at some future time.

Walsh then offered a feeble attempt to credit this dichotomy of thinking. Alluding to our dismantled ABM system he claimed it would be "less impossible" for the Soviets to achieve a disarming first strike than the US. "Disarm does not necessarily mean deprive of all weapons," he said, going on to point out that the US could not now stop a "single" Russian reentry vehicle (RV) while they, the Soviets, can stop "several tens of RVs."[14] That impressive sounding number comes to a grand total of 64, the number of ABM interceptors stationed around Moscow at the time (later reduced to 32), if they were one-hundred percent effective. To suggest that such a capability could significantly reduce the threat posed by approximately 7,500 US strategic warheads delivered by missiles is like saying a lake holds significantly less water after a bucket-full has been removed.

Defense Secretary Harold Brown also has a penchant for saying something in one sentence and retracting it with the next. A pointed example of this give-and-take information occurred in September of 1977. After emphasizing the threat of all the new Soviet ICBMs he said: "I should add that the United States has no desire for a plan to develop a first strike, disarming capability against the Soviet Union. Accordingly, we shall not seek such a capability *provided that the Soviets show similar restraint toward the United States*."[15] (Emphasis added.) From the description he gave of Soviet activities which preceded that statement, it is obvious that Secretary Brown does not interpret Soviet programs as showing "restraint."

For there to be a *counterforce gap* the Soviets would need a tremendous lead in technology over the United States and that is obviously not the case. In August 1977, Admiral Stansfield Turner, Director of the CIA, confided to the Joint Economic Priorities and Economy in Government subcommittee of Congress that the Soviets lag the US in most areas of military technology.[16] Figure 10-3 illustrates how the US led and still leads in making many war technologies operational. In addition to what is shown, the US has a significant superiority in electronics micro-miniaturization, nuclear effects hardening, warhead miniaturization, computer technology, and sensor development. These fields are essential to a first strike capability.

In the example cited above, Dr. Currie alluded to the secrecy needed to launch a disarming strike and indicated that that was not possible in the United States. Yet when Pentagon officials are challenged on sensitive points they quickly retreat behind the cloak of secrecy and plead the inability to comment because of *national security*. Meanwhile, military spokesmen consistently refuse to engage in public dialogue and open forums where spontaneous responses might injure their credibility. The Navy, for instance, has repeatedly been invited to appear with me at speaking engagements and on television shows to defend its position that Trident is only a defensive weapons system. It has always declined to do so.

The Pentagon Papers and Watergate are classic examples of what secrecy can hide when any branch of the government is not held responsible to the people. In another case, former President Gerald Ford and the House Intelligence Committee had a disagreement over secrets involving the October 1973 Mid-East war. When Chairman Otis G. Pike asked Assistant Attorney General Rex E. Lee how the committee could operate without control over classified information, Lee replied that it should respect the secrecy rules all congressional committees have followed for decades. "That's exactly what's wrong, Mr. Lee," retorted

Figure 10-3
Comparison of US-USSR Technological Developments

	U.S.	U.S.S.R
First deployed tactical nuclear weapons in Europe	1954	1957
First ICBM flight	1958	1957
First satellite in orbit	1958	1957
Acquired low penetrating bomber	1959	1975
Acquired supersonic bomber	1960	1975
Deployed solid propellant in missiles:		
SLBMs	1960	1977*
ICBMs	1962	1968
Placed satellites in geosynchronous orbit	1963	1974
Put MRVs on missiles:		
tested	1963	1968
operational	1964	1973
Put penetration aids (chaff and decoys) on missiles	1964	not to date
High speed reentry vehicles:		
tested	1968	1973
operational:	1970	1975
Put MIRVs on missiles:		
tested	1968	1973
operational:		
ICBMs	1970	1975
SLBMs	1971	1978
Developed stellar inertial guidance (SIG)	1969-70	1972-73
Put on-board computers on missiles	1970	1975
Number of foreign military bases	hundreds	few

*Deployed 12 SS-N-17 SLBMs on one Yankee class submarine only.

Pike. "For decades committees in Congress have not done their jobs and you've been loving it. You come up here and whisper in one friendly congressman's ear and in my opinion that's why we're in the mess we're in."[17]

In early 1976 the House Select Committee on Intelligence concluded, after a year-long investigation, that federal intelligence agencies, as they are currently constituted, operate in such secret ways that they are beyond the scrutiny of Congress. Retired Admiral Gene LaRocque once said that 95 percent of the Navy's secrets are illegitimate. "About 50 percent of what is classified in the Navy is designed to keep it from the Army and the Air Force and the Secretary of Defense," explained LaRocque. "About 25 percent is designed to be kept secret from Congress and about 20 percent from the State Department and the public." He summed up that only 5 percent of all secrecy in the Navy is justified by security regulations.[18] That is how the military operates in our "open society."

The campaign to maintain the fear of the "Soviet Threat" took a more activist turn after Jimmy Carter won the presidential election in 1976. The *Committee on the Present Danger* was born. Consisting of 141 original members it started under the co-chairmanship of former Deputy Defense Secretary David Packard and AFL-CIO Secretary-Treasurer Lane Kirkland, with another former Deputy Defense Secretary Paul Nitze in charge of policy studies. Some hard-line anti-communist members are Jay Lovestone, director of AFL-CIO's International Department; W. Glenn Campbell, director of the Hoover Institution of War, Revolution and Peace; and Richard V. Allen, a senior staff member of the Hoover Institution and former foreign affairs advisor to Richard Nixon.[19] Other members are former Secretary of State Dean Rusk, former Chief of Naval Operations Admiral Elmo Zumwalt, General Maxwell Taylor, Eugene Rostow, and Dr. Edward Teller, father of the H-bomb. Claiming to be wholly independent, this committee released a statement saying: "In the nuclear age enough may not be enough and time may run out unless our efforts keep pace."[20] This committee campaigned strongly againt SALT-2 as giving the Soviets too much of an advantage. Now, under the Reagan Administration, Eugene Rostow was director of the Arms Control and Disarmament Agency and Paul Nitze is the chief arms control negotiator for theatre nuclear weapons.

In contrast, former director of the US Arms Control and Disarmament Agency Paul Warnke has expressed fear that new developments in strategic weapons may tempt one of the two superpowers to launch a preemptive first strike against the other. He pointed out that there is the temptation to strike first because of the fear you won't be able to strike second.

This brings us to the question of whether the Soviet Union actually has a strategic counterforce capability. Since counterforce is a matter of degree, we must say that they do have some. Their bigger bombs are a variable in the lethality equation. But it is not the most important variable. The degree of counterforce their large warheads confer is moot when we consider that the United States is approaching the ultimate in counterforce—the unanswerable first strike. The U.S. should have that capability by the end of the 1980s. The Soviet Union, meanwhile, seems to be trying to keep pace but there is no available evidence that it has the missile lethality, the anti-submarine warfare potential, the ballistic missile defense network, or the space warfare technology to attain a disarming first strike before the end of this century, if then.

In closing this chapter I would like to quote extensively from Dr. William J. Perry, recently retired Under Secretary of Defense for Research and Engineering. Pay close attention to this testimony from the Pentagon's chief research scientist as he tells of US superiority over the USSR. The following is excerpted from a lengthy comparison of capabilities:

> . . . We spend a lot of our time looking at the capabilities of the Soviet Union and I am sure they spend a lot of time looking at our capabilities. I would have to say that if I were a Russian looking at the US I would be very impressed and maybe even have a bit of an inferiority complex.
>
> I think what they fear is the technical capability of our weapons and they try to compensate for that by manufacturing lots of weapons. The difficulty of that approach is that . . . if they don't have a chance to use them in the next few years, they have made the wrong decision because they have today, for example, maybe 20,000 tanks deployed in Europe. In the meantime we are developing something called precision guided weapons which will allow 155 millimeter artillery shells to destroy tanks . . . 20,000 tanks of the design they have will be the wrong thing to have in the early '80s . . . I think they have made the wrong decision in going to the massive deployment of equipment but they have made that decision . . .
>
> . . . It has reached the stage now where we see them building four ICBMs at once. Now, even the most enthusiastic supporter

> of ICBMs in the United States would not propose that we build four in parallel. I would simply submit that is an enormous waste of money on their part . . . I can come up with no rational reason for why they should have to design four ICBMs simultaneously and then actually proceed to build them.
> . . . They are building, for example, surface effect ships. They have an enormous program in that area which, as nearly as we can determine, is a colossal failure . . . I would hate to be the person who has to come in and defend that program. I think I would get massacred . . .[21]

This is the Soviet capability which has been inflated by the Pentagon to justify its most ambitious projects. This is the Russian threat that we hear so much about—particularly when the military budget is coming up for debate. Nevertheless, in the short run, an unpredictable response to aggressive US programs by a frightened Kremlin may hasten the unthinkable. Soviet planners may be stampeded into firing their nuclear weapons in time of crisis before they can be destroyed by a superior US arsenal. That, in the final analysis, may be the greatest danger of all.

Notes

1. For a fuller history of the nuclear arms race see Chalmers M. Roberts, "The Road To Moscow," Chapter 1 of *SALT: The Moscow Agreements And Beyond,* edited by Mason Willrich and John B. Rhinelander, (N.Y.; The Free Press, 1974).
2. Sources for figure 10-1: *World Armaments And Disarmament: SIPRI Yearbook 1977,* (Stockholm International Peace Research Institute, Sweden, 1977), pp. 24-25; *United States Military Posture For FY 1977,* by Chairman of the Joint Chiefs of Staff General George S. Brown, 20 January 1976, pp. 37-38; *SALT: The Moscow Agreements And Beyond,* op. cit., p. 52; *Fiscal Year 1975 Authorization for Military Procurement, Research and Development, and Active Duty, Selected Reserve, and Civilian Personnel Strengths,* hearings before the Senate Armed Forces Committee, 23 April 1974, Part 7, p. 3865.
3. Speech at Georgia Institute of Technology. Published in US State Department publication *Current Policy,* No. 57, dated March 1979.
4. Speech by Averill Harriman at "The Capitol Hill Seminar," sponsored by the Coalition for a New Foreign and Military Policy, February 1977. Published in the *Congressional Record,* 9 February 1977 and 3 March 1977.

5. *World Armaments And Disarmament; SIPRI Yearbook 1974,* (Stockholm International Peace Research Institute, Sweden, 1974), p. 430. (UN Resolution 3093A/XXVIII)
6. Ibid. (UN Resolution 3093B/XXVIII)
7. United Nations Document A/9770.
8. AP dispatch, "Warning Handed to UN," *San Jose Mercury,* 7 December 1974.
9. For further details see S. Kawasaki, "Report of Proceedings of Commission 3," *Scientific World,* (40 Goodge St., London, W1P 1FH, England; Number 3/4 1975), pp. 40-42.
10. Most of the above information on Diego Garcia and the Indian Ocean was obtained from a study of that area by New Zealand researcher Owen Wilkes; from a draft copy of his 22-page report entitled "US Militarization of the Indian Ocean and Australasian Involvement."
11. Congressman Les Aspin, "Budget Time At The Pentagon," *The Nation,* 3 April 1976, pp. 399-402.
12. Dr. Frank Barnaby, "The Mounting Prospects Of Nuclear War," *Bulletin of the Atomic Scientists,* June 1977, pp. 11-20.
13. *Fiscal Year 1977 Authorization For Military Procurement, Research And Development, And Active Duty, Selected Reserve, And Civilian Personnel Strengths,* hearing before the Senate Armed Forces Committee, 11 March 1976, Part 11, p. 5921.
14. Ibid, p. 5936.
15. Remarks by Defense Secretary Harold Brown at the Thirty-Fourth Annual Dinner of the National Security Industrial Association at the Sheraton-Park Hotel in Washington, D.C. on 15 September 1977. Published in the 15 September 1977 *New Release* from the Office of the Assistant Secretary of Defense for Public Affairs.
16. "Congress told Soviets Trailing Technologically," *Aviation Week And Space Technology,* 5 September 1977, p. 55.
17. AP dispatch, "Four Little Words May Create Crisis," *San Jose Mercury,* 13 September 1975.
18. UPI dispatch, "95% of Navy Secrets Said Illigitimate," *San Jose Mercury,* 1 January 1975.
19. Column by TRB from Washington, "Present Danger," *Watsonville Register-Pajaronian,* 23 November 1976.
20. AP dispatch, "Russian Arms Edge Predicted," *San Jose Mercury,* 4 April 1977.
21. *Department of Defense Appropriations For 1979,* hearing before the House Appropriations Committee, 23 February 1978, Part 3, pp. 646-648.

THE PROFIT IMPERATIVE

The philosophy which has ruled government groups, and individuals for the past three-hundred years has not taken as its guide the moral law; has not considered the rights of man. Money, not men has been the supreme consideration and the justifying end.

—Peter Marin

The Pentagon rationalizes its appetite for new and more deadly weapons as being "in the national interest" and necessary for "national security." These are the charmed phrases that are supposed to conjure public support for the arms race. Although these slogans have been part of America's political lexicon for decades few of us could agree on their exact meaning. In fact, it is their inexactitude that accounts for their political potency. Is there a singular "national interest"? Is our nation's military and foreign policy in our "national interest"? Is our foreign and military policy necessary to our "national security"? My experience overseas both during and after WW II was important to my discovery of the true parameters of our military policy.

In July 1946 I left war-torn Manila after having seen combat and the beginning of post-war reconstruction. Manila had been reduced to slums with over-crowded housing, inadequate transportation, and a scarcity of food. Young children were in the streets begging, stealing, and hustling for prostitutes. Crime was high.

Thirty years later I returned to those islands expecting to see a rebuilt Manila. I had seen Moscow, Tokyo, Hiroshima and Nagasaki all rebuilt since WW II. But in the Philippines I was disappointed. Conditions were actually worse in some respects—aggravated by the increased population. About one-fifth of Manila's population are squatters who are forced to live in tar-paper and tin shacks hastily erected on any vacant lot they can find. That statistic is typical of every major city in the Philippines and many other parts of the world. The rich, on the other hand, have walls around their houses topped with broken glass, spikes and barbed wire. The one exception to this destitution is the Makati area of Manila where banks and multi/transnationals have their offices in modern high-rise buildings. And the residential areas adjoining that sector are a typical suburbia except for access being controlled by armed guards to keep out the poor.

In Manila a three-room hut often houses a family as large as eight people and it is not uncommon to find ten living in a single room. These people's daily calorie intake is 35 percent below U.N. nutritional standards. One-million in the country's 12½-million work force are unemployed and another five-million are underemployed. Youth vagrancy is particularly high and young men graduating from college feel fortunate to be hired as houseboys or barkeepers in tourist hotels. The suicide rate among young people is abnormal. Crime is rampant.

Economic exploitation of these circumstances is frightening. It has actually suppressed the economic development which would alleviate these conditions. Approximately 800 American companies own fifty percent of all business enterprises and constitute eighty percent of all foreign investment. US petroleum companies control ninety percent of all energy sources. And the biggest incentive to attract foreign companies is the low wage which is blatantly illustrated in the following excerpt from a six-page *Fortune* magazine advertisement designed to lure investment:

> . . . Incentives like plentiful, inexpensive labor that is English-speaking and therefore a cinch to train . . . The minimum age for employment is fourteen years. The law provides for a seven-day work week with one day of rest for each employee. The minimum wage is $1.20 per day. Unskilled workers receive the minimum rate. Semi-skilled workers receive between $1.48 and $1.77 daily, while skilled workers earn $1.77 to $2.22 and above.[1]

Note that those wages are *per day,* not per hour. And American agribusiness is also capitalizing on these destitute conditions. The best land in the Philippines is used to produce pineapple, coconuts, bananas and sugar to sell to the industrialized nations while the Filipino people don't own enough good land to raise their basic food grains. Resources are exploited in similar fashion. The lumber industry, for instance, denudes half-a-million acres a year, causing the Philippines to have the most rapid rate of deforestation of any nation in the world. Japan and America get the lumber while the Filipinos have floods when it rains and drought during the dry seasons.

The Philippines is typical of many other countries in Asia, South America and Africa. Their exploitation was pointed out by Brazilian Archbishop Dom Helder Camara:

> The economic and cultural structures that dominate the world are suppressing more than two-thirds of humanity. They are killing and destroying more people than the bloodiest wars —and doing all this under the cover of democracy.
>
> Multinational companies only seem to be democratic because they have thousands of share holders, but in reality, they are controlled by a small group of men.
>
> They refine production methods and exploit raw materials with only one aim: to extract the greatest possible profit. Human considerations and human costs have little or no place in the decisions of the ruling groups.[2]

In 1941, just prior to the United States' entry into World War II, there were 1,000 companies which controlled two-thirds of the manufacturing assets of the United States. Thirty-five years later that same share of production had conglomerated to only 200 companies and if the trend continues it will be only 100 corporations by the latter 1980s. The upshot of these mergers was that small businesses were squeezed out of the picture while middle-sized corporations were absorbed. Free enterprise gave way to price-fixing and monopolies with the consequent devastating effect on the consumer and the public at large. American corporations have grown so big that they are insensitive to human needs and immune to legal sanctions. They merely pursue their own measurement of success, which is profits.

As manufacturing and agribusiness swelled in power they discovered that undeveloped countries offered a lush source of cheap labor, fertile land, and abundant resources. General Motors, AT&T, Standard Oil, Ford, Sears Roebuck, General Electric, IBM, Mobile Oil, Chrysler, and IT&T are among the corporations that operate billions of dollars worth of business annually on foreign soil. If each of these ten corporate giants were individual nations they would be among the fifty richest in the world.

Investment of giant US corporations in the Third World has become the overriding consideration in forming US foreign policy. This investment is euphemistically called our "national interests." US "national interests" are measured in billions of dollars of investment in foreign countries. It is an activity which can only be carried out under the protection of a strong military umbrella. During his February 1975 Pentagon budget presentation to Congress, then Defense Secretary James Schlesinger alluded to the military role in protecting foreign business involvement:

> We live in an interdependent world economy, and our foreign economic interests are substantial. US assets abroad amount to more than $180-billion. Annually, we export more than $70-billion in goods and services, and our imports are of equal or greater value . . .[3]

These "foreign economic interests," first of all, drive the United States toward an interventionist foreign policy which tends to support regimes in the countries involved that are sympathetic to US business interests. Secondly, investment in the Third World leads the US to guard against political and economic competition which might threaten that investment, particularly from the USSR.

Let us look first at the interventionist aspect. In 1974 US Senator Alan Cranston pointed out that: "Among the governments we've been supporting are 56 military dictatorships and authoritarian regimes which, to one degree or another, have used military aid money, intended for defense against outside aggression, to terrorize and subjugate their own people."[4] More recently, a survey by the Center for Defense Information revealed that "of the 41 military-dominated governments in the world with records of violating citizens' rights, the United States has been a major supplier of 28."[5]

The US must support these repressive regimes, of course, to prevent nationalist movements from upsetting US business arrangements. Commercial and government sales of military equipment have jumped from $1.2-billion in 1970 to over $17-billion in 1981. More than half went to the oil-rich countries of the Mideast. Under President Reagan's relaxed controls, the Pentagon estimates that figure will top $23-billion in 1982. The Center for Defense Information estimates that with loans and grants tacked-on, foreign military transfers will exceed

$30-billion.[6] In July 1981 President Reagan proclaimed: "The United States therefore views the transfer of conventional arms . . . as an essential element of its global defense posture and an indispensable component of its foreign policy."[7]

Congress has control of very few of these transactions. Most are cash sales conducted under the Foreign Military Sales Act with the US Defense Department acting as intermediary after a license has been obtained from the State Department. US corporations actually promote the business. The top ten US arms exporters account for about one-quarter of these sales by over a thousand companies holding arms export licenses. The act also allows the President to guarantee the loans which private companies extend to foreign governments.

Commercial arms sales amount to about 10 percent of the dollar figure in arms sales abroad but they have far more than 10 percent of the effect. These sales usually involve small arms which only need an export license from the State Department. These, of course, are the weapons used most by dictatorships to repress their own people in order to maintain a favorable climate for US business.

There are still other types of foreign sales which are not directly military and which are handled through the Commerce Department. These include such items as transport aircraft and helicopters which can, however, be used to support military operations. In some cases they are actual stripped-down military vehicles which the purchasing country equips itself.

Now let us turn to the other aspect of US foreign policy brought about by American investment in undeveloped countries—the elimination of political and economic competition. About the only way to keep other developed countries out of the poor countries being exploited is by being #1 in global military strength. Nuclear weapons have been a principal tool to deter such competition—particularly *Soviet* competition. Since World War II the promotion of a "Soviet Threat" has been the chief means by which a series of administrations have created public support for an interventionary and confrontational foreign policy.

The arms race resulting from this foreign policy has created opportunities for corporate profits on the domestic scene. Trillions of dollars have been extorted from the taxpayers' pockets to finance the arms race and provide the military umbrella necessary for corporate ventures abroad. The Pentagon budget rose from $80-billion in 1973 to requested outlays of $215.9-billion for 1983, and the Defense

Department predicts that outlays will soar to $356-billion by 1987. Military expenditures today amount to over half the money appropriated by Congress and about 40 percent of the Pentagon's cut is channeled to American businesses in the form of defense contracts.[8] Military contracting has grown into a lucrative $100-billion a year business and is still climbing. In addition, there are more billions of dollars in military work buried in such agencies as the National Aeronautics and Space Administration, the National Oceanic and Atmospheric Administration, the Department of Energy, and the National Science Foundation. Here are a few examples.

The National Science Foundation has granted contracts to research centers like Scripps Institution of Oceanography to study such things as sound propagation through the ocean and mapping the magnetic field of the ocean. We have seen how these technologies are being used for anti-submarine warfare. The Department of Energy (and its predecessors, the Energy Research and Development Administration and the Atomic Energy Commission) has done all the research, development and production of tens of thousands of nuclear bombs for the US stockpile. They also develop and produce the reactors which propel nuclear-powered submarines and warships. The National Aeronautics and Space Administration has, through the years, supplied the military with space flights and satellites. We have seen how Landsat, Skylab, and Seasat satellites, to name a few, fit into this category. Probably the most striking example right now is the space shuttle which receives wide media coverage as a civilian space project. But the truth is that during the 1980s it will become the only vehicle used to put *all* Pentagon satellites in orbit. It will support 100 percent of the rapidly expanding military space work. Furthermore, the missions which have been cut over the past year to maintain schedule and budget restraints have not been military.

Lockheed Corporation, which ranked as the largest of defense contractors in eleven of the past twenty years and is currently one of the six largest defense contractors, will provide a good example of the dynamics and profitability of weapons contracting. Lockheed is a highly diversified conglomerate with plants spread from coast to coast and numerous offices overseas. In 1971 Lockheed allegedly faced bankruptcy due to cost overruns on the C-5A Air Force transport; three years after Deputy Assistant Air Force Secretary Ernest Fitzgerald told Congress that the C-5A fleet was going to cost the government $2-billion more than it should.

Price overrun claims were at that time handled by the US Government Renegotiating Board. Most of the claims, according to former director of the Naval nuclear Propulsion Program Admiral Hyman G. Rickover, are grossly overpadded. He says that contractor employees "are encouraged to search out and report actions and events that may be used as a basis for a claim . . . Even minor technical matters are now treated as contract matters."[9] According to Rickover, "various people might brag of settling claims for only thirty cents on the dollar. They know that by upping their claims two or three times, they will get really more than they need, and this is what is being done."[10] Admiral Rickover used Lockheed in one of his examples:

> In 1971, the then Commander, Naval Ship Systems Command, personally negotiated with officials at Lockheed Corporation and tentatively agreed to pay the company $62 million in settlement of shipbuilding claims totaling about $160 million. This was the infamous "Golden Handshake" made without benefit of a legal, technical, and financial audit of the claim.
>
> Based on subsequent audit of the claim, the Navy contracting officer determined that the Navy owed only about $7 million, not $62 million. Lockheed appealed to the Armed Services Board of Contract Appeals. The Board, without reviewing the merits of the Lockheed claims, ordered the Navy to pay the $62 million on the basis that Deputy Secretary of Defense Packard had made statements which led the company to believe it would be paid that amount.[11]

As a result of concentrated lobbying by military contractors the Renegotiating Act is now defunct. Pressure is now concentrated on keeping the 1934 Vinson-Trammell Act from being re-implemented. It would place a 12 percent profit ceiling on aerospace contracts and 10 percent on shipyards. In the absence of statutory restraints the military contracting climate is most favorable to profit maximization.

Now let us return for a clear look at the C-5A. In early 1973 the General Accounting Office (Congressional auditor of government spending) reported that the 1965 estimate of $3.4 billion for 120 C-5A aircraft would rise to $4.9-billion for only 81 planes. Furthermore, those planes turned out to be of inferior quality. Two-and-a-half years later the General Accounting Office again said that because of weakness in the wings the service life of each C-5A will only be 8,750 flying hours instead of the 30,000 specified in the contract. It would cost an additional $1.1-billion, the Air Force estimated, to strengthen the wings to meet the 30,000 hour goal. But even after that is accomplished, the General Accounting Office noted, the C-5A's cargo capacity would still have to be set at only 174,000 pounds, instead of the design load of 220,000 pounds, in order to ease the strain on the wings. If that is not done the entire fleet will have to be grounded by 1983. The Air Force requested $190.2-million for fiscal 1983 to rework another 18 aircraft. The total repair job, now estimated at $1.5-billion, is the costliest in Pentagon history.

The C-5A story is a classic example of how inefficiency in fulfilling government contracts is rewarded by more business and more profits. It is interesting to note, however, that the commerical market has no counterpart of the renegotiating board. Competition in that area is unforgiving of cost growth.

At the same time that Lockheed was negotiating for C-5A overruns, it was also having difficulty with sales of its new commerical L-1011 jetliner. However, the company extricated itself from its 1971 C-5A problems by "absorbing" a $200-million loss. Immediately thereafter Rolls Royce, engine builder for the commerical L-1011, went bankrupt and saddled Lockheed with another $190-million in unplanned expenses. At Richard Nixon's prompting, Congress passed the Emergency Loan Guarantee Act that backed a $250-million loan to save the aerospace giant. This famous "bail-out" raised loud debate in Congress and among the public and served to focus attention on the inefficiency of Lockheed management. By the end of 1973 Lockheed's long-term debts were $853-million. Ernest Fitzgerald, the person who exposed the C-5A scandal and lost his job as a result, pointed out:

> Regardless of their performance, the bumbling giants demand that the taxpayers furnish whatever money they say they need. Worse, the national administration seems always to end up supporting their demands. Sometimes, to anesthetize the public, there is a little carefully staged fighting—the Lockheed bail-out is one example—but in the end the Pentagon and its supporting cast of contractors unite to pick the public pockets.[12]

In 1976 Felice Cohen, director of the Military Audit Project, a nonprofit research group, filed suit against Lockheed under the False Claims Act charging that "as a direct result of the false, fictitious or fraudulent claims of Lockheed, the US Treasury has been unlawfully drained of many millions of dollars and the taxpayers . . . have been forced to shoulder additional tax burdens as a result of Lockheed's unlawful activities."[13] The Military Audit Group obtained access to volumes of information which, they claimed, was invaluable in understanding the process by which the government has continually protected Lockheed; such as by shielding it from investigations that would uncover the corrupt and wasteful nature of Lockheed's operations and relationship with the government. The group later provided affidavits contending that Lockheed, among other things, diverted funds, materials, machines and personnel from the government subsidized C-5A project to work on its commercial L-1011 program.[14]

Later in 1976 the US Government filed a motion to dismiss the case because (1) most of the information is not new and (2) the case might prejudice some future action against Lockheed by the Justice Department. While the attorney for the plaintiff vigorously opposed the government's motion he said: "The government is acting as a surrogate for Lockheed which is, in itself, a scandal."[15]

Let us now look at how Lockheed has prospered since it has been saddled with a huge debt and a bad reputation. Profits have risen from a $188-million *loss* in 1970 to a $65-million gain eight years later. (Figure 11-1) In 1975 Lockheed's earnings almost doubled over the previous year despite serious losses in its commercial sales and only a slight increase in overall sales. Nevertheless, Lockheed was one of eleven major corporations which took advantage of numerous deductions, write-offs and exemptions that riddle the tax code to avoid paying any income tax for 1975.*

Earnings dropped somewhat in 1976 as its commercial L-1011 airliner program suffered new losses—probably because of the foreign payoff scandal in which Lockheed had figured prominently. Nevertheless, because government contracts, which account for sixty percent of Lockheed sales, were on the upswing, total sales dipped only slightly. Lockheed's net profits surged again to an all time high in 1977 and 1978 even though commercial airliner losses were still significant. The slight gain in total sales is attributable to C-130 Hercules military transport aircraft sales and, in particular, to production of Trident-1 missiles.

According to *Forbes* magazine, Lockheed's average return on equity over the five years ending with 1979 was 57.6 percent.[17] For 1976 alone, Lockheed's slump year for net profit, its return on equity was a whopping 49.6 percent.[18] When compared with the *all-industry* median

*Lockheed also avoided taxes for 1974. And, by carrying forward losses from 1970, kept its adjusted taxable income below zero from 1970 through 1973.[16]

of 12.9 percent that put Lockheed firmly in first place of all US corporations for profitability, a position it held for several years despite the complaints of corporate executives that it was barely making ends meet.

Figure 11-1
Lockheed Sales and Earnings

Year	Sales (billions of $)		Net Earnings (millions of $)	L-1011 Loss (millions of $)
1970	2.5		– 188.0	41.7
1971	2.9		– 40.0	78.3
1972	2.5		– 7.0	80.5
1973	2.8		18.2	70.0
1974	3.3		23.2	49.2
1975	3.4		45.3	93.8
1976	3.2		38.7	124.8
1977	3.4	(3.0)*	55.4	120.0
1978	3.5	(3.2)*	64.9	118.8
1979	4.1	(3.5)*	56.5	188.4
1980	5.4	(4.5)*	27.6	199.4
1981	—	(5.2)*	– 288.8	128.6

*Figures shown in parenthese are adjusted sales reflected in the 1981 Lockheed Annual Report which do not include L-1011 sales.

Source:
Lockheed Annual Reports, 1971 through 1981.

Net profits for Lockheed dropped from $64.9-million in 1978 to 56.5-million in 1979, largely because production of the L-1011 Tri-Star jetliner was increased from a 1977-78 rate of six aircraft per year to 14 in 1979.[19] Accordingly, net sales for the airliner increased from $294.3-million in 1978 to $526.3-million in 1979—but the cost of the latter was $569.1-million. It cost more to build the planes than was realized in sales even though the aircraft had been in production for almost a decade. That, along with increased development costs and general administration expenses, deepened the L-1011 program loss from $118.8-million in 1978 to $188.4-million in 1979.[20] The loss on that one commercial program was more than three times the overall net profits for the whole corporation. Clearly, Lockheed's inefficiency has multiplied as production has increased but because of the corporation's reliance on military sales it was still able to retain the top position in profitability for the Aerospace and Defense Industry for 1979 (although it dropped to #3 place when compared to *all* US corporations).[21]

The L-1011 program continued to pull down Lockheed's net earning for 1980 and 1981. Finally, on December 7, 1981 management cancelled the program and wrote off all remaining costs which left the net earnings for that year in the hole by $288.8-million. It looks like Lockheed has come full circle back to its 1970 position. Nevertheless, total sales—mainly military—are higher than ever.

Before leaving the discussion of profitability there is still another fringe benefit which is unique to defense contractors. Much of the manufacturing equipment and many of the facilities are furnished by the government. There is no investment necessary for the contractor and they are free from taxation. For instance, at Lockheed's missile plant in Sunnyvale the main manufacturing building for submarine-launched ballistic missiles is owned by the Navy, as is much of the machinery within. At Marietta, Georgia where the C-5As were built, a good share of the facilities and manufacturing equipment are government owned. Not having to invest in those assets, of course, makes business more profitable.

That the arms race is profitable for corporate executives and investors cannot be disputed. Its effect on employment is another matter. The general belief that we need weapons contracts to create jobs stands in stark opposition to the facts. Although legislators and the public remain reluctant to cut the military budget because they think unemployment will rise, the truth is that weapons building is inefficient at producing jobs.

In 1972 the Library of Congress made a study of the number of jobs generated for each billion dollars spent in various sectors of the economy.[22] The jobs included all operations from the cutting or mining of raw material to the manufacture of the finished products. The result of that study indicated that $1-billion would furnish employment for 132,000 public service jobs, 100,000 teachers, 77,000 nurses, and between 50,000 and 76,000 jobs in the various construction industries. The Defense Department first estimated that a billion dollars spent on military contracting would provide 35,000 jobs, which did not compare favorably with the other catagories. That figure was quickly modified upward to 55,000 jobs per billion spent and that put military contracting in the same ball park as the building trades. When we look at the overall spectrum of military contracting, however, we find that much of it is to provide labor-intensive goods and services to military personnel. These jobs should drive the defense jobs per $1-billion well above the 55,000 mark. The fact that they do not suggests that some sectors of defense contracting—weapons contracting in particular—produce very few jobs per $1-billion spent. The impact of Lockheed's missile plant in Santa Clara County, California on the local job market provides a vivid example.

During fiscal year 1977 Lockheed's plant in Santa Clara County had a $1.1-billion contract to manufacture 80 Trident-1 missiles. According to information received from Lockheed, there will be 8,000 people working on Trident-1 at its peak production. Santa Clara County's 160,000 manufacturing jobs were expected to produce $9-billion worth of goods during that year. While Trident missiles comprise 12 percent of that manufacturing output, the production of these missiles employ only 5 percent of the work force. Clearly, when compared to other sectors of industry, weapons production provides fewer jobs per investment dollar.

One reason that manufacturing weapons does not produce many jobs is because it is capital-intensive as opposed to labor-intensive. The highly automated production lines are designed to reduce labor costs. New manufacturing technologies such as numerical control and computerization of machines significantly reduces the number of people required to produce a missile or other weapon. Even the engineering and design of those devices is becoming highly routine through the use of conventional computer technology as well as the more exotic computer graphics which reduce many-fold the effort required to make concept evaluations, run trade-off studies, and perform basic engineering drafting. The trend toward capital-intensive industry has been growing over the past decade. In 1968, for example, the entire Lockheed Corporation hired 95,404 employees and turned out $2.2-billion in sales.[23] In 1980 the number of workers was 74,600 while sales jumped to $5.4-billion.[24] To cancel out inflation the sales for 1968 can be converted to 1980 dollars which would figure out to be $4.97-billion.[25] In "real" terms, sales increased 8 percent during those 12 years but employment decreased 22 percent. This is a striking example of how capital-intensive industry can reduce labor costs which means reducing employment.

In the previous paragraphs I've sketched an outline of the impact of the arms industry on US society—an impact that every US citizen feels when he or she pays taxes or faces the prospects of unemployment. Beyond this the intersection of this industry with the foreign policy and military establishments holds implications for the formation of public policy at every level. In his farewell radio and television address to the nation, President Dwight Eisenhower issued a warning regarding this powerful interest group:

> This conjunction of an immense military establishment and a large arms industry is new in the American experience . . . we must guard against the acquisition of unwarranted influence, whether sought or unsought, by the military-industrial complex. The potential for the disasterous rise of misplaced power exists and will persist.[26]

Coming from a man who held the highest military rank as well as being President of the United States, that warning is most cogent.

Probably the most obvious manifestation of the military-industrial complex is the flow of people back and forth between corporations and the Pentagon. In 1969 Senator Proxmire insisted that the Defense Department survey the number of senior retired military officers (Colonel and Navy captain and above) who work in industry. The results showed that the number had tripled in ten years—that 2,122 former top military men were working for the top 100 defense contractors. Lockheed hired ten percent of them, or 210. Boeing had 169, McDonnel Douglas 141, General Dynamics 113, and North American Rockwell came in fifth with 104. Those five companies, alone, hired one-third of all those former senior officers working for the top 100 companies.[27] The number continues to increase—433 more flocked to defense work in 1975 and 715 in 1976. Meanwhile, the Council on Economic Priorities concluded in 1975 that twenty-seven percent of all those cases were actually conflict of interest situations. The Council also revealed 32 cases which apparently violated federal statutes prohibiting retired officers from selling to the armed service branch from which they retired.

To look at the flow in the other direction we can again call upon the testimony of Admiral Rickover before the Joint Economic Committee:

> . . . the great difficulty in conducting defense business is most of the top officials come from industry. They naturally have an industry viewpoint . . . Since most of the positions are filled by business people, naturally, we are going to have a business flavor in government.[28]

That certainly calls attention to a more subtle form of influence that enhances business. Today in the newspapers we can read about Rockwell taking generals and admirals to its hunting lodge in Maryland,

Boeing treating top NASA officials to fishing trips, fraud and collusion in buying beef for the armed forces, Air Force officers attending golf tournaments as guests of Northrup, and the Director of Defense Research and Engineering accepting favors to help Rockwell sell Condor missiles. An October 1976 Associated Press dispatch even reported that on Jimmy Carter's Lockheed-paid trip to South America, when he was Governor of Georgia, he offered to help promote sales of the cargo planes manufactured in the company's Georgia plant.[29]

Throughout this chapter I've argued that the parameters of the arms race are not set by the requirements of "national security" or "national interests" as these things are commonly understood, but rather by the commercial interests of a small sector of the US public. Throughout this book I've suggested that these interests, when translated into military terms, are leading our nation, and indeed our world, toward nuclear catastrophe. Yet even if we can set aside this very probable outcome of a continuing arms race and just consider its present effects we are still confronted with a reality that diverges from any humane calculation of our "national interests." As noted by Dwight Eisenhower only three months after he became president:

> Every gun that is made, every warship launched, every rocket fired signifies, in the final sense, a theft from those who hunger and are not fed, those who are cold and are not clothed.
>
> This world in arms is not spending money alone. It is spending the sweat of its laborers, the genuis of its scientists, the hopes of its children . . .
>
> This is not a way of life at all, in any true sense. Under the cloud of threatening war, it is humanity hanging from a cross of iron.

NOTES

1. *Fortune*, October 1975, pp. 41-49.
2. From speech by Archbishop Dom Helder Camara when he accepted the People's Peace Prize in Oslo, Norway, 10 February 1974. Cited in *Fellowship* magazine, March 1974, p. 11.
3. *Statement of Secretary of Defense James R. Schlesinger to the Congress on FY 1976 and Transition Budgets, FY 1977 Authorization*

Report, and FY 1976-1980 Defense Program, 5 February 1975, p. 6.

4. Cited in *Parade,* 8 September 1974.
5. *The Defense Monitor* (Center for Defense Information, Washington, D.C.; 1982), Volume XI, Number 3, p. 1.
6. Ibid, p. 5.
7. Ibid, p. 3.
8. The Department of Defense presents its fiscal year 1983 budget as only 28½ percent of the federal budget but it is referring to the Federal Unified Budget which includes trust funds such as Social Security and Railroad Retirement. Those funds are already committed and beyond the control of Congress.
9. Cited in *Notes from the Joint Economic Committee,* 31 August 1976.
10. *Defense Procurement in Relationships Between Government and Its Contractors,* hearings before the Subcommittee on Priorities and Economy in Government of the Joint Economic Committee of Congress, 2 April 1975, p. 4.
11. *Opening Remarks of Admiral H.G. Rickover before the Subcommittee on Priorities and Economy in Government of the Joint Economic Committee of Congress,* 29 December 1977, pp. 12-13.
12. Ernest Fitzgerald, "The Pentagon as the Enemy of Capitalism," *World,* 27 February 1973.
13. *The Wall Street Journal,* 23 February 1976.
14. *New York Times,* 21 February 1976.
15. *San Francisco Examiner,* 29 November 1976.
16. *Congressional Record,* House of Representatives, 26 January 1978, Congressman Charles Vanik testimony.
17. *Forbes,* 7 January 1980, p. 129.
18. *Forbes,* 1 January 1977, p. 133.
19. "Tristar Production Costs Offset Lockheed Profits," *Aviation Week and Space Technology,* 15 October 1979, p. 32.
20. *Lockheed Annual Report 1979.*
21. *Forbes,* 7 January 1980. pp. 62 and 129.
22. For a more detailed analysis see Marion Anderson, *The Empty Pork Barrel: Unemployment and the Pentagon Budget,* a report by the Public Interest Research Group in Michigan, 615 E. Michigan Ave., Lansing, Michigan 48993; April 1975.
23. *Lockheed Annual Report 1968.*
24. *Lockheed Annual Report 1980.*
25. Inflation factor determined from *Department of Defense Annual Report Fiscal Year 1980,* by Harold Brown, Secretary of Defense, 25 January 1979, charts 14-1 and 14-2, p. 318.
26. Excerpt from farewell speech of President Dwight David Eisenhower, 17

January 1961.

27. "A Roll Call of Colonels that Industry Hires," *Business Week,* 27 November 1971, p. 20.
28. *Defense Procurement in Relationships Between Government and its Contractors,* op. cit., p. 2.
29. AP dispatch, "Carter's Debt To Lockheed," *San Jose Mercury,* 10 October 1976.

EPILOGUE

The greatest power which nuclear weapons have, their power to kill us spiritually, can be taken away from them right now by a living faith . . . Nuclear weapons have the power of spiritual death so long as we despair at overcoming their physical and political power . . . .

—*James W. Douglass*[1]

I do not view the nuclear arms race as the root problem in our society. I believe it is a manifestation of a deeper sickness just as poverty, starvation, crime, immorality, and other evil things are also effects of that same sickness. I do recognize the nuclear arms race as a very dangerous manifestation, however, which needs immediate correction before it destroys all of us.

The root problem, as I see it, is more basic. I can most succinctly describe it as personal selfishness and the urge to control. These traits are ingrained in each of us since birth. We are taught all through our formative years to "Look out for #1," to establish ourselves in a good job, and to achieve financial security. We are urged to get ahead in the world and impressed with the need to compete—for grades, in sports, to achieve recognition, and in many other, sometimes subtle, ways. Above all we are taught blind patriotism and not to question authority. These traits work their way up the societal ladder to become corporate greed and militarized power—the military-industrial complex.

Throughout this book I have focused on the technologies which are moving us closer to nuclear war. But we don't have to wait for the bombs to drop to have casualties—nuclear weapons are killing people right now. They are killing people, first of all, through radiation poisoning throughout the entire weapons production cycle from the mining of uranium to the testing of the weapons. A friend of mine, a spiritual leader of the Dakota Sioux, told me how little Indian children playing on their reservation are breathing the radioactive tailings from uranium mining as they are whipped from the waste pile by the winds. "Atomic Veterans" are now suffering the effects of exposure to nuclear tests 2 or 3 decades ago, and we are hearing more and more about government coverups of radiation exposure.

Another way nuclear weapons are killing people right now is through misplaced use of resources. While hundreds of billions of dollars are going toward preparation for war, people are starving by the millions. UNICEF's annual *State of the World's Children* message reports that 17-million children under five years of age from the poorest countries died in 1981, and 1982 is not expected to be better.[2] That is comparable to the World War II "Holocaust" happening over and over again every 4½ months. As you read this a child is dying every two seconds. During that same interval the Pentagon spends $11,600. It would only take $100 of that to provide the necessary health and nutritional care to save that child's life. But those children continue to die. "Whoever they once were, whatever religion they were growing up in, whatever language they were beginning to speak, and whatever potential their lives held, they were simply failed by the world into which they were born."[3]

Millions more people are dying because they cannot obtain the necessities of life. Even more are struggling for survival. Meanwhile, nuclear weapons epitomize the greed in our affluent society. We Americans are only six percent of the world's population but we consume 40 to 50 percent of the available resources. Nuclear weapons are used to sustain that lifestyle in a troubled world.

The real and immediate harm from nuclear weapons is that they are killing us spiritually. Psychologists refer to this phenomenon as "psychic numbing." Something has to be dead within us to allow the gross injustices on this planet to continue. At the same time, the looming threat of nuclear war has created a sense of hopelessness.

No place is this hopelessness more prevalent than in youth. Most parents in this country would be shocked to know what really goes on in their children's minds. Dr. Robert Jay Lifton, a professor of psychiatry at Yale University Medical School, described the double life children are growing up in: "They grow up with the usual mixture of a sense of security and elements of insecurity and expect to live out their lives in traditional fashion. But they have another mind-set that includes the possibility of everything, themselves and their parents and everyone they have known or touched, being suddenly annihilated."[4]

This hopelessness in youth was vividly exemplified in a September 1981 *Fellowship* magazine article by Harvey Cox. He described a California poll taken in the spring of that year in which youth were asked two questions: (1) Do you believe there will be a nuclear war? and (2) if so, do you think you will survive it? Eighty-four percent of the youth polled said yes, they thought there would be a nuclear war and no, they didn't think they would survive it.

Professor Cox described his shock and skepticism at that poll's results. He decided to ask his class at Harvard those two questions and was astounded that he received the same results. He said:

> . . . There were students there from the medical school, the education school, the law school, divinity school. These are people who are staying up late nights working on projects and term papers and yet, in some dark region of their hearts, they don't believe there's any future they are really preparing for.[5]

Those were college students. I decided to also try those questions when I gave a presentation to a mentally-gifted class at a middle-school in San Jose, California. There were about eighty 6th, 7th and 8th graders in the assembly. I started with a different question—asking how many of them thought often about nuclear weapons and nuclear war. Only 5 or 6 hands went up. Then I asked how many thought there would be a nuclear war. Almost all the hands went up. I didn't have the stamina to ask how many thought they would survive. Several 6th graders stayed afterward to talk with me and it was heart-rending to hear them share their fears.

This is a real hopelessness—a real cancer in our society. If parents or teachers want to get some idea of how their children feel I suggest they ask them to draw a picture of the world as they visualize it in twenty years. Some sociologists attribute many problems in youth to this hopelessness. Because they don't perceive a future, young people are looking for immediate satisfaction and that is leading to many evil things—drugs, alcohol, sexual promiscuity, crime, and a general "don't give a damn" attitude. And we wonder about the increase in suicides among children and young people.

It is not just in America where youth feel hopeless. In Japan, for instance, the Prime Minister's Office recently ran a survey of young people. One of the questions asked was if they had an objective in life. A "No" reply came from 72 percent of those queried although about 7 percent added that they would like to have a one.

This feeling of powerlessness claims more than just the young. The general attitude of people seems to be that they would like things to be different but feel the whole issue is too much for them—too overwhelming. Most people seem to think that what they could do would have no effect whatsoever, and that we just have to learn to live with the bomb. Norman Cousins aptly described that dilemma: "The era of Strangelove is upon us. The greatest danger to the American people today is not a surprise attack but a steady erosion of the principles that went into the making of a free society and that alone can sustain it."[6]

This leads to the inevitable question of whether there is any hope. Two years ago I wasn't too sure. But since sometime in 1979 or 1980 critical consciousness regarding nuclear weapons has begun to surface. It has appeared at the personal level in all walks of life—religious leaders, former government officials, educators, physicians and, most important, among the grass roots people. Accompanying this rising consciousness has been a willingness to make personal sacrifices. The numbers are not great, yet, but they are growing. This has been a tremendously hopeful sign for me. It has firmed my conviction that the decision to stop nuclear weapons will not be based on political negotiations, economic considerations, or technical advances. All of these have been thoroughly tried with consistent failure. They have stimulated division and increased hopelessness.

I am convinced that the decision to end the nuclear arms race will be a spiritual/moral decision. What will turn this country, and eventually the world, around will be a multitude of people flatly saying "NO!—this is not right, nuclear bombs are not what I believe in, nothing is worse than what nuclear weapons are causing right now!"

What does it mean to say a flat-out "No!" to the Pentagon and Big Business? In the Christian tradition there is a story about a rich young man who told Jesus he obeyed all the commandments and asked what else he needed to do to be perfect. Jesus told him he should sell all he has, give the money to the poor, and then follow him. The rich young man found that sacrifice too much to pay for perfection. I have always wondered how Jesus' answer would be paraphrased today. I believe it would go something like this:

> Reduce your consumption of goods to where you do not

provide a market for big business. If it can not sell the goods it will not be profitable to exploit the land, labor and resources of the Third World.

—Reduce your consumption of goods to where you use only your share of the world's resources. Then you will not be taking what belongs to someone else.

—Reduce your consumption of goods to where you will not need a large salary. Then you will not need the high-paying jobs offered by weapons factories.

—Reduce your consumption of goods to where you can live below the taxable level. Then you will not have to pay for those weapons of war.

This formula is the interior aspect of nonviolence and the ultimate dimension of personal noncooperation with corrupt practices. Those who have the faith to take these steps will find new dimensions to living. But of course we also need to exteriorize nonviolence through actions aimed at the ending of the nuclear arms race. That is necessary because more public understanding of the underlying reasons behind that threat is necessary. Public action by those who are already enlightened is critical because all too few are presently working at this educational process. A whole lot depends on those few.

It is essential that Americans begin to ask questions. The appropriate questions might be: How much importance do I attach to freedom? Am I happy being enslaved to a weekly paycheck while subordinating important values to economics? What is my most important duty to my children and their children? Will the world be a better place because I have lived in it?

These are the beginnings of interior searching which can turn the tide of public attitudes. These are the questions which can eventually lead to unilateral US initiatives toward disarmament and foster the sincerity to negotiate meaningful treaties toward peace. The actual danger as well as the potential solutions are not "out there." Both lie within us and taking responsibility for our personal behavior is just about the only thing in this world over which we have 100 percent control.

When I started writing this book I had a fairly clear idea of the first strike scenario and the role of industry and banks. But several years of intensive research to tie all the facts together have had a profound effect on me. Among other things I feel the need for urgency. I wish all this were science fiction, but it isn't. I hope this book has disturbed the reader enough to start the process of questioning and change.

NOTES

1. Jim Douglass, "Christ is Risen from Nuclear Holocaust," *The Catholic Agitator,* (Los Angeles Catholic Worker), August 1981, p. 6.
2. *The State of the World's Children, 1981-82,* by James P. Grant, Executive Director of the United Nations Children's Fund (UNICEF), released in December 1981, p. 1.
3. Ibid.
4. Cited in New York Times News Service article by Olive Evans, "Children Feel Threat of Nuclear Annihilation," *Watsonville* (CA) *Register-Pajaronain,* 28 May 1982, p.4
5. Harvey Cox, "Let People Cry Out," *Fellowship,* September 1981, p. 4.
6. Editorial by Norman Cousins, *Saturday Review,* 12 May 1979, p. 12.

GLOSSARY

ABM—Anti-Ballistic Missile

AMB Treaty—A SALT-1 document which puts restrictions on ABM interceptors, launchers, and radar.

ABRES—Advanced Ballistic ReEntry Systems. Now renamed Advanced Strategic Missile Systems, ASMS.

ABRV—Advanced Ballistic Reentry Vehicle. A new warhead designed for MX and possibly Trident-2. Now called Mark-21 RV.

ACE—Advanced Control Experiment. An early maneuvering reentry vehicle developed on the ABRES program.

ACIS—Arms Control Impact Statements.

Advanced Development—The phase of development following concept definition and preceding full scale development.

AFSATCOM—Air Force SATellite COMmunications system.

AGOS—An improved model of T-AGOS. Small, slow ships used to tow the SURTASS anti-submarine warfare sensor arrays.

AIRS—Advanced Inertial Reference Sphere. The newest generation inertial guidance package designed for MX.

ALCM—Air-Launched Cruise Missile.

Alpha—A Defense Advanced Research Projects Agency program to develop a pulsing, chemical high-energy (killer) laser for use in space.

Altair-3—A US rocket booster motor which will be used as the second stage of the Air Force's anti-satellite missile.

ALWT—Advanced Light Weight Torpedo. Planned successor for the Mark-46 anti-submarine torpedo.

AMARV—Advanced Maneuvering Reentry Vehicle.

AMPA—Advanced Maritime Patrol Aircraft. Concept studies of a potential successor to the P-3 anti-submarine airplane.

ANZUS—Australia-New Zealand-United States mutual defense treaty.

Apollo—A US space program administered by the National Aeronautics and Space Administration.

ASALM—Advanced Strategic Air-Launched Missile.

ASMS—Advanced Strategic Missile Systems. Formerly known as ABRES. An Army/Navy/Air Force research and development program reoriented and renamed in early 1982 to promote greater interplay between ICBM and SLBM research and development and the ballistic missile defense technology.

ASROC—Anti-Submarine ROCket fired from surface ships.

ASTOR—Anti-Submarine TORpedo. The Mark-45 nuclear torpedo now believed to be retired from use.

ASW—Anti-Submarine Warfare.

ASW/SOW—Anti-Submarine Warfare Stand-Off Weapon. A Tomahawk cruise missile being developed to attack submarines.

ATB—Advanced Technology bomber. The Stealth bomber.

Atlas—An early US missile still being used for tests.

Austere ELF—A Former extreme-low frequency communication program of the US Navy. Now abandoned in favor of Project ELF.

AUTODIN—AUTOmatic DIgital Network. A component of the Defense Communications System.

AWACS—Airborne Warning And Control System. A Boeing-707-type radar aircraft. Also called the E-3A.

B-1—A new US supersonic bomber.

B-1B—A version of the B-1 bomber designed as a cruise missile carrier.

B-52—A current US strategic bomber.

B-70—A strategic bomber proposed before the B-1 but never built.

Baker-Nunn Camera—A telescopic camera used to photograph satellites in orbit.

Ballistic Missile—A rocket-powered missile that, after being boosted to speed, coasts through a ballistic arc.

BAMBI—BAllistic Missile Boosts Intercept. An early 1960s program to investigate intercepting hostile ballistic missiles in their boost phase (i.e. while their rocket motors are still burning).

BAMM—Balloon Altitude Mosaic Measurements. A US program to test mosaic infrared sensors raised aloft by balloons.

Big Bird—A US reconnaissance (spy) satellite.

Big Bird—A conceptual study of a large aircraft which can stay aloft for an extended period as an air-mobile concept for MX.

Block—Used to designate production runs of classes of a satellite. Navstar Block-1 satellites, for instance, are development spacecraft. The Block-2 are slightly redesigned for the production buy.

Block-5D—Used to designate a US meteorological satellite.

BMD—Ballistic Missile Defense.

BMEWS—Ballistic Missile Early Warning System.

Boeing-707—A commercial jet airliner.

Boeing 747—A commercial jet wide-bodied airliner.

Burner-2—An upper stage used with thrust-augmented Thor missiles for maneuvering in space. Part of an early US anti-satellite system.

Bus—That portion of the missile which releases the multiple individually-targeted reentry vehicles (MIRVs). The technical name is the Post-Boost Control System (PBCS).

C-4—Navy designation for the Trident-1 missile.

C-5A—A Lockheed-built military cargo aircraft—the largest in the world. Also called the "Galaxy."

C-130—A Lockheed-built military cargo aircraft. Also called "Hercules."

C-141—A Lockheed-built military cargo aircraft. Also called the "Starlifter."

CAFE—Code name for a 1970 secret project at Lockheed to investigate alternative warheads for Poseidon missiles in case multiple warheads on missiles were banned by the SALT-1 treaty.

CAPTOR—enCAPsulated TORpedo. A deep water anti-submarine mine.

C-cubed—Command, Control and Communication.

CEP—Circular Error Probability. The radius of a circle, centered on the target, within which the warhead has a fifty percent chance of hitting.

CIA—Central Intelligence Agency of the US government.

Clarinet-Pilgrim—A coding of Loran-C navigation signals for communications use.

Cobra Dane—A large US phased-array radar on Shemya Island of the Aleutian group.

Cosmos (Or Kosmos)—A series of Soviet satellites of which about seventy percent perform military missions.

Counterforce—A nuclear strategy in which the attack missiles are aimed at the opponent's military forces.

Countervailing—Another name for counterforce used in Presidential Directive Number 59 (PD-59) to connote a limited nuclear exchange as opposed to a disarming first strike.

Countervalue—A nuclear strategy in which the attack missiles are aimed at the opponent's value targets—cities and industrial areas.

Cruise Missile—A guided missile using an "air breathing" engine and supported by the atmosphere. It flies like an airplane.

CTP_k—Cross-Target Probability of kill.

D-5—US Navy designation for the Trident-2 missile.

Damage Limitation—A strategic nuclear doctrine intended to limit damage to American cities by destroying Soviet nuclear weapons before they are launched. A euphemism for counterforce.

DARPA—Defense Advanced Research Projects Agency.

DC-10—A commercial wide-bodied jet airliner manufactured by McDonnell Douglas.

Delta-1—A Soviet nuclear-powered ballistic missile submarine which carries twelve SS-N-8 missiles.

Delta-2—A stretch version of the Delta-1 which carries sixteen SS-N-8 missiles.

Delta-3—Another version of the Delta class which carries sixteen SS-N-18 missiles.

Deploy—to make a weapons system or component operational.

Deterrence—A nuclear strategy whereby a potential aggressor is "deterred" from attacking because of the massive and unacceptable retaliation that will follow.

DEWLINE—Distant Early Warning LINE of radars for bomber and cruise missile warning.

Dimer—A high density fuel used in sea-launched cruise missiles.

Directed Energy—A term used to describe high energy (killer) lasers and subatomic particle beams; or any other type of energy that is directed to a target to destroy it or render it inoperable.

Discoverer—An early US surveillance satellite.

DMA—Defense Mapping Agency.

DMS—Defense Meterological Satellite.

DOE—Department of Energy.

DOD—Department of Defense.

DOT—Designating Optical Tracker. A mosaic infrared sensor launched on a missile to track incoming warheads for ballistic missile defense.

DSCS—Defense Satellite Communications System. A US military communications satellite.

DSP—Defense Support Program. DSP satellites are the current US early warning satellites.

E-3A—Airborne Warning And Control System (AWACS) aircraft. A Boeing-707-type radar airplane.

E-4A—The Advanced Airborne Command Post aircraft. A specially-equipped version of the Boeing-747 jetliner.

E-4B—An improved version of the E-4A with improved C-cubed and EMP hardening capabilities.

Early Spring—A Polaris missile modified for anti-satellite tests during the early 1960s.

EC-121—An older US radar surveillance airplane.

EC-130—The TACAMO aircraft. A version of the C-130 cargo airplane.

EC-135—A special modification of the Boeing-707 airplane that is used for airborne command posts.

Echo-2—An old class of Soviet nuclear-powered submarines which carry Shaddock SS-N-3 cruise missiles.

EHF—Extreme-High Frequency.

ELF—Extreme-Low Frequency.

EMP—ElectroMagnetic Pulse. A high voltage generated in missile and reentry vehicle circuitry when traveling through the environment from a nuclear explosion.

Engineering Development—All work necessary, including testing, which leads to a production decision. Now more commonly called full-scale development.

Equatorial Orbit—The orbit of a satellite which always stays over the equator.

Evader—A name given to the Mark-500 maneuvering reentry vehicle for Trident-1 to imply its purpose is to evade defensive interceptor missiles.

EXPO—EXtended-range POseidon missile. A 1971 task force study at Lockheed which developed into the Trident-1, C-4, missile.

F-4—An older Air Force fighter plane.

F-15—A modern US Air Force fighter plane.

F-111D—A US fighter plane.

FAA—Federal Aviation Administration. The US civil aviation administration.

FB-111A—An existing US fighter-bomber.

FB-111B/C—A proposed stretch version of the FB-111A fighter bombers and the F-111 fighters for carrying cruise missiles.

FB-111H—A proposed stretch version of the FB-111A to carry cruise missiles.

Fiscal Year—The fiscal year for US budgetary purposes runs from October 1st through the following September 30th.

Fission—A nuclear reaction where heavy atoms (such as uranium or plutonium) divide to form smaller atoms of about half the weight. (Cf. An atomic or A-bomb explosion.)

FLTSATCOM—FLeet SATellite COMmunications system. Formerly a Navy system but now integrated into a space agency managed by the Air Force.

Fratricide—The destructive effect, from debris, EMP, etc, of a nuclear explosion on subsequent incoming warheads.

Fusion—A nuclear reaction where light atoms fuse together to form heavier atoms. (CF. A hydrogen or H-bomb explosion.)

FY—Fiscal Year.

Galosh—A Soviet anti-ballistic missiles interceptor. Thirty-two are currently deployed around Moscow.

GAO—General Accounting Office. The congressional watchdog on financial expenditures.

GEODSS—Ground-based Electro-Optical Deep Space Surveillance system.

Geosynchronous Orbit—An equatorial orbit where the satellite's orbit revolutions are synchronized with the earth's rotation so that the satellite appears to stay over a certain spot on the equator. Also called earth-synchronous orbit.

GLCM—Ground-Launched Cruise Missile.

Golf—An old Soviet class of diesel powered ballistic missile-launching submarine. It carries three SS-N-5 missiles.

GPS—Global Positioning System. (Navstar)

H—The symbol for silo hardness in the probability-of-kill equation.

HALO—High Altitude Large Optics. A future satellite-based sensor array for detecting and tracking ballistic missiles, bombers, and satellites.

Harpoon—A sixty-mile range anti-ship missile.

HF—High Frequency.

HI-CAMP—Hi-resolution Calibrated Airborne Measurements Program. A test program using mosaic infrared sensors in a U-2 airplane.

HIT—Homing Interceptor Technology. A nonnuclear interceptor to destroy ballistic missiles and satellites. A US program.

HOE—Homing Overlay Experiment. A US concept for mid-course (exoatmospheric) ballistic missile defense.

Hotel—An early Soviet class of ballistic missile submarine. It carries three SS-N-5 missiles.

Hydra—An early 1960s program to launch missiles from capsules floating in the ocean.

ICBM—InterContinental Ballistic Missile.

Illiac-4—The Navy's powerful anti-submarine warfare computer.

Interim Agreement—A SALT-1 document limiting strategic weapons for a five-year period.

IOC—Initial Operational Capability.

IONS—Integrated Operational NUDETS (nuclear detection) System.

IUS—Inertial Upper Stage. To be used with the space shuttle to put satellites into higher orbit.

JP—Jet Propulsion fuel. Correctly, JP-4, JP-5, JP-9, etc.

K—Symbol for lethality of a missile or warhead.

KH-11—A modern US reconnaissance (spy) satellite.

Kiloton—The nuclear explosive force equal to one-thousand tons of conventional high explosives.

Kneecap—Jargon for NEACP (National Emergency Airborne Command Post).

Ladar—A combined use of laser and radar.

LAMPS—Light Airborne Multi-Purpose System. ASW helicopters carried on frigates, destroyers and cruisers.

Landsat—The US earth resources satellite series.

Laser—A highly concentrated beam of coherent light. An acronym for Light Amplification by Stimulated Emission of Radiation.

Lethality—A number, expressed as "K", denoting the ability of a missile or warhead to destroy a hard target. The higher the number, the more lethal the weapon.

LF—Low Frequency.

LoAD—Low-Altitude Defense. A terminal (endoatmospheric) US ballistic missile defense program.

LODE—Large Optics Demonstration Experiment. A DARPA program to develop the mirror to steer and control a high-energy (killer) laser.

Looking Glass—Code name for the Strategic Air Command's airborne command posts.

Loran-C—A low-frequency navigation system which can also be used for emergency communication. Loran is an acronym for LOng RAnge Navigation.

LRCA—Long-Range Combat Aircraft. A new name for the B-1 bomber.

LWIR—Long-Wavelength InfraRed.

Mach—Mach numbers are used to denote the speed of rockets and aircraft relative to the speed of sound; Mach-1 being the speed of sound. The speed of sound varies with temperature and altitude but for practical purposes it is about 750 miles per hours.

MAD—Mutual Assured Destruction. (Originally: Mutual Assured Deterrence.)

MAP—Multiple Aim Point. A defunct basing proposal for MX.

Mark-12 reentry vehicle—The MIRV originally deployed on Minuteman-3 ICBMs.

Mark-12A reentry vehicle—a new warhead designed for Minuteman-3 missiles and possibly for MX and Trident-2.

Mark-21 reentry vehicle—The ABRV.

Mark-37 torpedo—Converted to make the Submarine-Launched Mobile Mine (SLMM).

Mark-45 torpedo—A nuclear anti-submarine torpedo launched from submarines. Also called ASTOR. Believed to be out of service.

Mark-46 torpedo—A lightweight anti-submarine torpedo launched from aircraft and surface ships and delivered by ASROC.

Mark-48 torpedo—The latest anti-submarine torpedo launched from submarines.

Mark-57 depth bomb—A nuclear depth bomb carried by anti-submarine patrol aircraft.

Mark-62 mine—A Quickstrike shallow water mine converted from the Mark-82 bomb.

Mark-64 mine—A Quickstrike shallow water mine converted from the Mark-84 bomb.

Mark-65 mine—A 2,000-pound Quickstrike shallow water mine.

Mark-82 bomb—A US Air Force bomb.

Mark-84 bomb—A US Air Force bomb.

Mark-101 depth bomb—a nuclear depth bomb carried by anti-submarine patrol aircraft.

Mark-500 reentry vehicle—A maneuvering reentry vehicle (MARV) being developed for the Trident-1 missile.

MARV—MAneuvering Reentry Vehicle.

Maser—A concentrated beam of energy at microwave frequency. An acronym for Microwave Amplification by Stimulated Emission of Radiation.

MEECN—Minimum Essential Emergency Communications Network.

Megaton—The nuclear explosive force equal to one-million tons of conventional high explosives.

MF—Medium Frequency.

MIDAS—MIssile Defense Alarm System. The first US early warning satellite.

MILSTAR—MILitary Strategic-Tactical And Relay satellite system. A future replacement for AFSATCOM, SDS, and possibly FLTSATCOM.

Minuteman—US intercontinental ballistic missiles. Minuteman-2 and Minuteman-3 ICBMs are currently deployed.

MIRV—Multiple Individually-targeted Reentry Vehicle.

Missile-X—A new mobile intercontinental ballistic missile which the Pentagon hopes to put into production. Sometimes referred to as MX.

MOL—Manned Orbital Laboratory.

MPS—Multiple Protective Shelters. A defunct MX basing scheme.

MRASM—Medium-Range Air-to-Surface Missile.

MRV—Multiple Reentry Vehicle (not independently targeted).

MSR—Missile Site Radar. Once used at the Safeguard ABM site in North Dakota.

MWIR—Medium-Wavelength InfraRed.

MX—Missile-X.

Mya-4—A Soviet strategic heavy bomber. Also known as "Bison."

NASA—National Aeronautics and Space Administration.

NATO—North Atlantic Treaty Organization.

Nautical Mile—1.15 statute miles, 1.85 kilometers, or 6,080 feet.

NAVSTAR—The US global positioning system of satellites being developed.

NCA—National Command Authority.

NEACP—National Emergency Airborne Command Post.

NEARTIP—NEAR Term Improvement Program for the Mark-46 torpedo.

Nike-X—An early US Army anti-ballistic missile.

Nike-Zeus—The US Army's first anti-ballistic missile.

NORAD—NORth American Aerospace Defense Command.

NOSS—Naval Ocean Surveillance Satellite.

NRL—Naval Research Laboratory.

NTS—Navigation Technology Satellite.

NUDETS—NUclear DETection System. A network of detectors placed on host satellites to detect and assess damage from nuclear explosions.

Omega—a very-low frequency navigation system.

ORICS—Optical Ranging, Identification and Communication System. A US laser system being developed to detect and communicate with submarines.

Orion—A US land-based anti-submarine patrol airplane. The P-3.

OTH—Over The Horizon radar.

P-3—The Orion anti-submarine warfare airplane.

PAR—Perimeter Acquisition Radar. A phased-array radar formerly part of the North Dakota ABM site; now assigned to NORAD for missile early warning.

PAVE PAWS—New phased-array radars for detecting submarine-launched ballistic missiles. (An acronym for Precision Acquisition of Vehicle Entry—Phased-Array Warning System.)

PAVE PEPPER—A US Air force program which tested seven MIRVs on Minuteman-3 missiles.

Payload—Same as "throw weight."

PEPE—Parallel Element Processing Ensemble. A high capacity computer system being developed for the US ballistic missile defense program.

PD-59—Presidential Directive #59. Signed by President Carter in 1980 to codify limited nuclear war.

PGRV—Precision-Guided Reentry Vehicle. A target-homing MARV being developed by the United States.

PINETREE LINE—A line of bomber early warning radars in mid-Canada.

Pisces—An extreme-low frequency (ELF) communications concept once studied by the US Navy. It would have used existing power transmission lines as an antenna. (An acronym for Pacific Intertie Strategic Communications ELF System.)

P_k—Probability of Kill.

Polaris—The United States' first nuclear-powered ballistic missile submarine. Also the first US submarine-launched ballistic missiles.

Polar Orbit—The orbit of a satellite which passes over the north and south poles of the earth.

Poseidon—A class of US ballistic missile launching submarines converted from Polaris subs. Also, the Poseidon submarine-launched ballistic missile; successor to Polaris.

Project ELF—The US Navy's current extreme-low frequency (ELF) communications system project.

p.s.i.—Pounds per Square Inch pressure.

Quickstrike—A family of shallow water mines.

Radar—RAdio Detection And Ranging.

RDSS—Rapidly Deployable Sensor System. A new US anti-submarine warfare sensor array in development.

REGAL—REmotely-Guided Autonomous Lightweight torpedo. Apparently the same as and a new name for the ALWT program.

Rhyolite—A US satellite to intercept telemetry signals from Soviet missile tests.

RV—Reentry Vehicle.

S-3A—The US's current carrier-based anti-submarine warfare airplane. Also called Viking.

SABER PENETRATOR VII—A Pentagon study of new strategic bomber concepts.

SAC—Strategic Air Command.

SACDIN—Strategic Air Command DIgital Network.

Safeguard—The Nixon Administration's ABM system. Now dismantled.

SAINT—SAtellite INTerceptor. A US anti-satellite program of the early 1960s.

SALT—Strategic Arms Limitation Talks.

SAM—Surface-to-Air Missile.

SAMOS—Satellite And Missile Observatory System. The first US spy satellite.

Sanguine—An extreme-low frequency (ELF) system which was never deployed.

SCRAMJET—Supersonic Combustion RAMJET.

SDS—Satellites Data System. U.S. Air Force communications Satellites.

Seafarer—A follow-on proposal to Sanguine for an extreme-low frequency (ELF) communications system. Abandoned in favor of Austere ELF.

Seaguard—a US Navy/DARPA anti-submarine warfare research program.

Seahawk—The newest LAMPS anti-submarine warfare helicopter designated SH-60.

Sea King—The SH-3 anti-submarine warfare helicopter based on aircraft carriers.

Seasat—A US ocean dynamics satellite program discontinued after the first satellite was launched.

Seasprite—The SH-2 existing anti-submarine warfare LAMPS helicopter.

SEATO—SouthEast Asia Treaty Organization.

SEEK FROST—A program which updated and replaced US DEWLINE radars.

SEEK IGLOO—A program to replace Air Force bomber warning radars in Alaska.

Sentinel—The Johnson Administration's proposal for an ABM system.

SES—Surface Effect Ship.

SH-2—The existing LAMPS anti-submarine warfare helicopter called Seasprite

SH-3—US carrier-based anti-submarine warfare helicopters called Sea King.

SH-60—The new LAMPS anti-submarine warfare helicopters called Seahawk.

Shaddock—The Soviet SS-N-3 cruise missile.

Shelldyne—A new fuel being developed for cruise missiles. Correctly: Shelldyne-H.

SHF—Super-High Frequency.

SIG—Stellar Inertial Guidance.

SIOP—Single Integrated Operational Plan. The master targeting plan for nuclear weapons.

Sipapu—An American Indian word meaning "sacred fire." The code name for the Army's neutral particle beam weapon for ballistic missile defense in space; now renamed "White Horse."

Skylab—A large US space station; no longer in orbit.

SLBM—Submarine-Launched Ballistic Missile.

SLCM—Sea-Launched Cruise Missile.

SLMM—Submarine-Launched Mobile Mine. A modified Mark-37 torpedo.

SOLRAD—A US Navy satellite to measure solar radiation.

Sonar—An acoustic device for sending and detecting underwater sound signals. (An acronym for SOund Navigation and Ranging.)

SOSUS—SOund SUrveillance System; for detecting and tracking submarines.

SPADATS—SPAce Detection And Tracking System.

Spartan—A US ABM interceptor with 400-mile range. No longer operational.

Sprint—A US ABM interceptor with 25 mile range. No longer operational.

Sputnik—The first series of Soviet satellites. Sputnik-1 was the first artificial satellite in orbit.

SRAM—Short-Range Attack Missile.

SRB—Special Reentry Body. An early MARV concept and forerunner to the Mark-500.

SS-7—An early Soviet ICBM. No longer operational.

SS-8—An early Soviet ICBM. No longer operational.

SS-9—An early Soviet large throw weight ICBM. No longer operational.

SS-11—A Soviet ICBM.

SS-13—A Soviet ICBM using solid fuel.

SS-16—A new solid-fuel Soviet ICBM never deployed.

SS-17—A new Soviet ICBM.

SS-18—A new Soviet large throw weight ICBM.

SS-19—A new Soviet medium weight ICBM.

SS-20—A new Soviet intermediate-range ballistic missile being deployed against Western Europe. It uses the first two stages of the SS-16.

SSBN—A nuclear-powered ballistic missile submarine.

SSGN—A nuclear-powered guided missile (cruise missile) submarine.

SSN—A nuclear-powered attack submarine.

SS-N-3—The Soviet Shaddock cruise missile.

SS-N-5—An old Soviet SLBM carried on Golf and Hotel class submarines.

SS-N-6—A Soviet SLBM carried on Yankee submarines.

SS-N-8—A Soviet SLBM carried on Delta-1 and -2 submarines.

SS-N-18—A Soviet SLBM caried on Delta-3 submarines.

SS-NX-12—A possible follow on to the Soviet Shaddock SS-N-3 cruise missile.

SS-NX-17—A Soviet solid-fuel SLBM only deployed on one Yankee submarine.

SS-NX-20—A new Soviet SLBM in development for use on the new Typhoon submarine.

SSP_k—Single Shot Probability of Kill.

START—STrategic Arms Reduction Talks

Stealth—An aircraft or cruise missile using new technologies to make it less visible to radar.

Strategic—Having to do with strategy: the planning and directing of large scale military operations, as distinguished from tactical. In the case of nuclear weapons this is global in scope.

Strategic Triad—The combination of land-based intercontinental ballistic missiles, air-breathing intercontinental bombers and cruise missiles, and submarine-launched ballistic missiles: land, air and sea. Both the US and USSR operate with a strategic triad of nuclear weapons.

Strategic Weapons—The weapons in the strategic triad. Long-range weapons designed for a confrontation between the US and the USSR.

Strat-X—The Strategic Exercise Study started in 1966 by Defense Secretary McNamara to modernize the strategic triad.

SUBROC—SUBmarine ROCket. An anti-submarine rocket fired from submarines.

SUM—Shallow Underwater Missile. A Mobile concept for strapping ICBMs in cannisters to the sides of submarines for patrol in the shallow waters of the continental shelf.

Sun-synchronous Orbit—A polar orbit of a satellite whose orbit plane always intersects a line between the sun and the earth at the same angle.

SURTASS—SURveillance Towed Array Sensor System for open-ocean anti-submarine warfare detection.

Tacamo—An airborne very-low frequency broadcasting system to communicate with US submarines; an EC-130 aircraft. (An acronym for TAke Charge And Move Out.)

Tactical—Having to do with tactics: arranging and maneuvering military forces in action or before the enemy. Usually associated with theatre operations such as Europe, the Pacific, or the Atlantic.

Tactical Nuclear Weapons—Nuclear weapons designed to be used in a theatre of operations. They are shorter range than strategic nuclear weapons.

T-AGOS—Small, slow ships used to tow SURTASS anti-submarine warfare sensors.

TALCM—Tomahawk Air-Launched Cruise Missile. An unsuccessful competitor for the strategic air-launched cruise missile.

Talon Gold—A DARPA program to develop the aiming and tracking system for the high energy (killer) laser in space.

Teal Amber—A visible wavelength mosaic sensor being developed by the US to be used for ground-based satellite tracking.

Teal Ruby—A mosaic infrared sensor being developed by the US to detect and track bombers and cruise missiles from space.

TEL—Transporter-Erector-Launcher for a missile.

TERCOM—TERrain COntour Matching. A sensor used by cruise missiles to follow the ground with a digital map in their computers' memories to get to their targets.

Thor—A US rocket booster motor.

Throw Weight—The weight of a missile after the last booster motor has separated. Also called payload.

Timation—An early name for the Navstar system.

Time-Urgent Targets—ICBM silos which would have to be destroyed before they launch their missiles.

Titan-2—The US's oldest ICBM still in service, also the largest. They will be retired about one-per-month until they are all gone by 1987.

TLAM—Tomahawk Land Attack Missile. A sea-launched cruise missile.

TLAM/C—A TLAM with a conventional warhead.

TLAM/N—A TLAM with a nuclear warhead.

Tomahawk—Name for the General Dynamics cruise missile.

Trajectory—The ballistic arc through which a ballistic missile travels.

Transit—The current US navigation satellite.

Transponder—A radio or radar set which, upon receiving a signal, transmits a signal of its own. Used on satellites to relay messages.

Trident—The new sea leg of the US strategic triad. The new submarine is called Trident. The first and second generation missiles are called Trident-1 (C-4) and Trident-2 (D-5) respectively.

Tu-95—A Soviet strategic heavy bomber. Also known as "Bear."

Typhoon—A new Soviet ballistic missile submarine which will probably carry twenty SS-NX-20 SLBMs.

U-2 airplane—A high-flying US reconnaissance (spy) airplane.

UHF—Ultra-High Frequency.

ULMS—Underwater Long-range Missile System. Later renamed Trident.

V-2—The German World War II "buzz bomb"—the first cruise missile.

Vela—A US satellite in deep space (70,000 miles high) to detect nuclear explosions.

Viking—The United States' carrier-based anti-submarine patrol airplane. Also designated S-3A.

VHF—Very-High Frequency.

VLF—Very-Low Frequency.

V/STOL—Vertical/Short Take-Off and Land aircraft.

War Fighting—A term for counterforce with a more aggresive connotation, as opposed to "damage limitation."

Warhead—The explosive charge of a weapon. For strategic and tactical nuclear weapons it is the nuclear bomb. In the case of missiles, the reentry body containing the bomb is often referred to as the warhead.

White Horse—The US Army's neutral partical beam weapon program for space-based ballistic missile defense. Formerly called Sipapu.

Wimmex—Jargon pronunciation for the World Wide Military Command and Control System (WWMCCS).

Y—Symbol for the explosive power or "yield" of a nuclear weapon, expressed in kilotons or megatons.

Yankee—A class of Soviet nuclear-powered ballistic missiles submarine which carries sixteen SS-N-6 SLBMs each.

YC-14—A medium transport designed for short take-offs and landings.

YC-15—A medium transport designed for short take-off and landing.

Yield—The explosive force of a nuclear bomb expressed in kilotons or megatons. Designated by the letter "Y".

INDEX